ALCHEMY OF THE MODERN RENAISSANCE

*Symbolism - Symbolism is all around us, it is the world's hidden language. Symbols can be either good or evil, depending upon the message they are intended to convey. Some of you may have noticed that on the front cover of this book, there is an evil symbol that has been perverted and distorted to change the message contained within that symbol to something positive.

The shapes on the front cover are a replication of the ancient symbol for alchemy. Since the triangle looks to be a pyramid with a capstone, it is similar in appearance to the all Seeing Eye symbol that is seen on our currency. The difference between the symbol on our currency and the one on the front of the book is the placement of the eye. This is important because the eye is a representation of "light" or "information."

When the eye is at the capstone of the pyramid, the symbol is telling a story about a small group of elites that sit atop that pyramid and horde all of the power and information from the rest of society. This is the story that is depicted on every single dollar bill.

However, on the front cover the eye has been brought down to the base of the pyramid. This change represents a transfer of information and ultimately power from the elite back to the people. This book is just one small step along the way, in bringing that hidden information back to society.

ALCHEMY OF THE MODERN RENAISSANCE
By J.G. Vibes

Alchemy of the Modern Renaissance
Leilah Publications
Copyright © 2012 J.G. Vibes Leilah Publications
All rights reserved.

To order wholesale, please contact:
American Wholesale Book Company (205) 956-4151
Ingram Book Company (800) 937-8000
Baker & Taylor (800) 775-1100

Leilah Publications P.O. Box 1863 Tempe, AZ 85280 U.S.A.

Leilah Publications brings a global vision of art & writing for the 21st century, publishing & investing in avante-garde artists, writers, and visionaries. The company was founded on 13 October 2006 to publish the visions of prodigies, leading us into the 21st century under a new generation of visionary artists, lyricists, writers, actors & actors, and poets.

ALCHEMY OF THE MODERN RENAISSANCE:
A HISTORY AND FUTURE OF CIVIL RIGHTS IN RELATION TO ART, PHILOSOPHY, AND CULTURE.

By

J.G. VIBES

TABLE OF CONTENTS

Introduction
1. -Alchemy of the Modern Renaissance
2. -Disclaimer
3. –Alchemy
4. -Ethics and the Basic Philosophical Principles of Peace and Freedom
5. -Human struggle for civil rights

The Past
6. -Occult History and Nationalistic Folklore
7. -Powerful people commit crimes and lie to you about it…. This is no theory
8. -The Banking Backstory of Friday The 13th
9. -America Was Not Discovered, It Was Stolen
10. -The Nazi Corporate Fallout
11. -Darwinism, Eugenics and the Silent Genocide

Social Engineering & Psychological Warfare
12. -Inhuman Nature?
13. -Education as Indoctrination
14. -Social Engineering and The Scientific Dictatorship
15. -Propaganda, Public Relations and Psychological Warfare
16. -Advertising and The Subliminal Culture
17. -Mainstream Media is Mass Mind Control
18. -Television Programming is Programming Your Mind
19. -The Entertainment Industry
20. -Parental Propaganda
21. -Inner Child

Economics
22. -Feudalism: From the Dark Ages to the New World
23. -Who's The Man
24. -Fabian Socialism and the New World Order
25. -North American Serfdom
26. -The Birth of the Corporate Beast in America
27. -Central Banking in Early America
28. - End the Fed
29. -Controlled Economic Collapse
30. -Third World By Design
31. -The Sweatshop Economy
32. -Royal Landlords
33. -Cursed Dinosaur Blood
34. -The Climate Industrial Complex and the Hoax of State Sponsored Environmentalism

Politics
35. -Newspeak: A Language of Deception
36. -Right? Left? WRONG!
37. -Beyond the Good Guy and the Bad Guy
38. -Classified Corruption
39. - Illegal Information
40. -Who Owns Congress?
41. -Illegitimate Bureaucracy
42. -Fascism…For your safety
43. -The Prison Industrial Complex
44. -Dare to Resist the War on Drugs
45. -Tricks of the Trade

War
46. -Who Wins In War?
47. -The War Industry
48. -The Privatization of War
49. -Order Out of Chaos
50. -False Flag Attacks
51. -The Only Way to Truly Support the Troops is to Save Them from War
52. -Controlled Conflict in the Middle East

Peace
53. -An Error in Communication
54. -Peer Pressure in a Divided Culture
55. -The Global Consciousness Crisis
56. - The Illusion of Race
57. - Who are you calling crazy?
58. – Future Physics
59. - Positive Vibrations

Shamanism
60. - The Psychedelic Inquisition
61. - Why Shamanism?
62. - Meditation
63. - Responsible Shamanism in the 21st Century
64. -Marketing Illness and Addiction
65. -Fundamentals of Firewater
66. -Marijuana: Miracle not Menace

Imagination
67. -Living The Dream Awake
68. -Synchronicity

Legend
69. -Mythological Origins of Modern Religion
70. -Your Prophets Were Shaman Revolutionaries?
71. -Jesus the Peaceful Revolutionary
72. -The Birth of Islam and the Arabian Empire
73. -Holy Wars

New World Weapons
74. -Water as a Weapon
75. -Monsanto's Monopoly
76. -Frankenfood Politics
77. -Fluoride: The Poison in the Well
78. -Quit Smoking
79. -Air Pollution and Chemtrails
80. -MK Ultra

The Future
81. -2012: Do not Fear the Renaissance
82. -The Culture Battle Between Art and Propaganda
83. -Peaceful Economics
84. -Peaceful Politics
85. -Kindness and Cooperation
86. -We Are Winning
87. –About the Author: J.G Vibes

*"In this concrete jungle we live, our survival is love that we give
Now my instinct is guiding my way, it is true what they say, the world is your chance to create"* - DubFX

Section 1

Introduction

1. -Alchemy of the Modern Renaissance
2. -Disclaimer
3. -Alchemy
4. -Ethics and the Basic Philosophical Principles of Peace and Freedom
5. -Human Struggle for Civil Rights

"We are unraveling our navels so that we may ingest the sun. We are not afraid of the darkness. We trust that the moon shall guide us. We are determining the future at this very moment. We know that the heart is the philosopher's stone. Our music is our alchemy." — Saul Williams (Poet) [0]

Alchemy of the Modern Renaissance

Today the human race finds itself in a constant state of worry and fear. It seems that humankind has now spiraled so far out of control that no one can grasp the reality that it does not have to be this way. A superficial world has been created for us, a world that has corrupted our perception of ourselves, and the world around us. Ideals that we base our lives around such as authority, time, money, and status are nothing but a cancer in the soul of humanity. Yet we are conditioned to accept these diseases as absolutes, because we simply do not know any better. We do not know any better because our perspective is limited. Much like a fish born in an aquarium could not imagine the existence of an ocean, it is almost impossible for a human in the 21st century to conceive what lies outside of our conventional reality. With limited perspective comes limited possibility, which is our species is caught in a cycle of misfortune, never understanding our full potential. This cycle will be broken when the human consciousness as a whole is in a state of peace. Then and only then will we be able to live in a peaceful world.

Throughout history, there have been many groups that have worked to create a positive shift in consciousness to bring about a peaceful world. Many times these revolutionaries disguised their message in various forms of art and culture so they could still reach the people without being condemned by the state. During the times of ancient Greece, they were called "Philosophers," and then towards the end of the middle ages into the start of the renaissance they were called the "Alchemists," while today they go by many names. The alchemists were a collection of scientists who studied many mystic areas of research that had been banned by the government and church. However, this cunning group of rebels publicly told the government and church that they were not studying mysticism, but were actually learning how to change base metals into gold using science. Since this was a very attractive offer to both the government and church, the alchemists were given complete freedom to research whatever they wanted.

Though their front was gold making the alchemists were primarily interested in esoteric traditions such as astrology, numerology, shamanism, and other mystic practices. These are traditions that have been kept alive through various cultures and counter cultures since the times of ancient Egypt and Mesopotamia. This ancient knowledge was later uncovered by the alchemists through their research into the forbidden teachings, which have many times been called "the mystery schools." These ancient secrets are known and harnessed by both good and evil forces.

Similar to the times of the last alchemists, humanity is living in a dark age, an age that needs a rebirth in order to correct itself. History is a cycle of dark ages and golden ages, separated by times of rapid intellectual and spiritual growth that we refer to as a renaissance. The word "renaissance" represents the idea that a civilization can be reborn stronger and more conscious then before. During the renaissance of the middle ages, the alchemists managed to raise the consciousness level of an entire civilization without the knowledge of their oppressive government or religious regime. They did this by building an underground culture imbedded with their mystic ideals, which assimilated with the contemporary culture of the time. Even the most famous artists of the time such as Michelangelo for example were deeply involved in the alchemical teachings and used their art to bring revolutionary messages to the people.

In present times, the alchemists manifest themselves as the artists, musicians, philosophers, and independent journalists of the counter culture. This is our generation's movement that will carry on "the great work" to transform and uplift the human consciousness just as the alchemists did before us. As we near the end of this dark age of materialism and oppression, history repeats itself and the counter culture is starting to assimilate with the traditional mainstream culture. The messages of the modern alchemist are reaching the hearts of millions through the music, art, and philosophy that the counter culture embodies. The message is one of peace, personal freedom, and universal connectivity that have been silenced for generations by the slave driving financial regimes that are still in power today. Our oppressors know that once humanity as a whole accepts peace that they will no longer be needed, and no longer be in control. We will control our own consciousness, and our own destiny as we lead future generations into a more free and positive world.

This book is a call to action for anyone who thinks a better world is possible. We have the power to make a difference; we outnumber our oppressors by roughly a million to one. They stand absolutely no chance; their only power comes from their control over our thoughts and actions. We are incarcerated in an invisible prison, where our society and learned bias's act as the bars and prison walls. So in order to free humanity from this rat race we must first educate and enlighten as many people as possible about the true nature of our existence so they are able to think and act in a way that empowers them and the rest of their human family. YOU can be a part of this movement, and in order for this to work, you MUST be a part of this movement. Every human being has the creative energy within them to move mountains even if they do not realize it. So take that creative energy, and become a part of the movement any way that you can, use the natural gift within you to spread the message that a revolution of love and compassion is not only possible for this world, but necessary.

If you are already an artist of some kind, stop for a minute and think about what rather purpose your art is serving, notice if your art sends any particular message. Now think about your beliefs and see if your art lines up with those beliefs. Since art has a profound impact on the minds of the people it reaches, the artist has a responsibility to make sure that they are not sending any negative or self-destructive messages. This is the idea of the new counter culture movement, to replace our obsolete, destructive, and materialistic culture with a more peaceful and unifying one. When this day comes, we can finally put an end to war, poverty and the mass manipulation that is responsible for the nightmare our species is experiencing. This book and the work I have done with my company "Good Vibes Promo" is my humble contribution to the movement, and I'm really looking forward to seeing yours!

QUOTE SOURCES AND SUGGESTED READING
----
[0] Saul Williams – Coded Language

"I did not come here to chill; I came here to rock, to smash the empire with my boom box!"
- Michael Franti (Rock Musician) [0]

Disclaimer

First, this book is dedicated to you and every other soul that has been a victim of war, financial slavery, and genocide. I would also like to acknowledge the people who have made me feel sane and encouraged me to continue with this project despite the many roadblocks and discouraging situations that I have encountered during the three years it took me to finish writing this. There are many ideas in this book that may be unpopular. These ideas may question everything you know to be true. Since I am aware that so many of the issues that I touch on are extremely controversial I make sure to back up my claims with specific examples that have been proven and are on public record for you to research yourself.

Some of the most damning evidence that I present herein are the direct confessions and public statements of the culprits themselves. As you will discover, that which we learned through our "education," media, cultural institutions and even our family and friends is mostly disinformation that has been handed down by our illegitimate rulers, so it is important that you approach this information with an open mind. These essays are best read in order, but the book does start out with some very heavy subject matter, so feel free to use the table of contents to bounce around if you are in the mood to learn about a particular subject.

By providing this research I am in no way saying I am any kind of authority, and you are completely welcome to disagree with me all that you wish. This book is simply one of my attempts to speak out about the injustice that is going on in the world, and offer a few simple ideas that I think would improve the quality of life for our whole species. You're also welcome to disagree with my solutions, and if you do, I encourage you to organize your ideas to create an alternative to share with the world.

The issues facing our generation are so abundant and so complex that I felt it was best to briefly explain a wide variety of those issues. These short essays will introduce you into the world that has been hidden from our view by the cultural institutions that dominate modern societies. The information you are about to read is only the tip of the iceberg, the very surface of the rabbit hole. This is merely one resource of many, and after you finish reading, I urge you to continue your research so you can form your own unique opinions about what is going on in the world. No one source of information should be the foundation of your worldview, when that happens you is giving another person the power of thinking for you.

The specific facts that I offer up in this book and the confessions that I reveal I will stand by as fact, but I still suggest everyone does their research to confirm mine. That is not to say that everything contained within this book is absolute truth, especially some of the metaphysical aspects of my philosophy. Metaphysics still plays an important role in what is going on in the world today, and in order to branch off into that realm of philosophy it is necessary to venture beyond the limitations of our five senses, and beyond measurable phenomena. My assumptions on spirituality and various legends are simply assumptions based on my research and my own personal experience.

I personally believe these things to be true but can't prove them because they are in the realm of the supernatural. I feel that these topics are still important to bring up, because they are related to some of the deeper issues that many people are afraid to consider. For your convenience, I have grouped these more metaphysical discussions in two sections, Imagination and Legend, so remember to read with an extra critical eye when you get to that part of the book. With that being said when it comes to my research on politics, the history of banking and the current plan that the elite has for global society, I am 100% confident that these facts are correct. However, all these areas should be read with a critical eye as well, every word you read anywhere should be approached this way.

In the following pages, I will break down how many aspects of modern culture create a prison for the human family. Some of the things I say may challenge your most sacred beliefs and your favorite pass times. By revealing this information to you, I'm not telling you to completely change your life, but I want you to be aware that there is more going on then you have been told. The society that we grew up in was built upon lies so we would be powerless and ignorant of what was really taking place on the global stage. If one is able to set aside the cultural assumptions that have been instilled in us by our oppressors and think for ourselves the true nature of our struggle will come into focus.

Many of us have a vested interest in maintaining these cultural assumptions because they act as a defense mechanism, protecting us from the harshness of reality. Unfortunately, the longer that we ignore the problems that face our species and leave them for someone else to deal with, the direr our predicament becomes. At first glimpse, these issues may seem overwhelming and insurmountable but simply knowing that they exist is the first step towards freeing your mind and creating a better world for all of us to live in. Contraire to what we have been led to believe ignorance is not bliss; it is actually the reason for the majority of the suffering that has taken place throughout history.

If we are not fully aware of what is going on then there is no way that we can possibly improve the quality of life on this earth so our children can live in a better world. Everyone wants to be positive and it is definitely in our nature to put off things that may be difficult, sad, or painful. However, this is no excuse to ignore legitimate problems that need to be fixed and it is certainly no reason to allow crimes to be committed before our very eyes.

One of the biggest obstacles between humanity and a better future is the corrupt governments and financial systems of the world. Today almost everyone is somehow connected to these systems and depend upon them for survival. Most of the jobs available are related to the government, military, corporation, or other system of control, there are not many other options. When I discuss the crimes of the government and aristocracy in this book, I am specifically referring to the evil of the system itself and the people at the very top who have been corrupted by that system, not the average person who's working a nine to five job for the government or the person on unemployment.

When a person initiates violence or fraud, they then enter a territory where they can rightfully be exposed and brought to justice for their crimes. So it may seem like I am "attacking" or "slandering" various people throughout this book, but that is only because their actions have justified this sort of reaction. I am simply pointing out their aggressions and suggesting that we do something about it, while those that I criticize are the ones who are initiating violence. That is not to say that there are not many good people who are simply trying to survive and provide for their family and they are left with no choice but to work a government job or collect a welfare check. Some of these people even understand the failings of the system and do have the good intentions of making changes from within the system, but unfortunately, the system is designed to prevent that from happening.

You cannot use a broken system to fix it; it just does not make sense. Either way, this book is not an indictment of the average person, who is simply a cog in the wheel and a mere victim themselves. If you are one of these people, remember that just because you are forced to depend on the establishment for survival in some way or another does not mean that you have to agree with and support their actions. When I criticize these things that we are all forced to do I am no way attacking you. When I say that the education system is, corrupt I am in no way condemning people that have no choice but to send their children to public school, I understand that there are very little options in this society. By saying that gas and oil is used to control us and is harmful for the environment, I am not condemning the construction worker who is forced to use a gas guzzling truck for work. Car emissions are nothing compared to the billions of gallons of crude oil that have been dumped into the ocean by multinational oil corporations.

Due to the way this whole system has been created, we oftentimes have no choice but to live within the boundaries of the establishment and the status quo if we wish to survive, I understand that. However, that does not change reality, it does not change the fact that we are being taken advantage of, and it does not change the fact that a better world is actually possible. If we do not fully understand the nature of our reality, then we will be unable to avoid the common social pitfalls and we will fail to create a better world for our children.

There are some of you that will read this and think my ideas are "all over the place" because I do not subscribe to a particular political ideology and adhere to all the ideas of a Republican, Democrat, Communist, or Anarchist. Things are much more complicated than simply picking a political party or social clique and subscribing yourself to a whole system of beliefs based on other people's ideas. It is important that everyone knows about what is going on around the world and has an opinion of their own. This is a situation that is much more important than the vast oceans of junk culture that people have extremely complicated opinions about. So if you disagree with me about something that is great! I'm glad that you feel strongly about something that is not on TV! Please research that topic the best that you can and bring your informed opinion to the rest of us so we can make some progress, which is what a free society is all about!

QUOTE SOURCES AND SUGGESTED READING
----
[0] Michael Franti & Spearhead - Hey World (Remote Control) - All Rebel Rockers (2008)

"The true alchemists do not change lead into gold, they change the world into words." - William H. Gass [0]

Alchemy

All alchemy starts with the mind, or more specifically the application of the mind to achieve some kind of productive or creative goal. If this is the case then it is safe to say that this has probably been taking place in various forms since the beginning of time. Although little facts are known about life in ancient Egypt, we can tell from their ruins that alchemy played a very important role in their society.

The first alchemists in western culture were the early philosophers of ancient Greece, the great thinkers who brought the concepts of logic, reason, and philosophy into the realm of mainstream society. Aristotle, Plato, and Socrates were among the most influential of the ancient philosophers because their ideas greatly improved our ability to make sense of reality. Many researchers believe that these great thinkers actually picked up a lot of their ideas from the mystery schools of ancient Egypt, where some of them spent time studying. This is quite possible considering Greece is fairly close to Egypt and the ancient Egyptians had an extremely advanced philosophy that was similar to that of the Greeks.

In ancient Greece, the tools of the alchemist were far more accessible to everyday citizens than ever before. Although there was still aristocracy and slave labor in ancient Greece, there was also a wealth of information that was rarely seen in the ancient world. The use of logic and philosophy was definitely one of the primary factors in the development of this early democracy. Tyrants thrive in times of violent insurrection, as it adds legitimacy to the idea that people need to be controlled, but when their authority is logically examined, it is revealed to be illegitimate and will no longer be tolerated.

Logic was a new way of thinking about the world through closely examining the language that was used to describe reality. By removing contradictions from their philosophies and exposing lies in their culture, they were eventually able to construct a clearer vision of reality that resulted in one of the most independent civilizations that the world had ever seen. Unfortunately, this intellectual power and freedom among the commoners forced the aristocracy to become even more deceptive until they eventually conned their way back into supreme power, which ultimately resulted in the downfall of their civilization.

After the fall of ancient Greece and then Rome the entire western world descended into a dark age where there was no philosophy, logic, or intellectual self-defense whatsoever for the mass majority of the population. It was not until centuries later when the age of enlightenment and European renaissance revived the long lost arts of logic and philosophy, which eventually grew into the infamous "Alchemy" that many of us are so familiar with today.

The early European renaissance was defined by the explosion of art, culture, and expression that took place just after the dark ages. In a short time, Western Europe was transformed from a dreary, hopeless wasteland into a thriving center for business, education, and technology. This transformation was the result of the public becoming more informed and aware about history, alchemy, and philosophy. Prior to the renaissance, only the nobility was able to learn about these subjects, the rest of the population was cut off from this kind of intellectual study. This suppression of information had a profound impact on the worldview that most of the public shared throughout the middle ages. Once the information spread to the masses and they became more cultured it was like a veil had lifted and many people saw the world in an entirely new and different way. These new insights were shared with the peasants through art, music, and other forms of culture. Through this revolutionary subculture, everyday peasants were transformed into artisans and alchemists who brought life to their ideas with their newfound knowledge.

Aside from philosophy, astrology is by far the oldest form of alchemy. Some of the earliest civilizations were expert astrologers who had knowledge that in many cases surpassed today's most accomplished astrophysicists. The modern concept of astrology that is found in tabloids and newspapers is really a cheap knock off when compared to the work of real astrologers. Expert astrologers have a deep knowledge of how people's moods are affected by the movement of our planet in relation to other celestial bodies. Although the idea of astrology is ridiculed in most mainstream circles, the most wealthy, and powerful people in the world have personal astrologers. Infamous robber baron J.P. Morgan had it right when he said, "Millionaires do not have astrologers, billionaires do. " [1]

It is even rumored that Morgan's astrologer advised him not to get on the Titanic, a voyage that killed many of his friends and business associates. Ronald Regan is another powerful public figure who was obsessed with astrology as was documented in the Washington post, Time Magazine, and People magazine during his presidential term. The elite have long been obsessed with the supernatural although they typically dismiss this publicly. One glaring example in recent history is the case of Hitler, who we now know to be obsessed with the occult and the supernatural, yet kept this fact secret during his rule. In typical "do as I say not as I do", fashion Hitler outlawed any kind of literature on the supernatural while at the same time sending his troops around the world in search of the Holy Grail and the Spear of Destiny.

Sacred Geometry is another extremely old form of alchemy that is as old as life itself in the natural world, but was not discovered by humans until ancient times. In many ways, sacred geometry is being completely rediscovered today and could possibly be the key to some amazing new technologies. Since prior to the rise of ancient Egypt sacred geometry has been used in advanced art, music and architecture. In nature, sacred geometry can be seen in shells, flowers, beehives and even in your own mind during meditative states.

Today the knowledge of sacred geometry has paved the way for the forms of fractals. Fractals are kind of an advanced form of sacred geometry in which there is a "fragmented geometric shape that can be split into parts, each of which is a reduced sized copy of the whole" [2] Today fractals are used in advanced computer technology, graphic simulations, art, and music. In nature, fractals can be found in snowflakes, spider webs, river networks, clouds, mountain ranges, crystals, leaves, lightning, systems of blood vessels and even DNA.

DNA itself is an amazing development of modern science and shamanism that is constantly unraveling deeper mysteries into the nature of life and our existence. I say shamanism because Francis Crick, the scientist who discovered DNA, was actually on LSD when he made his groundbreaking revelation. Shamanism when combined with critical thinking skills and a definite purpose can lead to many more of these unbelievable discoveries. This practice is also age old, psychedelic use and deep meditation has been common among alchemists and philosophers in various cultures throughout history, although these areas of research were typically forbidden. The alchemists and philosophers had access to much more information than the rest of society did, but there were still many areas that were forbidden even to them.

In the dark ages, any higher education or cultural expression was reserved strictly for the ruling class. In suppressing this knowledge, the elite have actually slowed down the evolutionary process as well. If over 90% of the population is not given all the tools and all the information that is necessary for them to do their part in pushing along civilization, then there will not be much of a civilization. Sure, the physical labor you get out of the population will bring great roads and palaces, but if their creativity is not fueled then there will be very little cultural advancement. That is the kind of society you have during a dark age, one where a small group of people are responsible for the direction of the civilization while the rest are exploited and dehumanized.

The artists and alchemists brought the renaissance to Europe. They were on the cutting edge of knowledge and would hide sensitive information in their works. This was a way of peacefully bringing revolutionary ideas to average people who had not yet been exposed to them. It was this spreading of ideas through art that was responsible for a complete change in society and upheaval of the old cultural norms. This is the only true revolution, because any revolution that is born in violence will continue in violence and just result in another oppressive government. Although the alchemists were not able to bring a completely free and humane society to Western Europe they were able to greatly improve the quality of life for average people within their civilization just by expressing their ideas.

A revolution of ideas is what these people brought to the struggling society of the dark ages, and it was that revolution which saved that society from total collapse. Without one weapon being drawn, these thought warriors radically changed the whole structure of society. There is so much that can be learned from this period in history and the people that made it what it was. We are on the brink of total collapse because people do not have all the information and are not given a fair shot to express themselves.

Our economic, political, and religious institutions have been hiding information from us for ages and it has limited our perception of reality. This is the same sort of knowledge suppression that was occurring in the dark ages. This kind of intellectual oppression lasted for hundreds of years until the renaissance when that forbidden information was revealed to the masses through art.

A violent revolution will only bring more pain and human suffering. The only way to change the structure of society without violence is with a revolution of ideas. Our thoughts are our greatest asset and our most powerful weapon in the fight for freedom and every single one of us has the ability to make a positive change. Bring history to the people and share your insights into philosophy just as the alchemists and artisans did in the past. This is the peaceful way to a different society, to create instead of destroy.

QUOTE SOURCES AND SUGGESTED READING
----
[0] A Temple of Texts - William H. Gass (2006)
[1] J.P. Morgan: Signs of success By Steve M. Weiss
[2] Mandelbrot, B.B. (1982). The Fractal Geometry of Nature. W.H. Freeman and Company
[SR1] Logic: A Very Short Introduction by Graham Priest
[SR2] Sacred Geometry, Philosophy, and Practice by Robert Lawlor
[SR3] Serpent in the Sky: The High Wisdom of Ancient Egypt by John Anthony West
[SR4] Alchemy: An Introduction to the Symbolism and the Psychology (Studies in Jungian Psychology) by Marie-Louise Von Franz
[SR5] Alchemy & Mysticism: The Hermetic Museum (25th) by Alexander Roob
[SR6] Hermetic Philosophy & Alchemy (Kegan Paul Library of Arcana) by M.A Atwood
[SR7] The Emerald Tablet: Alchemy for Personal Transformation by Dennis William Hauck

"There is no reason why the future generation should be instructed in how to live by an older generation that is committing suicide." - Manly P. Hall [0]

Ethics and the Basic Philosophical Principles of Peace and Freedom

What is morality? This question has been debated by philosophers since the beginning of time. Today, it is one of the most confusing and volatile topics in western culture. Throughout human history, our course of action has been directed by our sense of morality and our code of ethics. In other words, our concept of "right and wrong" or "good and evil" has had a direct impact on our behavior.

Ethically speaking, our species has come a very long way since the dark ages, but the progression is far from over, and has unfortunately slowed to a screeching halt in the 20th century. Sure, the slave trade has slowed down, authoritarian psychopaths now have a velvet glove over their iron fist, and people are at least starting to pretend that civil liberties have a place in our society. However, this only shows that we are a species just beginning to discover ethical principles, not a species that fully understands these principles and is able to put them into practice. If our collective direction is not founded on consistent ethical principles then we still have a very long way to go before we can truly call ourselves "civilized."

Humanity is at a very interesting crossroads, we now know right from wrong but we continue to allow immorality to take place for the sake of convenience. This is much in the same way that the cigarette smoker knows that they really should quit, but just can't bring themselves to actually do it. What we are lacking here is an objective and universal code of ethics that holds every human being to the same moral standard and is consistent in all circumstances. Throughout time, there has existed a double standard, in which the average people have been subject to a completely different set of rights and expectations than their rulers experienced.

A double standard is basically the idea that different people are subject to different rules and expectations based on their class position, race, sex, or social status. This idea becomes even more complicated when you throw "proxies" into the mix. A "proxy" is basically a group or organization that accepts blame and responsibility for the actions of individual people. To put this term into perspective, many people see the word "proxy" as another way of saying "barrier" or "shield."

Governments and corporations are the most obvious and oppressive examples of this phenomenon in our society. When people do something on behalf of the government or a corporation they are almost never held accountable for their actions, this is one of the primary purposes of governments and corporations to begin with. These proxies legitimize the unethical actions of individual people and protect them from any legal consequences.

The double standards created by governments and corporations are at the very root of human suffering and environmental destruction. We have come to the understanding as a species that murder, theft, kidnaping, and other forms of violence are completely unacceptable human behaviors. Unfortunately, it is not that simple. This is where the double standards come in, because the aforementioned violent acts are excused if they are carried out by agents of the State or the corporate establishment. This is why none of the people who were responsible for the financial collapse or the murder of civilians in Iraq have been brought to justice. Murder is seen as justified if it takes place on a battlefield; theft is seen as charity if it takes place at the hands of an IRS agent; and kidnapping is seen as justice if the police are locking up a nonviolent offender.

This is the insane world that we have found ourselves in: a world of subjective law and subjective morality where the most heinous atrocities are given a pass if they are ordered or allowed by someone in "authority." Gang members and serial killers account for a very tiny percentage of the violence that takes place on the entire planet, as these people are forced to do their deeds in secret and they are subject to the consequences of law. On the other hand, State-sponsored thieves and murderers like the IRS, the army, or the police are cloaked by the false legitimacy that is created by the proxy of government. Corporations work very much the same way thanks to a little-known legal loophole called "corporate personhood." This is why no one is held accountable when the CEOs at Exxon make decisions that bury tropical islands in crude oil, or the CEOs at Goldman Sachs make decisions that cause millions to be homeless.

On the other hand, your average citizens are under constant scrutiny and are always 10 steps behind the tiny few who are given a license to murder, cheat, and steal. This is why there is so much inequality and violence in the world, because some people are allowed to cheat, steals, and commits violence without consequence. It really is that simple.

This subjective legal structure is quite effective in keeping people in their place, but it only goes so far because it does not affect people's behavior when they are in private. This is where morality comes in. Moral arguments have long been used by religious or political organizations to manipulate people and dictate their personal decisions, even when "the law" is not looking. These various establishments constantly twist the definitions of "right and wrong" depending on the circumstance to suit their own needs and steer human behavior in a direction of their choosing. Strict judgments about victimless actions and obedience to authority have been imposed on us and our ancestors and sold to us as moral virtue. At the same time, those in power and authority have been given a pass to violate these established moral values as a matter of contrived necessity.

Generally, when a violent crime is committed, the suspect is at least sought after to face punishment for their crime. However, if that criminal is sanctioned by the state their aggression is overlooked and considered to be perfectly moral. This is nothing new; control systems throughout history have used inconsistent moral standards to warp the minds of their subjects. One of the primary objectives of any government is to justify or legitimize their own aggressions and to ultimately develop a monopoly on the use of force so no one is able to challenge their power. This is why the idea of a clear and consistent moral standard is so repulsive to those in power, because they know it will ultimately negate their double standard, hold them accountable for their unjust actions, and revoke their license to threaten and kill.

In short, authority figures establish ethical guidelines based on their own self-interest and then tell the public *"do as I say, not as I do...because I said so."* This is a completely unjust and illogical way of evaluating ethics, because it is NOT intended to evaluate ethics, it is simply a con intended to make obedience a virtue in the eyes of the oppressed. Obedience is never a virtue. When ideas about morality are forcefully imposed and are not practiced by those who enforce them, it is not just those particular ideas that are rejected by the population, but the whole concept of morality altogether is rejected with it. This is a natural reaction to counter the cognitive dissonance that has been created by years of contradictory ethical standards and inconsistent moral codes. After so many generations of suffering under the false moral codes of different ruling classes, many people nowadays just shut off and roll their eyes at the mere mention of morality.

This multi-generational corruption of morality has left the majority of people generally confused and frustrated with ethical concepts, thus giving way to the philosophies of pragmatism and solipsism. Both of these philosophies basically equate to moral relativism, the idea that there is no such thing as objective morality. This has been the doctrine of solipsism for ages; pragmatism is just the newer reformatted version of this same philosophy. These ideas did not naturally develop in the human consciousness but were injected into mainstream culture through the media and education system. When adopted in the early 20th century pragmatism implicitly justified state violence and actively demoralized future generations by ruling that ethics were subjective and a matter of opinion.

Moral relativism is essentially the idea that morality does not exist and cannot be defined, but rather is only a matter of agreed upon social convention. This is the core principle that was embodied in the philosophical Trojan horse of pragmatism. Pragmatism is one of the most popular and misunderstood concepts in western thought. It sounds nice, if you look up the definition of "pragmatism," you will see the word "practical" used multiple times without establishing exactly what that means. Let us take a look; here is the definition of "pragmatism" from the Merriam Webster online dictionary.

" An American movement in philosophy marked by the doctrines that the meaning of conceptions is to be sought in their practical bearings, that the function of thought is to guide action, and that truth is preeminently to be tested by the practical consequences of belief" [1]

This definition is rather confusing, but when you sift through the newspeak, you will find a philosophy that does not really stand for anything but just "goes with the flow" and disregards the search for truth and morality. The pragmatist blindly seeks out the path of least resistance without attempting to properly understand how that path came to be. This mentality is obviously reckless, irrational, and nihilistic yet is unbelievably popular because it allows people to take a passive role in reality without feeling any guilt or shame.

If a person believes that, there are no moral absolutes they are then able to justify their own unethical actions, as well as turn their back on the unethical actions of others, if that is what feels good for them at the time. This is obviously a very appealing philosophy for people who have been trained from birth to accept authority and feel incapable of achieving any good in this world even if they tried. It is also somewhat understandable that people would adopt this mindset considering they have been subject to a lifetime of watching various religious sects battle over subjective moral standards. Likewise, they have seen corrupt political organizations use moral arguments to oppress nonviolent people and justify their own violence at the same time.

Most peaceful and rational people get very turned off by these kinds of situations and rightfully so. Yet this is the very reason that pragmatism and ideas of moral relativism are so attractive to the current generation, because people are understandably sick and tired of having their personal lives governed by irrational and subjective moral edicts. This is most likely the same reason why many of the philosophers and academics who got any attention during the 20th century embraced these ideas, but there were still a few rebels who saw these ideas for what they really were.

One such rebel was libertarian philosopher Ayn Rand. She not only rejected moral relativism but actually developed her own way of describing the existence of absolute truth. This is embodied in her "objectivist" philosophy that states that absolute truth can be determined by applying a logical process to observable and verifiable facts. Objectivism has been a popular worldview for rational people since the advent of philosophy, but Rand was the first person to put it in clear terms. She developed this philosophy at a time when pragmatism was extremely popular so naturally she was a relentless critic of the pragmatist outlook. In her book "For the New Intellectual," she gives a brilliant description of the pragmatist philosophy and its implications on ethics in society. She said: *"They [The Pragmatists] declared that philosophy must be practical and that practicality consists of dispensing with all absolute principles and standards—that there is no such thing as objective reality or permanent truth—that truth is that which works, and its validity can be judged only by its consequences—that no facts can be known with certainty in advance…….whatever one wishes to be true, is true, whatever one wishes to exist, does exist, provided it works or makes one feel better….. and anyone who holds any firm convictions of his own is an arbitrary, mystic dogmatist, since reality is indeterminate and people determine its actual nature."* [2]

Ayn Rand rightfully diagnosed this morally bankrupt mentality as the unspoken menace that plagues the soul of humanity. While I do not personally agree with every single aspect of Ayn Rand's work (specifically her ardent defense of big business and avocation of egoism), she did have many great ideas that have made it a lot easier for future generations to understand philosophy. More recently, in 2011 a world-renowned scholar and educator named John Taylor Gatto shared similar thoughts in an interview with Richard Grove of Tragedy and Hope media.

Gatto Said *"If you now connect pragmatism with the concept of justified sinning, you have an absolute blank check in any situation, to invent truth, invent justice, sacrifice biologically inconsequential people and invent any excuse for doing anything that you want. It seems to me that is been the driving force in American affairs for a long long time, but interestingly enough it is been the driving force of an intellectual elite, I believe, through history."* [3] So in other words, people in power use these philosophies to control the minds of the entire human population, in order to justify their crimes and rationalize the abhorrent civilization that they have created.

The philosophy of moral relativism has been embedded in our culture for several generations, so by now it has become an unquestioned and unconscious convention. Today children grow up learning this philosophy without even realizing it, much in the same way that they learn other cultural traits like accents, slang terms or even personality traits or nervous habits. These are all things that we pick up unconsciously from the culture we grow up in, as we are constantly exposed to these ideas through the media, education, family and our peers.

Many children who adopt this philosophy still manage to become intelligent adults who openly reject culturally imposed dogma, without realizing that their whole worldview is corrupted by the subliminal dogma of pragmatism. Our lives are filled with encounters where people use pragmatic arguments to explain their actions or defend the status quo, so naturally this mindset becomes quite popular without ever being explicitly described or understood. Unfortunately, moral relativism, solipsism, and pragmatism are the dominant ethical philosophies of the modern age, which has rendered our generation, and several before it demoralized, hedonistic and apathetic.

If a consistent moral standard is necessary to create a truly free and civilized society then those standards must apply to everyone equally. Interestingly enough, such a standard has already been proposed and is practiced by pacifists and freedom seekers worldwide. That standard is known as the Non-Aggression Principle or NAP for short. The common law institute describes the non-aggression principle as "do not initiate force or fraud," or "if it harms none, do what you will," or "treat others as you'd like to be treated," or "live and let live." In more detail, "Do not initiate force or fraud against anyone else's person or property." In other words, except for self-defense, *"do not harm others, do not harm or steal their property, do not break your word, and do not try to coerce anyone by threatening to do any of these things, and do not delegate or encourage anyone to do any of these things."* [4]

Do not hurt anyone, be honest and do not take anything that does not belong to you, this sounds like an incredible ethical guideline to me! In reality, this is all common sense to most average people and the good majority of the world's population would prefer to live their lives according to these principals. These standards are also generally accepted by most religions and social groups. Some people will even argue that our society is already functioning according to these principals, and for the most part they would be right. However, there are a few exceptions to this rule that have thrown our world into chaos, that being authority figures who claim the privilege to initiate force without consequence or legitimate claim of defense.

By this non-aggression standard, we can say, "*if you initiate the use of force and harm another person, or you violate their property you are acting immorally.*" This rule applies to every human being regardless of what title they happen to have or costume they happen to be wearing. This is a moral standard that aims to protect the individual rights and personal property of every human being, regardless of class or social position. This would be recognized as fair, only customs that are seen as fair will actually be respected by society, which is why subjective and inconsistent standards are never fully respected and encourage chaos. These guidelines are universal so therefore more honest than moral codes in the past that have been subjective and centered around force, obedience, or sacrifice.

Subjective ethical standards are seen as optional by most people, so they fail to create any kind of social order, which is apparently what they are intended to do. The reason that most people see these standards as optional is because they are rarely followed by those in power. If the most powerful people in the world are behaving like savages, then that sends a message to the rest humanity that behaving like a savage will bring you power, wealth, and happiness. This seems like a natural psychological reaction to me, as disturbing as it is, it does make a lot of sense.

No one wants to be a victim of violence, theft, or fraud; it is these fears that are responsible for the development of law and morality in philosophy to begin with. Unfortunately, neither law nor morality is currently achieving this goal because their honest intention is not to protect people but to fleece and control them. Only a subjective law can be used by one to control another, a universal law on the other hand is a common understanding that encourages honest and peaceful interactions. When someone steps outside of these guidelines for any reason and initiates the use of force or fraud they can then be held accountable for their aggressions, no matter who they are.

The Non-Aggression Principle does not only protect us from harm and fraud but it also encourages honesty and integrity because it holds everyone to the same standard. People cannot be honest with one another in the face of a double standard because in order to accept that double standard in the first place they must already be lying to themselves. Morality has continued to be a messy, confusing, and divisive topic because it has remained subjective and oppressive. Applying Objectivism to the Non-Aggression principle will establish an ethical framework that will be respected for its fairness and will actually achieve the goal of promoting honest and peaceful interactions in society.

QUOTE SOURCES AND SUGGESTED READING
[0] Manly P. Hall – personal collection of audio lectures
[1] Merriam Webster Online Dictionary
[2] For the New Intellectual –By Ayn Rand
[3] Peace revolution 43 john Taylor Gatto the ultimate history lesson interviews

[4] http://common-law.net/nap.html
[SR1] The Ethics of Liberty by Murray N. Rothbard
[SR2] Ethics for the New Millennium by Dalai Lama
[SR3] For the New Intellectual by Ayn Rand
[SR4] Law, Liberty, and Morality by H. Hart
[SR5] Bright-sided: How the Relentless Promotion of Positive Thinking Has Undermined America by Barbara Ehrenreich
[SR6] The Nicomachean Ethics by Aristotle
[SR7] Universally Preferable Behavior by A Rational Proof of Secular Ethics by Stefan Molyneux

"Conventional wisdom would have one believe that it is insane to resist this, the mightiest of empires, but what history really shows is that today's empire is tomorrow's ashes; that nothing lasts forever, and that to not resist is to acquiesce in your own oppression. The greatest form of sanity that anyone can exercise is to resist that force that is trying to repress, oppress, and fight down the human spirit." - Mumia Abu Jamal [0]

Human Struggle for Civil Rights

Since the beginning of civilization, the majority of the world's population has been in a constant fight for equality and civil liberties. It has been the same story all along in many different cultures; small groups of people have been obsessed with dominating the rest of us, and have successfully done so by using force, words, and mind games. Since ancient times there have been tyrants and power hungry elitists committing the most horrific human rights violations to satisfy their greed and dominate their fellow human beings.

Many steps have been made in the right direction since the days of slavery, human sacrifice or the witch-hunts, but we really haven't come all that far. Consumerism is the new slavery and war is the new form of human sacrifice where billions of souls are wasted in the name of conquest. We still live in an inhumane world where a ruling class dominates and enslaves the rest of us. Through all the hardships that our ancestors have endured over the past few millennia we have realized that the kind of life that we were being offered before was unacceptable. In the past few hundred years we have voiced this realization and demanded that the ruling class allows us to live in a more peaceful and free society. This kind of situation usually presents itself as a revolution where whoever is in power is removed and replaced with another tyrant and the system stays completely the same.

If there are ever any changes after a revolution, they are very small, although the "leader" may change the concept of authority and the "justified" violence that comes with it continues. If any rights are granted to the population it is a very select few liberties given to a small portion of society. We have seen this all throughout history, the elite has told the public that they will now have rights, but that you are only entitled to those rights if you meet certain "criteria". Usually their criteria leave out over half of the population. This trick is tragically obvious when looking at the aftermath of the European monarchies collapsing or the end of slavery in America.

Before all of the revolutions took place pretty much no one had any rights except for the monarchy. Then after various revolutions broke out all over Europe the monarchy was forced to give a small percentage of the population some kind of say in government. That group of course being white land owning males , everyone else was considered "unfit" to have any kind of say in how the society was ran. This continued until women had to fight for their rights, then African Americans and all the way down the line.

The elite was certainly in no hurry to give any kind of rights or privileges to any of these groups, but were forced to do so individually as each group demanded them. When the elite finally felt threatened enough they gave small amounts of freedom to the people and made minimal concessions on their social policy, but again not much changed, the elite still had an immense amount of power and control over everyone on the planet. Even though they allowed the public to have limited rights they did not give up their taste for control that easy. History tells us that despite what they say, the elite are not particularly in favor of the commoners having civil liberties; they have taken every opportunity to keep us from having them. Public concern for human rights is not in their favor either because they count on having a dehumanized population that is willing to go to war and give up their basic rights.

Now the public will no longer accept the kind of conditions that our ancestors dealt with. Since the elite can no longer tell us to our faces that they believe they are our "divine rulers" they must now pretend to be the voice of reason so we will still listen to them, and they have done a very good job at fooling most of us. They have made most of us think that we are free and that our civil rights have already been won but this is far from the case.

Average people that do not come from high-income families are typically going to have an extremely hard time getting any kind of job in the political system. Not only that, they have a far greater chance of becoming a victim of our corrupt legal system. To be treated fairly, to have equal opportunity and an equal say in politics are certainly basic civil liberties that our culture does not provide. Even the rights that are apparently available to us today such as free speech, privacy, or the right to bear arms are systematically being taken away because these freedoms threaten their control system.

Ensuring that not everyone living on this planet has their basic human rights violated should be a priority for the world community. How can we say that we are living in a "civilized" society when war, genocide, slavery and other forms of exploitation are taking place all over the globe? These atrocities are unfortunately still a sad reality for the majority of the people on this planet. To top it off, all of this is actually being carried out by various elites and their puppet regimes who tell the world that the only way to peace and prosperity is by following their orders.

Although most of history has been a cycle of oppressive, dominating societies, there have been those times when we managed to win some freedoms from the powers that be. Those emancipating times have led to some of the most impressive civilizations seen in the human story. Unfortunately as we saw with the Greek and Roman Empires, after a few generations of flourishing under self-governance a civilization comes to a crossroads. The wealth and progress of the society attracts greedy souls that wish to use the nation's power to create an empire. This situation is a recipe for disaster because once a civilization reaches this point it is very easy for it to be hijacked by corrupt warmongers. This process is inevitable when centralized control is present, because it is then easy for a psychopath to come along and hijack the civilization simply by gaining political power and establishing themselves as a so-called "authority."

The struggle for human rights is a struggle against the exploitation of people. It is a struggle towards the freedom of autonomy and self-ownership, the right for people to live as they wish without bothering anyone else. We are all important and vital to the essence of this planet, none of us deserve to be killed, oppressed, or marginalized because of the color of our skin, the language we speak, the size of our bank account or the politics of our so-called "leaders."

This kind of mentality where small groups of people are given the power to use force on others without consequence is depraved and is responsible for the dismal state of our civilization. We are making progress, but we must continue to demand that we are given the freedom that we deserve. Many generations of our ancestors have fought to end inequality and oppression, it is our responsibility to carry on that legacy so our children will live in a more peaceful and free worlds then we see today.

QUOTE SOURCES AND SUGGESTED READING
----

[0] the executed god: the way of the cross in lockdown America - Mark Lewis Taylor (2001)

"2000 years of history could not be wiped away so easily"
– Bob Marley & the Wailers

Section 2

The Past

6. -Occult History and Nationalistic Folklore
7. -Powerful people commit crimes and lie to you about it.... This is no theory
8. -The Banking Backstory of Friday The 13th
9. -America Was Not Discovered, It Was Stolen
10. -The Nazi Corporate Fallout
11. -Darwinism, Eugenics and the Silent Genocide

"History will be kind to me for I intend to write it." - Sir Winston Churchill [0]

Occult History and Nationalistic Folklore

Having an accurate view of history is extremely important in making sense of what is going on in the world today. Every situation that is taking place today is the result of something that happened in the past, and those past situations are the result of something that happened before that. This may seem very simple but among our politicians and the general public there is no respect for the great lessons of history. If there was a proper respect for the lessons that history has taught us then most people's opinions about global policy would change drastically. Without a clear picture of how we got here it is completely impossible to figure out how to get to where we need to be, which is why everyone is so confused about the state of the world. Think back to our discussion on pragmatism while reading these next two chapters. It is extremely relevant because pragmatism basically insists that history and causation have no value whatsoever.

In school and in the media history is generalized by random and mostly trivial events. This results in a mainstream view of history, where there is a disconnected series of events that seem to take place for absolutely no reason. Many of the extremely important events in history that had a big impact on the world have been left completely out of the history books. This shortsighted historical dialogue in the public arena causes people to have a distorted vision of why things are the way they are. If you are going to see a movie and you arrive to the theater late and miss the beginning, then the middle and the end of the film will make no sense to you.

The history that is acknowledged by our schools, media, and other social institutions is a very superficial and biased account of what actually happened. There are countless stories that have been intentionally hidden from our view for many ages. These stories make up what many have called our "occult history," as the word "occult" simply means hidden. When hidden information is revealed the dots of the past are connected and history is no longer a confusing blur. If the occult history is the version of events that is factual and hidden, then the version of events that is false and presented to the general population through the media and education system should be considered "nationalistic folklore." This idea of nationalistic folklore goes back before the times of Plato, who used the phrase "noble lies" to describe the false reality that is presented to society by the ruling class. The purpose of a noble lie is to maintain social order and keep the working class in their place. This same idea was prevalent in Nazi Germany, only Hitler referred to the noble lie as "the big lie."

"*Voting allows the people a say in government*," "taxes are spent on public services not war and bureaucratic budgets," "the government always acts in the best interest of the public," "the government cares about the public and is here to protect them" and "financial success is the only route to happiness." These are just a few of the blatant noble lies that work to maintain the social structure of western civilization. Possibly one of the worst noble lies to infect our generation is the idea that "there is no such thing as truth or morality." It does not take much investigation to discover that those statements are untrue, but due to intimidation, social engineering, peer pressure and other methods of coercion, the lies are never exposed so they continue to perpetuate.

We are now a country that is torn apart by war, poverty, and corruption. The politicians and elite tell us that we only have ourselves to blame for these hellish circumstances and that we are an out of control society. We are told that we should hate and fear our neighbors, but our neighbors are not to blame and neither are we. There are many times throughout history that we can look back on and see that specific political organizations and financial dynasties are completely responsible for the chaotic world that we are seeing develop. To cover up their responsibility these dynasties and organizations create nationalistic folklore in which they are the protectors of humanity who no one can live without, when in reality the complete opposite is true.

With all the manipulation that takes place in shaping our view of the past it is apparent that what has happened in history is still open to debate in many cases. It is also a widely accepted idea that those in power write history in a way that makes them seem honorable, and if that is true it would reaffirm that mainstream, history is only one side of the story. The establishment is very open about the fact that they are in control of the public perception of reality. George W. Bush blatantly lied to the American public about Iraq developing weapons of mass destruction, and when news became known that there were in fact no weapons of mass destruction Bush simply accused anyone who criticized him of attempting to "revise history." On June 16th while giving a speech about that very issue Bush said "Now there are some who would like to rewrite history; revisionist historians is what I like to call them"[1]

He made this statement knowing that it did not match up with the facts that had recently been made public. This is because the facts are completely irrelevant to the establishment; the only version of events that is accepted in discussion is their side of the story. Karl Rove, one of the top aides in the Bush white house took this idea a step further when he described to a New York Times reporter how the establishment literally controls reality. The Reporter Ron Susskind happened to be critical of the dishonest Bush administration and Rove responded by claiming that Susskind belonged to "what we call the reality-based community," which he defined as people who "believe that solutions emerge from your judicious study of discernible reality. That is not the way the world really works anymore. We are an empire now, and when we act, we create our own reality. Moreover, while you are studying that reality—judiciously, as you will— we will act again, creating other new realities, which you can study too, and that is how things will sort out. We are history's actors ... and you, all of you, will be left to just study what we do." [2] What Rove is saying here is that he and the rest of the establishment decide what reality is and what fiction is, using absolutely no logical process and basing none of their stories on verifiable facts?

Most Americans are extremely confused about the plummeting economy and an ever-growing unemployment rate because the history of money has been neglected by our education systems and completely rewritten by the corporate controlled media. If we look back at the history of the US economy and banking system, which has been hidden, from us, then everything makes a lot more sense. Our economic downfall is a result of our country being sold out to corporate banks over a hundred years ago. Because of the pyramid scheme that they have created in our economy it is impossible for our country to get out of debt. These banking cartels have been around since before the discovery of the new world, and since the days of the American colonies they have been obsessed with controlling this nation's economy just as they do in Brittan and now the rest of Europe.

Many of the most popular US presidents greatly opposed the banks and became very popular with the people because of their strong stance on the matter. Andrew Jackson may have been a slave-owning aristocrat and he is far from a champion of the common people, but he was one of the biggest challengers of the English banking cartels. In the 19th century Jackson gave us a warning about the banks that puts the current crisis into focus, he said "The bold effort the present bank had made to control the government ... are but premonitions of the fate that await the American people should they be deluded into a perpetuation of this institution or the establishment of another like it." [3]

A hundred years later during the great depression president Franklin Roosevelt admitted that the financial sector had successfully gained control of the entire country. In a letter to white house regular Edward Mandell House; Roosevelt wrote, "The real truth of the matter is, as you and I know that a financial element in the large centers has OWNED the Government of the U.S.

since the days of Andrew Jackson."[4]

This will become even more interesting when we learn in a later chapter that House was actually a front man for the bankers who was a mentor to many American presidents most notably Woodrow Wilson and Franklin Roosevelt. He was more or less the Henry Kissinger of the early 20th century. Understanding the history and looking at the corruption within the financial sector today it is possible to connect the dots and make sense of what is going on with the economy. With just one small piece of hidden information the story seems to come together and this is just one quick example of how discovering some of this occult history can shed light onto confusing or overwhelming situations.

Even more confusing than the economic situation is the endless cycle of senseless wars taking place all over the world. Again, many people do not have a proper historical reference when it comes to the military industrial complex. What is taking place right now is what has been taking place for the past few thousand years, conquest. Powerful governments and the financial interests that back them are creating empires all around the world, while making a fortune selling weapons and pillaging natural resources. They are invading lands that they are confident they can conquer and once they do so they set up their companies and start taking any resources of value that they can find. This is what the banking dynasties, the US and the United Nations are doing and it is nothing new. Since the days of Alexander the Great or the Roman Empire power hungry political and financial groups have set off around the world in conquest.

The similarities between the ancient Roman Empire and the current American society are astonishing. A quick look at the history of the Roman Empire can really clear up a lot of confusion about the radical expansion of the US military. Despite the government-generated myth that war is good for the economy, war is in fact the absolute worst financial predicament that a country can get themselves into. There is nothing more costly than a war, especially these days. Looking back at almost every empire that has ever collapsed including ancient Rome, an excessive wartime policy has always been the downfall of the civilization.

The Roman warmongers had convinced their people that they were spreading "civilization" and that foreign enemies were a threat to their everyday life. Even closer to our own time we can see how the British empire used military force to destroy the lands of millions of native people in the name of "colonization" or "democracy". Even America itself is a British colony where an untold number of native shaman people were murdered and had their land stolen by the government. Sadly America has followed in the footsteps of the British, spreading our corrupt system of pseudo democracy around the world by the barrel of a gun. Regardless of what excuse they give us they are still doing the same thing that has been done in the past, just because the language involved and excuses given are different does not mean that anything has changed.

George Orwell said, "He, who controls the present, controls the past. He, who controls the past, controls the future."[5] What he meant by this statement was that if someone can control how a society sees their history, it would then be easy for them to control the direction that the society would take. This has been the situation throughout western civilization, the elite has been able to get away with the same crimes again and again by distorting our view of history and having a tight control of which historical information reached the masses. As we have been told many times before, "those who are not aware of their history are doomed to repeat it." With a clear view of the past we can make responsible decisions for the future, so we do not have to be faced with an unfortunate history repeating itself.

QUOTE SOURCES AND SUGGESTED READING
----
[0]Secrets of superstar speakers: wisdom from the greatest motivators of our time - Lillet Walters (2000)
[1]The lies of George W. Bush: mastering the politics of deception - David Corn (2003)
[2]Faith, Certainty and the Presidency of George W. Bush By Ron Suskind October 17, 2004 New York Times
[3] Jackson closed the second Federal Bank (est. 1816) with these comments in 1836; his speech was published in the Annals of Congress, Volume 1, pages 1140-1143.
[4]President Franklin D. Roosevelt in a letter to Col. Edward Mandell House (21 November 1933) Source: F.D.R.: His Personal Letters, 1928-1945 (1970 edition) edited by Elliott Roosevelt
[5] 1984 - George Orwell
[SR1] Secret Societies and Psychological Warfare by Michael A. Hoffman II
[SR2] The Politically Incorrect Guide to American History by Thomas E. Woods Jr.
[SR3] The Republic by Plato
[SR4] Matrix of Power: How the World Has Been Controlled By Powerful People Without Your Knowledge by Jordan Maxwell
[SR5] A Peoples History Of The United States Of America by Howard Zinn
[SR6] Common Sense by Thomas Paine
[SR7] The making of the English working class by E.P. Thompson

"When a well-packaged web of lies has been sold gradually to the masses over generations, the truth will seem utterly preposterous and its speaker a raving lunatic."
- Dresden James [0]

Powerful People Commit Crimes and Lie About It.... This Is No "Theory.

Large-scale crimes are complicated and very difficult to carry out, so they require multiple people working together in secret in order for them to be successful. Something on the scale of a bank heist would require a handful of people, while something like a mass murder or drug trafficking operation requires a much larger network of more well connected and well protected criminals. Whether they are street gangs, mafias, cartels, or governments, these crime syndicates all go through great lengths to keep the vital details of their operations a secret and to provide a cover story that justifies their existence and excuses the atrocities that they are unable to hide.

It is not uncommon for criminal groups to present a drastically different picture of themselves to the public because ultimately the fate of their mission is dependent upon public opinion. When a criminal or criminal group has the support of the public they can go on undetected until they eventually grow arrogant and cross the line, exposing themselves in the process. The government, the mafia, a banking cartel, and a street gang may look like different groups but they behave in very much the same way and use many of the same excuses to justify their violent actions. If you ask any of these groups why they exist and what purpose they serve, the answer will always be protection, security, and financial necessity. The only thing that separates these groups in reality is a difference in resources, public image, and scale of operations. All of the previously mentioned groups use intimidation, force, and manipulation as they battle rival groups over dominance, resources, and territory.

If you are having a hard time wrapping your mind around the fact that the major politicians and financial interests are criminals then simply look at it from a business perspective. It is no secret that big business works so closely with the government that they are arguably the same entity; this fact is highlighted by the revolving door that exists between these two different factions of the state. Most people who find themselves in high-level political positions were once CEO's of fortune 100 companies and those who are not will likely become a well-connected lobbyist upon leaving office.

Dick Cheney, vice president and top executive at Halliburton or Goldman Sachs CEO turned treasury secretary Henry Paulson would be among the most obvious examples of this revolving door. Both of the crooks in question undoubtedly used their political positions to influence events in such a way that would greatly benefit their respective businesses, this is commonplace in Washington. It is even more typical for those involved in business to develop quiet and cooperative relationships with people who already have political power;

this allows them to direct national policy from behind the scenes by simply befriending or bribing decision makers. The relationships between the world's most powerful people are blurred in the public, but behind the scenes many of them work very closely together, went to the same colleges, go to the same social clubs, attend the same meetings and send their children to the same schools. What this tells us is that beyond political parties and campaign rhetoric there are many connections and relationships that are rarely discussed in the public. As I said before public opinion is basically the only thing that is holding a criminal back from committing their next crime, which is why people who carry out large scale violence or theft are so interested in learning how to control and manipulate public opinion.

Taking this process a step further, the government has been able to develop a forced monopoly on education while big business has been able to develop an equally damaging monopoly over the media. Since big business and government both represent different arms of the same ruling class we can say that together through their control of various social institutions, such as the media and education system, they are able to direct public opinion away from their crimes and establish a nationalistic folklore in the public consciousness that is favorable to their worldview. This nationalistic folklore is nothing but a collection of cover stories with very little supporting evidence, and sadly these cover stories have been accepted as truth by the general public.

One of the basic defense mechanisms of the criminal establishment is to ridicule and attack anyone who dares to question the false reality that they have meticulously created. The term "conspiracy theorist" developed during the early 20th century and was used to describe people who did not believe in the "mafia." That is correct, for the majority of the 20th century the government completely denied the existence of organized crime. This is most likely due to the fact that the mafia was the government's underground army. Later "conspiracy theorist" was used to describe the people who did not believe the official story of the JFK assassination. This term is intended to automatically discredit a person or their ideas without actually taking a look at the arguments or evidence that they are providing. This is a relatively new shortcut in thinking, but it is similar to terms like "heretic" or "traitor" which were used to discredit truth seekers and dissenters throughout history. It was not until 1997 that the term conspiracy theory appeared in the English dictionary, the same year that a Hollywood film was released of the same title.

By definition the word conspiracy means "a secret agreement between two or more people to perform an unlawful act." So we can say that the definition of conspiracy theory would be "an accusation of a secret agreement between two or more people to perform an unlawful act." When a conspiracy theory ends up being true it then turns into a conspiracy case, because conspiracy is considered a crime in most cases. Every day in our corrupt judicial system people are sent to jail on counts of "conspiracy." Mob bosses, drug dealers, gang members, stockbrokers, and politicians alike get charged with conspiracy when they are found to be planning illegal acts in secret. Technically a lawyer who is working to prosecute suspects in a bank robbery could be considered a conspiracy theorist. Yet the term "conspiracy theory" has such a negative stigma attached to it that it is used as an argument ender in the media and political circles. What this implies is that we are not allowed to make accusations of unlawful acts on the part of our government or the elite. It seems the discussion is over once you start making claims about people who have power and wealth.

The term conspiracy theory is often associated with stories like big foot, the loch ness monster, or Hollywood gossip found in supermarket tabloids. These fantasies are all designed by the corporately owned media in order to create fictitious controversy. This is necessary in order to establish a public bias so when real controversy presents itself the public is reliant on the story that is seen as most popular or easiest to believe. The unfortunate thing about how this works is that the "official story" is always created and presented by the people who are in question of committing the crimes. This is like allowing a criminal to be their own prosecutor, judge, jury, and press.

Much of the stigma surrounding conspiracy theories comes from government intimidation. The government is just like one big gang or mafia organization. They use the same tactics to keep their wrong doings secret, including murder and witness intimidation. It is normal for activists to get death threats and be otherwise victimized through government fear tactics. Nonviolent revolutionary and civil rights hero Martin Luther King JR. had his phone tapped by the CIA, received regular death threats and even had several bombs left at his house. Later, classified documents came to surface showing how many of these threats were actually ordered by the US government as a part of their counter activist program called "COINTELPRO." COINTELPRO waged war against the US population in an attempt to slow down the social and civil progress that threatened the goals of the establishment.

When it comes to political conspiracy theory whoever is making the accusation is many times on point, and if they're not it is still possible that the government just did a really good job covering their tracks. Luckily for us, a lot of times they slip up or someone on the inside is brave enough to bring information to the surface, so some of the incidents that people once considered conspiracy theories are actually now proven to be true. The Manhattan Project was the military program that developed the atomic bomb. This project was considered by most people to be a conspiracy theory for years, until the bombs eventually dropped. Whole towns were built to test the first nuclear weapons. All of the residents were sworn to secrecy and spread out between one of the 30 testing sites across North America and the UK. The Manhattan project started out as a small testing operation in 1939 but in the few years it was in operation it grew to have over 130,000 people, all under strict secrecy.

There is also a very popular misconception in the mainstream consciousness that the weight of evidence is on the side of the establishment when in reality this is far from the case. The amount of evidence that proves government corruption and conspiracies against the people far outweighs any evidence defending the establishment against the claims of "conspiracy theorists."

As an example ill start with a controversial issue that continues to divide people all over the world that being the destruction of the World Trade Center buildings on 9/11. There is no hard evidence whatsoever linking CIA asset and patsy Osama Bin Laden to the attacks, yet according to the media, education systems and other arms of the establishment, he has become the "undisputed mastermind" of the attacks. In fact the only evidence that the establishment rests upon is their "9/11 commission" which has since been exposed as a sham.

Most of the people who oversaw this commission have since came forward and admitted that they were forced into presenting a version of events that was scripted by the establishment. One of these commissioners named John Farmer even wrote a book called the ground truth, detailing how evidence was intentionally left out of the report and how the blame was intentionally placed on Arabs in order to foment war in the Middle East. The flimsy 9/11 narrative suffered another fatal blow when the US government claimed to have killed Osama Bin Laden in 2011 without offering any evidence and changing the story multiple times. These few circumstances illustrate important cases where there was no evidence to back up the version of events that was handed down by the establishment, now let's take a look and see what kind of evidence is presented by those who dare question the "official versions" of world events.

The mainstream culture will lead you to believe that things like mind control, eugenics, depopulation programs, false flag attacks, the establishment of world government, and other claims of corruption are unfounded theories with no evidence behind them. However, there is a substantial amount of evidence proving that all of the aforementioned claims are verifiably true. Declassified government documents, admissions of guilt and studies carried out by the members of the establishment in question offer direct insight into these issues. Throughout the rest of this book I will be citing those documents, quoting those confessions and laying out all of the evidence to prove the claims that I am making. I will also discuss the work of propaganda experts and scientists who developed mind control techniques and aristocrats who openly admit their crimes against humanity. If this kind of information was actually brought out in a trial it would prove beyond doubt that the establishment is implicit in subverting public opinion using nefarious methods and guilty of conspiring with other members of the ruling class to expand their power and wealth.

So what is so hard to believe about powerful corporations and members of our government secretly getting together to plan global events? It seems like it is almost necessary for these parties to have meetings about their future policies. These plans are obviously more effective when carried out in secret so the culture of lies in politics seems to be a natural result of self-preservation. Yet when someone brings this point to light they are ridiculed in the media and their observation is labeled as "conspiracy theory", which one immediately associates with big foot type stories.

Many of the accusations that are brought up against the government that are labeled as conspiracy theories are eventually proven to be true way after the fact, just like the Manhattan project. The gulf of Tonkin incident, The Watergate scandal, The Tuskegee experiments, The Iran contra situation and other world changing events have all been exposed as conspiracies. Before the truths of these events were exposed the government and puppet media organizations labeled all these stories as "conspiracy theories" that the public should not take seriously. When evidence was finally uncovered that proved otherwise it became apparent that there was an actual conspiracy taking place and that the government and media were lying all along. Our "leaders" tell us to not give any thought to conspiracy theories just as anyone who is hiding something will tell you not to look for it or the wizard of Oz will tell you not to mind the man behind the curtain. Corruption exists within all levels of our government and within our corporations. This is no theory, and to call it one is to assume that there are no facts or documented evidence to back it up when they are in our face every single day and have been documented for centuries.

QUOTE SOURCES AND SUGGESTED READING
----
[0]Liberty Quotes - Christopher Kalabus (2009)
[SR1] American Assassination: The Strange Death of Senator Paul Wellstone by James H. Fetzer
[SR2] JFK: The CIA, Vietnam, and the Plot to Assassinate JFK by L. Fletcher Prouty
[SR3] None Dare Call it Conspiracy by Gary Allen
[SR4] Behold a pale horse – William Cooper

"The Bankers own the earth. Take it away from them, but leave them the power to create deposits, and with the flick of the pen they will create enough deposits to buy it back again. However, take it away from them, and all the great fortunes like mine will disappear and they ought to disappear, for this would be a happier and better world to live in. But, if you wish to remain the slaves of Bankers and pay the cost of your own slavery, let them continue to create deposits." [0]
- Sir Josiah Stamp

The Banking Backstory of Friday The 13

The unlucky Friday the 13 is one of the most well recognized superstitions in the western world. This tradition is over 700 years old and has a very interesting origin. During the 12th century there was a massive religious war that consumed most of Europe and Asia. Europeans referred to these times as "the crusades." This war lasted centuries and allowed an elite class of knights to accumulate so much power and wealth that their influence rivaled both the monarchy and the church. The knights of the temple of Solomon, or more commonly known as "The Knights Templar" were the most influential political force of their time. They were the world's first international bankers and were the corporate giant of the middle ages.

The Templar Knights were a military force throughout the entire crusades, but did not become a strong political organization until they were given diplomatic immunity by the church in 1126. Their close relationship with the church was unusual for the time, as the lifestyle of a knight was usually associated more with the monarchy. The Knights Templar represented both the warrior and the priest, and was often referred to as the "fighting monks." This best of both worlds diplomacy allowed the knights to form their own political dynasty that transcended the established powers of the time. They did not have to abide by the same rules as the church or the monarchy but they had the advantage and privileges of both institutions.

During the crusades it was rumored that the Templars studied alchemy and discovered forbidden knowledge on their journeys. This would not be the first time that this has happened in history, it is actually quite common for conquerors to return home with ancient artifacts, just like napoleon did with the Rosetta stone, for example. Some say that instead of offering their discoveries to museums the Templars kept the artifacts and knowledge within their own order. This is all speculation and legend, but what we do know for certain is that the Templars were sneaky executives and became the world's first multinational bankers.

They had most of the known world caught in a complex pyramid scheme that is eerily similar to the scams that are being run by international bankers today. They collected taxes for protecting trade roads, bankrolled both sides of all the wars and exploited the massive peasant class and used them as workhorses to build their fortunes. Through these shady practices the knights ended up having more money than the monarchy and the church combined. Both the church and the monarchy were deeply in debt to the Templars from loans they had taken out, so one would be able to argue quite easily that the Templars were the most dominant political institution of the time.

Eventually the monarchy grew very threatened by the immense power of the Knights Templar. The person to finally take action against the Templars was King Phillip the 4th of France. Since the Templars were under the protection of the church, King Phillip needed papal permission to overthrow them. In order to get this blessing Phillip covertly murdered two popes in less than a year until a candidate of his choice was in power. With all the necessary steps taken King Phillip made his move. On the morning of Friday, April 13 1307 there was a surprise raid on all the Templar offices. The knights were being arrested on over a hundred different counts of heresy and treason and confessed after being brutally tortured. After a short, rigged trial the Templars were sentenced to burn at the stake. The grand master of the Knights Templar cursed the king and pope before he was executed, and synchronistical both died within the year.

It is said that a fleet of Templar warships managed to escape France the night before the raids, and continued to control world events from behind the scenes. They apparently did this by changing their names and moving to various different parts of the known world. In fact, it is said by many that the Templars who managed to escape the inquisition fled to Switzerland and reestablished their international banking cartel there.

This theory makes sense considering that the country has been a safe haven for bankers and robber barons for centuries. There are over 500 major banking institutions in Switzerland, the majority of them are owned and controlled by various elite bloodlines and covert organizations that I'll describe in detail later on. It is estimated that around 35% of all the private wealth globally is held in Switzerland. The world trade organization or WTO is also based in Switzerland. These banks are among some of the only financial institutions in Europe who are not subject to audits and investigations from the new European Union government. The financial district in London called "the city," as well as the Vatican in Italy is also given the same kind of protection and secrecy, but they are the only areas in Europe that have those kinds of privileges. It is also rather interesting that the Swiss Guard is responsible for guarding the pope (located in Italy, not Switzerland), a task that was once the job of the Knights Templar.

The flag of Switzerland is actually an inversion of the Templar's shield, the flag being red with a white cross and the shield being white with a red cross. The banking elite may have ties to the areas government and economy, but they have nothing to do with the people of Switzerland. They do not represent them and their actions should not be held against the people of this country. In fact Switzerland is one of the best places on earth to live, with very free social policies. They have a low crime rate because everyone in the country is armed and drugs are legal. They also remain neutral in all major wars, but still, when there is smoke there is usually fire. Although I would not mind living in Switzerland myself and imagine it is filled with wonderful people, there are just too many clues pointing to this region as playing a vital role in the many worldwide banking schemes. With this being a very realistic possibility, Templar influence would seem to put the puzzle together nicely, but it is not something that we have been able to prove yet. Switzerland is just one of the many places where the elite have established a stronghold to operate from; the same goes with "The City" in London, the Vatican, Washington DC, and Zionist Israel. The people that live in these places have nothing to do with the elite's plans, aside from being used as workhorses, cannon fodder, and political pawns.

Since the days of their fall from grace the Templar Knights and their predecessors have learned their lesson, and have continued their work in secret. Even if the official order went underground their business model and diplomatic strategies are still very much alive today and have a deep impact on our way of life. The Templars became an all-powerful "invisible government" by mastering and manipulating economics much like the bankers that influence world events today. In fact, today's multinational bankers follow the Templars model precisely and use all of the same age-old tactics to exploit the masses.

QUOTE SOURCES AND SUGGESTED READING
----
[0] The Legalized Crime of Banking - Silas W. Adams (1958)
[SR1] Babylon's Banksters by Joseph P. Farrell
[SR2] The Place of Enchantment by Alex Owen

"Illegal aliens have always been a problem in the United States, ask any Indian."
- Robert Orben [0]

America Was Not Discovered, It Was Stolen

The shaman people that inhabited North and South America prior to its brutal Anglo European takeover built a vast and organized civilization. They lived in structured societies that were democratic and very connected with spirituality and nature. There was very little sickness and they had medicinal plants for every condition that were far superior to today's pharmaceuticals. The indigenous people were extremely happy, things like depression, mental illness, crime, or greed were not nearly as prevalent in their culture, as is seen in ours. Now I'm not so naive as to think that all the natives were totally peaceful, but the kind of mass violence seen in the west was certainly not present. There were many different tribes scattered throughout North and South America, some of them peaceful, some of them violent, it was literally a whole new world inhabited by a vast network of societies each with their own unique culture.

There were definitely some tribes that employed slave labor and practiced human sacrifice, but these groups were more hierarchical in structure then the rest of the native populations. To say that there was just one civilization here before colonization began would be a disservice to the diverse culture of the pre Columbus Americas. Making the generalization that every tribe in that hemisphere was the same would be like saying that Canada, Mexico, and the United States had identical cultures today. Contrary to the Europeans claims that the Americas were a vast uninhabited wilderness, there was actually a massive native population that numbered in the hundreds of millions. Traces of this large population seemed easy enough to destroy at first, considering the natives put a great deal of care into making as little an impact on their environment as possible. However, as time passes archeologists are continuing to uncover evidence that the pre Columbus civilizations were much more advanced and populated then the historical record tells us. Even the ship logs of early European explorers show us a much different story than we were told in history class.

That is not the only thing we were lied to about in history class. The ruling elite were also well aware that there were unexplored continents on the other side of the Atlantic Ocean. Many early European civilizations took voyages to the other side of the Atlantic over a thousand years ago; it is even believed that early Irish and Norse cultures actually had trade established with some Native American tribes. All of this information was hidden from most of the general public, only the nobility who were literate and had a decent understanding of history knew that the world was twice as big as most people believed. As I discuss many times throughout this book, oppressive warmongering rulers always hide important information from their subjects so they are easier to control and more willing to accept subpar living standards, this situation is no different. The myth that the world was flat was merely propaganda to keep explorers from traveling west and discovering the new world before the monarchy was able to claim it.

Due to lack of resources and the extensive crusades and inquisitions that were raging in Europe for many centuries, it took the elite until 1492 to make their official move across the Atlantic Ocean. Prior to this, only exploratory voyages were taken to the new world in order to prepare and gather information for future colonization. When the elite were ready for conquest they sent an inquisitor and mapmaker by the name of Christopher Columbus to begin the Native American genocide and colonization process. Columbus was not an explorer but one of the few elite members of society that had access to occult information such as the existence of the Americas.

He knew exactly where he was going when he set sail across the Atlantic Ocean. He most likely obtained this knowledge through a secret society he belonged to called "the Knights of Christ," which was apparently a surviving order of the Knights Templar. This connection would explain why all of the ships from his famous first voyage were flying the colors of the Knights Templar, the Maltese Red Cross. Regardless of where Columbus got his information his mission was certain, to harvest natural resources using native slave labor and to claim land for the monarchy. This colonization would be the start of the most brutal genocide in known human history.

When Columbus reached the new world he arrived in the Caribbean islands and established his first settlement in what is now Haiti. Upon their arrival the Europeans immediately started looking for gold and began persecuting the native people. Columbus was under extreme pressure to return to Europe with as much gold as possible, in order to repay the monarchy for funding his voyage. To speed up the process Columbus and his men became even more brutal with the native people. They ordered every man, woman and child they found to collect a certain amount of gold every three months. The natives that reached their quota would receive a copper token that they would wear around their neck. If they were found without these tokens they were brutally tortured and murdered. Because of the trusting nature and disposition of the native people, the barbarian conquerors easily took advantage of them. In old ship logs we can see the ignorant and ruthless attitude that the European invaders had towards the indigenous people.

In his journal Columbus wrote, "they are so naïve and so free with their possessions that no one who has not witnessed them would believe it. When you ask for something they have, they never say no. To the contrary, they offer to share with anyone. They brought us parrots and balls of cotton and spears and many other things, which they exchanged for the glass beads and hawks' bells. They willingly traded everything they owned…. They do not bear arms, and do not know them, for I showed them a sword, they took it by the edge and cut themselves out of ignorance. They have no iron. Their spears are made of cane. They would make fine servants. With fifty men we could subjugate them all and make them do whatever we want." [1]

The atrocities committed by Columbus and his crew were just the beginning of the American holocaust that eventually destroyed a vast and thriving civilization. Over the half millennia that followed different European nations set up colonies in lands that did not belong to them and killed hundreds of millions of people to do so. Hundreds of years of murder and displacement have left the native shaman people with a fraction of their population, all of which have been forced onto small concentration camp like reservations. The age of imperialism saw the genocide of many civilizations in Africa, Australia and Asia as well as the Americas.

QUOTE SOURCES AND SUGGESTED READING
----
[0] Robert Orben - Patterns in prehistory by Robert J. Wenke (p. 587)
[1] A Peoples History of the United States - Howard Zinn
[SR1] 1491: New Revelations of the Americas Before Columbus by Charles C. Mann

"When fascism comes to America, it will be wrapped in the flag and carrying the cross"
- Sinclair Lewis [0]

The Nazi Corporate Fallout

Our whole lives we have been told in school, at home and through the media that America is the greatest country in the world and is a beacon of moral integrity on the planet earth. We were taught that our society is the most humane and free type of civilization that is physically possible. Yet this same story has been told in the most fascist dictatorships, so who's to say that America is any different? History shows that our government has certainly not acted much different from some of the harsh dictators we have seen throughout the world in the 20th century. In fact, the government and major American corporations have done business with these regimes and in many cases even carried out the same oppressive policies themselves.

The most reviled of all fascist regimes in recent history is that of Adolph Hitler and the Nazi party of Germany. Hitler's regime took advantage of the terrible economic situation that Germany was riddled with after World War 1 and used advanced propaganda to generate public support for his insane policies. Many have even deemed this man to be an "antichrist," and rightfully so. If such a thing exists then Hitler is a prime candidate. He is responsible for building concentration camps, committing genocide and creating a totalitarian police state for the German people. It is also important to note that most of the German people were duped by the Nazi propaganda machine and actually believed that these oppressive policies were for their safety and for the good of the country. This was a horrible situation where a savage oligarchy took advantage of millions of people.

If there ever was a political institution that was a threat to freedom and civil rights it was the Nazi party. But this is not the reason why the Americans decided to fight them in World War 2. In fact, the Americans and the Germans had extremely good diplomacy before Japan bombed Pearl Harbor. Many American businesses and politicians worked very closely with the Nazis even after the two countries were at war with each other. The holocaust had already claimed the lives of millions of German people by that point, and a police state had long since been established, so whoever was doing business with the Nazis in the late 1930s and early 1940s knew exactly who they were getting involved with.

The war really had nothing to do with ideological differences or "liberating" populations from oppressive rulers but it was a massive business move for governments and big corporations. There was some level of conquest, with various elites attempting to redraw Europe and the Middle East, but there were also a lot of short-term gains for those involved through kickbacks from arms manufactures. War is never a "moral" issue, it is always about the ruling classes of different countries fighting over wealth and power, every single time, and both world wars are no different.

Prior to the Americans getting involved in the war there were corners of the political arena that were actually big supporters of the Nazi party, both for business purposes and common interests. The most prominent American politician to work with the Nazis was actually George W. Bush's grandfather Prescott Bush. There is no doubt that he was funding and working with the Nazis because his company's assets were seized in 1942 by the United States government under the "trading with the enemy" act. He worked at the head of a financial firm called Brown Brothers Harriman that acted as a US base for the Nazi business interests. Brown Brothers Harriman was one of the biggest international investment firms in the 1930's and they sent millions of dollars in gold overseas to rebuild the German army and fund the Nazi party. This racket was finally exposed on July 30 of 1942 when the New York Herald Tribune posted an article called "Hitler's Angel Has three million dollars in US Bank." This article raised suspicion about the bank being a "secret nest" for Nazi elite's and eventually sparked the investigation that took down the operation.

Some of Americas largest corporations also contributed to the atrocities committed in Nazi Germany during the Second World War. They saw the Nazi party as a rising political and financial force in Europe and they wanted a piece of that business. Many of them also had similar political and social interests as well. Among those corporations IBM was by far the most heavily involved with Hitler. In 1933, the very same year that Hitler came to power, IBM invested a million dollars into Nazi Germany and built a factory in Berlin. Once established in Germany the IBM Company began building the cataloging machines that Hitler would need to organize his genocide.

This technology was used to process and register which citizens would be sent to ghettos or concentration camps. Without the IBM cataloging devices known as the "Hollerith" machines the Nazis would have still carried out the holocaust but it would not have been nearly as organized, widespread, or deadly. IBM was not the only company that helped Hitler and his Nazi regime rise to power. Without the help of companies like General Electric, Standard Oil, I.G Farben, and Ford Motors the Nazis would have never had the resources or the technology to build a militarized empire from the ashes of the collapsed Weimar Republic.

There were many minds and organizations behind the Nazi policy of world domination, this brutal regime was not just the work of one lone crazed individual, and it was a network of elite powers that have been trying to take over the world for many centuries. Hitler just happened to be the front man of the group. This network includes royal bloodlines and the few elite families that dominate international business, as well as various "think tanks," secret societies, intelligence organizations and other esoteric groups. These groups have no loyalty to the countries that they represent. Eventually these international groups do not even want these countries to exist anyway; their goal is a global dictatorship that is controlled under one political, economic, and military force. This was Hitler's stated goal and the mission of many supporting organizations that outlived the Nazi regime and moved on to implant their fascist ideals into other governments that showed potential for power.

The multinational network behind global policy does not "choose sides" like they force the rest of us to do. They try to influence as many "sides" as they possibly can to increase the odds of them completing their mission. For example, in World War 2 they backed the US, the UK, the Soviets, the Nazis, and others to ensure that no matter the outcome, they would have a strong influence on the winner of the war. All of these aforementioned countries have a strong history of imperialism and racism that is in part due to the influence of the elite nation builders that sit behind their governments. It is important to note that they use racism as a weapon against every single ethnicity; they change the heritage that they vilify depending upon the political climate in order to suit their agenda. Any group or race of people that happens to be in the way of their plans becomes a target for racial discrimination. During the times of colonization it was the native tribes, during the times of slavery it was Africans, in Nazi Germany it was the Jews, and now in the "war on terror" it is the Muslims.

The same forces were behind all of these atrocities although different regimes may have led the various campaigns. We know that these events have been put into motion by the same groups because of transactions that take place between businesses (i.e. IG Farben, GE, and Standard Oil) and families (i.e. Bush) who have strong ties to the elite. These companies are still around today but have had to change their names various times due to their unscrupulous practices. Standard oil has splintered out into most of the major oil companies and IG Farben is now involved with big pharma and GE is still causing trouble under the same name.

After the war the Nazi military power in Germany came to an end but many key figures in the regime were scouted and recruited by governments and corporations from all over the world. Many of the primary influences, backers, and financiers of the Nazi party also went on to coach new world "leaders" on how to handle their military and foreign policy. The Americans rounded up dozens of Nazi scientists, economists, and special forces to give them jobs for the U.S government. In many cases the government had Nazis excused from war crimes so they could begin working for America. These Nazi transfers took place under a classified government project called "operation paperclip." Through this project many top ranking members of the Nazi party became integrated into the American government. One notable example is that of Wernher von Braun, a Nazi rocket scientist who was hired by the US through operation paperclip and who later worked with NASA as the chief engineer for the Saturn-V launch rocket that sent the Apollo spacecraft to the moon.

America was not the only country to be infected with the Nazi mentality after the end of World War 2. The United Kingdom also maintained contact with the elite circles that financed and encouraged Hitler's rise to power, which makes sense considering the UK, had a longer relationship with these groups than the Nazis did. It could be argued that the whole Nazi party was a creation of Anglo-American interests. This has been confirmed by the research of economics professor Antony C. Sutton in his book "Wall Street and the rise of Hitler."

When it was time for peace treaties to be signed and territorial lines redrawn at the end of the war it only makes sense that the elite which have been influencing all sides from the beginning would have a strong influence in this process, that is one of their main objectives in creating these wars to begin with. The elite pretty much ran the entire diplomatic process and used their influence over the established governments to create the United Nations. I'll get more into the specifics of this later, but the UN would become the groundwork for their next attempt at global domination. Through the UN the elite was able to create the structure and draw the borders for the post war nations as well as police the world according to their politics. Sadly, these same elite now have a strong influence in the United States, Israel and the whole continent of Europe, with many puppet regimes throughout the Middle East and Africa.

QUOTE SOURCES AND SUGGESTED READING
----
[0] It Can't Happen Here - Sinclair Lewis (1935)
[SR1] Leanord Piekoff – The Ominous Parallels
[SR2] The Rise of the Fourth Reich by Jim Marrs
[SR3] Unholy Alliance: A History of Nazi Involvement with the Occult By Peter Levenda
[SR4] Wall Street and the Rise of Hitler - Antony C. Sutton

"If I were reincarnated I would wish to be returned to earth as a killer virus to lower human population levels."
- Prince Phillip [0]

Darwinism, Eugenics, and the Silent Genocide

Charles Darwin is one of the most respected figures in scientific history and his ideological theories have changed the way we look at the world and how we practice science. Although "Darwinism" consists of more theory and assumption than scientific law, it is still held to be absolute truth in the western world. Charles Darwin did make some incredible observations about the natural world that no one in the west had even approached at the time. However, these natural observations were corrupted by his own ideological assumptions. There is a lot of truth in Darwin's work, but the truth that exists within his research really does not do anything to prove his materialistic assumptions.

Darwin's painfully damaging assumptions did not come from his research in the wilderness but from his upbringing as a white wealthy Englishman under the strict rule of the Catholic Church. Darwin belonged to a popular movement at the time that was fed up with the churches tyrannical rule. The aristocracy also had economic and strategic reasons for wanting to break down the established religious order, as the divine right of kings prevented the nobility from attaining more wealth and power then they already had. Darwin and his colleagues belonged to that privileged class which sought to disprove any kind of spirituality and remove the spirit from serious intellectual discussion. This was an understandable goal considering the extremely repressive nature of the church at the time, but what they did was throw the baby out with the bathwater, for lack of a better term.

It is true that the Anglo Saxon church in its many variations was unrealistic, outdated, and oppressive even at the time of Darwin, but for some reason he did not draw the line with organized religion but wanted to rule out the supernatural altogether. Darwin and his colleagues assumed that since spirituality in their culture was represented by an oppressive control system that the idea of spirit was somehow damaging to the human condition. In reality it was just the corrupted mainstream versions of religion that Darwin was exposed to that shaped his whole spiritual view. Even if the idea of spirit was some kind of menace, Darwin's observations have nothing to do with spirituality. Yes, Darwin's observations do disprove many specific points of the King James Bible, which did totally cripple that institution. However, the Christian bible or any other holy book for that matter is not any kind of representation of human spirituality. It is simply a book that was written by rulers and then passed along to the public as the "word of god. " Therefore, Darwin's findings only disprove the said "truths" of specific organized religions but have no implications for spirituality in general.

In Darwin's time there was an idea among the nobility that their genetics were superior to those of the rest of society. Many families including Darwin's took this belief to extreme levels by practicing incest as a tradition. They thought that if adolescents were to marry within their own family then not only would all the wealth stay in the family, but the "good" genes would also. This also ensured that the family fortunes would be retained for many future generations. This practice is very common in aristocratic families, which explains why they are all extremely mentally unstable. Darwin came from a very classist and racist elite level of society and that is reflected in his work, especially "The Descent of Man."

One of the most famous cases of royal incest is found in the Hapsburg dynasty that produced rulers in Spain, Austria, Hungary, Belgium, the Netherlands and the German empire. Around 1700 the Spanish branch of this empire fell apart suddenly and died off. Recent studies of the Hapsburg Family Tree show that sickness and deformity due to incest was responsible for the sudden demise of this "royal bloodline." The most successful political dynasty in America, the Bush family is notorious for inbreeding. In fact, George Bush Sr. and his wife Barbara Bush are actually in the same bloodline, which is the Pierce or Percy bloodline. The British house of this bloodline is named Percy and the American house is named Pierce. The elite's family structures are very complicated with many "houses" and surnames that are omitted from the public dialogue to avoid scrutiny and cover up their ongoing eugenics experiments. I am only singling out the Bush family because it is an example that those of you in the west will recognize, but in countries all over the world, in every continent there are elitists and monarchs who hold this worldview.

The ruling class of every nation is obsessed with breeding and is using the best of our advanced technology and medical science to guarantee that their heirs will be somehow thoroughbred. Since the aristocracy has been practicing selective breeding for centuries they are under the impression that they are already of a superior stock to the rest of humanity, thanks to the "care" that their ancestors took in breeding. This is of course just an egotistical delusion that justifies their exploitative treatment towards the rest of humanity.

Darwin's other dehumanizing ideology is his "survival of the fittest" mantra. Darwin did not just come up with this philosophy out of thin air; this was actually an idea that has been traditionally held by families of nobility since before the Middle Ages. It was this philosophy that the aristocracy used to justify their inhumane treatment of the serfs and peons that built their empires and tended to their fields. The saying "survival of the fittest" was actually coined by an aristocrat named Thomas Robert Malthus who was openly brutal and inhumane in his descriptions of the poor or as he called them "the lower races."

In a 1798 publication called "An Essay on the Principle of Population" Malthus suggested that planned food shortages could be used to decrease the population of the poor through starvation. This was the root for the idea of "population control," because a large population is very difficult for the elite to manage while retaining their own wealth and power. Malthus suggested that the streets should be made narrower and more people should be crowded into living quarters to encourage conditions that would bring back the plague. In that same essay he said that villages should be built next to stagnant pools where germs could fester and all remedies and cures would only be available to those who could afford it. In his own words "we are bound in justice and honor formally to disclaim the right of the poor to support. To this end, I should propose a regulation be made declaring that no child born should ever be entitled to parish assistance. This infant is comparatively speaking, of little value to society , as others will immediately supply its place…All children beyond what would be required to keep up the population to this level must perish, unless room be made for them by the deaths of grown persons." [1]

In so many words what he was suggesting was establishing a national limit on childbirths, and executing any child that was born past that limit. In the times of Malthus many elite circles were publicly speculating that if the world's population were to exceed 3 billion people there would be mass famine and destruction of all the resources on earth. Obviously, they were all very wrong. Malthus was wrong about many things, but nonetheless he was one of Darwin's primary influences and one of the most racist and arrogant aristocrats of the Victorian age. Without the writings of this brutal feudal lord and his predecessor Herbert Spencer it is very possible that population reduction would have played no part in Darwin's philosophy. Their racist and classist tendencies were prevalent even in Darwin's early work. In fact, his most famous work "Origin of Species" was originally titled "Preservation of Favored Races."

The true danger of Darwin's philosophy was exposed during the Second World War when "Social Darwinism" took Germany by storm and became the cornerstone of Hitler's most inhumane policies. Social Darwinism applies the survival of the fittest idea to human society and implies that our species would be stronger if the weaker end of the gene pool were to be eliminated. The pursuit of this "stronger species" would come in the form of an institution called "eugenics" which is still around today. Eugenics is defined in most dictionaries as "the study of or belief in the possibility of improving the qualities of the human species or a human population, especially by such means as discouraging reproduction by persons having genetic defects or presumed to have inheritable undesirable traits or encouraging reproduction by persons presumed to have inheritable desirable traits." This sadistic philosophy resulted in the sterilization, institutionalization, and genocide of millions of people throughout the world who were marked as subhuman by the ruling class.

Although Darwin's philosophy laid the groundwork for the eugenics movement it was not him who actually coined the term "eugenics," but it was his cousin Francis Galton. Galton's vision for the eugenics movement was to develop it into a science that would influence public policy until it eventually became a kind of religion. Galton defined eugenics as "the study of agencies under social control that may improve or impair the racial qualities of future generations, whether physically or mentally."[2]

In the beginning of the 20th century Galton began to introduce his new science to various intellectual circles around the world. He was gaining prominence around the time of Charles Darwin's death, and seeming as if it were planned Galton was there to carry the torch. Towards the end of Darwin's life his writings became darker and he was much more open about the ultimate social goals of his philosophy. His final book "Descent of Man" is obviously the work of a eugenicist, in it he clearly suggested that the evolution of humanity should be engineered by the Anglo-Saxon aristocracy, which he saw as a superior race.

There are many quotes in that book that illustrate his point of view, but none as clear and concise as this. Darwin published the following words "With savages, the weak in body or mind are soon eliminated; and those that survive commonly exhibit a vigorous state of health. We civilized men, on the other hand, do our utmost to check the process of elimination; we build asylums for the imbecile, the maimed, and the sick; we institute poor-laws and our medical men exert their utmost skill to save the life of every one to the last moment, Thus the weak members of civilized societies propagate their kind. No one who has attended to the breeding of domestic animals will doubt that this must be highly injurious to the race of man. It is surprising how soon a want of care, or care wrongly directed, leads to the degeneration of a domestic race; but excepting in the case of man himself, hardly any one is so ignorant as to allow his worst animals to breed." [3]

If Darwin had lived longer his rhetoric would have undoubtedly grown as blatantly racist as that of his cousin. Correspondence between the two shows that Galton was the one who introduced the philosophy of eugenics to Darwin. Just two years after the Descent of Man was published and nearly a decade before Darwin's death, Galton wrote a letter to the Times of London suggesting that the British move Chinese immigrants into Africa as a more stealthy way of carrying out genocide on the native population.

The letter read in part "My proposal is to make the encouragement of the Chinese settlements at one or more suitable places on the East Coast of Africa a part of our national policy, in the belief that the Chinese immigrants would not only maintain their position, but that they would multiply and their descendants supplant the inferior Negro race. I should expect the large part of the African seaboard, now sparsely occupied by lazy, palavering savages living under the nominal sovereignty of the Zanzibar, or Portugal, might in a few years be tenanted by industrious, order loving Chinese, living either as a semi-detached dependency of China, or else in perfect freedom under their own law." [4] Sadly, this letter was actually published, as this was the prevailing kind of attitude among the aristocracy at the time so that was what the papers printed.

The eugenics movement swept across Europe and the US, it was taught in schools, praised in the media, and finally pushed through as government policy almost everywhere. The Nazi party was not the only regime during those times that were guilty of forcing harsh eugenics policies on their people. All over the United States during World War 2 people who were depressed, handicap, alcoholic, or even children who were as young as 7 years old that happened to score too low on standardized IQ tests were singled out and sterilized. More than 42,000 people were sterilized in America between 1941 and 1943 under the guise of eugenics, so Germany was not the only country at the time that had sick master race schemes. In fact one of the most influential books to Hitler's ideology was a book called "passing of the great race" by an American named Madison Grant. Hitler called passing of the great race his "bible" and wrote Grant numerous fan letters.

Madison Grant was another eugenicist disguised as a philanthropist who was very influential in American politics. He was friends with numerous presidents, including Theodore Roosevelt and Herbert Hoover. It is no secret that the American government has an extremely racist track record and subjected the Native American and African population to the same inhumane treatment that the population of Europe received from Hitler. Grant was not alone either; Eugenics was a matter of national policy and still is today, though under various different names and disguises.

The first birth control efforts in America were motivated by Eugenics policies, and were specifically targeted at minorities and the poor working class. A Eugenicist by the name of Margaret Sanger established the countries first birth control bureaucracy "Planned Parenthood." Today this organization enjoys the respect of most progressives because they see it as providing an affordable service to the community. While this may be true for some, the sinister roots and intentions of this organization are not to be ignored. Margaret Sanger was surprisingly profane when discussing her ideas about eugenics in writing or public speeches. It was a stated goal of hers to limit the number of births among minorities; she called this effort "The Negro Project." It is terribly ironic that Planned Parenthood is seen as a philanthropic organization because Sanger was extremely clear about the fact that she was not a charity worker.

In "The Pivot of Civilization" she writes, "Even if we accept organized charity at its own valuation, and grant that it does the best it can, it is exposed to a more profound criticism. It reveals a fundamental and irremediable defect. It's very success, it is very efficiency, it is very necessity to the social order, are themselves the most unanswerable indictment. Organized charity itself is the symptom of a malignant social disease. Those vast, complex, interrelated organizations aiming to control and to diminish the spread of misery and destitution and all the menacing evils that spring out of this sinisterly fertile soil, are the surest sign that our civilization has bred, is breeding and is perpetuating constantly increasing numbers of defectives, delinquents and dependents. My criticism, therefore, is not directed at the failure of philanthropy, but rather at its success." [5]

It is true that there is some positive impact that Planned Parenthood has on many individuals, but that is merely an unintended consequence. Again, this was all revealed by Sanger in her writings. In that same book she writes "Every single case of inherited defect, every malformed child, every congenitally tainted human being brought into this world is of infinite importance to that poor individual; but it is of scarcely less importance to the rest of us and to all of our children who must pay in one way or another for these biological and racial mistakes." [6]

In these difficult times that we are living in birth control and abortion are a very real option for most people, and I'm in no way condemning anyone who chooses either. However, that does not change the intentions behind these programs, and it is important that we have all of the right information before we make life-changing decisions. These are the only methods of population reduction that operate in the light of day; the darker eugenics programs are carefully disguised and largely unknown to the general public.

The darker goals of eugenics were explored deeper by the works of Bertrand Russell, an author who championed many ideas of the ruling class. In "The Impact of Science on Society" Russell writes, "I do not pretend that birth control is the only way in which population can be kept from increasing... War... has hitherto been disappointing in this respect, but perhaps bacteriological war may prove more effective. If a Black Death could be spread throughout the world once in every generation survivors could procreate freely without making the world too full... The state of affairs might be somewhat unpleasant, but what of that? Really high-minded people are indifferent to happiness, especially other people's... There are three ways of securing a society that shall be stable as regards population. The first is that of birth control, the second that of infanticide or really destructive wars, and the third that of general misery except for a powerful minority..." [7]

When most people hear this kind of talk their first instinct is to ask "why would they do this?" or "what do they have to gain that they do not already have." Russell's next suggestion reveals the dark endgame of eugenics, he writes "Gradually, by selective breeding, the congenital differences between rulers and ruled will increase until they become almost different species. A revolt of the plebs would become as unthinkable as an organized insurrection of sheep against the practice of eating mutton."[8]

According to this testimony the elite have been seeking to branch humanity off into two different species with the most of humanity descending into a slave race or race of "plebs," and the Anglo-American aristocracy being the dominant "master race." This is why to this day elite families only breed with each other and in many cases breed within their own families. This is also why they dumbed down public education and are poisoning the general population, in hopes to speed along this process of creating two separate human species, the slaves, and the slave drivers.

In that same book, Bertrand Russell reveals how poisons of various kinds would help to speed along the evolutionary divergence and reduce the population. On page 66 he writes, "Diet, injections, and injunctions will combine, from a very early age, to produce the sort of character and the sort of beliefs that the authorities consider desirable, and any serious criticism of the powers that be will become psychologically impossible. Even if all are miserable, all will believe themselves happy, because the government will tell them they are so."[9]

These are among some of the most complex descriptions of eugenics to date, giving us some insight behind the plan and ultimate goal of this genocidal social movement. As with Darwin, Bertrand Russell is very popular among modern atheists for his criticisms of the church and organized religion, but most are not aware of his support for oligarchy and political control.

Eugenics was openly a social policy for most of the industrialized nations in the world until the peak of World War 2. At this time Hitler's extreme implementation of eugenics exposed the true nature of this sick pseudoscience and forced it underground. In the United States the eugenics movement changed its name and splintered off into various branches including genetics, population control, transhumanism, and social biology, among others. The Rockefellers, Rothschild's and Carnegies were some of the primary financiers for eugenics programs in the west and after World War 2 they just renamed their foundations to avoid public scrutiny. The "American Eugenics Society" became the "Population Council" and the aristocracy began funding their eugenics operations through tax-exempt foundations and parading their expenditures to the public as "charitable contributions to society." Today these same organizations and many others force sterilizing vaccinations onto third world populations, all the while acting like they are providing humanitarian aid to the people.

When straight foreword eugenics failed they moved it under the umbrella of population control and the working class was told that they were poor not because of corruption, but because there were just too many of them and not enough resources to go around. This lie is incredibly offensive when you take a look at the vast disparities within our societies where there is literally a ruling class and a serf class. Today the leading causes for hunger and poverty are war, displacement, lack of infrastructure and overexploited resources (usually on the part of large corporations and governments), but nowhere internationally is overpopulation officially recognized as having any part in world hunger.

In fact, there is more than enough food produced in today's industrialized agriculture industry to feed the whole world and then some, but unfortunately some people can't afford that food and others live in areas where there is not even proper infrastructure to transport it. Reducing the global population would still not help the remaining people get food; therefore it would have no effect on world hunger or poverty. Thinning out the population and making it easier to maintain has been a goal of the aristocracy since ancient times and it continues to this day, but would honestly do nothing to improve quality of life for those of us who are suffering.

The new face of eugenics was extremely deceptive and its advocates were more secretive about the true intent of their work. The eugenics movement grew more dangerous at this time, not only because of their disguised approach but also as a result of the growing influence of international bureaucracies. The United Nations is the largest of these, but there are also various other satellite groups that work on the behalf of the UN but under different names. One such organization was UNESCO, an Educational, Scientific, and Cultural establishment with underlying eugenic goals. The first director of this organization was Julian Huxley, a eugenicist from a prominent English family.

His writings had the same kind of master race themes that were expressed by his predecessor's, showing a continuation of the eugenics agenda over the span of many generations. In one published interview he said, "The lowest strata are reproducing too fast. Therefore… they must not have too easy access to relief or hospital treatment lest the removal of the last check on natural selection should make it too easy for children to be produced or to survive; long unemployment should be a ground for sterilization."[10] UNESCO is just one of the many international organizations who are working to reduce the world's population.

This is the kind of danger that is embodied in the deceptive ideologies that Darwinism represents. Yes, creatures do evolve over time and adapt to their environment but that fact should not change how we feel spiritually and it should not alienate us from our fellow human beings by upholding divisive and self-destructive ideals. What Darwin did was point out obvious scientific observations and used those observations as proof to hold up his own political and idealistic agenda. I will agree that Darwin's legitimate findings about evolution logically assassinated the claims of most organized religion. I see this as a very positive and important contribution to the philosophic dialogue, because most organized religions are simply political groups that use our desire for natural spirituality to manipulate our perception of the world, thus influencing our actions.

However, this contribution does not mean that everything he said was true and it does not mean that he had benevolent intentions with his work. An enemy of your enemy is not always your friend. Even the best philosophers in history like Aristotle, and Plato believed in slavery and other forms of subjugation. So while certain philosophers may make meaningful contributions, it is important for us to dissect every word they say and compare it with our own values instead of just accepting every aspect of someone's philosophy without question, just because they happened to do something that you respect.

Today the ideas of Darwin, Galton and other early eugenic scientists are still very much alive among the aristocracy in almost every single part of the world, as it is a philosophy that justifies their authority and allows them to tamper with human evolution. The typical mainstream assumption about eugenics is that it was some misguided but well-meaning social experiment of the past. However, overpopulation fear mongering and government depopulation programs are very much alive today and are being implemented before our very eyes. Current President Barack Obama picked a man named John Holdren as his "Science Czar" who helped writes a book called 'Ecoscience" in the 1970's that took the social goals of eugenics and gave it the language of the environmental movement, which was starting to grow in popularity. He and other eugenicists at the time sought to hijack the momentum of the environmental movement so they could use it to justify depopulation policies. They knew that if they could convince the public that their policies were for the good of the environment they would be able to advance their eugenics agenda with minimal public resistance.

The book "Ecoscience" discusses forced abortions and mass sterilization as possible "solutions" to the apparent "overpopulation problem." Holdren has backpedaled on some of these statements now that he is in public office, but only because those ideas are becoming more unpopular as the public begins to do their own research. Talk of "master races" and "social engineering" has become taboo in the mainstream culture, so people who advocate these kinds of ideas needed a new way of presenting their social policies. Typically eugenics policies are now sold as environmental protection efforts or charity to the poor, things that everyone would be in support of. Sadly, this is all just the new public relations spin that has been applied to eugenics propaganda. The government and their parent corporations are responsible for most of the environmental pollution that takes place on this earth; environmental protection can't possibly be a goal for them. It is a traditional role of government and ruling class to tell the working class whatever they want to hear in order to justify new policies that would otherwise be unpopular; this is one of those cases.

Many of today's top eugenicists are actually seen as "philanthropists" or charity workers because their public relations are so persuasive. Bill Gates is a perfect example of this situation; he has established depopulation programs across the world, but disguised them as social programs that are apparently for the "good of the people." If you listened to what the mainstream media had to say, you would believe that Bill Gates was spending his fortune trying to "cure AIDS" or bring "medical care" to third world countries with large vaccination programs. On the other hand if you actually listened to what Bill Gates was saying about these vaccination programs then you would see that his goal is not to improve public health, but actually to stop population growth. This is achieved by adding sterilization chemicals to the vaccinations and then forcing those vaccinations on the population at the barrel of a gun.

At the invitation only TED2010 Conference in Long Beach, California, Bill Gates revealed the true intentions of his vaccination programs. In a speech titled "Innovating to Zero!" he said, "First we got population. The world today has 6.8 billion people. That is headed up to about 9 billion. Now if we do a really great job on new vaccines, health care, reproductive health services, we lower that by perhaps 10 or 15 percent."[11]

If you look back at what he said you will see that he is suggesting that vaccines will actually work to lower the world's population. This statement makes absolutely no sense if the vaccines were intended to help people and extend their life expectancy. This was a quote that never made it into the headlines because it offers a glimpse into the true nature of modern eugenics, which is very popular among the media tycoons that control the headlines. For example, in a 1996 interview for the Audubon nature magazine the owner of CNN, Ted Turner said that the population should be reduced by 95%! Since then he has slightly retracted his statement but not much, saying that a population reduction of 2/3 would be more "reasonable." Ted Turner has also advocated a one-child policy, despite having five children himself. These two are simply following in the footsteps of the aristocrats who came before them and are just a few of the many who are still advancing the eugenics agenda today.

Various tax-exempt foundations waste billions of dollars every year on untested vaccinations, genetically modified food projects, and birth control, instead of spending that money on improving water systems and infrastructure. If a child gets vaccinated and is still forced to survive on contaminated water every day, they really are not much better off at all, even if the vaccines were safe, which they are not. Sterilizing vaccinations are not just hearsay, in 1995,

UNICEF's anti-tetanus vaccinations were contaminated with B-hCG, a pregnancy hormone that can permanently sterilize women. The cost of improving basic public services would actually be much less than the vaccination projects and would greatly improve health, but it would not reduce the population, so that option is not considered. This is especially startling when we remember Bertrand Russell's predictions about using diet, vaccinations, and biological agents to cull the population. The people who created some of the first vaccines like the small pox antidote for example, actually refuse to take most modern vaccinations due to the harmful toxins that they now contain.

Today most eugenics projects are filtered through tax exempt foundations and international organizations like the United Nations, Club Of Rome, Rockefeller Foundation, Ford Foundation or the Bill and Melinda Gates Foundation, just to name a few. In the early 1990's the Club of Rome published a book titled "The First Global Revolution," which was the follow up to their fear mongering best seller "Limits of Growth" from 1972. The First Global Revolution gave a very up-front description of their plan to use the environmental movement as a means to promote depopulation policies. The report read, "It would seem that humans need a common motivation, namely a common adversary, to organize and act together in the vacuum; such a motivation must be found to bring the divided nations together to face an outside enemy, either a real one or else one invented for the purpose. New enemies therefore have to be identified.

New strategies imagined, new weapons devised. The common enemy of humanity is man. In searching for a new enemy to unite us, we came up with the idea that pollution, the threat of global warming, water shortages, famine and the like would fit the bill. All these dangers are caused by human intervention, and it is only through changed attitudes and behavior that they can be overcome. The real enemy then, is humanity itself. The old democracies have functioned reasonably well over the last 200 years, but they appear now to be in a phase of complacent stagnation with little evidence of real leadership and innovation Democracy is not a panacea. It cannot organize everything and it is unaware of its own limits. These facts must be faced squarely. Sacrilegious though this may sound, democracy is no longer well suited for the tasks ahead. The complexity and the technical nature of many of today's problems do not always allow elected representatives to make competent decisions at the right time."[12]

What is being discussed here by one of the most influential think tanks in the world is forced population reduction justified by "real or invented" environmental concerns. In some areas of the world, where there already is very little social freedom, these policies are already beginning to take effect. Even today in China there is a "one child policy" in which families are forced to have abortions if they get pregnant and already have a child. This policy has led to a crisis where the males greatly outweigh the females and created a situation that many have called "gendercide." Despite the dangers of the one child policy it has been embraced by the UN and major tax-exempt foundations, as they are both determined to stifle the human population.

In many oppressive societies throughout history the ruling class has sought to control every aspect of the citizen's life, even breeding. This was suggested by Plato in "The Republic," so we know that selective breeding and controlling the population growth of the underclass has been an obsession of elites since at least the time of ancient Greece. Through the centuries the idea of selective breeding has grown into a silent method of warfare, waged over centuries against the working class and third world populations. Many of the major contributors to the eugenics movement are praised as great progressives by the education system, media, and pop culture. Despite their popular status these people have introduced some very negative and destructive ideas into the human consciousness, ideas that have been unquestioned and uninvestigated by mainstream culture.

According to Professor Steven W Mosher of the international Population Research Institute the populations in Europe and North America would actually be in decline if it were not for people migrating into the country. The number of births taking place worldwide has been in sharp decline over the past 20 years. If this trend continues then the world's population will quickly peak and then begin a mysterious and dangerous decline. Furthermore, to suggest that reducing the global population will actually improve the quality of life for the people here is resting upon the misconception that poverty is a result of overpopulation. To improve life for people on earth we need to find ways to get people what they need, reducing the amount of people will not help the ones left get what they need. There is more than enough room and resources for all of the people on earth and then some, but unfortunately the people in control of those resources are not using them responsibly.

QUOTE SOURCES AND SUGGESTED READING
----
[0] *Trashing the Planet,* by Dixy Lee Ray with Lou Guzzo, 1990, page 169.
[1] An Essay on the Principle of Population - Robert Malthus
[2] The Eugenics Review, a journal published by the Eugenics Education Society (1909)
[3] The Descent of Man – Charles Darwin
[4] Francis Galton to the Times of London, June 6, 1873 (http://galton.org/letters/africa-for-chinese/africa-chinese-1.gif)
[5] The Pivot of Civilization - Margaret Sanger (1922) Chapter Five
[6] The Pivot of Civilization - Margaret Sanger (1922), p. 274.
[7] The Impact of science on society - Bertrand Russell
[8] The Impact of science on society - Bertrand Russell
[9] The Impact of science on society - Bertrand Russell
[10] Huxley J.S. 1947. Man in the modern world. Chatto & Windus, London. Originally published in The uniqueness of Man, 1941.
[11] http://www.voltairenet.org/Bill-Gates-talks-about-vaccines-to
[SR1] Foundations: Their Power and Influence by Rene A. Wormser
[SR2] In the Minds of Men: Darwin and the New World Order by Ian T. Taylor

[SR3] The Descent of Man by Charles Darwin
[SR4] The Impact of science on society by Bertrand Russell
[SR5] The Molecular Vision of Life: Caltech, the Rockefeller Foundation, and the Rise of the New Biology by Lily E. Kay
[SR6] The Next Million Years by Charles Galton Darwin
[SR7] The Pivot of Civilization by Margaret Sanger (1922)
[SR8] Forbidden Gates: How Genetics, Robotics, Artificial Intelligence, Synthetic Biology, Nanotechnology, and Human Enhancement Herald The Dawn Of TechnoDimensional Spiritual Warfare by Thomas R. Horn
[SR9] Callous Disregard: Autisms and Vaccines: The Truth Behind a Tragedy Callous Disregard: Autisms and Vaccines: The Truth Behind a Tragedy By Andrew J. Wakefield
[SR10] Vaccination The Issue of Our Times By Peggy O'Mara
[SR 11] The First Global Revolution: A Report by the Council of The Club of Rome - Alexander King, Bertrand Schneider

"In a society that tries to standardize thinking, individuality is not highly prized."
-Alex Grey

Section 3

Social Engineering & Psychological Warfare

12. -Inhuman Nature?
13. -Education as Indoctrination
14. -Social Engineering and the Scientific Dictatorship
15. -Propaganda, Public Relations and Psychological Warfare
16. -Advertising and the Subliminal Culture
17. -Mainstream Media is Mass Mind Control
18. -Television Programming is Programming Your Mind
19. -The Entertainment Industry
20. -Parental Propaganda
21. -Inner Child

"The whole deal's like some crazy game. They put you at a starting line, and the name of the game is "Make It Through Life," only everyone's looking out for themselves and looking to do you in at the same time."
- Frank Armitage {They Live - Film} [0]

Inhuman Nature?

Our culture has molded us into manipulative, envious, and self-destructive souls, we are so confused and out of touch with our origins and our purpose that we write this depraved mentality off as "human nature" or "just the way it is." Billions of people on this planet now accept war, poverty, corruption and greed as "human nature" but no one really stops to think about how we got here and where these ideas came from. Even as we look into history one must be careful because the history books were still mostly written, edited or published by tyrants, monarchs and politicians. This is just one small example of how the ruling elite control the information that a population receives in order to keep them satisfied with the distorted reality they are living.

For thousands of years authoritarian rulers have suppressed knowledge on a mass scale through rewriting religious texts, wartime propaganda or when subtle forms of manipulation did not work, they would simply wipe out civilizations. By keeping everyone ignorant of where we came from and where we are headed, these empires are actually holding back the natural process of human development. We have been led to believe that the meaning of life is to fight with one another, to climb on top of your brothers and sisters, and to capitalize off of others misfortunes. Obviously, they have it all wrong, the meaning of life is to overwhelm people with love and respect, to learn from one another, learn from our environment, and see where it takes us. Sure, that is very different from what we are experiencing today, but it is still within our reach.

The idea that violence and dominance is a part of our genetic makeup is obsolete and stifling the process of evolution. It is these kinds of assumptions about the nature of our species that justify the most horrific behavior. For example, war is the most inhumane and unnatural phenomena on the planet, yet due to endless propaganda and indoctrination it is revered as honorable in most cultures. Dehumanizing programs such as the American "boot camp" are used by governments to remove any traces of empathy, compassion, or free thought from the minds of potential soldiers. During these programs the military conditions soldiers into accepting violence through imposing racist and hateful ideologies. This kind of psychological manipulation coupled with the horror of war often results in what doctors describe as post-traumatic stress disorder, a severe emotional condition in which extreme circumstances cause severe depression and panic attacks. If violence was a natural part of the human condition then soldiers would not be coming home from war with post-traumatic stress disorder.

In the rest of this chapter I'm going to be discussing the concept of human nature using the terms "competition" and "cooperation." These are vague terms that can have very different meanings for different people so to avoid confusion I'm going to redefine these terms for the purpose of this discussion. Competition will be defined as a mindset where one *"achieves their goals by violating the rights of others, using force or fraud"*. Cooperation will be defined as a mindset where "everyone achieves their goals by their own merit, without violating the rights of others." In the case of cooperation it would be common for people to achieve their goals with the voluntary help of others, since it is completely possible to have situations where everyone wins. Cooperation by this definition does not necessarily require all parties involved to be on the same team working towards the same goals, it simply requires them to be civil and honest with one another in their interaction.

It is the cooperative nature of our species that is responsible for our technological way of life and our understanding of the world. Language and communication has allowed humanity to pass information between each other and to future generations that result in a steady increase in knowledge over time. This knowledge is obtained through cooperative communicative processes that are necessary in order to achieve the kind of advanced societies that we live in today. Much more progress can be made through positive human interaction and cooperation then through fighting and coercion. In reality it is this kind of aggressive lifestyle that has held us back in so many ways. The time and resources spent on war are indeed wasted, if applied towards something productive instead of something destructive these efforts could bring unimaginable positive change to the world.

Some argue that our aggressive tendencies may have been necessary during the beginning stages of humanity, but even if that is the case they are now obsolete because we are no longer living in the wilderness and we have the capabilities of avoiding conflict by using our intellect. Most of the popular ideas about a violent human nature have been handed down by power seekers to justify their immoral business plan. It is these people who stand in the way of us achieving freedom and peace, so we must not look to them for answers about the nature of our species. Their assumptions are loaded with ulterior motives and they have not once throughout the course of history led us in a positive direction with their limiting and self-destructive ideologies.

The human mind is a very malleable thing and is dramatically affected by propaganda, indoctrination and other environmental factors. Therefore, how can anyone form assumptions about human nature by observing human behavior, when human behavior has been manipulated on a mass scale for centuries? If people were naturally brutal and violent than they would not have to be trained to deal with killing people in boot camp. Likewise people back home would not need constant pro war propaganda to convince them that violence was virtuous, they would naturally admire this kind of activity.

Even in today's world, with seemingly limited resources we can still all get by without slaughtering each other and stirring up trouble. Frankly, the reason why we are still dealing with limited resources and possibilities is because we are constantly trying to be better than one another instead of actually focusing on fulfilling our needs and using our imaginations. Is not it possible for everyone to just do their own thing, and use their intellect to work things out when they get in each other's way? This seems like a far safer and more productive way of doing business than we see today. The mainstream culture has yet to catch onto this concept, but that does not mean that we have to stagnate with them. In our everyday encounters, business interactions and especially our conflicts, we can take the high road by using our intellect to meet our needs without violating the rights of others.

QUOTE SOURCES AND SUGGESTED READING

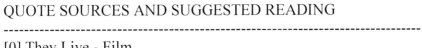

[0] They Live - Film

"If I was educated I would be a damn fool."
- Bob Marley [0]

Education as Indoctrination

The education system in America and most of the rest of the world is a corrupt establishment that does a lot more harm than it does good. The main focus of public education is to mold young minds into accepting authority and to teach them the very basic skills that they will need to be a part of the work force. Schools do not teach people how to think but only what to think, or more accurately how to remember and regurgitate information that has been fed to them. The useful information that is taught in schools would realistically only take a few months per year to go over, but passing along this information is not what is important to the public school system. What is important to them is the day-to-day structure of how the school is run which "socializes" and indoctrinates the children. This structure is designed to break the child's spirit and teach them to be submissive to authority figures. It is also specifically designed to groom working class children for their future jobs, which will be at a corporation or bureaucracy of their choosing.

The first public education system was developed in 1819 in Prussia, which is now Germany. This country was very much under authoritarian rule and it is obvious to see that their education system was developed to refine social control. The public education system was separated into three different levels, where students were divided based on which class of society they were born into. The nobility would receive the highest level of education where they had an advanced curriculum including the arts and various critical thinking exercises. They were actually arrogant enough to call this level "Real Schulen," which is actually German for "Real School"; you just can't make this stuff up! The middle tier, which did not teach critical, thinking, was reserved for the assistants and professionals that served the elite. Then finally the public education system was for the majority of the population. This was the least advanced tier in the education system where creative thinking was completely eliminated. The lower classes were taught how to be obedient and were only given the information that was needed to do their mundane jobs.

The public indoctrination system grew ever more complicated with the industrial revolution and the need for factory laborers. America at the time was at the forefront of manufacturing and the owners of the country's largest factories felt it would be in their best interest to redesign the public education system so that they could mold their future workforce from their youngest and most impressionable years. The usual suspects were involved in this corporate infiltration of the schooling system. Between 1900 and 1920 Andrew Carnegie and John D. Rockefeller alone pumped more money into the education system than the federal government did.

The elite also created foundations to fund the educators and the academics that would push this new ideology forward. One of these foundations, John D.

Rockefeller's General Education Board had this to say in their opening mission statement "In our dreams, people yield themselves with perfect docility to our molding hands. The present education conventions of intellectual and character education fade from their minds and unhampered by tradition we work our own good will upon a grateful and responsive folk. We shall not try to make these people or any of their children into men of learning or philosophers, or men of science. We have not to raise up from them authors, educators, poets or men of letters, great artists, painters, musicians, nor lawyers, doctors, public officials, politicians, creatures of whom we have ample supply. The task is simple. We will organize children and teach them in a perfect way the things their fathers and mothers are doing in an imperfect way." [1]

Again you can feel the elitist bigotry seething in those words; they are describing their wishes to "mold" their servant class into the perfect slaves. Remember the elite looks at us as a different, inferior race that is only here for their personal use and exploitation. There is no doubt that their eugenics-based philosophies are deeply woven into the fabric of our education system.

The connection between eugenicists and early educators is well documented. One of the early corporate scholars was a man named Edward Thorndike; he was a strong proponent for introducing dehumanizing eugenics projects and social engineering efforts. These projects include population control, sterilization and other age-old practices that have been adopted by the most brutal dictators in history. He is the man responsible for "educational psychology," a school of psychology that established that certain areas of history, logic, and philosophy made students resistant to manipulation because it encouraged the children to develop their own independent intellect and made their minds less pliable. This was seen as a problem as the whole point of the public education system was to mold the minds of the working class for the assembly lines and the battlefield.

In an essay for Columbia's Teacher College in 1911 Thorndike suggested that schools should have a role in "selective breeding." In the essay Thorndike talks of how schools should be "instruments of managed evolution, establishing conditions for selective breeding before the masses take things into their own hands"[2]. Thorndike was not the only educator to adopt these eugenics based philosophies, this was in fact the dominant attitude within the many government bureaucracies that were developing at the time. Although the rhetoric is toned down these days, the basic result of public education remains the same. Another one of these phony intellectual puppets was Edward Ross a sociologist who published a mind control manifesto in 1906-called "social control." In it he says, *"plans are underway to replace family, community and church with propaganda, mass-media and education...people are only little plastic lumps of dough"* [3]. These were people who were promoting Hitler's ideas when Hitler was a teenager!

In Nazi Germany standardized testing was at the very center of the indoctrination process, and the same tradition continues today in schools throughout America and Europe. If schools were truly designed to educate then standardized testing would have never been introduced. Testing and grading are techniques that are used to TRAIN, CONDITION, and CATEGORIZE, not to teach or educate. The propagandized ideologies of the establishment tell us that ridged structure and standardized testing is necessary "for the children" to succeed. That is because the approach their suggesting is the only way to create the society that they wish to create, so they will accept no other way of doing business and will do their best to downplay the advantages of any alternatives.

Standardized testing was championed by yet another front man for the elite H. H. Cadard, who was chair for the Psychology Department at Princeton. He was another eugenicist who saw public education as a tool for creating a worker class hive. In his writings he openly shared his elitist views as if they were not a gross violation of human rights, he once said, *"standardized testing would cause the lower classes to confront their biological inferiority, sort of like wearing a dunce cap. In time that would discourage reproduction of the ants on the anthill."*[4].

Many people believe that the current public education system is something that we have chosen as a society because we want to teach our children about the world, but sadly like many public institutions it is not something we have asked for but something that has been forced on us by the ruling class. When public schooling started being discussed in the United States, the majority of the public was opposed to it and saw it as an attack on their civil liberties. This is why specific curriculum is required by law, contradictory curriculum is banned by law, and children are forced to go to school by law. When something is required by law you can tell that it is a top priority for the establishment and will specifically serve the elite, this is because the needs of the ruling class are the government's main concern. When the working class needs something to survive there is a mountain of red tape and endless debate, but when the elite throw a temper tantrum about their economy they get a multi trillion-dollar blank check in the form of a bailout or subsidy.

America's public indoctrination system has gotten progressively worse as time has passed, and as the elite has better mastered the art of social engineering. After World War 2 the establishment made another push to bring the education system deeper into their control by infiltrating the U.S Department of Education using their private foundations and powerful corporations. By 1967 public education was dominated by industrial forces, and in that year "the behavioral teacher educational project" was launched, which outlined in detail the true goals of the schooling system. This programs self-stated mission was to achieve "the impersonal manipulation through schooling of a future America in which few will be able to maintain control over their own opinions" [5]. It also stated, "each individual receives at birth, a multipurpose identification number which enables employers and other controllers to keep track of them". [6]

According to the language of their own programs they are grooming the youth of the country for a tightly controlled "worker bee" lifestyle. This system was being designed specifically to create factory workers and crush creativity. This all makes sense when you notice that awards are not given out in school for creativity and self-expression but for perfect attendance and obedience. This is the same reason why the school bells between classes are reminiscent of early factory bells and whistles that would separate shifts in the sweatshops of the industrial age.

More recently during the Clinton administration the government made a move to take over the education system so it was under even more extreme control. This attempt is well documented because On Sept. 25, 1998, Rep. Bob Schaffer submitted an 18-page letter to the congressional record outlining the Clinton administration's plans for the education system. It came to be known as "Marc Tucker's Dear Hillary letter," named after Marc Tucker president of the National Center on Education and the Economy. This letter was from Marc Tucker to the Clintons on November 11, 1992 just a week after Bill Clinton was "elected" president.

In the letter he talks of "training" and "human resources" and asks for the implementation of three different laws. In the following years Clinton passed these laws, they were the "Goals 2000 Act, "the "School-to-Work Act, "and the "Elementary and Secondary Education Act". These acts made standardized testing nationally required and set up a nationwide database for keeping track of students. Tucker said the plan was designed to "remold the entire American system into a seamless web that literally extends from cradle to grave." [7] As usual this plan was to be implemented over an extended period of time as to avoid public resistance to any sudden change. The system would be built to eventually use "job matching" programs that would place students in certain job categories depending upon their standardized test scores.

The Clinton education policy was not specific to just his administration, like many efforts in Washington this has been a bi-partisan effort slowly built over many different presidential terms. It has long been the goal of the establishment to put these measures into place, but they work incrementally so small steps are made one by one over long periods of time in order to make the moves seem unrelated and to keep a relatively low profile. When these politicians and self-appointed "experts" speak of "human resources" and "social engineering" that is exactly what they mean they see us as a "resource" to be "engineered" or controlled. Their motives and goals are hidden in plain sight in the very language of the laws that they pass and the philosophies they endorse.

The overall curriculum and structure in public schools has remained the same from the first Prussian model all the way to present day. Critical thinking is not only suppressed but it is almost completely condemned within school walls. Students that exhibit signs of creativity are often times singled out by teachers as troublemakers because they are typically more resistant to authority and more independent. Sometimes when a student's creativity cannot be broken they are forced to take mind numbing psychoactive drugs like Ritalin or Adderall.

Repetitious training exercises are also hidden within the basic structure of a school day. In America children are forced to "pledge allegiance" to the flag every single day, this exercise is designed to implant nationalistic tendencies into the conscious mind of the student. Demanding students to walk in a straight line or ask before going to the bathroom is a more subtle form of training, however it also sets them up to "fall in line" when they graduate school and move on with their lives. Homework is given so students are so consumed with the mandated material that they have no time to learn anything on their own. Later, when they get out of school their curiosity is totally destroyed and they no longer have any desire to learn anything at all because they associate learning with the forced repetitious bore that public schooling is. Students leave school thinking that they have already learned everything of importance in the world, and they look forward to being relieved of the stress that they now associate with learning.

  The authoritarian nature of the public education system also works to further polarize the class structure by rewarding conformist who are willing to obey and punishing nonconformists who wish to seek their own answers and form their own opinions. Eventually when these children grow up those who were willing to conform to the teachings of the system often find themselves with better jobs and more money that result in an easier, less stressful lifestyle and a higher position in society. People of high positions in society, so called experts often receive more respect for their opinions whether that respect is deserved or not, while the rest of us struggle to have our voices heard. The people who are able to shut up and do as they're told are rewarded, thus encouraging them to reinforce the status quo and project the teachings of the establishment onto the rest of society. This is how propaganda becomes philosophy and the ideas of the elite are assimilated into culture and turn into the norms that are worshiped by society.

  Along with the indoctrinating structure of the public school system the curriculum is also distorted to fit a political agenda. In 2010 in the state of Texas there was a lot of controversy surrounding a textbook company that was trying to rewrite history in order to advance a neo-con agenda. The NAACP was completely infuriated by a few textbook changes in particular regarding slavery and the celebration of Jim Crow laws. Since most text books printed in America come from Texas this was a very serious issue that affected the minds of millions of impressionable children.

  Generally the historical curriculum in government school is skewed to portray the establishment in a positive light. History lessons make warmongers look like martyrs because the warmongers have control over the formation of these lessons. Many of the harsh realities involving the civil war, the great depression, and the civil rights movements were completely left out along with the real history of slave owning aristocratic presidents and robber baron industrialists. These are pivotal points in history that one must have a clear picture of in order to make sense of what is going on in the world today. Without a proper understanding of the social injustice that our species has overcome in the past, we will not be able to overcome the social injustices that we are experiencing in the present.

  The most vital lesson that has been removed from our education system is not made up of a list of facts like one may believe, but is actually a step-by-step process in critical thinking called the "trivium." The trivium allows one to become autodidactic, which simply means "self-taught." This process was removed from the public education system because as I mentioned, the people who were in charge of the curriculum were not interested in teaching our children how to think, but rather what to think. Prior to the Prussian schooling model, the classical education was comprised of two parts, the trivium, and the quadrivium. The trivium consisted of grammar, logic, and rhetoric while the quadrivium was arithmetic, geometry, music, and astronomy; together they make up the seven liberal arts. This time tested learning process is still taught in many elite universities but has been intentionally removed from government schooling for social engineering purposes.

One of the main proponents of modern "education" was President Woodrow Wilson. He admitted very plainly *"We want one class of persons to have a liberal education, and we want another class of persons, a very much larger class, of necessity, in every society, to forego the privileges of a liberal education and fit themselves to perform specific difficult manual tasks."* [8]

When he mentioned a "liberal education" he was most definitely referring to the *trivium* and *quadrivium*, most specifically the *trivium*. Logic and critical thinking were considered to be useless or dangerous skills for the working class to be developing, so these studies were occulted from the mainstream and reserved for the ruling class. Without learning the proper critical thinking skills the general population is left vulnerable to psychological attack and manipulation. This is especially apparent when one class of people is given these tools and everyone else is not, it allows those who have the information to easily prey on those who do not. Today the trivium is unknown to most, but thanks to the excellent work of independent researchers like Jan Irvin, Richard Grove, Bob Tuskin, and Mark Passio, this lost tool is becoming available again.

Good, honest people that want to educate and make a positive impact on people's lives are naturally drawn to becoming a teacher. Unfortunately, when they eventually get into that position they realize that their hands are tied in a lot of ways in regards to what can be taught to the students. Teachers are more or less forced to uphold the status quo and pass the establishments line onto the students. Most of the people that end up being teachers are great people with the best intentions but they are simply being used as a spokesperson for the state mandated curriculum. When a teacher steps out of those narrow boundaries they risk losing their job and tarnishing their reputation, this is because those boundaries are in place to "mold the minds" of the students. This is not to say that a legitimate community school system is impossible, but it certainly is not going to happen with the kind of subversive culture and corrupt establishment that we are faced with today. These laws and the overall way we look at education needs to be challenged. We can no longer just buy the excuse "oh we are doing it for the kids" and look the other way without taking a serious look at what exactly is being done.

The truth is that government schooling is not designed to help children in any way; it is intended to train them. This training process is actually very damaging to children, as many educators have noticed. John Taylor Gatto was

New York City Teacher of the Year in 1989, 1990, and 1991, and New York State Teacher of the Year in 1991. After years of struggling with the state mandated curriculum he eventually decided to quit teaching in government schools. He quit at the height of his teaching career by posting an article in the wall street journal op Ed pages entitled "I quit, I think." In his resignation he admitted that he could no longer continue a career where he was forced to hurt children and ruin their minds year after year. The harm that he felt he was inflicting on children was not directly physical but was a kind of subliminal brainwashing that took place through what Gatto referred to as "the hidden curriculum." Gatto recognized that the structure of modern schooling was designed in such a way to discourage creativity, independence, and individuality while reinforcing obedience to authority. His Wall Street journal article started with the following:

"I've taught public school for 26 years but I just can't do it anymore. For years I asked the local school board and superintendent to let me teach a curriculum that does not hurt kids, but they had other fish to fry. So I'm going to quit, I think. I've come slowly to understand what it is I really teach: A curriculum of confusion, class position, arbitrary justice, vulgarity, rudeness, disrespect for privacy, indifference to quality, and utter dependency. I teach how to fit into a world I do not want to live in. I just can't do it anymore. I can't train children to wait to be told what to do; I can't train people to drop what they are doing when a bell sounds; I can't persuade children to feel some justice in their class placement when there is not any, and I can't persuade children to believe teachers have valuable secrets they can acquire by becoming our disciples. That is not true. Government schooling is the most radical adventure in history. It kills the family by monopolizing the best times of childhood and by teaching disrespect for home and parents. An exaggeration? Hardly. Parents are not meant to participate in our form of schooling, rhetoric to the contrary. My orders as schoolteacher are to make children fit an animal training system, not to help each find his or her personal path."[9]

Proper education is a necessary part of our advancement on this earth. If we are not able to better educate our children then they will be doomed to repeat the same madness that came before them. The whole structure of our education system must be redesigned to empower the minds of the students instead of shackling them. We need to drop the competitive grading system and allow our children to have a less oppressive learning environment. Given the right conditions to grow a child's mind would be able to do incredible things, but they will become thoughtless drones if they are forced into a strict regimen where they are not able to think creatively and freely.

We must develop an education system that celebrates creativity and individuality and actually works to educate, instead of indoctrinate. Until that day comes we cannot trust these institutions with the minds of our children. This is why now more than ever parents are choosing to home school their children or use alternative education centers. In 2010 the number of children being home schooled was 2 million and rapidly climbing as the public is becoming more aware of the faults in the government education system.

Homeschooling is still frightening to a lot of people because the idea of sending children off to a state institution for 12 years has become so deeply ingrained in western culture, even though the government is obviously a horrible candidate for a babysitter. However, this is a relatively new practice and literacy rates have actually plummeted since the government got involved in education and forced parents to send their children to specific schools by law. That is not to say that organized group learning is not a valuable thing, but there's no need for government involvement for organized group learning to take place. If experience has taught us anything it is that the government has not achieved their goals in regard to education, even dumbing down and slanting the curriculum for their own self-interest. Due to this failure there are a growing number of alternative learning centers popping up all over the world in response to the inadequate state education system.

Many of the alternative learning centers popping up worldwide have adopted the Montessori Method of education that to some extent allows children to direct their own path in learning. This method is named after and was developed by an Italian educator and physician by the name of Maria Montessori. Her work rested upon the idea that when given freedom and independence children will grow into far more responsible adults and will have a continued interest in learning. Montessori took what she knew about developmental psychology and applied that to her work with children and had great success with improving the outlook and learning abilities of her students. There are many affordable options available for parents who do not want to put their children through government schools and even more options will develop as more people begin to understand the disadvantages of state education.

Homeschooling and alternative learning centers are the best options that we have as individuals to ensure that our children have access to the proper learning environment. These are solutions for the everyday person; however the public schooling system will still remain and still continue to wreak havoc on our youth and our society, so this is still a problem. The American governments plan for education has obviously failed, so instead of waiting to go down with a sinking ship, we need to be proactive and start discussing possibilities for the future of schooling. The best option would be a decentralized network of community schools, where everything regarding curriculum and school structure was decided by those in the community as opposed to a government bureaucracy.

QUOTE SOURCES AND SUGGESTED READING
----
[0]As recorded in Time Will Tell (1992) a documentary by Declan Lowney
[1] The Underground History of American Education (2001) - John Taylor Gatto
[2]The Underground History of American Education (2001) - John Taylor Gatto
[3] Social Control (1901) - Edward Roth
[4] Dumbing Us Down: The Hidden Curriculum of Compulsory Schooling (1992). - John Taylor Gatto
[5] The Underground History of American Education (2001) - John Taylor Gatto
[6] The Underground History of American Education (2001) - John Taylor Gatto
[7] None dare call it education, John A. Stormer
[8] "The Meaning of a Liberal Education," Address to the New York City High

School Teachers Association (9 January 1909). The Papers of Woodrow Wilson: 1908-1909, Princeton University Press, 1974

[9] The Wall Street Journal, July 25, 1991

[SR1] A Different Kind of Teacher: Solving the Crisis of American Schooling (2000). by John Taylor Gatto

[SR2] Against School' (2001) by John Taylor Gatto

[SR3] Dr. Montessori's Own Handbook by Maria Montessori

[SR4] Dumbing Us Down: The Hidden Curriculum of Compulsory Schooling by John Taylor Gatto

[SR5] How the Order Controls Education by Antony C. Sutton

[SR6] The Absorbent Mind by Maria Montessori

[SR7] The Deliberate Dumbing Down of America by A Chronological Paper Trail by Charlotte Thomson Iserbyt

[SR8] The Dodd report to the American people by Norman Dodd

[SR9] The Exhausted School (1993). by John Taylor Gatto

[SR10] The Montessori Method by Maria Montessori

[SR11] The Underground History Of American Education by John Taylor Gatto

[SR12] Weapons of Mass Instruction by John Taylor Gatto

"Technological progress is like an axe in the hands of a pathological criminal."
- Albert Einstein [0]

Social Engineering and the Scientific Dictatorship

Since the first power hungry tyrant took the throne the establishment has always used the most advanced technology of its time as a weapon against anyone who threatens their authority. The most powerful tools and deepest knowledge have always been horded by the elite because they fear that if they were to lose the technological advantage then they will also lose their social dominance as well. Since technological advancement itself has been pushed along primarily by warmongers, most of the tools and techniques that have been developed throughout history have been designed to help a small group of people to dominate a larger group of people.

This goes for all weapons like the atomic bomb as well as neutral devices like the printing press, modern computers, or the Hollerith machine that IBM made for Hitler. The neutral devices that I mentioned can be used for both good and evil depending on how they are applied. Unfortunately, for most of the people on earth the elite have always used any technology they could get their hands on to advance their totalitarian agenda. Likewise, they are usually able to weaponize any kind of peaceful technology that comes about, and then subsequently horde that technology for themselves.

Technological advancement and scientific progress are among the primary sources for human power on the planet earth, this is not inherently good or evil, but it depends on how that science or technology is applied in the world. Using the Einstein quote from the beginning of the chapter as an example, an axe is a tool that can be applied positively if in the correct hands but could also be used as a weapon if it falls into the wrong hands. As Einstein recognized, science and technology have been monopolized and controlled by different psychopathic rulers for a very long time. An unbelievable amount of time, human energy and resources are poured into scientific research that has been requested by the government or the ruling oligarchy that sits behind it. Most of this research is applied to military technology as well as a myriad of social control mechanisms, psychological warfare techniques and other means of maintaining power.

In addition to disseminating propaganda and developing new methods of controlling people, the social planners were also responsible for steering the direction of technological progress. This was achieved by strictly controlling the process by which one joins the scientific establishment and then monopolizing their time with military or eugenics projects once they were finally certified. This is how the militarization of technology and scientific progress has accelerated in the past hundred years.

In the 20th century weapons of war and systems of control were able to grow more threatening than ever before with the help of electricity, air travel, quantum physics, industrial manufacturing, and other breakthroughs. For the first time in history the tools that were available to power hungry tyrants had the ability to affect entire civilizations and severely damage the environment. Warfare and despotism were horrific in previous centuries but now with the ability to instantly spy on anyone or attack anywhere in the world at any time an unprecedented level of power has been achieved by our illegitimate rulers.

Today we are certainly dealing with a different breed of authoritarianism, one that many have rightfully described as a "scientific dictatorship." Aldous Huxley was mainly responsible for popularizing this term; he is the author who wrote Brave New World, a dystopian novel in which a scientific dictatorship ruled over humanity. However, his interests in these topics were much deeper than just science fiction, as his family was actually heavily involved in the scientific industrial complex. Aldous may have been the black sheep of the family because in his writings he always seemed to portray the scientific dictatorship in a negative light while his family openly praised eugenics and psychological manipulation techniques. How Aldous truly felt on these subjects is not known for sure, but in his books and his speeches he condemned these oppressive applications of science. It is a personal theory of mine that Aldous may have been more humane than the rest of his family due to his psychedelic experience that was documented in the book "The Doors of Perception."

Brave New World depicted a society where citizens were subject to constant state propaganda and were coaxed into taking mood-stabilizing drugs that kept them apathetic. On March 20, 1962 Aldous Huxley gave a speech at Berkley University and revealed that his book was based on actual research that was taking place within the scientific industrial complex, by order of the government and ruling class.

During the Speech Huxley said "It seems to me that the nature of the ultimate revolution with which we are now faced is precisely this: That we are in process of developing a whole series of techniques which will enable the controlling oligarchy who have always existed and presumably will always exist to get people to love their servitude. This is the, it seems to me, the ultimate in malevolent revolutions shall we say, and this is a problem which has interested me many years and about which I wrote thirty years ago, a fable, Brave New World, which is an account of society making use of all the devices available and some of the devices which I imagined to be possible making use of them in order to, first of all, to standardize the population, to iron out inconvenient human differences, to create, to say, mass produced models of human beings arranged in some sort of scientific caste system. Since then, I have continued to be extremely interested in this problem and I have noticed with increasing dismay a number of the predictions that were purely fantastic when I made them thirty years ago have come true or seem in process of coming true.

A number of techniques about which I talked seem to be here already. And there seems to be a general movement in the direction of this kind of ultimate revolution, a method of control by which a people can be made to enjoy a state of affairs by which any decent standard they ought not to enjoy. This, the enjoyment of servitude, Well this process is, as I say, has gone on for over the years, and I have become more and more interested in what is happening." [1]

This knowledge was coming from a well-respected scientist and multi-generational insider of the establishment; he was one of the brightest minds of his time. Huxley's credibility and experience behind the scenes made this speech a stunning revelation that shed new light on the darkest corners of scientific research. His brother Julian was a biologist, as well as the first Director of UNESCO and a founder of the World Wildlife Fund. As I described earlier these particular organizations especially UNESCO have been slowly working to create a scientific dictatorship since well before Aldous spoke at Berkley, which makes his speech even more interesting.

The Huxley's ran in the same circles as another prominent Eugenicist Bertrand Russell, who was also extremely open about his elitist views. In his book "The Impact of Science on Society" Russell discussed social engineering and a scientific dictatorship.

Russell writes, "*I think the subject which will be of most importance politically is mass psychology. Mass psychology is, scientifically speaking, not a very advanced study... This study is immensely useful to practical men, whether they wish to become rich or to acquire the government. It is, of course, as a science, founded upon individual psychology, but hitherto it has employed rule-of-thumb methods that were based upon a kind of intuitive common sense. Its importance has been enormously increased by the growth of modern methods of propaganda. Of these the most influential is what is called 'education'. Religion plays a part, though a diminishing one; the Press, the cinema and the radio play an increasing part. What is essential in mass psychology is the art of persuasion. If you compare a speech of Hitler's with a speech of (say) Edmund Burke, you will see what strides have been made in the art since the eighteenth century. What went wrong formerly was that people had read in books that man is a rational animal, and framed their arguments on this hypothesis. We now know that limelight and a brass band do more to persuade than can be done by the most elegant train of syllogisms. It may be hoped that in time anybody will be able to persuade anybody of anything if he can catch the patient young and is provided by the State with money and equipment. This subject will make great strides when it is taken up by scientists under a scientific dictatorship.*" [2]

A few pages later he continues "*Apart from the danger of war, I see no reason why such a regime should be unstable. After all, most civilized and semi-civilized countries known to history have had a large class of slaves or serfs completely subordinate to their owners. There is nothing in human nature that makes the persistence of such a system impossible. And the whole development of scientific technique has made it easier than it used to be to maintain a despotic rule of a minority. When the government controls the distribution of food, its power is absolute so long as it can count on the police and the armed forces. And their loyalty can be secured by giving them some of the privileges of the governing class. I do not see how any internal movement of revolt can ever bring freedom to the oppressed in a modern scientific dictatorship.*" [3]

Bertrand Russell advocated the idea of a scientific dictatorship because as a member of the oligarchy he stood to gain a lot of power through becoming a social engineer. He belonged to a privileged group of intellectuals who would ultimately become the new priest class in western culture, molding public opinion according to their personal philosophies. This new expert class was filling the philosophical void that was created when the ideas of the church fell out of favor, leaving the aristocracy with very little influence over the minds of their subjects. Instead of being encouraged to apply the methods of science to their own lives people were asked to depend on statements from the "experts" to dictate their opinions. This kind of mentality has consumed today's culture to the point where no one trusts their own judgment about anything, but will trust every word that comes from an establishment "expert" without doing any background research of their own. Despite the impressive intellectual credentials held by the so called 'experts", many of them are on the establishments payroll and would not dare speak out against the status quo even if they know in their hearts that it is right and just to do so.

The "expert" classes of scientists, educators, politicians, and other prominent intellectuals have been working to deceive the general population for almost an entire century. That is not to say that every single member of the scientific community is a part of this plan, but the people at the very top, at the heads of foundations, those who control the bureaucracies, they are the ones who I am referring to. One such social engineer is Zbigniew Brzezinski, a tyrant who is still wreaking havoc in geopolitics. In 1970 he wrote of a scientific dictatorship, laying out his goals for the 21st century by saying "society would be dominated by elite whose claim to political power would rest on allegedly superior scientific know-how. Unhindered by the restraints of traditional liberal values, these elite would not hesitate to achieve its political ends by using the latest modern techniques for influencing public behavior and keeping society under close surveillance and control. Under such circumstances, the scientific and technological momentum of the country would not be reversed but would actually feed on the situation it exploits. [4]

As I have pointed out many times so far, the elite make no mistake about revealing their goals, and have stated on the record that they wish to establish a worldwide scientific dictatorship. It only makes sense that they will take advantage of their incredible wealth to develop technology that will assist them in achieving their goals. This is not mere speculation either but has been documented by various members of the scientific establishment over many generations. The fact that scientific advancement is presently monopolized by the most corrupt element of our society should not push us to vilify science itself, but the lessons of this unfortunate predicament should teach us to be much more careful with such an important responsibility and to not allow this kind of power to be centralized in a few hands. The vast knowledge and ever-growing technology that humans take for granted is an extremely powerful gift that seems to be specific to our species, at least as far as this planet is concerned. This power and responsibility has been greatly disrespected by those who have forced their will on the rest of humanity and directed the course of civilization. Primarily the most expensive and time consuming technological projects undertaken by humankind have not been for the betterment of society but were designed to kill, control and otherwise dehumanize innocent people.

When children grow up dreaming of becoming scientists they have the purest of aspirations and if they were left to pursue their own studies they would be able to accomplish the unimaginable. Unfortunately, to become a member of the scientific community one has to jump through many bureaucratic hoops until they are eventually inducted into an establishment that is tightly regulated and directed by warmongers and control freak aristocrats. People spend half of their lives taking classes, passing tests and filling out applications in hopes that one day they can become a scientist and cure a disease. After years of struggling to make the cut they realize that there is no funding for their charitable projects and if they dare step outside of the established guidelines they will be exiled from the scientific community.

In order to send scientific progress in a more positive direction it is necessary to develop a more open, transparent and decentralized scientific establishment. Influence from the government and military industrial complex is the primary reason for our dismal technological outlook and like many things science would flourish in the absence of the state. Think about the resources that are used for war and social control, now imagine if those resources and that energy were applied to curing diseases, space travel, free and clean energy solutions, food production and sustainable agriculture. Amazing things would be able to take place if only human beings were allowed to use their intellect and the resources of the earth to achieve positive goals instead of destruction. This is not a radical concept, it was understood by President Eisenhower as he revealed in his 1961 farewell address to the nation, when said:

"Today, the solitary inventor, tinkering in his shop, has been overshadowed by task forces of scientists in laboratories and testing fields. In the same fashion, the free university, historically the fountainhead of free ideas and scientific discovery has experienced a revolution in the conduct of research. Partly because of the huge costs involved, a government contract becomes virtually a substitute for intellectual curiosity. For every old blackboard there are now hundreds of new electronic computers. The prospect of domination of the nation's scholars by Federal employment, project allocations, and the power of money is ever present – and is gravely to be regarded. Yet, in holding scientific research and discovery in respect, as we should, we must also be alert to the equal and opposite danger that public policy could itself become the captive of scientific-technological elite." [5]

QUOTE SOURCES AND SUGGESTED READING
----

[0] The handbook of conflict resolution: theory and practice - Morton Deutsch, Peter T. Coleman, Eric Colton Marcus (2006)

[1] Aldous Huxley, March 20, 1962 Berkeley Language Center - Speech Archive SA 0269

[2] Bertrand Russell, The Impact of Science on Society, (Routledge, 1985), page 40

[3] Bertrand Russell, The Impact of Science on Society, (Routledge, 1985), page 66

[4] Zbigniew Brzezinski, Between Two Ages: America's Role in the

Technetronic Era. (Viking Press, New York, 1970), page 97
[5] Dwight D. Eisenhower, Eisenhower's Farewell Address to the Nation. January 17, 1961
[SR1] Brave New World – Aldous Huxley
[SR2] Brave New World Revisited by Aldous Huxley
[SR3] Social Control (1901) by Edward Ross

"Today the tyrant rules not by club or fist, but disguised as a market researcher, he shepherds his flocks in the ways of utility and comfort."
- Marshall McLuhan [0]

Propaganda, Public Relations and Psychological Warfare

Public Relations, better known as advertising is one of the most important industries to spring up in the 20th century and most people actually know very little about it. It has changed the way we are governed and has laid the foundation for our materialistic consumer culture, as well as opened the floodgate for advanced psychological warfare. From propaganda to deceptive marketing the field of public relations has allowed politicians and corporations to manipulate the desires and opinions of the working class. These practices were put in place so the ruling class could have better control over the much larger serf population.

In the early 20th century there was growing discontent among the general public, who had finally become tired of being treated like second-class citizens. The people began to hold strikes, boycotts and take any action they could to weaken the establishment, in hopes to bring about a more humane society and working environment. This was bad news for those in control because they need the cooperation of the working class to build their industries and fill the ranks in their armies. The government and corporations needed a more respectable image, and that need gave rise to the public relations movement.

There were many minds that made this movement possible, but the field itself is most typically associated with a man named Edward Bernays. Bernays is known as the father of public relations not because he was the first or only person to study propaganda, but rather because he was the first person to explain its practical use in a published work. He was also the first person to use the term "public relations" to describe the work of the propagandist. In his famous book bluntly titled "Propaganda" Bernays highlighted his own work and the works of many other prominent figures in the public relations industry.

It is important to mention that Edward Bernays came from a very prominent family in the field of psychology, as he was the nephew of Sigmund Freud, the "father of psychology." Freud's discoveries about the human unconscious were the basis of his nephews work. Bernays used what he knew about the inner workings of the mind as a tool of persuasion to control the masses through their subconscious. In "Propaganda" Bernays does not even attempt to sugarcoat his sinister plan when he makes statements like this one:

"The conscious and intelligent manipulation of the organized habits and opinions of the masses is an important element in democratic society. Those who manipulate this unseen mechanism of society constitute an invisible government that is the true ruling power of our country. We are governed, our minds are molded, our tastes formed, our ideas suggested, largely by men we have never heard of…in almost every act of our daily lives, whether in the sphere of politics or business, in our social conduct or our ethical thinking we are dominated by the relatively small number of persons…who understand the mental processes and social patterns of the masses. It is they who pull the wires that control the public mind." [1]

Before Bernays published "propaganda" in 1928 advertisements was far less complicated than the ones that were seen after. While advertisements in the past would just describe a product and its uses, now they would appeal to the viewer's subconscious fears and desires in order to make a mental connection between product and consumer. Do you ever wonder why commercials often times have absolutely nothing to do with the product they are trying to sell? It is because they are trying to sell an image that you can relate to, not just a product. An unbelievable amount of thought, time, and energy is put into every advertisement. Just think about how much money a 30-second commercial spot during the super bowl costs. These corporations know exactly what they are doing. They are playing on your emotions and subconscious through their advertisements so you buy their product, whether you want to or not.

Edward Bernays clients were some of the most successful businesses of the time, thanks to Bernays cunning advertisements. Betty Crocker approached him when they were having trouble selling their instant cake mix. Bernays instructed them to change the recipe by adding an egg, which would make the consumer feel that they were not just using an "instant mix." Bernays trick worked, and sales soared. His next client though, was far less innocent. A short time later Bernays was approached by the American Tobacco Company who was trying to figure out how to convince females to smoke cigarettes.

Apparently at the time there was a stigma attached to females smoking as it was not "lady like." Bernays and the ATC wanted to end this taboo and open up the tobacco market to the feminine half of the human population, which would double sales. Bernays exploited the women's civil right struggle by making advertisements that claimed it was liberating and empowering for women to smoke cigarettes. In his advertisements Bernays called cigarettes "torches of freedom" and encouraged young feminists to "light up." Again his deceptive marketing worked and the American Tobacco Company got incredibly rich.

One of the other PR masterminds that Edward Bernays mentions in his book is none other than Ivy Lee who was also working to build the propaganda industry, but from a slightly different angle. Where Bernays was focused on creating the psychology of consumerism, Lee was more interested in "crisis management" or in other words getting his billionaire clients out of trouble and restoring their public image. Today both trains of thought have converged to create a well-rounded system of deception and public perception management where an underclass of consumers is almost entirely convinced that their corrupt masters are wonderful people.

Ivy Lee's most infamous clients were the Rockefellers, and his first order of business for them was to repair their tarnished reputation. The Rockefellers were America's first billionaires who acquired their wealth by exploiting their workers, exploiting natural resources and operating cartels within the railroad, banking and oil industries. Their reputation took a turn for the worse after Colorado's "Bloody Ludlow" massacre in 1914 in which the ruthless aristocrats ordered the national guard to attack striking workers who were protesting outside the factories. When the battle was over 20 people were dead, only one of them was a trooper and many of them were children. Historian Howard Zinn called the massacre "the culminating act of perhaps the most violent struggle between corporate power and laboring men in American history." After this incident it became apparent to the Rockefellers and other titans of industry that they needed help with perception management and damage control.

There was rightfully a growing distrust for the corporations and the ruling class among the majority of Americans at the time and the elite knew they had to do something to change it. The Rockefellers acted by hiring Ivy Lee to manage and improve their public image. Lee was probably chosen for the job because years earlier he came up with an idea that would revolutionize how corporations communicated with the peasant class. That was in 1906 when a horrible train accident happened in Atlantic City, Lee suggested that the company issue a statement presenting their side of the story to the press; this was to be the first "press release".

The disaster was caused by negligence on the part of the railroad company and was witnessed by hundreds of people, so the press release was a special measure taken in hopes to get their side of the story out first. The press release scheme was a success and two days later the New York Times just printed the company's statement word for word! This kind of insanity continues to this day where "news" reporters simply regurgitate the statement from the white house or from Exxon about what they're doing instead of making any attempt at investigative journalism!

Lee certainly had his hands full with the Rockefeller family because unlike an isolated train wreck this aristocratic dynasty was hurting and exploiting the people on a daily basis, and have been for generations. Starting with the Ludlow Massacre Lee began to change the public image of the family and their businesses even if it meant telling blatant lies. Lee sent out mass bulletins claiming that the people who had been killed in the Colorado protests were the victims of a house fire caused by an "overturned stove." He also accused a popular union worker named "Mother Jones" of being a prostitute and running a brothel.

In addition to lying, Lee suggested that the families make high profile donations to various charities and have photographs taken of them handing out money to the commoners to make the public think that they were good hearted and generous people. Again the plan worked and the application of public relations was able to resurrect Rockefeller's reputation and then build it to the point where it is today. At the time of his death Lee was being investigated by congress for his work with the Nazis through the company IG Farben and a proxy firm called the German Dye Trust, he was also a founding member of the Council on Foreign Relations, which I will explain in detail later on.

It was common for the public relations tycoons to be involved in various competing political organizations as well as competing corporations, and that same tradition continues today. Even non-government organized crime syndicates have used public relations techniques to keep themselves in the good graces of the public. For example, famous gangster Al Capone was loved by his community because he ran soup kitchens and made sure he was seen as a generous and upstanding citizen. Public relations for a government sponsored crime syndicate are far more complicated, of course.

One early public relations expert Walter Lippmann worked closely with Edward Bernays and was specifically interested in the use of propaganda to push the public into a war or to agree with other unpopular political policies. In his work Lippmann was explicit in defending the ruling classes "need" to control the behavior of the working class, in his thinking this kind of control was "necessary in a democracy." Lippmann's book "Public Opinion" opens with Plato's "allegory of the cave," which is very telling if your familiar with the story.

For those of you who are not familiar with the allegory of the cave I'll take a minute to summarize this wonderful parable. The story describes a group of people who have been held prisoner in a cave for their entire lives. In the cave the prisoners are chained to the floor in such a way that they can only face a blank wall and cannot move or look in any other direction. All day they are forced to watch shadow figures that are projected onto a wall by puppets parading in front of a fire positioned at the back of the cave. In simpler terms this would be like a modern day television or projector screen. The prisoners actually believe the shadows in front of them are the only thing that is real as it is the only thing they have been exposed to for their entire lives.

They have given the shadows names and have a whole system of beliefs built around them. The philosopher is represented by the person who is freed from his chains and escapes the cave to see the outside world for what it is. When the philosopher returns and attempts to explain the outside world to his cellmates he is met with disbelief and hostility. Even if the philosopher were to unchain another prisoner and show him the outside world it would be too difficult to describe and so far outside of their frame of reality that they would still insist on remaining in the comforts of their familiar cave. The released prisoners would be hurt and confused by their new discovery and may even become angry with the philosopher for showing him the outside world.

When the philosopher returns to the cave after being exposed to the true nature of reality Plato concludes that *"Would not he remember his first home, what passed for wisdom there, and his fellow prisoners, and consider himself happy and them pitiable? And would not he disdain whatever honors, praises, and prizes were awarded there to the ones who guessed best which shadows followed which? Moreover, if he to return there, would not he be rather bad at their game, no longer being accustomed to the darkness? Would not it be said of him that he went up and came back with his eyes corrupted, and that it is not even worth trying to go up? And if they were somehow able to get their hands on and kill the man who attempts to release them and show them the outside world, would not they kill him?"* [2]

The allegory of the cave shows us that our thoughts and beliefs can be shaped and molded according to someone else's will if that person (or group of people) has the ability to control all of the information we receive from a very young age. Furthermore, it shows us that when the prisoners are conditioned enough to their way of life and their frame of reality then they themselves will act as a guard or warden for themselves, and any fellow prisoners who might dare to question the status quo.

The fact that Lippmann opens public opinion with this parable shows us that he feels its teachings are extremely important to his whole philosophy; otherwise he would have started the book out some other way. In relation to the allegory of the cave Lippmann's goal is to be the force manipulating the "shadows on the wall" thus controlling the minds of those in the "cave," or world. The term public opinion was meant to describe the false version of reality that is created by the propagandists on behalf of the ruling class.

This is not merely speculation, but was described by Lippmann himself when he wrote that *"We have learned to call this propaganda. A group of men, who can prevent independent access to the event, can arrange the news to suit their purpose... ...In order to conduct a propaganda campaign; there must be some barrier between the public and the event. Access to the real environment must be limited, before anyone can create a pseudo-environment he thinks wise or desirable."* [3] This "pseudo-environment" is similar to what I referred to earlier as "nationalistic folklore," or what is known in the military as psychological operations or "Psy-ops," for short.

Lippmann was interested in shaping public opinion in such a way that the general population could be easily forced into doing whatever was asked of them, or in his words he was trying to "manufacture consent." If you are familiar with the brilliant activist and scholar Noam Chomsky then you will recognize the term "Manufacturing Consent," as it is one of his most popular books. I highly recommend it, as well as all of Chomsky's work, but the term was actually originally coined by Lippmann.

In his own words Lippmann discusses the process of manufacturing consent, in public opinion he writes *"That the manufacture of consent is capable of great refinements no one, I think, denies. The process by which public opinions arise is certainly no less intricate than it has appeared in these pages, and the opportunities for manipulation open to anyone who understands the process are plain enough. . . . As a result of psychological research, coupled with the modern means of communication, the practice of democracy has turned a corner. A revolution is taking place, infinitely more significant than any shifting of economic power. . . . Under the impact of propaganda, not necessarily in the sinister meaning of the word alone, the old constants of our thinking have become variables. It is no longer possible, for example, to believe in the original dogma of democracy; that the knowledge needed for the management of human affairs comes up spontaneously from the human heart. Where we act on that theory we expose ourselves to self-deception, and to forms of persuasion that we cannot verify. It has been demonstrated that we cannot rely upon intuition, conscience, or the accidents of casual opinion if we are to deal with the world beyond our reach."* [4]

Basically what he is saying is that democracy is a bad thing because the commoners can't make proper decisions, so it is necessary for the ruling class to manipulate the public in order to build the kind of society that they want to build. These sentiments are echoed in Bernays work as well, In Propaganda he writes

"In theory, every citizen makes up his mind on public questions and matters of private conduct. In practice, if all men had to study for themselves the abstruse economic, political, and ethical data involved in every question, they would find it impossible to come to a conclusion about anything......It might be better to have, instead of propaganda and special pleading, committees of wise men who would choose our rulers, dictate our conduct, private and public, and decide upon the best types of clothes for us to wear and the best kinds of food for us to eat.

We have chosen the opposite method, that of open competition. We must find a way to make free competition function with reasonable smoothness. To achieve this society has consented to permit free competition to be organized by leadership and propaganda. Some of the phenomena of this process are criticized—the manipulation of news, the inflation of personality, and the general ballyhoo by which politicians and commercial products and social ideas are brought to the consciousness of the masses. The instruments by which public opinion is organized and focused may be misused. But such organization and focusing are necessary to orderly life." [5]

This twisted worldview was common among the intellectual elite at the time and still resonates today through their teachings. "Propaganda" actually was not a bad word until it was picked up and used by Hitler, who was an avid reader of the work coming from western PR experts. Prior to Hitler it was a totally acceptable word that was used by politicians and advertisers frequently.

In the work of both Lippmann and Bernays they suggested that advanced psychological techniques had already been applied to propaganda since prior to World War 1, and they knew first hand. It was these two professors who convinced President Woodrow Wilson to establish the Tavistock Institute of Human Relations, an organization that was designed to use psychological techniques against the American people in order to get them to comply with unpopular policies.

The first main objective of the Tavistock Institute and its team of professional con men were to convince the American people that it was a good idea to get into World War 1. This was quite an undertaking considering that most American's were opposed to any war, especially one that was halfway around the world and did not concern them. President Wilson was also "elected" on an antiwar platform so Tavistock really had their work cut out for them. This effort was funded by the British royal family, the Rothschild's, the Milner Group and the Rockefeller family trusts.

The propaganda created at the Tavistock Institute was so effective that the organization would continue to get support and funding until eventually growing to become an integral part of the military industrial complex, as it is to this day. The research that took place here has shaped our lives and our society more than anyone can imagine. Things that are often taken for granite were actually a direct result of this research, like the opinion poll for example. The opinion poll was a creation of the Tavistock Institute, and was developed with the intention of molding public opinion, not measuring it. Today the Tavistock Institute still exists, but now it is only one of many psychological warfare interests that have extensive geopolitical influence.

While the Tavistock camp focused on the group mind and the nature of public opinion there was a similar group of psychologists performing lab experiments with animals and human beings in order to develop future methods of controlling the mind. These lab studies provided research on human behavior that would later be used by public relations firms when they developed new techniques for social manipulation. The psychologists that specialized in these studies became known as "behaviorists," a term that was coined by wannabe Dr. Frankenstein John B. Watson.

In the very opening paragraph of one of his famous articles Watson summarizes his studies. He writes "*Psychology as the behaviorist views it is a purely objective experimental branch of natural science. Its theoretical goal is the prediction and control of behavior. Introspection forms no essential part of its methods, nor is the scientific value of its data dependent upon the readiness with which they lend themselves to interpretation in terms of consciousness. The behaviorist, in his efforts to get a unitary scheme of animal response, recognizes no dividing line between man and brute. The behavior of man, with all of its refinement and complexity, forms only a part of the behaviorist's total scheme of investigation.*" [6]

So the stated goal of behaviorism is more or less to predict and control the behavior of human beings. To meet this goal Watson would conduct experiments on animals and even human beings. He obsessed over the idea of one day being able to create and study a "baby farm" in which he would train groups of infant children from birth. Watson is famous for saying "Give me a dozen healthy infants, well-formed, and my own specified world to bring them up in and I'll guarantee to take any one at random and train him to become any type of specialist I might select – doctor, lawyer, artist, merchant-chief and, yes, even beggar-man and thief, regardless of his talents, penchants, tendencies, abilities, vocations, and race of his ancestors. I am going beyond my facts and I admit it, but so have the advocates of the contrary and they have been doing it for many thousands of years." [7] Watson and other establishment scientists even used their own children for experimentation to avoid public attention. It was the controversial work of the behaviorists that laid the foundation for a whole new realm of experimental psychology, which would then be taken advantage of by the largest governments and corporations in the world.

By the time that Watson retired from psychology and advertising an equally twisted individual named B.F. Skinner was ready to carry the torch and continue behaviorism research. Skinner is known best for his development of "operant conditioning," which is based on the idea of psychological training and conditioning by reinforcement. Skinner believed that all learned behavior is rooted in either a positive or negative response to certain actions that could be both predicted and conditioned. In other words, a behavior will increase if it is followed by positive reinforcement and will decrease if it is followed by negative reinforcement. He demonstrated this with his "operant conditioning chamber" which is now popularly known as the "skinner box." He would place animals in a chamber that contained a lever that the animal could press in order to obtain food or water as a type of reinforcement. It was also possible to deliver punishments like electric shocks through the floor of the chamber.

Skinner openly admitted that his research was going to be used to manipulate and condition human beings, but he argued that this was always going to happen in societies anyway, he just wanted to make sure that people were "manipulated correctly". Skinner had picked up where Watson left off and brought a whole new dynamic to the development of psychological warfare and mass mind control. Their unethical studies have joined the works of Bernays and Lippmann to become the dogma for the new generation of public relations consultants. Together their studies have delved so deep into the human consciousness that they seem to know more about the rest of society then we know about ourselves. These propagandists are among the most influential people of the past hundred years, even though their names have remained under the radar. This is by no mistake, the education system and the media are vital in keeping these historical figures and their impact on society a tightly guarded secret.

Public relations are now one of the most profitable and ruthless industries in the world and ethics have not improved at all since the mid-20th century, if anything they have progressively deteriorated. To find examples of these unethical practices one need look no further than today's leading PR firms. Among those firms is Burson-Marsteller a group that specializes in playing damage control for the world's worst corporations, torturers, and dictators. A 2002 article by John Vidal in the UK's Guardian newspaper paints a fairly accurate picture of the company's activities.

The article states that "Burson-Marsteller is the company that governments with poor human rights records and corporations in trouble with environmentalists have turned to when in crisis. The world's biggest PR company was employed by the Nigerian government to discredit reports of genocide during the Biafra war, the Argentinean junta after the disappearance of 35,000 civilians, and the Indonesian government after the massacres in East Timor. It also worked to improve the image of the late Romanian president Nicolae Ceausescu and the Saudi royal family. Its corporate clients have included the Three Mile Island nuclear plant, which suffered a partial meltdown in 1979, Union Carbide after the Bhopal gas leak killed up to 15,000 people in India, BP after the sinking of the Torrey Canyon oil tanker in 1967 and the British government after BSE emerged. In the past few years it has acted for big tobacco companies and the European biotechnology industry to challenge the green lobby and counter Greenpeace arguments on GM food."[8] These kinds of activities are the rule for today's PR firms, not the exception. The most violent people and corporations on the earth seem to have infinite resources, which allow them to pay off the arresting authorities and then hire expert propagandists to clean up their public image afterwards.

Some of the most iconic news images of our time surrounding war were not actually real but were simply public relations stunts, designed as psychological warfare operations. No one in America can forget the image of Saddam Hussein's statue being toppled and covered with an American flag, yet few people realize that this was a hoax, a staged psychological operation coordinated between the military and the media. In July of 2004 journalist Jon Elmer exposed an internal army study of the war showing that this whole statue scenario was indeed a set up. In the article Elmer writes "the infamous toppling of the statue of Saddam Hussein in Firdos Square in central Baghdad on April 9, 2003 was stage-managed by American troops and not a spontaneous reaction by Iraqis. According to the study, a Marine colonel first decided to topple the statue, and an Army psychological operations unit turned the event into a propaganda moment… The Marines brought in cheering Iraqi children in order to make the scene appear authentic, the study said. Allegations that the event was staged were made in April of last year, mostly by opponents of the war, but were ignored or ridiculed by the US government and most visible media outlets. "[9]

The statue hoax was just one example in a long list of lies and psychological operations surrounding the multiple wars in Iraq. At the onset of Operation Desert Storm in 1990 a public relations firm by the name of Hill and Knowlton spent millions of dollars on the government's behalf, constructing news pieces that would sell the war to the American public. One of the most moving pranks to come from this push to war was the testimony of a 15-year-old Kuwaiti girl, known only by her first name of Naira. In a videotaped testimony that was later distributed to the media she said *"I volunteered at the al-Addan hospital, While I was there, I saw the Iraqi soldiers come into the hospital with guns, and go into the room where . . . babies were in incubators. They took the babies out of the incubators, took the incubators, and left the babies on the cold floor to die."*[10]

Sounds horrible huh? Well, luckily it never happened, this too was a fabricated event designed to dehumanize the Iraqi people. The whole thing was exposed when the journalists discovered that the witness Nayirah was actually the daughter of a US ambassador who was being coaxed by military psychological operations specialists. If the government and media cooperate to deceive the American public during times of war then there should be no doubt in your mind that the same techniques are used during times of peace, and especially elections.

Psychological warfare and mass manipulation have surely been taking place since Plato's time, as his allegory of the cave provides a clear analogy to describe how the few have controlled the many for thousands of years. Our whole modern society is a replica of the early Greek and Roman empires, so it should come as no surprise that Plato's stories are just as relevant today as they were in ancient times. In Both ancient societies the elite owned slaves and the vast majority of the population was also in servitude to the ruling class, though they may have had a bit more freedom then slaves. Despite this inhumane class structure and relentless conquest the "leaders" of these civilizations proclaimed to be champions of freedom and democracy.

To maintain the illusion of a free and open society the elites retained a high level of education while at the same time suppressing the knowledge that was exposed to the indentured public. As with many feudal systems the commoners were mostly illiterate and although they were not forbidden from learning most of them were always working so hard that they had no time to study. This created a situation in which the ruling few used their superior education to manipulate the masses that unknowingly had their intellect subverted by the establishment.

The practice of using the intellect to rule by mental coercion became known in ancient times as "sophism." The sophists of the ancient world were expert deceivers and that tradition has carried on today within almost every government on the planet. The term sophist has roots in the Greek word *sophisma* that means "I am wise." Today we use the word "sophisticated" to describe people who are more affluent and cultured than the rest of society, this word is also derived from the same place. After time sophism became closely associated with politics because the ruling class took advantage of their superior knowledge and used it to manipulate the commoners into accepting high taxes, war, and unfair living conditions.

This was no accident; the elite knew exactly what they were doing. It is even said that the great philosopher Aristotle was harshly reprimanded by Alexander the great for sharing too much of his powerful information with the commoners. Aristotle was actually Alexander's teacher but the young conqueror knew that the lessons he received were more valuable to him if he and his court were the only people who had access to them. Today's ruling class is no different from Alexander the great; they are still suppressing and manipulating information with the intent of dominating the minds of others.

Now in the 21st century psychological warfare invades every aspect of modern life. It has made its way into every form of media and even into our education system; it is now deeply embedded in our culture. It has also extended deep into the political arena and has helped politician's further master the art of deception. Our thoughts are constantly being manipulated using these techniques. Many of us have trouble separating our own thoughts from those that have been implanted into our consciousness by the many subversive external stimuli we encounter on a day-to-day basis. How do you protect yourself from this invasion of the mind? The best place to start is to turn off the TV, resist having a materialistic attitude, and do your own research into the history and practices of the advertisement and PR Industries. Their propaganda has no effect on an informed and self-aware human being.

QUOTE SOURCES AND SUGGESTED READING
----
[0] The Mechanical Bride: Folklore Of Industrial Man - Marshall McLuhan (1967)
[1] Propaganda - Edward Bernays
[2] The Republic – Plato
[3] Public Opinion - Walter Lippmann

[4] Public Opinion - Walter Lippmann
[5] Propaganda - Edward Bernays
[6] Psychology as the Behaviorist Views It - John B Watson
[7] Psychology as the Behaviorist Views It - John B Watson
[8] http://www.guardian.co.uk/science/2002/jan/08/gm.activists
[9] http://newstandardnews.net/content/index.cfm/items/641
[10] Second Front: Censorship and Propaganda in the Gulf War (1993) - John R. MacArthur
[SR1] Manufacturing Consent by Noam Chomsky
[SR2] Merchants Of Discontent by Tamara R. Piety
[SR3] Propaganda and the Public Mind by Noam Chomsky, David Barsamian
[SR4] Propaganda by Edward Bernays
[SR5] Public Opinion by Walter Lippmann
[SR6] The Father of Spin by Larry Tye Crown
[SR7] The Tavistock Institute For Human Relations by Dr. John Coleman
[SR8] World as Laboratory: Experiments with Mice, Mazes, and Men by Rebecca Lemov

"The Matrix is everywhere. It is all around us. Even now, in this very room. You can see it when you look out your window or when you turn on your television. You can feel it when you go to work... when you go to church... when you pay your taxes. It is the wool that has been pulled over your eyes to blind you from the truth. That you are a slave, Neo. Like everyone else you were born into bondage. Born into a prison that you cannot smell or taste or touch. A prison for your mind." – Morpheus {The Matrix - Film} [0]

Advertising and the Subliminal Culture

Today the teachings of the modern propagandists have taken on a life of their own and become the number one secret weapon used by corporations against their customers as well as governments against their citizens. As a result of the culture that was created by public relations pioneers the western world greatly underestimates the power of the subconscious mind. Many believe that they have total control over everything they think and do. However, if this were a fact then addiction would not be such a problem in our society, tobacco use would not be the leading cause of death. This kind of situation illustrates how our will power is not stronger than our subconscious minds in many cases, and it goes a lot deeper than that too.

We are being constantly bombarded with a swarm of images every single hour! Whether it is from the TV or billboards, magazines, internet or even clothing, you are being spoken to through what we call the media. The people who are assembling these messages are doing so in hopes to make you act in a certain way, or to buy in a certain way. So if these stimuli can trigger buying impulses, then what is to say they are not triggering other impulses to?

It seems foolish to think that if someone watches a horror movie that they're going to go on a murder rampage, but that is not exactly what I'm suggesting here. What I am suggesting is that these images do have some effect on our opinions, desires, and actions. This is a known clinical fact and is taken advantage of by PR firms, politicians, newscasters and anyone else who wishes to control your conscious thought and action through your subconscious mind. If these powerful people spend this much time and energy discovering how to manipulate your subconscious through market research, which they do, then there must be some truth to all this.

Someone who surrounds themselves with violent or materialistic media may be more predisposed to violent or materialistic thoughts. Maybe they have some self-control; maybe they do not act on these thoughts, but the information is still there, stored in the subconscious mind of the consumer, only to surface later in the form of stress, illness, or bad mood. People do not want to hear this, though; they like their slasher movies and violent video games. Vicariously living through an on-screen character playing out a dramatic war scene gives them a rush, setting off triggers in their brains that are naturally designed to react to threatening or surprising situations.

There is a complex public relations effort behind every powerful industry. In fact, advertising is a huge and secretive industry all in itself. Most "good salesmen" know more about the art of persuasion then they do about the product their selling, most times they actually know very little about the product their selling. There are literally volumes of books, filled with deceptive maneuvers and sneaky persuasive tricks for advertisers to use. A handful of these books have been revealed to the public, but the contents of most of them remain a mystery to most of us, because the courses that one must go through to become a certified sales representative are very private and not offered in any college. To learn the tricks of this trade one must apply and be accepted before taking any courses. The art of persuasion is used by advertisers, politicians, and bankers alike to ensure that the public accepts their worldview.

In the past few years since the western occupation of the Middle East there has been a barrage of military propaganda in every corner of American culture. Children are a primary target for this propaganda, mainly through the use of "combat simulator" video games. Combat simulators are commonplace at the top of the sales charts, and oftentimes bring in more money than big Hollywood blockbusters. These Video games glorify the military and have helped the rest of the media to desensitize a whole generation from the horrors of war. In late 2010 a video game by the name of "Call of Duty Black Ops" made headlines as one of the top grossing games of all time. This game was a hypnotic gore fest that millions of young people became obsessed with, many of whom did not even agree with America's imperialistic wars in the Middle East, but were just caught up in the flashy advertising and the mob frenzy surrounding the game.

The reason why these games are able to take hold of people and transcend their political barriers is because the consumers are grossly underestimating the power of their unconscious minds. People are caught up in the mentality that "it is just a game" and think that they have the good sense to separate fiction from reality. The only reason why they feel such a connection to this kind of media in the first place is because they are familiar with the rush that they get when a fight or flight situation on the screen sets off brain triggers to release endorphins into their bloodstream. That does not sound much like a conscious decision to me. Just because you're not going on a shooting spree in a shopping mall like you saw on the video game does not mean that you will not be more likely to get road rage, depression or generally have unsettling thoughts because you have surrounded yourself with violent media.

People will argue that this violence has been with us for centuries and say that it is natural for humans to seek out violence for entertainment, but this is not the case. While it is true that violence is deeply entrenched in history, violent media tends to only becomes popular in a violent militaristic culture where the population is already predisposed to aggression because they are exposed to so much of it, and trained to embrace it from an early age. In a society where aggression is not encouraged and the military does not have a strong presence in the pop culture there is very little interest in violent media among the population. It should come as no surprise then that civilizations without strong central governments and frequent war have very little violence to deal with in their everyday lives. While imperialistic empires such as America are flooded with violent media and struggle with high violent crime rates, which are all a direct result of the aggressive culture that is created by a wartime atmosphere.

QUOTE SOURCES AND SUGGESTED READING
----
[0] Morpheus – The Matrix
[SR1] Mind programming by Eldon Taylor
[SR2] Subliminal adventures in erotic art by Wilson Bryan key
[SR3] The secret sales pitch by August Bullock

"If you're not careful the newspapers will have you hating the people who are oppressed and loving the people who are doing the oppressing." – Malcolm X [0]

Mainstream Media is Mass Mind Control

Most people form their opinions about world events based on the information that they get from television, newspapers, and other mainstream media sources. This situation is very dangerous considering the bias and corruption that exists within that industry. The media holds an incredible power to manipulate the direction of world events through their control of public opinion. This power naturally draws the attention of groups that wish to sway public opinion in order to promote their agenda or whitewash their crimes.

The media has now become one of the biggest businesses in the world due to their influence of public opinion. Over the last century many large companies have been battling over media dominance, attempting to have total control over what is said in the public arena. These companies are almost always heavily involved in politics and international business affairs. Through controlling the dialogue in the media they are able to portray their business practices and political allies in a positive light, even if this is accomplished by telling blatant lies. It is even accepted in the general public that all of the corporate news outlets have their own political agendas. What is not realized is that even though they may have different party affiliations the major media sources are all on the same team and advertise the same general worldview.

In the early 1980s there were over 50 corporations that controlled all of the news media in America. This is a small number considering that it accounted for television, movies, magazines, books and music all combined. Before the First World War there were actually hundreds of corporations that made up the US media. In 1983 a man by the name of Ben Bagdikian published a book called "The Media Monopoly" which pointed out the consolidation going on in the media at the time. In his book Bagdikian predicted that the meager number of 50 corporations would dwindle very quickly to less than a dozen companies if the media takeover was not prevented. His predictions were met with a great deal of criticism in the mainstream circuit, and that was to be expected considering they were the target of his accusations. Sure enough, over the next 25 years the media would be consolidated into fewer and fewer hands. Now in 2010 the media is completely dominated by only six companies! Time Warner, Disney, Rupert Murdoch's News Corporation, Bertelsmann, Viacom, and General Electric are in complete control of the media in the western world.

The corporate takeover of the US media is verified in the Congressional Record for 1917, when Congressman Callaway said "In March, 1915, the J.P. Morgan interests, the steel, shipbuilding, and powder interest, and their subsidiary organizations, got together 12 men high up in the newspaper world and employed them to select the most influential newspapers in the United States and sufficient number of them to control generally the policy of the daily press ...They found it was only necessary to purchase the control of 25 of the greatest papers. An agreement was reached; the policy of the papers was bought, to be paid for by the month; an editor was furnished for each paper to properly supervise and edit information regarding the questions of preparedness, militarism, financial policies, and other things of national and international nature considered vital to the interests of the purchasers." [1]

This mass consolidation of media power took a turn for the worse in the late 80's during the Ronald Regan administration when the FCC dissolved a policy called "the fairness doctrine." The fairness doctrine was developed early in the 20th century to ensure that controversial issues were not presented in a one sided manner in the media. The need for this policy grew from the limited number of frequencies that were available for radio stations to broadcast on. Since there were so few spaces available for broadcasting, rules were put into place so news corporations did not take advantage of their media monopoly. Broadcasters were required to present controversial topics that were important to their audience and allow both sides a fair shot to make their case.

One of the early supporters of the fairness doctrine Rep. Luther Johnson said in a debate in 1927 "American thought and American politics will be largely at the mercy of those who operate these stations, for publicity is the most powerful weapon that can be wielded in a republic. And when such a weapon is placed in the hands of one person, or a single selfish group is permitted to either tacitly or otherwise acquire ownership or dominate these broadcasting stations throughout the country, then woe be to those who dare to differ with them. It will be impossible to compete with them in reaching the ears of the American people." [2] These words are prophetic when considering how the mainstream media works today.

Today's mainstream media is merely an avenue for the elite to distribute their propaganda; it works in the same way as the political system with two sides that are pushing the same agenda. They attack each other on trivial issues but still more or less tow the government line on major policies. A key example of this charade is seen with the three primary television news networks, FOX, MSNBC, and CNN. FOX is owned by Rupert Murdoch's "News Corp", this is the least trusted source for news in America but still has a great deal of influence on many people's opinions. This has been known to be a "right-wing" or "conservative" news source. MSNBC is on the other side, apparently. MSNBC is considered the more "liberal" or "left-wing" news source, while CNN is said to reside in the middle of the road. The way their programming is structured appeals to different demographics but overall they are promoting the same general ideas just with minor differences to suit their target audiences.

This is the same way that MTV appeals to a different demographic than Nickelodeon or VH1 but still have the same kind of political agenda and overtones, why you ask? Because their owned by the same company, Viacom. The news channels may not be this blatantly obvious, because they are owned by different companies. However, it should come as no surprise that all of these different companies have the same agendas considering how centralized our media is. So let's take a look at who owns CNN, FOX, and MSNBC to see what they may have in common politically. Which seems kind of important considering this is the primary place where Americans seem to get their political information from.

CNN is owned by AOL/Time Warner, MSNBC is owned by Microsoft and General Electric and FOX are owned by Billionaire news tycoon Rupert Murdoch. General Electric is owned and controlled mostly by the infamous Rockefeller banking & railroad dynasty who history has shown to be tyrants and robber barons. The News headquarters for General Electric's NBC studios are actually in a 70-story skyscraper called, The Rockefeller Center. This is of course, owned by the Rockefellers. This same building is also home to the offices of Time Warner. Time Warner also has close ties to the Rockefellers but is mostly controlled by the J.P. Morgan dynasty. Both of these families have worked together to rob the public blind for generations. It is also important to mention that the US government worked with the Rockefellers, General Electric and Westinghouse to finance and engineer the first hydrogen bomb.

So what does this information tell us? It tells us that most of the world's mainstream media sources are owned by multinational corporations and international bankers. This is extremely important considering that most of the problems in the world are being caused by the very corporations that own the media, so they are going to want to direct public opinion in a way that serves their business interests. Ending the private Federal Reserve Bank and withdrawing from the exploitative WTO trade policies are things that would benefit the American people directly and immediately but it would be a nightmare for the corporations that own the media. That is why these issues are completely ignored and marginalized by the mainstream media.

Think about it this way, on MSNBC you are seeing the views that would benefit Microsoft and General Electric, on FOX you are seeing views that would benefit News Corp and on CNN you are seeing views that would benefit Time Warner. There is no news source that presents views and ideas that would benefit the majority of Americans, who do not have billions of dollars and run multinational corporations. All of the companies I mentioned are multinational corporations so basically what we have in the media are a large drawn out advertising campaign for corporations and whichever corrupt political party they choose to support. On top of that you have more multinational corporations with their own agendas advertising on their network, providing a source of income that the broadcasters come to depend on. For example major military contractors like Northrop Grumman or Boeing have tons of commercials all over the mainstream news, but what average citizen has any interest in the products that these companies have to offer? Are rocket launchers and aircraft carriers on the average American's shopping list? Of course not! Well, then why do these military contractors spend so much money on television advertisements? So they can use those advertising dollars as leverage against the broadcaster, in order to control how their corporation is presented in the news. If a broadcaster is being paid millions of dollars per month by Boeing to run their commercials then they are not going to be able to say anything negative about the war, it is that simple.

You will not be able to find information that is critical of multinational corporations or the banking industry through sources that are owned and funded by multinational corporations and banks, its common sense. Sadly, these interests are the biggest enemies of freedom, yet it is them who are responsible for molding the opinions of people all over the world. It should come as no surprise that there is so much confusion!

If you think the print media might be better, think again. Most of the major print sources are also owned by these same companies. The two largest print news sources in the world, the Associated Press and Reuters are both owned by the Rothschild banking dynasty. These sources pass down information to subsidiaries that are owned by companies like Time Warner, General Electric, and News Corp. Rupert Murdoch, the same media tycoon who catches so much criticism for his slanted programming on FOX news actually owns almost 200 newspapers, including The Times of London, The Wall Street Journal, and the New York Post. He also owns100 cable TV channels including Fox and 19 sports channels, 9 satellite and 40 regular TV networks, 40 publishing houses, and a movie studio. His opinions are directly influenced by banking families, multinational corporations, and political donators.

So in short, control over publishing, recording, and top cable companies belongs to GE, Time Warner, Viacom, Disney, and Newscorp. These are directly or indirectly owned by the Rockefellers, Rothschild's, Morgan's and Oppenheimer's, all of which own multinational corporations and international financial institutions. These are the richest people in the world who live lives of luxury on the backs of the working class and the third world. Do not think for a minute that these same figures do not also have a hidden hand in politics, because they do.

It costs such an incredible amount of money to run for president, the kind of money that only multinational corporations and foundations have access to. So all would-be Presidential candidates, be it democrat or republican are forced to rely on multinational corporations for their campaign funding. This means when they get into office they are more or less indebted to multinational corporations and then they must make sure that their policies are in line with the wishes of those who funded their rise to power.

It has become apparent that the media is a big public relations tool for the big corporations and the politicians that they put into power. Digging deeper, most of these corporations have direct ownership connections to powerful industry and banking dynasties such as the Rockefellers, Morgan's, and Rothschild's to name a few. David Rockefeller said it all in his 1991 Trilateral Commission meeting speech *"We are grateful to The Washington Post, the New York Times, Time Magazine, and other great publications whose directors have attended our meetings and respected their promises of discretion for almost forty years. It would have been impossible for us to develop our plan for the world if we had been subject to the bright lights of publicity during those years."*[3] Statements like this show how the industry is deliberately keeping crimes against humanity away from public view by maintaining control of what is covered in the media.

This problem may seem overwhelming, but there are many solutions that are well within our reach. The internet allows anyone with some time and dedication to present his or her point of view to the rest of the world. Everyday independent media sources are popping up that are not afraid to question authority or the ruling business class that runs the media. Until the average person is given fair representation in the mainstream media we must use the internet as a tool to get our suppressed message to the masses. We must also continue to fight corporate control of the media and demand our place in the public dialogue. Most importantly we need to become the media ourselves, with cheap video cameras and the internet we can do this research for ourselves and bring the information to other people, just as I do on a very low budget.

QUOTE SOURCES AND SUGGESTED READING
----
[0] Malcolm X speaks: selected speeches and statements By Malcolm X, George Breitman
[1] The Congressional Record, February 9, 1917, Vol. 54, pp. 2947-2948
[2] Interview with Larry Bensky, KPFA, Berkeley, and Robert Knight 1/16/ 2003
[3] Matrix of Power By Jordan Maxwell
[SR1] The Mechanical Bride: Folklore Of Industrial Man by Marshall McLuhan (1967)
[SR2] The Media Monopoly by Ben H. Bagdikian

"Television is the new state religion run by a private Ministry of Culture, offering a universal curriculum for all people, financed by a form of hidden taxation without representation. You pay when you wash, not when you watch, and whether or not you care to watch."
- George Gerbner ({Dean of the Annenberg School of Communication} [0]

Television Programming is Programming Your Mind

Television has only been around for about 100 years and in that short amount of time it has drastically changed how human beings think and behave. Televisions impact on society has been far more negative than positive because of how it disconnects humanity from nature and promotes materialistic values through its programming. Everything that is shown on TV today has been selected by the government and multinational corporations that own the broadcasters. Everything that is put out by these broadcasters must be approved by the government boards that oversee the industry, namely the FCC. If a program is not approved by the FCC then it is not allowed to be aired. This conflict usually does not occur though because the FCC and the multinational media corporations generally have the same interests. What this basically means is that the only thing that is on television are things that the government or large multinational corporations want you to see, just as I explained with the news earlier. This is one of the establishment's best tools of social control to distract and manipulate the minds of the masses.

Many people are very naive in thinking that the things they see on TV have absolutely no effect on their mental processes. The human subconscious is much stronger than most people are willing to admit. This means that there is a very good possibility that the situations and imagery seen on television will have an impact on how they think and react to everyday life. What a lot of people do not know is that after watching TV for just a few seconds the viewer goes into a suggestive state of hypnosis. A recent study conducted by a Dr. Aric Sigman looked into the effect that television has on the brain chemistry and critical thinking skills. He published his findings in a book called "Remotely Controlled" which reconfirmed many point that were first brought up in 1971 by a Professor Herbert Krugman in his studies on television and the subconscious.

Their research shows that it only takes 30 seconds of watching TV to be put in a highly suggestible hypnotic state. This hypnotic state has been proven in studies by reading alpha waves that have been emitted from viewers. Alpha waves are and uncommon brain wave pattern also present in the state of "light hypnosis" that hypnotists use for suggestion therapy. Have you ever tried to get someone's attention while they were watching TV? Usually it is pretty difficult to detach someone from their fixed gaze because of the light hypnotic state that their brain is in. When considering the highly suggestible state of mind that television creates in people it becomes alarming that an average American sees over 20,000 commercials and 33,000 murders per year on TV. This fact is especially scary considering the biggest consumers of television are children, who have even less ability then adults to differentiate between reality and fiction.

Television induced hypnosis also disables the neo-cortex or "higher brain" and increases activity in the limbic system or "lower brain." The limbic system is the region of the brain that triggers desires and sexual arousal, it has often been referred to as the "reptile brain." This region is unable to differentiate between what is real and what is an act; it sees everything that it can visualize as being real. If you are watching something frightening on the television your heart will beat faster and you will begin to tremble, this is because the parts of your brain that are actually active are not the parts that can tell the difference between reality and fiction. So while you may consciously realize that what you're watching is not real your mind is not able to reasonably assess the information because the logical parts of your brain are in a state of sleep.

The vulnerable hypnotic state that television creates has been designed purposely by the politicians and advertisers that put their message out over the airwaves. These messages have been carefully crafted to play on your subconscious fears and desires in order to persuade you to buy their product or go along with their social policy. If you pay attention you will notice that news shows and commercials are even more hypnotic and entrancing then regular programming, this is no accident. If you think about it the whole point of a news program or commercial is not to inform or entertain you, but to persuade you. There are all kinds of complicated techniques that are used to help with this persuasion; some involve dialogue while others are related to the visual set up of the program. These subliminal influences are largely responsible for the materialistic, nihilistic, and violent culture that is so prevalent in most of the world today.

The subliminal threat that television poses on our consciousness is very real, but even on a more surface level it is easy to see how this device has impacted society negatively. Most people generally spend over 24 hours a week in front of the TV, that is over one whole day of every week wasted consuming pop culture that has been created by the establishment. In the past our ancestors would use that time to enjoy the company of the people they cared about, appreciate nature or use their imagination to create something, while now we sit in a hypnotic state watching violent and materialistic programming. This kind of activity is very unnatural for humans to be taking part in and is not healthy for our mind and soul. That day a week can be spent a lot better if it was not in front of the TV. Start by cancelling your cable subscription and minimizing the time you spends in front of the TV, you will feel an immediate difference in consciousness. TV has become an invisible government shackle for the psyche of millions and your mind is better off without it.

QUOTE SOURCES AND SUGGESTED READING
----
[0] Amusing Ourselves to Death Public Discourse in the Age of Show Business by Neil Postman
[SR1] Remotely Controlled by Dr Aric Sigman

[SR2] Dialectic of Enlightenment by Max Horkheimer, Theodor W. Adorno
[SR3] The Culture Industry Revisited by Deborah Cook

"Art is moral passion married to entertainment. Moral passion without entertainment is propaganda, and entertainment without moral passion is television."
-Rita Mae Brown [0]

The Entertainment Industry

For the past several centuries the elite has struggled in finding a system of government that allows them to carry out their imperialistic wishes while maintaining public support at the same time. If they had things their way every society that was under their control would be a feudal fascist dictatorship. The only reason this is not the case is because they have seen in the past that this kind of government does not last long, as the people become agitated by the obvious disparities that exist within their civilization.

Sports, entertainment, and overbearing work schedules are used to distract the public from what is going on in their government. This mind control tactic has been used since the time of Ancient Rome but has gotten more complex and powerful as technology progressed. The ancient Roman "leaders" had an imperialistic policy quite similar to that of modern America. In order to keep their subjects ignorant of the political details of their military programs the Romans built a powerful entertainment industry. This industry consisted of huge coliseums that hosted brutal sporting events as well as elaborate bathhouses and country clubs for the more timid citizens. These events kept the general public occupied while their corrupt "leaders" ran the country into the ground with poor economic policy and over militarization.

Today's entertainment industry has come a very long way due to technology, but it still serves the same purpose as it did in Ancient Rome. As our political and financial institutions have slowly advanced their world empire over the past few generations, most Americans have been distracted by various forms of media, all of which are filled with pro establishment propaganda. Most major record companies, television broadcasters and media outlets are owned by the elite and any of the performers that are featured through those channels are on the elite's payroll. So their scripts, lyrics, and even press releases are often times written by corporations that are owned by the elite. The capital of the modern entertainment world is a place called Hollywood. Interestingly enough magicians' wands are made of wood from a holly bush. This is no coincidence as everything that comes out of Hollywood is designed to cast a spell, just like a magician's wand. Furthermore the word entertainment itself means "a diversion for the mind," which is exactly what it is and what it is used for.

It is very common for celebrities to buy into this game and just project whatever kind of ideas they are told to without thinking twice. While it is very rare for celebrities to speak out against the establishment, if this does happen then they are vilified in the media and will face many obstacles in their career as a result of their dissent. One of the most successful celebrities in recent memory to take a stand was Dave Chappelle. His years in the entertainment industry had shown him the corruption that exists behind the scenes and how entertainers are used as pawns to advance the elites agenda. When leaving his show and turning down a 20 million dollar deal he said "I was doing sketches that were funny but socially irresponsible. I felt I was deliberately being encouraged and I was overwhelmed" and "I felt in a lot of instances I was deliberately being put through stress because when you're a guy who generates money, people have a vested interest in controlling you."[1]

I cannot speak for Chappelle, but from an outsiders perspective it seems that he came to realize that the ideas that are put forth through the mainstream media are intended to make the population more disorderly, materialistic, and obedient. It is possible that he began to see these kinds of degrading ideas in the scripts that he was getting from comedy central and wanted no parts in it, regardless of how much money they were offering him. Dave Chappelle is a remarkable human being for refusing to put a price on his artistic integrity and his protest should be a lesson to everyone in the entertainment industry.

Music is not free from propaganda either. While there are many independent rock and hip-hop artists who are actually making creative revolutionary music, the mainstream circuit is a direct representation of the ruling elite. Hip-hop pioneer Professor Griff of Public Enemy has recently exposed the elites infiltration of the industry that he helped create. His research shows how some of the biggest names in hip-hop are just puppets who are being paid to socially engineer their listeners.

His research makes a lot of sense considering that hip-hop originated from peaceful gatherings with break-dancers, graffiti artists, and MCs spreading a message of freedom and equality. That was a message that the establishment could not allow, so slowly as a generation or two progressed they used their vast financial resources to send hip-hop in a different direction. This is how in less than 20 years a culture went from being about good times, peace, and empowerment to materialism, violence, and misogyny. The same thing has happened with rock music as well, its frontrunners were transformed from antiwar hippies into materialistic, cocaine addict Satanists in just a decade.

Major league sporting events are also a part of the propaganda machine just as the gladiator battles were in ancient Rome. It is not the sports themselves that are detrimental to free thought, but it is simply the over-commercialization of the organized leagues. Getting together with some friends and playing a sport every now and then can be fun and very good for your health. However, sitting in front of a television watching hours of commercials in between millionaires playing a game is not good for your mental or physical health. If you have interest in sports call up some friends or join a local league and actually play the game yourself instead of sitting at home in front of the TV consuming pop culture. If watching sports is your thing though and that is what you enjoy, more power to you, but if you have ever asked yourself why athletes and entertainers make so much money, all this should clear up some of that confusion.

Billions of dollars pour into these industries on a monthly basis because it has become one of the most effective tools of social control for the elite. It is the corporate controlled mainstream media that is perpetuating aggression and fear in our society, which is why people who are aware of this situation should support independent media and underground culture. Surround yourself with the ideas and expressions of everyday people instead of the propaganda that is so apparent in popular culture. If possible find a way to express yourself and create something to bring entertainment to other people.

QUOTE SOURCES AND SUGGESTED READING
----
[0] Women know everything! By Karen Weekes (page 340)
[1] "The Oprah Winfrey Show" with Dave Chappelle February 3rd 2006

"The most loving parents and relatives commit murder with smiles on their faces. They force us to destroy the person we really are: a subtle kind of murder."
- Jim Morrison [0]

Parental Propaganda

The bond between a parent and a child is one of the strongest human relationships and since the beginning of time children would learn valuable life lessons from their families. It is for this reason that many authoritarian societies have guided the structure of the family to mold future generations, even before they enter the indoctrination centers that we call schools. The most effective form of propaganda that the establishment has is the ability to impose their values on young impressionable children through their parents.

Using the methods of propaganda that are already in place via the media, education systems and religious institutions, the establishment has created a society where authoritarianism and domination is a part of everyday life. When parents are raising their children they are drawing on a lifetime of propaganda and they feel a great sense of guilt when their child naturally does not accept the established norms in society. Children are free and full of spirit and it has been so long since many parents have felt that way that they simply do not understand. Their oppressive culture and its abhorrent values have brought them so far away from their spirit that they feel that something is wrong if their child does not conform to the establishment's ideals.

This causes parents to be authoritative with their children to encourage conformity. What they are really doing is breaking their child's spirit and preparing them to live in an oppressive world and accept authority. Parents take this aggressive route because of the example that has been set by the established control systems. In our society it is commonplace for people in power or authority to be controlling and close minded, so when someone puts their trust in that kind of society they are going to behave in that fashion when they fall into a position of authority themselves.

Many good people that only want the best for their family actually end up putting themselves and their children through a lot of pain and turmoil because they are under the impression that their child has to be a certain way. All this stress and oppression is many times all carried out under the best of intentions, but it is with corrupted perceptions that parents are projecting society's ideals onto their children. Today Parents are not passing earthly knowledge and wisdom to their children but instead they are passing down a long list of cultural assumptions, idiosyncrasies, and misconceptions. They are passing along the materialistic message of the corporate elite that has been instilled in them through years of propaganda and indoctrination. Even worse is the fact that these false values are instilled through constant abuse, sometimes physical, but usually emotional. This has resulted in a situation where in almost every household throughout time children have been psychologically abused. If almost everyone's childhood is like this, is it any surprise that most of the adults in our society behave in such an irrational way?

Now as the empire is crumbling and the middle class is disappearing it is obvious to everyone that the ideals of our society are corrupt. It is important that we do not instill that same set of ideals in future generations or we will be doomed to repeat this cycle of dominance and propaganda yet again. We should be protecting our children from the toxic culture that surrounds us instead of forcing them to conform to it. The values that drive our culture are the reason for a great deal of suffering across the world. So when these values enter a family they will not only have a detrimental personal impact but they will cause another human being to project the same oppressive energy that is destroying our planet and our species.

One of the most profound spiritual minds of our generation "Osho" has really summed up this issue of aggressive parenting better than I would ever be able to. Osho Says "The whole idea that children are your possession is wrong. They are born through you, but they do not belong to you. You have a past, they have only a future. They are not going to live according to you. To live according to you will be almost equivalent to not living at all. They have to live according to themselves — in freedom, in responsibility, in danger, in challenge." [1]This is the kind of approach that we should take when raising our children in these confusing and troubled times. If our children are able to think with their own minds uncorrupted by the cultural programming that our generation was subject to then they will be able to have a clear vision for a brighter future.

This is not a change that is happening overnight but is simply a part of a progression that has been evolving for centuries. For the most part, every generation treats their children with just a little bit more respect then they saw from their parents, with that trend speeding up in the 20th century. Physical child abuse, infanticide and child slavery were extremely common throughout history, but in the past century as society has become more conscious about the value of human life, those horrors are thankfully much less common. Physical child abuse still takes place today, but it is much more isolated due to the fear of legal punishment and its recent taboo nature. However, there is still a great deal of emotional and psychological abuse that is dished out to most children, even by the most well intentioned adults.

Children are a minority group who remain second-class citizens in the eyes of most of the world, their actions scrutinized, their opinions ignored and their existence is seen as not much more than a burden. Most adult's fear and envy children, even if they do not realize it. This is because the child is a free spirit that represents change, which the adult has been trained to fear. That fear is then suppressed by attempting to tame the child and train him just as the parent was before him. This "taming" process is extremely confusing and traumatizing for the child, but unfortunately most parents feel that it is their duty to mold their child to be obedient to authority. Not many have questioned the morality or efficiency of this parenting strategy, but it is still a question of extreme importance. Our children are the future of this world and if they are not treated with respect and given freedom, then there will never be freedom or respect in our societies.

My Goal here is not to criticize anyone who used a mainstream parenting strategy, as that would probably be most of the planet. However, it is important for us to know that the way that we treat children as a species is directly related to the kind of adults that we see in our society. There is an old saying that goes "the hand that rocks the cradle rules the world," and this is very true, which is why it is so important to reevaluate how we treat young people. Our children are the future of this world and if they are not treated with respect and given freedom, then there will never be freedom or respect in our civilization.

QUOTE SOURCES AND SUGGESTED READING
----
[0]The Doors companion: four decades of commentary - John M. Rocco (1997)
[1]The Art Of Parenting – Osho
[SR1] Raising children compassionately by Marshall B Rosenberg
[SR2] The History of Childhood by Lloyd deMause
[SR3] Punished by Rewards: by Alfie Kohn
[SR 4] Unconditional Parenting By Alfie Kohn

"When you were young, you took on the world, remember how you'd laugh and sing? You've replaced it all with an IRA, internet porn, and a job you hate."
- Misery Index [0]

Inner Child

Throughout the course of our lives we develop a lot of baggage from the various environments that we encounter. We come into this world as pure souls with a clean slate and as we grow we adopt various beliefs and idiosyncrasies from our culture that eventually manifest as our personal identities. Whether it is race, class, occupation or belief structure people identify with cultural labels and use those labels to build their personal model of reality. A child sees the natural world with a clearer perspective because their perception is not clouded with cultural conventions and other prejudices. This is why concepts like money, time, and authority make no sense at all to children and rightfully so, these are all manmade cultural abstractions that really do not make any sense if you actually think about it from a human perspective.

It is typical for authoritarian societies to condemn their youth because they have not yet been corrupted and molded into an obedient, mechanized citizen. If the youth of any oppressive nation were able to freely grow without being indoctrinated into the cultural control system then the whole system would be radically changed within one single generation. The establishment knows that their stranglehold on the human race is unnatural, immoral and insane which is why their ideals are always met with resistance by the youth culture. The elite knows that their only hope to maintain political dominance is to vilify their citizens until they have been indoctrinated into the system, or in other words until they "grow up."

It takes years of repeated propaganda and social manipulation for a human beings natural center to be replaced with a cultural ego. However, the human mind is resilient and many of us are able to slip into adulthood with minimal psychological corruption. This growing portion of society may not be popular but they are very often the source of most of the positive progress that has taken place throughout history. Some of the greatest minds to have walked the earth have recognized that the idea of "growing up" and "fitting in" places people in invisible cultural prisons and corrupts their natural personal philosophies. One of the most brilliant thinkers of the last century, Albert Einstein was one of these people. He himself said that imagination is way more important than knowledge and that *"Common sense is the collection of prejudices acquired by age eighteen."* [1]

He was well aware of the cultural games that were being played with people's minds. When he was 16 years old one of his schoolteachers told him that he would never amount to anything because of his rebellious, unorthodox attitude. So he did what any free thinking revolutionary would do, he dropped out of school and pursued his education on his own. He went on to become one of the greatest scientists ever, and maintained his rebellious attitude all throughout his entire life. Einstein was against war, elitism and any kind of authority whatsoever. If it was not for his incredible contributions to science he surely would have been considered insane or an enemy of the state by the establishment.

When someone makes it out of childhood without being corrupted by limiting cultural assumptions they are usually called naive and told that their unorthodox point of view is not welcome in their society. Many creative and rebellious people who are in touch with their inner child typically receive such negative feedback from family and peers that they actually knowingly submit to a culture that makes no sense to them. This is exactly why you have to be a certain age in order to vote or run for political office. The system makes sure to give people enough time to submit to the established cultural model of reality before they are able to have any impact at all on the direction of the society.

There are many cases where we do have much to learn from our elders and it is true that skills that we depend upon for survival have been passed down through the generations. However, when it comes to a government setting cultural norms, the information that is being passed down always has an ulterior motive. That motive is always the same, to maintain control of the population and to defend the power of the established institutions so they endure the next generation. It is very important to learn and mature and it is possible to do so without "growing up" and limiting yourself with cultural prejudices. Being responsible, respectful, and peaceful is what makes you a mature adult; it has nothing to do with fitting in to the established culture.

QUOTE SOURCES AND SUGGESTED READING
----

[0] Misery Index – Spectator - "Heirs to Thievery" (2010)
[1] The Oxford dictionary of American quotations - Hugh Rawson, Margaret Miner (2006)
[SR1] Emotional Life Of Nations by Lloyd DeMause
[SR2] The Case Against Adolescence by Robert Epstein PhD

"You have owners. They own you. They own everything. They own all the important land. They own and control the corporations, They've long since bought the senate, the congress, the state houses, the city halls, they've got the judges in their back pockets and they own all the big media companies so they control just about all of the news and information you get to hear. They got you by the balls."
– George Carlin

Section 4

Economics

22. -Feudalism: From the Dark Ages to the New World
23. -Who's The Man
24. -Fabian Socialism and the New World Order
25. -North American Serfdom
26. -The Birth of the Corporate Beast in America
27. -Central Banking in Early America
28. - End the Fed
29. -Controlled Economic Collapse
30. -Third World By Design
31. -The Sweatshop Economy
32. -Royal Landlords
33. -Cursed Dinosaur Blood
34. -The Climate Industrial Complex and the Hoax of State Sponsored Environmentalism

"I freed a thousand slaves; I could have freed a thousand more if only they knew they were slaves."
- Harriet Tubman [0]

Feudalism: From the Dark Ages to the New World

History is the long story of our past, a story that is told in many different ways, with different information depending on where the story is being told. If one does enough research they will find that our past is a cycle of dominance and revolution, of civilizations rising up against authoritarian "leaders" that control their lives and manipulate them into servitude. Though some forms of government are more oppressive than others, the citizens are always duped into believing that their ruler is doing the right thing, otherwise they would join together and overthrow the established dictatorship. A brilliant philosopher by the name of Johann Wolfgang von Goethe is known to have said "None are more hopelessly enslaved than those who falsely believe they are free."[1].

Goethe was one of the most famous writers of German history, but his ideas were so radical that they were often met with resistance from tyrants. When the Nazi regime was burning books prior to the Second World War many of Goethe's writings were targeted and destroyed. His words are as true today for your average person as they were for the serfs in the middle ages who lived their whole life to serve a master that would not allow them to read.

In the middle ages Europe consisted of large pieces of land that were owned by wealthy royal knights called "lords." The lords basically used slave labor to acquire great wealth, but instead of putting their subjects in bars and chains, the lords manipulated the "serfs" into servitude using fear and debt. Most average people living during this time led lives of slavery without even realizing it and yet they still feared and respected the oppressive rulers that were responsible for their difficult lives. The lords would achieve this social dominance through letting people build houses on their land and live there for a price. Once the subject entered the agreement he would be indebted for labor and military purposes.

In most cases the lords were far more educated than their subjects and would prevent them from reading or learning anything that would make it possible for them to achieve social independence. This is very similar to the sharecropping system that wealthy slave owners in early America used to manipulate people into slave labor. In the middle ages the plots of land that the lords ruled over were called "fiefdoms"; in the times of slavery they were called "plantations," same idea. This kind of feudal economic set up still takes place today almost everywhere, but of course the language to describe it has evolved in order to make the public believe that "serfs", "slaves", "lords" and "masters" are all things of the past. Sadly, they are just as much of a reality today as they were centuries ago.

Today's complicated economic & legal systems were devised by the "lords" as a method of maintaining their wealth. These systems were sold to the population as a means of developing personal financial freedom and protection when in reality they created a very complicated and deceptive form of slavery. The fact that there are a few subclasses among the "working class" or "serf's" seems to make the public believe that everyone has some level of opportunity, but all of these subclasses are peons compared to the people who print the money and control the economy. This works the same in both capitalist and communist societies around the world, a wealthy few live in luxury on the backs of their struggling citizens. With both systems the middle class is nonexistent and the upper class has a total stranglehold on the lives of the lower class. This financial enslavement has been achieved like it always has, through debt and fear. Evidence of these tactics is all around us, as I will explain later in this book.

The upper class still manipulates average people into working for them for their entire lives, receiving pathetic compensation that makes it impossible to maintain a comfortable life. Also, just as the lords of the middle ages controlled the information that their subjects had access to, the upper class in today's world own all the major media outlets and control the curriculum in the education system. They do their best to make sure it is their side of the story that is presented to the general population and use the many organizations that they are connected with to condemn anyone who offers another side to the story.

Some fiefdoms were better than others and some lords less ruthless than others. While the "leaders" would bicker over their petty differences their societies were all pyramid schemes that served an oligarchy at the expense of the majority of the population. Centuries later nothing has changed, almost every single nation in the world is controlled by a power hungry oligarchy that allows millions of citizens to live in poverty. The many "countries" across the planet today are controlled by an aristocracy who apparently keep their people "free" and "safe" while at the same time enslaving them with debt and sending them to war. Some countries are better than others, some governments more oppressive than others. While the various "leaders" may bicker over their petty differences, every single one of them are facilitating and benefiting from their own feudal society. Most countries are nothing more than modern day fiefdoms!

The big secret is that nothing about the relationship between lord and serf has changed since the days when feudalism was openly accepted as a political and economic system. Technological advancements over the last millennia have provided todays serfs with a far more comfortable lifestyle than that of their ancestors; however the relationship between the working class and the ruling class has changed very little. Today it is possible for someone to have wall to wall carpeting, running water, electronic trinkets and home appliances, but that does not change the fact that they have to hand over a majority of their earnings to someone who has an obscene amount of control over their personal lives. The people are still unjustly taxed, sent to war for no purpose, and subjected to a life of fear and confusion just as they were in the dark ages.

Thanks to human ingenuity and the steady advance of technology most of us in the west are not subject to living in straw huts scavenging for food, but again this does not mean that we are free or financially independent, it simply means we just happen to be slightly more comfortable than those who came before us. The tiny group of aristocrats that have ruled over Europe and its colonies for centuries have been continuously looting resources from the working class and developing a stranglehold on the private lives of everyday citizens in order to protect their wealth and positions of power. Nothing about the social structure or role of authority in everyday life has changed, so while technological advancement has given us immediate comfort and the illusion of wealth, we remain under the financial and legal control of a few powerful psychopaths.

When you take a close look at how global events have progressed over the ages you will find that many of the families who dominate politics and economics today have bloodlines that actually trace back to the feudal lords of the Middle Ages. In Middle Eastern and third world countries this is painfully obvious because there are still royal dynasties who openly claim that it is their birthright to rule over their country, while in the west the aristocrats are a bit less open.

However, the aristocrats in the United States and Great Brittan have blood as royal as a Saudi king. For example, let's take a look at the past few presidential candidates in America. Bush, Cheney, and Bill Clinton are all distant cousins and descendants of Charlemagne, a French monarch who ruled most of Europe during his lifetime (742-814). 35 US presidents have genes that trace back to this Charlemagne, while the other 10, or so trace back to Alfred the Great who was king of England in the 9th century. Many of the most prominent banking families also come from these bloodlines so the royalty dominates the business world as well as the political world.

In The election of 2004 George Bush and John Kerry were the options for US president but both candidates were distant cousins to the Queen of England and even belonged to the same secret society at Yale University, the morbidly named Skull and Bones fraternity! If that is not creepy enough for you I would also like to mention that all decedents of Charlemagne are also great, great, great etc. Grandchildren of Prince Vlad III Dracula of Wallachia (modern Romania). This was the sick and depraved ruler who was known as a butcher and who eventually became the inspiration for the most famous vampire stories in history. Dracula may have had an extra knack for theatrics but his kind of sadistic inhumane behavior is the norm not the exception within these royal bloodlines.

A genealogist at the New England Historic Genealogical Society in Boston by the name of Gary Boyd Roberts is one of the top experts on the royal ancestry of American presidents. His research links every American president's lineage to different bloodlines of royalty throughout Europe. His findings are also backed up by Burkes Peerage that is the world encyclopedia of royal genealogy. In fact, according to both of these sources, in every election the candidate with the most royal genes has won. The jury on President Barack Obama's lineage is still out because all records of his early life are shrouded in secrecy. Due to the many forged documents and name changes that we have seen from Obama, it is difficult to determine if he has royal blood.

Throughout the rest of the world the story is the same, people that are born into a place of privilege because of the wealth of their ancestors are the new aristocrats who dominate politics and international business. Over the centuries those in power have learned that they can't quickly and forcefully push their way into dominating a large group of people, they need to trick the population into begging for their own enslavement. Countless hours are spent by rulers around the world to find new ways of conning their citizens into giving up their rights and handing their lives over to the state.

Each and every flag-waving citizen of any random country throughout the world will tell you that corruption does not happen in their country and that their "leader" has their best interests in mind. Almost every government throughout the world is an oligarchy even within the western countries that claim to conduct their business "democratically. " The fact remains that from superpowers like the UK, US, Russia or China to monarchies like Saudi Arabia there is a small privileged class who makes all of the decisions and exploits the work and ingenuity of the majority of the unknowing population. Many of the actions taken by government are unpopular among the majority of the population, but the plan stays on course despite the backlash. That does not sound very democratic to me.

There are a few rare cases when a new face steps into an important role in the aristocracy but this is rare and limited to people who make groundbreaking discoveries, inventors, entrepreneurs, and other wild cards that happen to find themselves in the company of the elite. This ruling class makes up a very small portion of the population, they account for less than 1% of the world's population. Despite their small size this elite class has managed to amass most of the world's attainable wealth and land through centuries of conquest and social domination. The families at the very top of this class structure are richer than many of the world's governments combined and their wealth is incalculable in terms that would relate to almost anyone in the world.

The modern feudal lords who work for these families get a smaller slice of the global financial pie, which is still much larger than your average person could imagine. Meanwhile, BILLIONS of people who account for around 99% of the world's population are left to struggle for the remaining scraps that haven't been wasted and hidden away by the feudal dictators. Under these circumstances the vast majority of the population is divided and pitted against each other to battle over the small amount of remaining resources. The feudal masters would much rather see billions of people suffer and die then change the way they do business and risk losing their immense power over the world's population.

Now as has happened many times before, things are beginning to fall apart due to corruption and inequality. The cracks in the system are exposing the true nature of what has been happening all along. We have been used as workhorses and human shields for centuries, our rights taken away and given back with the cycles of revolutions and changes in public opinion. Regardless of our nationality or what country we call home, we have been the pawns of the ruling class for centuries without even realizing it. Even in countries like the U.S and the U.S we are only given the illusion of freedom and we still have very little say in what actually goes on in the government.

Most people have a hard time dealing with these topics and refuse to believe that their lives are being controlled, but in order to free ourselves we need to recognize what is going on and start educating ourselves. The most powerful tool we have in this battle is information, which is why they work so hard to control the information that we have access to. Progress is already being made to stop this vicious cycle of economic control and unnecessary war, because people are finally starting to educate themselves and others. In the rest of this section I will dig deeper and name some of the specific organizations and families who facilitate this global feudal system that I have just described.

QUOTE SOURCES AND SUGGESTED READING
----

[0]Voices of Hope: Timeless Expressions of Faith from African Americans - Honor Books, Niral R. Burnett (2005)

[1] Goethe: The History of a Man by Emil Ludwig
[SR1] Fire in the Minds of Men: Origins of the Revolutionary Faith by James Billington
[SR2] Against Oligarchy by Webster G. Tarpley
[SR3] Belated Feudalism: Labor, the Law, and Liberal Development in the United States by Karen Orren

"I care not what puppet is placed on the throne of England to rule the Empire, The man that controls Britain's money supply controls the British Empire. And I control the money supply."
- Baron Nathan Mayer Rothschild [0]

Who's "The Man"

Now that we have established that the world is controlled by a global feudal system it is time to take a look at the specific family lines and political organizations that are responsible for establishing and maintaining that system. Within this Control structure the world consists of two classes, the exploiters, and the exploited. The influence and loyalties of the exploiters transcend national borders, ethnic or racial backgrounds as well as religious and political affiliations. Through the ages many empires have fallen, many political regimes came and went, but for the most part, the power and wealth has remained in the same bloodlines and the centralized systems of control are still in place.

Even in times of revolution where kings have been taken from their thrones and removed from power, the wealth and influence of the banking elite has not been threatened for nearly a millennium. Many researchers believe that these lines date back to the time of Rome or even Babylon and I would not doubt that to be the case. If they have managed to stay in power for the past thousand years then I see no reason why they could not have for the 1000 before it, or a thousand years before that. Although, that would be getting a bit too deep down the rabbit hole for now, so I'm just going to focus on the past few centuries.

The last time anyone has stood up against a ruling-banking cartel was when the Knights of Templar were outlawed in the 14th Century, and even then it was an envious king not the citizens who removed the Templars from power. The citizens had very little understanding of just how powerful and influential the Templars were, just as today many people are unaware of who their masters really are. Most of us know that our governments and financial institutions are corrupt, but many people are not aware that there are specific families and organizations that have been controlling these institutions from behind the scenes for many generations.

Our idea of "the man" or "big brother" has remained limited to the authority figures we have to deal with in everyday life, the police, and the politicians. These authority figures are in reality only scapegoats and puppets for a group sometimes known as "the illuminati" or "black nobility" just to name a few on the long list of nicknames this group has been given. This elite network of wealthy families has managed to slip under the radar for many generations through the various different wars and revolutions that have taken place. Who are these ruthless exploiters? Who do our so-called "leaders" answer to? Who do our authority figures take orders from?

We know who these tyrants are; they have been hiding in plain sight, in the tallest buildings in every city, at the heads of the largest companies in the world. These families did not get their power strictly through brute force but by fraudulently acquiring control of different countries financial systems and political organizations. The people that play a conscious role in facilitating this global feudal system make up less than 1% of the world's population. Together they are the global oligarchy who even the harshest dictators dare not cross; they are the kings of kings. Their global control network is spearheaded by various financial and political organizations that are held in regard, thanks only to their billion dollar public relations efforts.

Today there are many organizations that work over top of our government which have been put into place by the modern day feudal oligarchy. Many times these organizations are called "think tanks" or "policy institutes. " Policy institute is the more appropriate term, because these are the organizations that set the political policy and hand it down to the politicians. This is where our politicians get all their wonderful ideas from! Bush did not come up with the 300-page patriot act all by himself, but it was actually the work of a think tank called "the project for a new American century. " Obama's infamous health plan was not something that good ol Barack spent half of law school working on, but that too was the work of a thank tank.

The foreign and economic policy is set by these organizations as well, so that means the government's stance on wars, tax plans or welfare is all decided upon by these groups. Memos and reports created at these organizations make their way through the pentagon and the white house where they eventually land on the president's desk. At this point the president signs to authorize the plan, and reads over the policy so he is prepared to explain it when asked by reporters.

The most powerful of these organizations are the committee of 300, the Bilderberg Group, The Council on Foreign Relations and the Trilateral Commission. There are plenty of other diabolical think tanks, but these are the most influential. The people who belong to these specific groups are the wealthiest people in the world who own and operate the world's largest multinational corporations. The families that sit at the head of these organizations belong to the royal bloodlines that I have been discussing. There are well over a dozen bloodlines who have been secretly working together to exploit the rest of humanity for many centuries.

Sometimes these families have rifts and disagreements about specific policies and sometimes they do get competitive with each other about who will get the bigger piece of the pie, but overall they have shared the same goal for generations. That goal is to establish a worldwide government and connected feudal economic system that will give them complete control of the planet. It is also important to mention that there are millions of people in the world that happen to share these last names, but all of those people obviously are not within these bloodlines and do not play a role in this exploitation. The commanding bloodlines of the global elite are as follows, Merovingian, Rothschild, Rockefeller, Astor, Bundy, Collins, DuPont, Freeman, Li, Reynolds, Morgan, Onassis, Oppenheimer, Russel, Van Duyn. In different places all throughout the world these bloodlines are in charge of the most influential political organizations and the wealthiest multinational corporations.

In the west the Merovingian, Rothschild's, Rockefellers, Morgan's are the most influential of these bloodlines. The Merovingian Bloodline is the line of the royal families in Great Brittan and other parts of Europe, this line is also shared by nearly 80% of American presidents. This is the bloodline that descended from Charlemagne and Count Dracula. The Rothschild's, Rockefellers and Morgan's should need no introduction, these are the infamous robber barons that have dominated western business culture for centuries and picked up where the Knights Templar left off. Many of the other families I have mentioned played a similar role but have recently stayed more in the background compared to the Rothschild's, Merovingian's, Morgan's and Rockefellers. The Rothschild's are by far the wealthiest of these bloodlines and share the biggest piece of the global pie with the Merovingian bloodline, with the Rockefellers following close behind.

These family lines can be traced back to the feudal nobility of the middle ages and they are still in control of the majority of the world's attainable wealth, they own most of earths land surface and they continue to influence global policy in every detail. So what has changed about the relationship between these families and the rest of society since the dark ages? The technology that we have developed has made our lives somewhat less difficult, but all in all we are still a serf class who is controlled by descendants of the tyrants that our ancestors served on the fiefdoms of early Europe.

To carry out covert operations and secretly pass down information through generations the elite uses a vast network of secret societies and so called fraternities as underground training centers for aspiring globalists. These are organizations where members must take vows of secrecy in order to join and once initiated they plan out global policies that will eventually be presented through the think tanks that they are closely related to.

Many people doubt the influence of secret societies and write them off as harmless "conspiracy theories", but history has shown us that secret societies play a major role in some of the world's most pivotal events. For example, the First World War had a direct impact on the entire world and set in motion a chain of events that would bring the earth's population under tighter control of the global elite. This war was started in 1914 when Archduke Franz Ferdinand of Hungary was assassinated by a secret society called "The Black Hand." The Black Hand had many ties to different elite families and its stated goal was to "unify" different nations and city-states throughout Serbia and the rest of Europe. It was also said that this secret society was in cahoots with the British intelligence office MI6, this is highly possible considering that intelligence organizations often work with secret societies without the knowledge of the public or government officials. More on that later when I discuss the intelligence networks more in depth.

Secret societies are used to carry out elite missions that can span over several generations. In the mid 1800's the Rothschild's hired a man by the name of Albert Pike to counter the abolition movement in the United States. The Rothschild's had a heavy hand in the US slave trade and stood to lose a lot of money if slavery was abolished. With Rothschild's money Albert Pike created a secret society called the Klu Klux Klan; their horribly racist group should need no introduction. Despite the fact that the KKK is one of the most rightfully vilified organizations in the world, there is a statue in Washington DC dedicated to Albert Pike. The statue stands on a pedestal near the foot of Capitol Hill, between the Department of Labor building and the Municipal Building, between third and fourth Streets, on D Street, NW. During his life this racist pawn was known as a humanitarian and philanthropist. What a joke! Although many of the people that call themselves humanitarians and philanthropists these days are also depraved individuals that live lives that are drastically out of line with their public image.

Pike was also very close to a man named Giuseppe Mazzini who would form the Mafia in 1860, another infamous secret society that works closely with the elite. These organizations are just the tip of the iceberg when it comes to secret societies established by elite bloodlines. Both Mazzini and Albert Pike belonged to a fraternity known as "Scottish Rite Freemasonry" this is not to be confused with the American Masonic "Blue Lodge's" which is used as social clubs in communities and that almost anyone can join. Scottish Rite Freemasonry is far more elite and they actually use the blue lodges as a diversion to hide the true purpose of their secret societies.

The influential freemasonry that most major politicians and aristocrats are involved with is very much a secret society within a secret society. On January 22, 1870 Giuseppe Mazzini wrote a letter to Albert Pike concerning freemasonry, the letter said *"We must allow all the federations to continue just as they are, with their systems, their central authorities and their diverse modes of correspondence between high grades of the same rite, organized as they are at the present, but we must create a super rite, which will remain unknown, to which we will call those Masons of high degree whom we shall select. With regard to our brothers in Masonry, these men must be pledges to the strictest secrecy. Through this supreme rite, we will govern all Freemasonry which will become the one international center, the more powerful because its direction will be unknown."*[1]

Albert Pike was known to study the occult and talk frequently of Satanism. This may sound crazy but as I will outline many times throughout this book Satanism is actually the most popular religion among those in power. This is because Satanism is essentially ego worship that holds power as a key value. Remember that when politicians and aristocrats claim to be of a certain religion it is highly possible that their words are simply political rhetoric just like everything else that comes out of their mouths. Satanism is also deeply intertwined with freemasonry despite the organizations claim that they are non-denominational. Some researchers say this was due to Pikes influence while others believe Satanism has been a part of the elite circles for much longer. Manly P. Hall is one of the best sources on the occult secrets of freemasonry as he himself was a 33rd degree mason, which is the highest possible level. Pike, Mazzini, George Washington, George Bush, Karl Marx, and various other powerful establishment figures in recent history are also 33rd degree masons.

In one of his books, Hall writes about the satanic nature of freemasonry, he writes "The day has come when Fellow Craftsman must know and apply their knowledge. The lost key to their grade is the mastery of emotion, which places the energy of the universe at their disposal. Man can only expect to be entrusted with great power by proving his ability to use it constructively and selflessly. When the Mason learns that the key to the warrior on the block is the proper application of the dynamo of living power, he has learned the mystery of his Craft. The seething energies of Lucifer are in his hands, and before he may step onward and upward, he must prove his ability to properly apply energy. He must follow in the footsteps of his forefather, Tubal-Cain, who with the mighty strength of the war god hammered his sword into a plowshare." [2] Manly P. Hall was most likely not a Satanist as he was a bit more of a humanitarian than many of his fellow masons and he actually spoke out about the injustices of authority.

The secretive and politically influential aristocracy has been popularly known as the "illuminati" for hundreds of years. The secret society began in Bavaria, in 1776 and was originally called "Order of Perfectibilists" until they changed their name to the illuminati just soon after. The goal of this order was to defend the existing class structure from the approaching revolt of the peasants. The long oppressed and manipulated masses were becoming literate and educated, so the aristocracy knew a revolution was imminent. The once illiterate and indoctrinated working class was starting to demand a better way of life, a more free and equal society. The establishment was seeking to subvert this popular uprising and ensure that things stayed as they were, even in the wake of revolution.

The first order of business for the illuminati was to build a structured education system so they could influence what the public was learning and guarantee that future generations would be less resistant to authority. The elite were aware that they could not prevent people from learning altogether, but if they could have control of the specific information that was established as "fact" through a structured education system, they would still be able to complete their goal and carry on business as usual. This idea resulted in the "Prussian Education Model" that I mentioned earlier, which makes sense considering that the illuminati was formed in Bavaria, and Prussia and Bavaria were in the same general area on maps of 18th century Germany.

As planned, the popular revolutions of the 18th and 19th centuries may have made the working class feel a bit better about themselves, but little has honestly changed about the existing class structure. There was no redistribution of wealth or power whatsoever, but the elite covered this up using politics and economics to obscure the true class structure. Divisions were created in the social structure to splinter the peasants into different classes so just enough people were comfortable enough to uphold the traditional order and convince the rest of society that the status quo was acceptable. Charters and declarations were drawn up by the nobility proclaiming that the popular revolutions succeeded and that equal rights were now guaranteed to the common people, but again these are only pieces of paper. Documents like the Magna Charta and the Constitution are seen by many as milestones, but while they may be useful for court cases they are rarely enforced when it is important and they do nothing to prevent or correct the perils of feudalism.

The Illuminati and its relation to the darker side of freemasonry was even recognized by America's first president George Washington. On October 24, 1798 he wrote a letter to a contact named George Washington Snyder (no relation apparently) where he revealed his knowledge of the Illuminati and its infiltration of the freemasonic lodges across America and Europe. In the letter he says "It is not my intention to doubt that the doctrine of the Illuminati and the principles of Jacobinism had not spread in the United States. On the contrary, no one is more satisfied of this fact than I am. The idea that I meant to convey, was, that I did not believe that the Lodges of Free Masons in this Country had, as Societies, endeavored to propagate the diabolical tenets of the first, or pernicious principles of the latter (if they are susceptible of separation). Those Individuals of them may have done it, or that the founder, or instrument employed to found, the Democratic Societies in the United States, may have had these objects; and actually had a separation of the People from their Government in view, is too evident to be questioned."[3]

There is no doubt that freemasonry has played a major role behind the scenes in American politics, this fact is made especially clear by the formation of the "Anti Masonic" political party in 1828. This political movement was set off by an incident known as the "Morgan affair" in which a man named William Morgan was preparing to print a book detailing the secrets of the freemasons before he mysteriously disappeared under suspicious circumstances. Like many third parties the Anti-Masonic party withered away in a short amount of time because they could not keep up financially with the two dominant parties and their corporate funding, but the fact that this party existed shows us that the public has always had a suspicion of these secret societies.

There are countless books and articles on the specifics of the many secret societies, and ill recommend some of them at the end of the chapter in the suggested reading section. Due to the overwhelming amount of information that is available on freemasonry I'm just going to cover the basics. Other secret societies that have been known to be used by the elite are Skull and Bones, Hidden Hand, The Round Table, and Bohemian Grove among various other groups that are well documented and fairly easy to find information on. Many of the same people belong to all these different groups and many of them are working towards the same end, a feudal world government ruled by a small group of elites.

With more wealth then any of us could possibly imagine, the ruling elite is looking towards World Empire just as so many tyrants have throughout history. Their goal is to gain even more control over the world's population, and create a one-world government through trade deals and the United Nations exactly as they already have with the European Union. This is not a matter of speculation; these goals are openly admitted by the ruling elite almost every time they are interviewed.

In 2002 David Rockefeller published his memoirs where he made this confession *"For more than a century, ideological extremists at either end of the political spectrum have seized upon well-publicized incidents to attack the Rockefeller family for the inordinate influence they claim we wield over American political and economic institutions. Some even believe we are part of a secret cabal working against the best interests of the United States, characterizing my family and me as 'internationalists' and of conspiring with others around the world to build a more integrated global political and economic structure - one world, if you will. If that is the charge, I stand guilty, and I am proud of it."*[4] The New World Order is no longer a "theory" but is in fact an openly admitted goal held by the elite and their cohorts.

The largest and most threatening organizations to the wellbeing of humanity are without a doubt, NATO & the United Nations. I agree with having a safe place for diplomacy between nations, but the United Nations is not the way to do it because it is directly influenced and controlled by the aristocracy of each nation. To give the illusion of an unbiased, fair, and equal organization some third parties and smaller independent countries are given a seat, but their power is limited in comparison to that of the industrial superpowers. This was made quite clear when every nation in the UN approved of a measure that would condemn illegal settlements on Palestinian land that is every nation except for the US who used their veto power to cancel the action. This is a privilege that is only awarded to America, China, Russia, France, and England but none of the African or Middle Eastern countries in the UN have the ability to veto any action.

This shows that for the most part the larger elite controlled superpowers have more influence in the UN than the weaker countries. In other words, the UN is just another place where the more powerful countries can bully the less powerful. The UN also serves as a foundation for world government by linking all the smaller countries together to be pushed around and investigated by the larger superpowers. Through the stronger superpowers the global aristocrats use their puppet regimes to advance their feudal agenda. The Council on Foreign Relations (which David Rockefeller is chairs of) is also heavily involved in influencing the policy at the United Nations. In fact, The United Nations headquarters sits on 18 acres of prime Manhattan land that was donated by the Rockefeller family.

I want to remind you that these accusations are not unfounded and in no means a "theory" this is well-documented fact that is constantly being covered up by the establishment and its institutions. Even some rogue politicians are now speaking out against this global fascist agenda. Congressman Ron Paul of Texas was asked in May of 2007 about the New World Order and its relation to the United Nations. Ron Paul responded, *"The first President Bush said the New World Order was in tune-- and that is what they were working for. The U.N. is part of that government. They're working right now very significantly towards a North American Union. That is why there's a lot of people in Washington right now who do not care too much about our borders. They have a philosophical belief that national sovereignty is not important. It is also the reason I've made the very strong suggestion the U.S. need not be in the U.N. for national security reasons."*[5]

If we were really being honest about things the elite would have their own seat at the UN right next to the US, the UK, China and Russia because they are in fact just in themselves a superpower to be compared with other nations instead of other families. They are the superpower that has the smallest population yet the largest net worth. This of course does not happen because the 7 billion other people in the world would realize what was going on and there would be outrage.

This is why the elite disguise their influence and their goals while spending billions of dollars cleaning up their public image. When I speak of the global elite, the establishment, the west, the globalists, the illuminati or any like terms I am referring to the feudal bloodlines who work together creating a fascist world government under their control, as well as the corporations and organizations that they use to advance this agenda.

Rarely people that do not come from these bloodlines are able to attain wealth and power that rivals that of the elite be it through either a stroke of luck, genius, or trickery. Surely people like Bill Gates who have amassed unbelievable wealth within a lifetime are approached to join the ranks of the global elite, or else. Bill Gates is just one of the many modern day "philanthropist" types who will aid the current aristocracy in their mission of globalization and eventually pass that mission onto his children in hopes they will continue to build the family fortune.

This is what the already established bloodlines have been doing for centuries, some are more powerful than others and some are more relevant than others during different times in history, but they are all working toward the same goal. Bill Gates has already revealed his true colors through his funding of various eugenics and depopulation efforts. What happens when a new recruit is offered an ultimatum to join the global elite and refuses? They are eliminated.

A historical example of this kind of "elimination" is found with the deaths of the Russian Imperial Romanov family. This entire bloodline was progressively destroyed by the Rothschild dynasty because the Tsar Alexander I of Russia thwarted their attempt to establish a world government in 1814. At this point many of the European governments were in debt to the Rothschild's so they were using that debt as an excuse to set up a world government through interlocked financial systems.

Kind of sounds exactly like what is happening today with the European Union, huh? Well unfortunately for the globalist, Tsar Alexander I of Russia managed to retain his own wealth and was not at the mercy of the Rothschild banking cartel. Due to Alexander's refusal to participate in the economic system and his outspokenness against the Rothschild's plan his whole bloodline was attacked and systematically killed. With the Romanov bloodline eliminated the Rothschild's were then able to establish their own puppet regime and gain control of the Russian government.

Most of us could not even begin to imagine the wealth that these families hold because it is beyond what most of us see as "money," currency actually has no value to them. They are the ones who create the currency and collect the taxes; their wealth is measured in continents and people not dollars and cents. Everyone is a slave to these people, even the politicians, and this generation of the banking elite is growing impatient.

They are advancing their plan even more quickly than in previous eras due to technological advancement and unquenchable greed. The seamless implementation of the European Union has given them more confidence that they can consolidate the whole world's economy within their lifetime. Economic consolidation would allow them to create a shadow government that will rule the entire planet from behind the scenes. This process has already began and these families already wield incredible power over the world's population, but creating a global economic empire will give them supremacy that will be nearly impossible to challenge. Now that you know the people involved in the exploitation it is time we get a bit more into the specifics of their plan, the global dictatorship which has been referred to as the new world order.

QUOTE SOURCES AND SUGGESTED READING
----
[0] Vile Acts of Evil - Volume 1 - Banking in America - Michael A. Kirchubel (2009)
[1] Occult Theocrasy by Lady Queensborough pages 208-209
[2] The Lost Keys of Freemasonry or The Secret of Hiram Abiff -Manly P. Hall
[3] The Writings of George Washington, vol. 20, p. 518
[4] David Rockefeller: Memoirs p.405
[5] http://www.infowars.com/articles/nwo/ron_paul_first_bush_was_working_towards_nwo.htm
[SR1] Pawns in the Game by William Guy Carr
[SR2] Morals and Dogma of the Ancient and Accepted Scottish Rite of Freemasonry - Albert Pike
[SR3] Bloodlines of the Illuminati by Fritz Springmeier
[SR4] Memoirs by David Rockefeller
[SR5] The Anglo American establishment by Dr. Carroll Quigley
[SR6] The Crisis of Democracy: Report on the Governability of Democracies to the Trilateral Commission By Michel Crozier, Samuel P. Huntington, Joji Watanuki
[SR7] The Grand Chessboard: American Primacy And Its Geostrategic Imperatives by Zbigniew Brzezinski
[SR8] The Last Will and Testament of Cecil J. Rhodes
[SR9] The Lost Keys of Freemasonry or The Secret of Hiram Abiff by Manly P. Hall
[SR10] The World's Banker: The History of the House of Rothschild by Niall Ferguson
[SR11] America's Secret Establishment: An Introduction to the Order of Skull & Bones by Antony C. Sutton
[SR12] The Lost Keys of Freemasonry (Also Includes: Freemasonry of the Ancient Egyptians / Masonic Orders of Fraternity) by Manly P. Hall
[SR13] The True Story of the Bilderberg Group by Daniel Estulin
[SR14] Tragedy & Hope: A History of the World in Our Time by Carroll Quigley

"We shall have world government whether or not you like it, by conquest or consent."
- James Warburg [0]

Fabian Socialism and the New World Order

Ruling the world is something that bloodthirsty tyrants and ruthless aristocrats have been trying to do since ancient times. When people are born into nobility and have every single thing they can ask for, they become unsatisfied with their riches and set their sights on the ultimate prize, world conquest. This is how empire was born.

The bloodlines of the black nobility believe that they are of a superior race than the rest of humanity and have been inbreeding for centuries to keep their wealth and "royal genes" in the family. This twisted worldview has allowed them to build their empires while committing countless human rights violations, in the form of war, slavery, and human sacrifice. All along the way the majority of humanity has been carelessly exploited and manipulated without their knowledge. And for what? They have told us it is the work of god, that "civilization" is being cultivated, that an evil menacing enemy is being defeated, or simply that "progress" is being made. The nation builders have given many different excuses for their conquest over the centuries, but the motive has remained the same, to control every person and resource on the planet.

After all this time the ruling elite has mass manipulation and exploitation down to a well mastered science. Behind closed doors these families pass on their goals of world domination and teach their children how to extort and deceive the serf class. Since ancient times their agenda has been to use their wealth and power to influence politicians from behind the scenes. This way, when the public disapproved of how the society was being run, the politicians would act as a scapegoat and the banking elite would retain their wealth and power without criticism.

For many centuries rulers have attempted to build their empires through bloody conquests, and for most of the human population it is gotten extremely old. After many cycles of revolutions, the elite began to realize that brute force was not enough to keep down the human spirit. If they wanted to be successful they knew that they would have to take a less obvious, more secretive approach to world conquest. This approach involves gaining control of every economy in the world, which will in turn give them control of both the politicians and the public.

Now that is not to say that the elite have given up on using force all together, they are still prepared to rule with an iron fist if someone does not comply "diplomatically" with their plans. When they are brought to use force the elite often hides behind their puppet governments and rationalizes the conquest by claiming that someone is being "liberated" or "protected".

These excuses lead the public to believe that the many military actions that are taking place around the world are merely isolated incidents as opposed to a planned conquest. These conquests are spread out over long periods of time because if everything were to take place in a short amount of time then the public would surely catch on. So they take small steps and incrementally advance their goal of global economic and political dominance, through "diplomacy" when they can and through unrelenting force when all else fails. This political strategy is known as "Incremental Socialism" or "Fabian Socialism," which is basically the establishment of an authoritarian welfare state through long-term deception and diplomacy, as opposed to carrying out just one massive, swift military action. Instead of waging high profile wars to take control of an area's population, business deals and political policies are established behind closed doors that will slowly but surely result in a stealthy conquest. This conquest takes place over the course of many generations and is handed down to the children of the elite, this way everything happens over such a long period of time to make the events seem unrelated and the agenda goes unnoticed.

To articulate this thought many researches have used the analogy of the boiling frog, which I hope, will better illustrate the point I am trying to make. If you try to put a frog into a boiling pot of water it will immediately jump out, but if you put the frog into a pot of water that is room temperature and heat it slowly then the frog will stay in the pot and eventually boil without realizing that the water is getting any hotter. This is exactly the situation we find ourselves in, where slowly but surely over various administrations we are pushed closer and closer towards complete tyranny.

This is definitely no new plot, and was actually recognized by various early American presidents. James Madison, for example once said "I believe there are more instances of the abridgement of freedom of the people by gradual and silent encroachments of those in power than by violent and sudden usurpations."[1] The idea of carrying out plots over multiple generations sounds irrational to most people, but how else would societies be built? Empires are very large projects that could not be built successfully in just one generation. In our history, large architectural projects such as bridges, temples, and city infrastructure would take many generations to build. This is how things work when someone is managing a civilization; plans are long term even though they have many short-term problems and motivations.

There is a think tank based in the UK called "the Fabian society," which includes many members of the western aristocracy and works towards consolidating their wealth and expanding their influence. The logo of this secret society is ironically enough a wolf, wearing a sheepskin on its back….a wolf in sheep's clothing. This ideology and political approach has extended far beyond the Fabian society and has reached almost every government in the world. The word "Fabian" comes to us from the name of an ancient Roman dictator named Fabius Maximus Cunctator. He came to power by defeating an overpowering enemy by slowly wearing them down and blocking them off from the resources that they needed to flourish. This brilliant strategy made Fabius a legend and left behind a template for future "leaders" to use in battle and in politics.

The goal of the modern Fabian Socialist is the same ultimate conquest that has been sought after by control freaks for centuries, to create a one-world dictatorship under their control. This one world dictatorship is often referred to as the "New World Order." The term New World Order has been used by various western elites in public for at least a hundred years to describe the global civilization that they were working to enact. This goal has been advancing over the course of many generations, through various organizations with a handful of different actors making contributions along the way.

One person who was instrumental in laying much of the foundation for this plan was a British aristocrat and Rothschild agent by the name of Cecil Rhodes. Rhodes was a staunch imperialist and spent his life sending mercenaries around the world plundering developing countries in the name of the British Empire. One of his most profitable ventures came through the conquest of Africa and the creation of the diamond market.

Cecil Rhodes founded the world's most powerful diamond company DeBeers, a cartel that maintains a tight monopoly over the entire industry to this day. To provide stability and slave labor for his diamond mines Rhodes used the British military to establish apartheid states that were filled with concentration camps and widespread chaos. South Africa and surrounding areas were the base of his operations. In the past they were even blatant enough to call a territory "Rhodesia" (named after Cecil Rhodes), although eventually the name was changed to Zimbabwe to present the illusion that it was not a British colony. After Rhodes died he left a great majority of his wealth to the Rothschild dynasty and established The Round Table secret society and the Rhodes scholarship, both of which were intended as a means to bring about world government.

Georgetown Professor Carroll Quigley has some of the best research on these groups as he had direct access to some archives of the Round Table groups through the Council on Foreign Relations. His epic book Tragedy and Hope is over 1000 pages and chronicles the history of these organizations. In Tragedy and hope he says *"In the middle 1890's Rhodes had a personal income of at least a million pounds sterling a year which he spent so freely for mysterious purposes that he was usually overdrawn on his account ... Cecil Rhodes' commitment to a conspiracy to establish World Government was set down in a series of wills described by Frank Aydelotte in his book American Rhodes Scholarships."* [2]

Quigley reveals his sources in the following passage *"The Rhodes Scholarships... are known to everyone. What is not so widely known is that Rhodes in five previous wills left his fortune to form a secret society, which was to devote itself to the preservation and expansion of the British Empire. And what does not seem to be known to anyone is that this secret society ... continues to exist to this day ...There does exist, and has existed for a generation, an international anglophile network which operates, to some extent, in the way the radical Right believes the communists act. In fact, this network, which we may identify as the Round Table Groups, has no aversion to cooperating with the Communists, or any other groups and frequently does so. I know of the operations of this network because I have studied it for twenty years and was permitted for two years, in the early 1960's, to examine its papers and secret records. I have no aversion to it or to most of its aims and have, for much of my life, been close to it and too many of its instruments. I have objected, both in the past and recently, to a few of its policies ... but in general my chief difference of opinion is that it wishes to remain unknown, and I believe its role in history is significant enough to be known.*"[3] I will remind you that Carroll Quigley is no fringe source; he was a very prominent educator and even taught Rhodes Scholar Bill Clinton. Clinton even mentioned Quigley in his inaugural address, and frequently referred to him as his "mentor."

  The original round table groups eventually branched out into larger think tanks such as the Council on Foreign Relations and the Bilderberg Group. For years the very existence of these groups were denied, but recently they have been forced to reveal their associations, thanks to the hard work of activists and the independent media. The CFR membership is now almost completely public and is a long list of influential politicians, business tycoons, military leaders, and media moguls. The Bilderberg Group is an even more elite group that has members in various aristocratic circles worldwide, including the Rothschild's, Rockefellers and multiple royal families. Every year their annual meeting gets even more and more negative attention as the world begins to understand how they have been deceived and manipulated by the people involved with this organization. In 2011 when they met in Switzerland they encountered resistance like they had never seen before, in addition to the scores of activists there were also various politicians from the European Union there to protest the meeting.

  Italian politician Mario Borghezio attempted to enter the hotel where the conference was being held and had his nose broken by the paramilitary private security staff hired for the event. Interestingly, the security company's logo was the occult symbol of the all seeing eye that appears on our money and has long been the unofficial logo for the "illuminati." As to what goes on inside, that has been revealed by many moles and investigators. Even former NATO Secretary-General and Bilderberg member Willy Claes has admitted that the group sets global policy. This was revealed by Claes in a June 4, 2010 radio interview with Belgian news website zonnewind.be. The influence of the Bilderberg Group is now mainstream knowledge, and it is becoming obvious that their agenda is not in our best interest.

  For the elite, global politics is a game for power and the planet is their giant chessboard, on which all of humanity are expendable pieces to be used and sacrificed for the sake of advancing the game. In this game they plan many moves ahead in order to deceive their opponents and always remain on top of everyone else. Many people have a hard time believing that this is going on, but the globalization plot is already in visible motion.

  The European Union gives us a glimpse into what the bankers want to do with the rest of the world. Many Americans still may think that the New World Order is just a "theory", but there are not a whole lot of skeptics left in Europe. Just decades ago every single nation in Europe had their constitutions dismantled and economy taken over by the banking elite. For all ceremonial purposes the countries still have their own governments and borders, but the real power lies in the international banking cartel that centrally controls every nation's economy. In fact, since the consolidation of Europe the governments of every European country are now subservient to the banking elite. This is what they want to do in every single continent across the globe, which will remind you is not a farfetched goal for international bankers to have.

This kind of economic and political union has already taken shape in Africa and they are constantly making steps to establish similar super states in both North America and Asia. The process has already began, through seemingly harmless "trade agreements" and "alliances," which are the same steps that set the European Union into motion. The plan in North America is called "The Security and Prosperity Partnership" and although it has been vehemently denied by most politicians, declassified documents show that this plan is definitely in the works.

All of the predominant political organizations, the education systems, and the media are all put into place by the elite, so globalization is obviously going to be portrayed in a positive light within those sources. That does not mean that the propaganda and public relations efforts are at all correct. Their sales pitch for global fascism is that it will "end wars", "end economic depression" and so on and so forth. However, the very people that are offering this sales pitch are the ones who are instigating the wars and creating the economic depressions. This is a scam, a set up that has been carefully planned to mold public opinion into accepting a worldwide dictatorship. Public opinion is extremely important; the will of the public is really the only force that has ever been able to subdue power hungry tyrants.

The elite may have all the financial, military, and political power in the world, but they are outnumbered to such a degree that they can only continue to build their plan as long as were willing to go along with it. This is why every single move that they make is designed to win us over and convince us that things are being done in our best interest, when in reality we are being exploited and played for fools. Globalization will not bring peace and prosperity as promised, it will only lead to more poverty, less freedom and a complete abandon of human rights all together.

In this section I have discussed many different organizations and groups that play part in facilitating this global feudal system, and each of them play their own specific role in the advancement of authoritarianism. To draw a comparison I will refer to an old mystery novel by Agatha Christie titled Murder on the Orient Express, released in 1934. This is an analogy that has been used by many great researchers in the past. In the story a detective is faced with the task of finding out who killed one of the passengers onboard the train. There were multiple stab wounds in the victim's body and multiple suspects who appeared to have nothing to do with each other; there were too many clues to make any kind of logical sense of the situation at a glance. Throughout the story the detective does his homework and discovers that all of the seemingly unconnected suspects had ties to the victim, to each other and they all shared the same motive. In the end they were all guilty and each played an integral part in the homicide.

This story is relevant because it provides the perfect analogy to represent the many different families and organizations that work together to bring about a common end. The elite have close ties to one another through their international foundations and they share the same goal in the sense that they are working to keep their long established feudal systems in power. At this point in time the

Council on Foreign Relations and the Bilderberg group are the most publicly active of these groups, so if you pay attention to what they are doing you can easily decipher the elite's agenda.

In the pseudo democracies of the west we are taught to take a "pragmatic" approach to the political and economic aspects of our world. The philosophy of pragmatism is a subtle form of surrender in which we are told to accept the status quo despite its many imperfections and sacrifice our ideals for more "practical" solutions that do not "rock the boat", so to speak. Meanwhile, the elite practice a contrasting approach that is relentless and uncompromising. Under these circumstances they are always on the offensive and we are always on the defensive, which is why they have continued to influence global politics for centuries with minimal opposition.

To work within the system and the boundaries laid out by the elite is to take part in a rat race, but at the same time even to attack these interests head on would play right into their hands as well. So what can we possibly do to take them from power? We must change the system in a way that does not empower the ruling class, but instead empowers the whole of humanity, because right now the whole planet is suffering as a result of the established way of doing things. The key to doing this is by establishing objective morality, holding everyone to the same standard, and no longer allowing these organizations a license to commit violence and fraud. To ascend beyond slavery every single one of us will also need to play an active role in the direction of our society, and hold self-education and free thought as core values.

QUOTE SOURCES AND SUGGESTED READING
----
[0] Statement by CFR member James Warburg on February 17th, 1950
[1] James Madison - Virginia convention of 1788
[2] -Dr. Carroll Quigley, "Tragedy and Hope"
[3] -Dr. Carroll Quigley, "Tragedy and Hope"
[SR1] Beyond the Conspiracy: the Committee of 300 by John Coleman
[SR2] Cecil Rhodes: a study of a career by Howard Hensman
[SR3] Superclass: The Global Power Elite and the World They Are Making by David Rothkopf

"The law, in its majestic equality, forbids the rich as well as the poor to sleep under bridges, to beg in the streets, and to steal bread."
- Anatole Franc [0]

North American Serfdom

There is a long history of poverty in North America, since colonial times the overwhelming majority of United States citizens have spent their lives as the workhorses of the elite. There have been short periods where a middle class was able to develop, but for the most part the gap between the rich and the poor has been very pronounced. The great majority of American history has been plagued with economic depression and working class suffering. There were economic depressions in 1837, 1857, 1873,1893,1907,1929, and again in the 1960's and 70's, except many times they were called "recessions," to make things sound better. It seems that with every generation more and more wealth is stripped away from the commoners. Early on in colonial times the richest British executives saw the new world as a great opportunity to expand their fortunes. They took advantage of the vast natural resources that North America had to offer and used slave labor to keep down production costs. Slavery was being outlawed all over most of Europe around this time, so the new world was seen as a kind of "safe haven" to conduct this kind of grotesque business.

Titans of industry such as the Rothschild's, the Morgan's, and the Rockefellers had already established themselves as the elite business class of America by the middle of the 19th century. With the help of state power they monopolized the railroad industry, the oil industries, the textile mills, and every other essential business in the country until they were able to completely dominate the market. Since just about every job in the country was at one of their companies they were able to set the price on all the goods and pay whatever kind of wages they wished. Thanks to many generations of political favors they have managed to preserve these monopolies to this day with very little outside competition.

In the midst of the most recent depression the establishment refuses to admit that something is wrong and continues to insist that our economy is not completely rigged. There has always been a very wide gap between the rich and the poor in America, but now with the economic collapse and Wall Street bailouts that gap has grown significantly. While once there was some kind of hope that the American dream existed, now there is only bitterness and regret in the hearts of millions. Billions of taxpayer dollars have went to pay Wall Street executives million dollar salaries, while record numbers of families are suffering in poverty. Now in the most dire economic times that this country has ever seen our politicians and financial systems show their true colors and real motivations. The situation is now undeniable; the establishment does not care about us. As long as their political allies, special interest groups, shareholders, and financial backers are taken care of then they do not give a damn about the rest of us.

Due to the policies that our government has put into effect under both democratic and republican rule, the aristocracy has become incredibly wealthy and the struggle of the working class has deepened severely. In the 1980s the richest 1% of the population who controlled most of the country's wealth saw their incomes grow by 87%, while the income for the poorer families has slowly declined. In that same decade, according to Forbes magazine the riches 400 families in America increased their revenue from 92 billion dollars to 480 billion dollars. This trend continued all through the Bush and Clinton years all the way up to the economic collapse of 2008 when it got even worse. In 2008 the Wall Street Journal published a "study of wealth" which showed that the top .01% (not 1% but .01 %!!) earners in America possessed 22.2% of the nation's wealth. Excluding that elite group the top 10% (all of which are millionaires and billionaires) control 73.8% of the nation's wealth. Then the rest of us, 90% of Americans possess only 4% of the nation's income. If this is not feudalism I do not know what is.

In a recent article, Ray B. Williams points out that *"The U.S. Census Bureau and the World Wealth Report 2010 both report increases for the top 5% of households even during the current recession. Based on Internal Revenue Service figures, the richest 1% have tripled their cut of America's income pie in one generation. In 1980 the richest 1% of America took one of every 15-income dollars. Now they take three of every 15-income dollars.... Income inequality has been rising since the late 1970s, and now rests at a level not seen since the Gilded Age (1870 to 1900), a period in U.S. history defined by the contrast between the excesses of the super-rich and the squalor of the poor."*[1]

This disproportionate society is becoming more and more obvious every day, especially in some of the country's most lavish cities. Atlantic City and Las Vegas are both home to some of the biggest hotels and casinos in the country, and also some of the biggest slums. On the same block where billionaires go to throw their money away, people are living in dilapidated housing or on the streets. Every day they struggle to survive while in the shadow of an outlandish yuppie playground.

In Las Vegas thousands of struggling Americans have been forced to live in the 200 miles of flood tunnels that run under the city. There is literally an underground village of homeless people in one of the country's richest cities. The sewers are broken into small sections where residents store their few worldly possessions. This subterranean community was discovered by a news reporter named Matthew O'Brien who was researching a murder case when he stumbled across a makeshift apartment in the aqueducts. Conditions in the tunnels are far worse than on the surface but if these people were to try to find shelter elsewhere they would be rounded up by police. The establishment does not mind these people living in an inch of standing water with moldy ceilings and poisonous insects crawling everywhere as long as the tourists can't see them.

This kind of callous attitude from government and law enforcement towards people struggling financially has been typical during the recent economic crisis. Soldiers and police in riot gear have violently ripped people from their foreclosed homes. Once being evicted people have no choice but to set up tents in the safest areas they can find. Eventually the police come and kick them out of there for trespassing, or loitering or a number of other erroneous charges. In multiple cities across the country just after the economic collapse in 2008, police in multiple cities were videotaped destroying tent cities that were established by the recently evicted. This horrific scene continues to happen again and again in the few years since the collapse.

Even the people that may be fortunate enough to have homes are still struggling to pay their bills and keep food on the table. According to the department of agriculture the amount of families suffering from hunger doubled in the 2 years between 2007 and 2009. Under the current economic conditions in America there are over 50 million people who have been unable to afford food at some point in their lives. ¼ of that figure of 50 million people experiences this struggle on a regular basis. That means at least 12.5 million people wake up every morning not knowing if they will be able to eat that day. To make matters worse the same people that are responsible for creating this inequality make a lifestyle out of capitalizing off of others misfortunes.

The "Morgan" family that I referred to early on in this chapter are the heirs to the infamous "J.P. Morgan" dynasty. Their company "J.P. Morgan" actually benefits in more ways than one, from a high unemployment rate and poverty stricken populous. They are the largest processor of food stamps in the country and are paid for each case they handle, so that means that the more Americans that go on food stamps, the more money J.P. Morgan makes. Today there are a lot of people on food stamps, which is basically the same concept as a bread line with a slightly more modern, more efficient feel. If people did not have the ability to go to the supermarket and cash in their food stamps whenever they wanted, then we would have breadlines that dwarf those seen during the "great depression."

On Bloomberg TV during an interview in 2011, one of the company's major executives Christopher Paton admitted that this was a very important business for J.P. Morgan, and that it was in fact doing very well in the current economic climate. Since the stock market crash of 2008 the amount of Americans on food stamps has jumped from 26 million to 43 million people in just a few short years. This is obviously very bad news for most Americans, but actually very good news for J.P. Morgan and their shareholders. To further compound their profits they actually outsourced the few jobs that are created through the food stamp industry, primarily telemarketing jobs. Now when someone loses their job in America and has to apply for food stamps their phone call will be connected to a call center in India where jobs are abundant because western corporations are able to pay their employees slave wages. These are the same companies that saw trillions of dollars' worth of taxpayer money in the form of government bailouts, like they needed it more than the people who are unemployed.

As the financial crisis deepens the United States is slipping into conditions reminiscent of the third world. All of the country's wealth has been concentrated in the hands of a few elite groups and the rest of the population is left to fend for themselves. Every single day people are losing their homes. Tent cities are popping up in metropolitan areas and rural communities are becoming ghost towns. It is becoming increasingly harder for average Americans to find work and it seems that people who do not already come from wealthy families are having a more difficult time climbing out of poverty. This rigged financial system has given most of us nothing but hardships yet we have been conditioned to worship this institution and the people that have enslaved us with it. They can no longer fool us; the corporate media can't convince us that this is not happening. We know what is going on, this is more real for us then it is for any of them. We are the ones who are losing our homes and having our lives torn apart by their con machine.

QUOTE SOURCES AND SUGGESTED READING
----
[0] The Constitution in the Supreme Court: second century, 1888-1986, Vol. 2 By David P. Currie
[SR1] Third World America by Arianna Stasinopoulos Huffington

"Fascism should rightly be called corporatism as it is a merger of state and corporate power."
-Benito Mussolini [0]

The Birth of the Corporate Beast in America

Our finances, food, water, government, media, communications, and almost anything you can possibly think of is tightly controlled by large multinational corporations and regulated by government. The corporations that dominate the global market are all owned and operated by the ruling class that I have exposed in previous chapters. These multi-national corporations use their financial power to influence government and world events to further their own agenda and stomp out any competition that may present itself. Sadly this has been taking place before our very eyes for many generations without anyone really noticing because this corporate entity is so strong that they are able to invest an unlimited amount of time and energy into cleaning up their public image. This corporate entity acts as a proxy through which the ruling class can hide behind to avoid accountability for their actions.

At the dawn of the corporate age even the politicians spoke out against the corporate influence on society. On November 12, 1864 just after the end of the civil war, Abraham Lincoln said *"I see in the near future a crisis approaching that unnerves me and causes me to tremble for the safety of my country. As a result of the war, corporations have been enthroned and an era of corruption in high places will follow, and the money power of the country will endeavor to prolong its reign by working upon the prejudices of the people until all wealth is aggregated in a few hands and the Republic is destroyed. I feel at this moment more anxiety for the safety of my country than ever before, even in the midst of war. God grant that my suspicions may prove groundless."*[1] Lincoln certainly was not perfect, he was a conniving politician just like the rest of them, but the fact that he was covering these issues show that they were important to the people at the time. In 1868, just a few years after Lincoln's assassination, congress passed the 14th amendment that was apparently designed to give rights to freed slaves. While freed slaves did receive some kind of legal recognition through this act, it still changed nothing about the reality of their situation.

What is very sneaky about the 14th amendment is the issue of corporate personhood. This was a point that corporate lawyers concealed within the language of the amendment to give corporations more legal power in the courts, as well as give the courts more power in the realm of business. The corporate personhood clause states that corporations deserve the same rights that are guaranteed to a "person" or "citizen" protected under the Constitution. Since this act was in place corporations have been legally considered a "person" in the court of law. This was such a serious implication because now the people that are actually behind the actions of the "corporation" can no longer be held accountable for the crimes they commit in the name of said corporation. This kind of idea is not new, this has always been the policy preferred by the ruling class, as it allows them to commit atrocities and get away with it.

In the 18th century in the parliament of England, Edward Thurlow said "Corporations have neither bodies to be punished, nor souls to be condemned; they therefore do as they like."[2] Thurlow was as right then as he is today, if people that run corporations are not personally held accountable for the actions they commit at the head of that corporation, then they will take advantage and do whatever they want. The same goes for government as well; governments and corporations are both proxies that the ruling class hides behind to avoid punishment for their crimes.

There's nothing wrong with owning and running a "business" or a "company," entities which are completely different from a corporation. A corporation is an entity that is legally protected and subsidized by the government, while a company is a privately owned business that depends on its reputation to survive, instead of special privileges and handouts. Unfortunately, in today's markets even the most well intentioned small business owners are forced to become corporate themselves just to contend with all of the licensing and regulation that is required by the government. When the government talks about "regulation" they are typically ignoring the major corporations, but regulating the small fry competition that threatens to disrupt the monopolistic nature of the current industry. These conditions result in a situation that many refer to as "corporate welfare."

It became apparent early in the 20th century that the 14th amendment had nothing to do with equal rights for freed slaves. By 1910 there were 307 cases brought before the judicial court in which the 14th amendment was cited, 19 of them cases were freed slaves fighting for equal rights, while 288 of them cases were corporations delegating for legal position. This legal loophole allows corporations to claim the same rights as a human being, which in turn undermines any checks and balances in place and makes it impossible to hold anyone accountable in the industry. This is one of the major reasons why we have monolithic monopolies in the energy, food, and medical markets. Through the course of American history the elite has consistently pushed for protections for their corporations and extension of their powers. Meanwhile the individual rights of citizens have been relentlessly attacked and continue to dwindle as time passes.

In the beginning of the 20th century corporate corruption was one of the most debated topics of the time. In 1906 in an attempt to gather support and distance himself publicly from the aristocracy, the president at the time Theodore Roosevelt said "Behind the ostensible government sits enthroned an invisible government owing no allegiance and acknowledging no responsibility to the people. To destroy this invisible government, to befoul the unholy alliance between corrupt business and corrupt politics is the first task of the statesmanship of the day."[3] Unfortunately, just like Lincoln and many other presidents; Theodore Roosevelt's time in the white house was spent protecting the aristocracy instead of policing it. What he was really looking to do was expand the size and reach of government and in order to gain public support for the cause he latched on to a key issue of the time and sought to exploit that issue for political gain.

Theodore Roosevelt came to be known as a "trust breaker" and a hero for the common man exactly as he had intended to, but this of course was only campaign politics, as it always is.

This kind of hypocritical pandering is a typical part of the American political process and is seen to this day. The same way that Obama got "elected" on promises of closing Guantanamo bay, ending the war in Iraq and getting tough on big business yet did nothing of the sort once he got into office. He actually ended up expanding the war into a half dozen different countries and signing a bill that authorized the indefinite detainment of American citizens without trial. The same way George Bush condemned the corrupt behavior of "a few bad apples" on wall street like Enron, but before Enron was exposed as a fraudulent organization the CEO Ken Lay was a top consideration for Bush's "secretary of energy". The government and corporations are on the same team. However, there is still one aspect of this that we have yet to discuss, and that is an organization far more powerful than both the governments and the major corporations. Even the murderous royal families throughout the world are still beholden to the banks.

QUOTE SOURCES AND SUGGESTED READING
----

[0]The Puzzle of Fascism by Eric D. Williams
[1] The Lincoln Encyclopedia, by Archer H. Shaw, letter to (Col.) William F. Elkins 11/21/1864.
[SR1] Corporatism: The Secret Government of the New World Order by Jeffrey Grupp
[SR2] Smartest Guys in the Room by Bethany McLean
[SR3] The Corporation: The Pathological Pursuit of Profit and Power by Joel Bakan

"It is well enough that people of the nation do not understand our Banking and Monetary system, for if they did, I believe there would be a Revolution before tomorrow morning."
-Henry Ford [0]

Central Banking in Early America

At the center of the global financial monopoly lies the Bank of England, an economic institution created and operated by the Rothschild and Warburg dynasties. It was this bank that our ancestors fought against in the revolutionary war. Sure, they were fighting for independence from English rule, but the Bank of England and their unfair taxes played an important role as well, as they were deeply tied in with the English monarch and still are to this day. Once the revolutionary war was won and America was born, the bankers were completely furious because this "new world" was supposed to be their pet project. So of course with nothing better to do with their time the elite get back to work to recapture the new world.

In 1812 the Bank of England hired the British army to attack America and force them to instate a central bank. At the onset of war Nathan Rothschild sent this message to the Americans, *"Either the application for renewal for the charter is granted, or the United States will find itself involved in a most disastrous war."*[1] When the colonies refused to renew the charter the chairmen said *"Teach those impudent Americans a lesson. Bring them back to colonial status."*[2]

With these orders the British invaded America in 1812 for the second time in less than 50 years. At the outcome of the war the British were able to secure their central bank in the new world. In 1816 the Rothschild controlled "Second Bank of the United States" was born, but only signed into action under a 20 year charter. When it came time to renew the charter the American people voted an extremely "anti-bank" candidate by the name of Andrew Jackson into office. Jackson successfully killed the central bank in America during his presidency and was revered as a champion of the people for doing so. He may have been popular for this reason, but he was no saint when you consider his horrible treatment of the natives and his strong support of slavery.

The banking cartels were not going to give up that easily, they came back in the early 20th century and this time would take our economy from right under our noses, instead of using force. After many failed attempts at passing financial legislation through congress, the banksters realized that they would have to build a whole administration from the ground up in order to achieve their economic takeover. So that is exactly what they did. The banking cartels fully funded Woodrow Wilson's 1912 campaign and when he was eventually "elected" they also appointed his cabinet. In 1913 Senator Nelson Aldrich, who was related to the Rockefellers, pushed the Federal Reserve Act through Congress just before Christmas when everyone was on vacation. Next the bill skated through the banker backed executive branch and became law. For 200 years a war was raging over control of the American economy, and in 1913 the bankers won.

QUOTE SOURCES AND SUGGESTED READING
---

[0] Wall Street Makes Money the Old-Fashioned Way...They Steal It! by Charles M. Klotsche
[1] Bankruptcy of Our Nation by Jerry Robinson (2009)
[2] Letters to Earth...You Can Survive Armageddon! by Peter Kling (2009)
[SR1] The Tycoons by Charles R. Morris

"Everyone is pointing to Barack right now, President Obama and saying, 'You gotta get the economy together, and you gotta get the economy together.' When in fact the president has very little to do with the economy. It is the Federal Reserve Chairman that at least sets the policy… that is a privately owned company. The Federal Reserve Bank, they set the agenda."
- KRS-One [0]

End the Fed

Since the Federal Reserve took control of our economy in 1913 there have been 2 major depressions, countless "recessions," and a massive devaluing of our national currency. The Federal Reserve has never been audited and no government board or "elected" official has any say in the Feds economic decisions. It is this private bank that sets the financial agenda for the country, not our politicians. The Federal Reserve has no obligation to the public at all; in fact this institution is willingly extorting the public to line the pockets of international bankers.

The fed is not only an unjust and immoral institution but it is also unconstitutional. The US constitution says that the power to issue and distribute currency can only be held by congress. The constitution goes on to say that money must be backed by some kind of tangible resource like gold or silver. The founding fathers specifically set the constitution up this way because they were very familiar with how the Bank of England was run and saw how central banks and fiat currency enslaved nations under debt. A fiat currency is described as "Currency that a government has declared to be legal tender, despite the fact that it has no intrinsic value and is not backed by reserves. Historically, most currencies were based on physical commodities such as gold or silver, but fiat money is based solely on faith."

In other words the government or central bank is actually counterfeiting the nation's currency, thus diminishing its value in the process. What they are doing is creating money out of thin air and using that money to dominate societies. This problem is further compounded by the use of a banking trick called "fractional reserve lending." Fractional reserve lending means that banks are lending out money that they do not have, in other words they only have a fraction of the funds in their bank. This is all perfectly legal under our current corrupt system of injustice. So a central bank or government that uses fiat currency and distributes money using fractional reserve lending can lend much more money than they actually have and then charge interest on the money that never existed in the first place. This really is one of the best and most well thought out scams of all time.

Lending money at interest whether it exists or not is called "usury," a practice that is no different than the "loan sharking" that is said to take place in organized crime. As I will lay out in the chapter about religion many of the most respected prophets of various different faiths were all opposed to usury and saw it as an obstacle for human rights and positive social evolution. What we have in the global financial market today is a system that takes usury to a whole new level because traditionally bankers and goldsmiths were limited to lending out only the money that they had in their coffers, but with fractional reserve lending they are now allowed to lend out as much money as they want, even if they do not have it.

It was Woodrow Wilson who signed the Federal Reserve Act into law after it was passed by congress. This was the president that sold the country out to the international banking cartel. Maybe this is why his face is on the $100,000 bill, a nod of recognition for the man who allowed America's corporate financial merger. There is no doubt that Wilson was inclined to take these actions because of his own place in the aristocracy, but he was also strongly influenced by members of his administration, especially Edward Mandell House. House was a vital part of Wilson's political team from very early on and it was ultimately House's connections to the international banking cartel that ensured Wilson's presidential nomination in 1912. House worked very closely with the Rockefeller and Rothschild families and shared many of their sadistic elitist beliefs.

Many people see the president as being a strong influential figure, but the truth is our "leaders" often get most of their ideas from other powerful people that they respect. Wilson considered House to be his mentor, so naturally most of the decisions that Wilson made were directly influenced by House's opinions. This presidential partnership oversaw the introduction of the Federal Reserve, the implementation of the federal income tax, the entrance into world war one and the treaty process following the war that redrew the world's boundaries. House would later have a profound impact on the presidency of Franklin Roosevelt as well, and he was the mentor of many other US "leaders."

Almost every time a government has used a fiat currency throughout history it has resulted in hyperinflation, massive public debt, and collection of wealth into a small elite section of society. It was this economic system coupled with exorbitant military spending which eventually led to the downfall of the Roman Empire and possibly the downfall of the American empire as well. Even Nobel Prize winning economist Milton Friedman admitted that America's draconian central bank was responsible for the nation's financial woes. In his book "Two Lucky People" Friedman says *"The Fed was largely responsible for converting what might have been a garden-variety recession, although perhaps a fairly severe one, into a major catastrophe. Instead of using its powers to offset the depression, it presided over a decline in the quantity of money by one-third from 1929 to 1933 ... Far from the depression being a failure of the free-enterprise system; it was a tragic failure of government."*[1] More recently, chairmen of the Fed Ben Bernanke admitted that this assessment was correct and that the feds mismanagement of the money supply actually was responsible for the great depression.

In October of 2008 we were officially sold out to Wall Street as the whole world was watching. While record numbers of Americans were out of work our government gave 700 billion tax dollars to various corporations that were directly to blame for the financial crisis. When all was said and done it turned out that they actually handed out 29 TRILLION dollars, but only told us about 700 billion of it. The excuse for this corporate welfare situation was that the economy would fall apart even more than it already had if those businesses were allowed to fail. However, this excuse was just as erroneous as the weapons of mass destruction in Iraq. The American people knew that this was a scam and protested in record numbers for their "representatives" not to pass the bailout bill. Millions of people lost their jobs and homes because of the shady business practices of the corporations in question. The American people felt that these businesses were in no way entitled to bailouts. Despite the overwhelming public backlash the government passed the bill anyway because they do exactly what the banking and financial interests tell them to do.

There were a few politicians that were not corrupted by wall street and actually stood by their constituents to fight the corporate takeover of America, mainly Dennis Kucinich, Ron Paul and Bernie Sanders. Because of the immense pressure that was put on the Fed they were forced to reveal other information surrounding the financial disaster. After 2 years of trying to stall and hide information the Fed was forced to release details about the "back door bailouts" that occurred in addition to the bailouts that the taxpayers actually knew about. The back door bailouts were still using taxpayer money but the American people had no say what so ever and this information would have remained completely hidden from the public had it not been for the determination of a few rogue congressmen.

When details of the backdoor bailouts were published through the independent media in late 2010 it was worse than anyone could have imagined. The released information showed "emergency lending programs" in which 29 Trillion dollars in tax payer money was paid to various large corporations all of which belong to the banking cartels that run the fed. This was a massive direct transfer of wealth from the people into the hands of the bankers who already have a monopoly on everything. The forced release of these documents was largely ignored by the mainstream media as most of it is owned and controlled by the same people that own and control the Fed. Luckily the story spread all over the internet thanks to the independent media.

Even by taking a quick look at the tax structure in our country it is easy to tell that a small class of people who have plenty are constantly extracting money from a larger class of people who are constantly struggling to get by. None of the elite or their business pay any taxes at all! This is a fact! David Rockefeller once smugly admitted "You know, gentlemen, that I do not owe any personal income tax. But nevertheless, I send a small check, now and then, to the Internal Revenue Service out of the kindness of my heart." [2].

None of the big corporations pay any taxes either. Most of them hide behind phony "nonprofit" organizations through which they are able to deduct billions of dollars from their owed taxes. In 2010 Bank of America earned 4.4 Billion dollars and paid nothing because they had so many deductions. This is one of the primary reasons why billionaires set up "philanthropic" organizations, so they can avoid taxes while still looking good in the press.

The Federal Reserve and their fiat currency are responsible for our economic collapses, inflation, unemployment, and poverty. Their system is rigged to serve the ruling class and is not in the best interest of the public. This is without a doubt one of the most corrupt institutions on earth, only surpassed by the central banks that do the same thing on an international level such as the World Bank or the IMF. This is an organization that has only been around for a short period of time, and the people never asked for it or wanted it. It has nothing to do with our government and is a private corporation owned by the elite, just like Bank of America or Halliburton. As many researches have pointed out there's nothing federal about the "Federal Reserve," just as there is nothing federal about "Federal Express."

The Federal Income tax is the first thing that should be done away with. This tax is totally unproductive and provides absolutely no money to public services. Income taxes are primarily used to pay off the debt on our currency, a debt that is completely unnecessary to begin with and would not exist if there was not a private bank distributing that currency. Gas taxes and tolls pay for roads, property taxes pay for schools and hospitals, and sales taxes pay for a myriad of public services. This oppressive tax has absolutely no productive value in our society so it should be eradicated immediately. That is not to say that those other taxes are legitimate, but the income tax is by far the worst and should be the first thing to go.

If we actually wanted to work towards creating a peaceful society we would make all taxation voluntary, and remove the violence and coercion from the equation. Presently, all taxes are collected under the threat of prison or even worse death, should you resist an immoral arrest. This is not only wrong and inhumane but it is also not at all practical. This coercive method of establishing a community chest of resources is inefficient because most of the overhead is spent on the enforcement of the tax laws, instead being used somewhere where it would benefit society. Also, when taxation is compulsory there is usually no guarantee that the money will be used correctly or wisely. This happens naturally because there is no incentive for the government to actually do a good job, because they get paid even if nothing gets done at all. In fact, the government usually gets paid more money when they make problems worse because their many failures are typically rewarded with more funding.

Holding a gun on people and taking their hard-earned money is not a productive way of solving social problems or creating a fund for community projects. If we really wanted to solve these problems and really wanted to see that our collective wealth was spent wisely, we would take out the middleman. When our money is taken out of our paychecks and is funneled through the government, a very small percentage actually makes it back to the community. This process is actually preventing any kind of real economic growth within the community and is stifling any kind of meaningful charity that would be taking place in the absence of taxation. The federal income tax is just one example of many that reveals the fraudulent and violent nature of state and banking power. As with all human interactions, removing violence, fraud, and coercion from the equation is the first step toward peace and freedom.

QUOTE SOURCES AND SUGGESTED READING
----
[0] KRS-One in interview that appeared on "The Obama Deception"
[1] Two Lucky People - Milton Friedman
[2] The Quotable Billionaire by Steven D. Price (2009)
[SR1] No More National Debt by Bill Still
[SR2] The Creature from Jekyll Island by G. Edward Griffin
[SR3] The Secrets of the Federal Reserve By Eustace Mullins
[SR4] Web of Debt: The Shocking Truth about Our Money System and How We Can Break Free
[SR5] The Lost Science of Money By Stephen A. Zarlenga

"The way to make money is to buy when blood is running in the streets."
- John D. Rockefeller [0]

Controlled Economic Collapse

The economic crisis occuring in America and across the world is reminiscent of one of the darkest moments in American history, the great depression. Things certainly haven't been this bad economically since those times, sure there have been dozens of depressions in American history, but the crashes of 1929 and 2008 are surely the most damaging. In both cases there was a lot of speculation in the media about where this mess came from, and who was to blame. I'm sure that mainstream coverage of the first great depression was just as vague and uninformative as what we see in the media today. However, in the many years following the stock market collapse of 1929 information began to surface that shed some light on what caused the market to fail and who was behind the crash. This information is what led Milton Friedman to conclude that the Fed and United States government was to blame, as I documented earlier. This is all vital in understanding the current economic crisis because a lot of the same factors are at play.

The very earliest controlled financial meltdown that I have been able to find occurred in Europe well before the American civil war. During the Battle of waterloo in the Napoleonic wars Nathan Rothschild was responsible for one of the oldest cases of "insider trading", which led to the Rothschild family robbing a whole nation blind. In 1815 when the battle of waterloo took place, there were no quick methods of communication like we have today so messengers were used for communication in times of war. The Rothschild's took advantage of this by having spies on the frontlines of the battle who would return information to the family faster than the messengers used by the military.

When the British won the war Nathan Rothschild was of course the first to know, and he immediately went to the stock exchange and started selling stocks while putting out the rumor that the French had won the war. This created a panic on the floor of the stock exchange and investors all over England began frantically selling their stocks. With the price of all stocks plummeting Rothschild was able to buy out the whole English market for a fraction of its cost. When word returned that the English had actually been victorious the value of the market soared, and overnight Nathan Rothschild became the richest man in the world. This is similar to the tactics used in America that caused the great depression in the 1930's.

During both great depressions in America a lot of people became very poor, but a small few became extremely wealthy. Those who got wealthy were the major banking interests who have been manipulating the stock market and the American economy for most of the 20th century. This certainly was not by mistake, both financial meltdowns were planned and orchestrated by the ruling elite as a hostile wealth grab. This wealth transfer was carried out in order to widen the gap between the rich and the poor and create a two-class system where the public was completely controlled by the upper class.

Franklin D. Roosevelt was in office during most of the depression, years after his death his son in law Curtis Dall wrote a book called "my exploited father in law" which gave an inside look into the politics of the great depression. In his book Dall says *"The depression was the calculated 'shearing' of the public by the World Money powers, triggered by the planned sudden shortage of supply of call money in the New York money market....The One World Government 'leaders' and their ever close bankers have now acquired full control of the money and credit machinery of the U.S. via the creation of the privately owned Federal Reserve Bank."* [1]

The traditional banking and industrial dynasties are of course the usual suspects in these scams and indeed they are involved in almost all of them, but there are many other oligarchs that play part in creating economic depression for personal profit. In our time George Soros is one of the most infamous feudal oligarchs, he is known worldwide for rigging markets and profiting off of the misfortunes of others. There are even various countries that he literally cannot even step foot in anymore because he will be arrested. It seems every time there is a massive crash in the market George Soros makes billions of dollars, it is a shame that more people can't put 2 and 2 together.

Through multiple high profiles financial scams the elite have successfully reinforced the modern feudal system. However, they have only managed to create this economic monopoly with our participation and support. Now that we can see the damage that they have created in our society we can make the conscious decision to seek a new way of doing business. The system they have left us is not the only way, it is the only way for them to get what they want, but it is not the way to run a productive and humane society. Every time in recent memory that there has been some financial disaster there was no food shortage, drought or anything natural, but the elite is red handed in plain sight every single time. Each time a transfer of wealth has taken place to return the majority of the world's people further towards the feudal enslavement that was suffered by their ancestors.

QUOTE SOURCES AND SUGGESTED READING
----
[0]The Fourth — And by Far the Most Recent 637 Best Things Anybody Ever Said - Robert Byrne (1990)
[1] F. D. R. My Exploited Father-In-Law: An Intimate Account of the Man, the Regime, and the Legacy - Curtis B. Dall (1983)

"In every scheme that worsens the position of the poor, it is the poor who are invoked as beneficiaries."
- Vandana Shiva [0]

Third World by Design

"Third World" is a term that originated during the cold war, to describe countries that were not allied with the Soviets or the west. Although they had no alliance or affiliation, these countries were still colonized by both sides of the cold war. During this time the governments of these countries were influenced by both the Soviet Union and the United States. Businesses from both nations had also moved in to exploit the people and resources of the colonized areas, a practice that had already been taking place for centuries. When the cold war was over the military and spy operations within the colonized countries ended, but sadly the exploitation did not.

Two of the largest corporations in the world, the International Monetary Fund (IMF) and the World Bank are the self-appointed "developers" of poor third world countries. However, under their carefully crafted public image these corporations are doing incredible damage to developing countries for their own political and financial gain. The IMF and the World Bank are actually holding back progress in these countries through their complicated international trade laws and bureaucracies. The decisions that are made by these companies disrupt the lives of millions in the third world, displacing them from their homes, staking claim to their natural resources and monopolizing their economy.

Prior to the establishment of these corporations in the third world, the people were able to grow food and hunt in the wilderness of their country, but those times are gone. These business interests have basically seized all of the land in these developing countries and claimed that they own it. This process can be described as neocolonialism or diplomatic imperialism. What ends up happening is countries who have starving populations are exporting vast amounts of food to industrialized nations via multinational corporations.

There is no reason why global poverty should be a problem, it is obvious here that there is something more to the situation. A population should only be in a time of struggle during some unpreventable natural disaster, like a drought, famine, or flood. Any other catastrophe is usually going to be manmade, and if it was manmade it is safe to say it should have never happened in the first place. In most cases it is not natural disasters that are responsible for the condition of the third world. Many of these areas were once abundant in natural resources, before western countries came in and industrialized their lands. Now the people are cut off from their homes and pushed off into unfertile wastelands because their corrupt government sold out to western corporations. After having their only means of survival taken away they are expected to pay money for food, water, and clothing, which they once had the ability to provide themselves with. There was once a time when these people were able to live naturally off the land and that was the life that they were accustomed to for many generations. Today, most of them have been forced off their land by the military or corporations and forced to contend in the weak job market and poor living standards within the overcrowded cities.

The people are hungry and have been chewed up and spit out by the corporate establishment. Now it is the corporate establishment who is responsible for seeing that they get "back on their feet"? It looks like the fox is guarding the henhouse. The politicians always have a heavy hand in the industry, many of them either owning multinational corporations themselves or directly funded by them, so either way they benefit as a result of imperialism.

Any third world country that you take a look at always has the same story; corrupt politicians have sold out the countries resources and finances to the elite western businesses. When multinational corporations enter into a third world country they set up sweatshops, pillage whatever resource it is that they are seeking and are protected because they are working with the local puppet regime. This is why it is so important to our government that countries be "co-operative" with the interests of the United States. By a "co-operative government" what they mean is basically a puppet government that will not stand up to western corporations.

Whenever a "leader" actually does stand up for their people they are vilified by western governments, even if they are the most humane person that the nation has ever seen. There is a great deal of wealth in 3rd world countries, but it is horded by the aristocracy and is not accessible to the overwhelming majority of the population.

This imperialistic global trade system is made possible by complex trade agreements such as the "North American Free Trade Agreement" or NAFTA. This agreement and many others like it come from a multinational group of elitists called the World Trade Organizations or WTO. The policies put into place by this organization benefit only the owners and shareholders of a few specific corporations. "Free trade agreements" allow large American companies to look for resources and workers outside of the country. This takes power out of the hands of the consumers and workers while allowing the corporations to create global monopolies by looting resources from foreign countries and using their citizens for slave labor. The working class back in America loses millions of jobs every year overseas, and the places where the companies move to are now forced to deal with environmental destruction and mass displacement of local populations.

One of the most articulate and on point descriptions of "free trade" that I have come across was from a researcher by the name of David Icke. In his incredible book "…And the Truth Shall Set You Free" he writes "free trade is the freedom of the strong to exploit the weak. It is the means through which multinationals, subsidized by their governments via the overseas aid budgets and other hidden channels, operate "cartelism" against the interests of the general population. It is the freedom to create dependency on a system that only the few control and use that dependency to manipulate at will. The freedom to move production from high wage industrialized countries to the sweatshops of the third world, savagely exploiting the native population. The freedom to steal their food growing land and to destroy the industries and incomes of those in the developed world also. In doing this, the elite create anger, despair, and division, the perfect combination for manipulation. That, my friends, is the "free trade" the economists, politicians, and news correspondents tell us we desperately need more of."[1]

The person who coined the term free trade was a Scottish economist named Adam Smith. This concept was formulated as a way to allow England to continue importing heroin into Chinese Harbors. It is these conditions that resulted in the "Opium Wars," which I will discuss at length in a later chapter. Of course, his idea caught on rather quickly because "free trade" would open the doorway for the elite to take advantage of every corner of the global market. This also allowed companies to do their dirty work, like slave labor, drug dealing, and environmental destruction on someone else's turf, so to speak.

Adam Smith's own writings show that he was well aware of the exploitation that his policies were encouraging, and he had no regrets. In one of his most famous works "Wealth of Nations" he writes "Wherever there is great property there is great inequality. For one very rich man there must be at least five hundred poor, and the affluence of the few supposes the indigence of the many. The affluence of the rich excites the indignation of the poor, who are often both driven by want, and prompted by envy, to invade his possessions."[2] This coming from a man who had an immense amount of property, it shows that the ruling class is traditionally more interested in maintaining their wealth than they are concerned with the plights of the poor or developing an economic system that is actually worthwhile for society. The only thing that they regret about their responsibility in creating poverty is that now they have a "problem" to "deal with," in the sense that they have to guard their wealth from the lower classes.

The British and United States governments are intent on maintaining dominance in the third world, through conquest and diplomacy both, because they depend on the regions resources and cheap labor for their global power. Many times throughout history the western imperial powers have proven that they will do anything to keep their colonies abroad. This is responsible for the vast majority of wars that take place, wars that are carried out against the will of the public in most cases. The US does business with tyrants but will call them saints in the press as long as they welcome multinational corporations into their countries. However, if a "leader" refuses to open up his borders to western trade he is vilified and marked as an enemy.

In the 1980s the CIA led covert operations to overthrow a popular "democratically elected" government in Nicaragua because they were less compliant with western businesses then the former totalitarian regime. The new regime was more progressive and did not want their people to be exploited by foreign corporations. Hundreds of thousands of innocent peasant farmers were killed simply so the US could establish a regime that was friendlier with their businesses. Some of the most brutal death squads in Central America during that time were trained by the US government so they could prevent the peasants from establishing a free society. This war for trade and political dominance continues in Central America to this day, and the government continues to support fascist regimes with financial military aid, weapons, and training. This is what they call "humanitarian aid," more of the deceptive language that is used to mask the harsh reality of what we are dealing with.

The same goes for the Middle East, Saudi Arabia has one of the most oppressive feudal regimes in the Middle East, but they are praised by American politicians and businesses because they play along with the global trade game. Africa is no different, in 2010, ten years' worth of classified diplomatic files were released through the whistleblower website Wikileaks showing discussions between American and European diplomats regarding Zimbabwe's natural resources. Throughout the whole decade of discourse between various diplomats it was apparent that the western governments had no interest at all in the human rights violations or poverty that was taking place in the country. All of the discussions were concerning how the current regimes policies would affect business and trade for multinational corporations. This is just one of the recent stories that have surfaced in the United States, but the pillaging of the third world is taking place every single day all across the globe.

The IMF, The World Bank and other multinational corporations make promises in the countries that they do business in, but have never followed through on any of them. As soon as they have conned their way into a country they immediately build infrastructure that western companies use when pillaging the areas natural resources, displacing millions of people in the process. Then they will claim that they are heroes because they have built the infrastructure that will allow the corporate world to better take advantage of the working people of the country. Even worse the corporations promise to bring more efficient utilities to these countries, but offer them at a price that only the colonizers and sweatshop owners can afford. These policies make life a struggle for the average people of the third world, many of whom pray constantly that they will just have clean water and food for another day.

Every year multinational corporations pay public relations firms millions to clean up their image and whitewash the cruel reality of globalization. PR consultants are masters of deception and are thoroughly educated in advanced persuasion techniques. Of course, this public image is only an illusion, built to protect the regimes that are pillaging the third world. If the multinational corporations that are impoverishing these countries were actually providing a public service and had nothing to hide there would be no need for a tremendous public relations budget.

The revitalization of the third world is only possible through allowing the people to have control over their own land, resources, and economy. Under the current system the odds are stacked against developing countries, leaving them vulnerable to exploitation from the dominant western business interests. We can no longer stand by and watch as the richest corporations on the planet feed off of people that are struggling to survive. It is this injustice that has brought incredible violence and turmoil to our doorstep; this is the reason why there is so much hostility towards US interests in developing countries. This kind of global economic policy creates a cycle of exploitation that is not just irresponsible, it is completely inhumane.

There should be an incredible public outcry across the whole world about this, but there is not because the issue is so misunderstood. The establishment shrouds the roots of poverty in mystery when the whole situation can be explained quite easily. Most third world countries are abundant in natural resources and are actually quite wealthy but all the wealth is held in the ruling class, who leave their people to starve. This ruling class gets huge payouts from western corporations to let them come into their countries and pillage their natural resources. The common people get nothing from these payouts and in the process lose their natural resources and their land to foreign corporations.

QUOTE SOURCES AND SUGGESTED READING
----
[0]Staying alive: women, ecology, and development - Vandana Shiva (1989)
[1]And the Truth Shall Set You Free - David Icke (1997)
[2] Wealth Of Nations - Adam Smith (1776)
[SR1] Wealth Of Nations by Adam Smith (1776)

"Foreign aid is when the poor people of a rich country give money to the rich people of a poor country."
- Johnny Hart [0]

The Sweatshop Economy

As the most recent great depression in America deepens there is a lot of confusion and misinformation about how the job market works, and why the unemployment rate is so high. Between World War 2 and the invasion of Iraq, the United States was at the forefront of industry, offering well-paying jobs and opportunity. Now it seems like the well has dried up, leaving a large number of Americans unemployed and in poverty. What is most interesting about this situation is the fact that all of the manufacturing and factory jobs seem to have vanished, yet corporations are still able to produce their products in record numbers. If these industries are no longer creating jobs, then where are the products being manufactured?

Most corporations have outsourced their factories to foreign countries where the authorities are extremely corrupt and there is already a culture of oppression and widespread slavery. Hundreds of Thousands of jobs every year are taken from this country and moved overseas where corporations take advantage of the desperate workers and basically run slave camps. In 2010 while the unemployment was at record highs US companies created 1.4 Million jobs abroad. Meanwhile, in the US those same companies struggled to create half that number.

The same organizations and policies that are responsible for third world debt and poverty are also responsible for the creation of the sweatshop crisis. The so-called "free trade" agreements allow for companies to hire outside of their own borders. These policies give the corporations an extremely unfair advantage not only over the employees of their sweatshops but also the citizens back home who are losing their jobs as well.

It is far more expensive to run a factory in the west where living standards are high and workers expect better pay. To eliminate this expense factories are moved to less developed countries where large corporations can put workers into slave camps, as long as they pay off the local regimes. In outsourced factories conditions are horrible; workers are subject to grueling 18-hour shifts for just pennies a day. Some of the biggest companies in the world such as Nike, Gap, and Monsanto have been fined millions of dollars after sweatshop operations have slowly been exposed over the past two decades. Unfortunately, even after paying steep fines like this it is still cheaper for these companies to outsource their labor then to run a legitimate business back home where better conditions are expected.

In addition to the economic problems caused by outsourcing, there is a significant environmental impact as well. In India for example, The Coca Cola Company has been found guilty in several lawsuits because of their negative impact on local villages and ecosystems. Coca Cola like many other multinational corporations completely devastate the local communities that they neighbor abroad. The company admits to using roughly 600,000 liters of water per day, depleting the water supply of local villages. They have also been accused of polluting the land, water, and air of nearby villages with toxic waste from their factories.

This is the kind of world we are living in, a world where unbelievably powerful people own large companies that hold their profit margin to be more valuable than human life or environmental conditions. Cutthroat practices are openly accepted if you have enough money or the right political connections. Manipulation, lying, intimidation and even murder are all commonplace in the corporate world. Multinational corporations take this behavior to a whole new level because they are completely above the law and very influential in politics. In developing countries corporations are oftentimes more powerful than the government and even have their own private armies to keep workers in line and reporters out of their factories.

Most of the people in this country believe that slavery is just an ugly part of our past, something that ended years ago and no longer affects them. However, Slavery did not end with the civil war like many of us would like to believe, it was just transferred to distant lands away from the concerned eyes of the American public. Sweatshops are the new corporate plantations that have for the most part stayed out of sight and out of mind because of the distant location of their factories. It is this modern slave industry abroad that is responsible for the high unemployment rate in this country.

If the multinational corporations that have outsourced their factories were to bring those factories back to the U.S there would be an obvious increase in the amount of jobs available. The only adverse effects that this move would cause would be on the profit margins of these large companies, which is why they spend a lot of money and fight very hard to cover up the nature of their operations. The disgusting facts of this industry are undeniable, which is why almost every major multinational corporation has been found guilty in lawsuits involving unfair working conditions and environmental destruction.

QUOTE SOURCES AND SUGGESTED READING
----
[0] Johnny Hart (BC Comic Strip)
[SR1] Slaves to Fashion: Poverty and Abuse in the New Sweatshops by Robert J. S. Ross
[SR2] Advocacy Across Borders: NGOs, Anti-Sweatshop Activism and the Global Garment Industry by Shea Garwood

"Three hundred men, each of whom knows all the others, govern the fate of the European continent, and they elect their successors from their entourage."
- Walter Rathenau [0]

Royal Landlords

The fact that a very tiny percentage of the world's population maintains control of all the land and resources on the planet is another one of the serious issues of the 21st century that no one wants to face. The facts are all on public record, and all of the statistics I used in this essay have been taken from the "world wealth report of 2007" released by Merrill Lynch/ Cap Gemini. The people who are responsible for poverty and hunger are in fact those who are keeping food and resources away from the rest of the human population. This group I am referring to consists of less than 1% of the population, they are the royal bloodlines and multinational corporations that covertly rule over the entire planet. Whether we want to admit it or not these people have total control over the world's population by maintaining a monopoly over everything they possibly can from energy resources to food and water.

Hundreds of years ago the royalty of Great Brittan were hell bent on world domination, like many other European nations at the time. After centuries of violence and conquest the British royalty were able to dominate most of the world through political and military force. It was said that "the sun never set on the British Empire" because there were so many areas throughout the world which the British had colonized that it was always daytime somewhere in an occupied territory of Britain. Even today the Queen of England's real estate takes up 1/3 of the earth's surface! That is one family owning more than a quarter of all the land in the world while 85% of the human race owns no land at all! This is not what humanity is about, something is horribly wrong with this situation. The royal family may have the lion's share of land to their name but other elite families also have a large wealth of property as well, which they have acquired and protected using their phony environmental organizations.

Land is not scarce, if it were to be divided up equally there would actually be 5.2 acres available to every man woman and child in the world, and that is not even including Antarctica. Now I'm not suggesting that we divide up the earth into 7 billion 5-acre sections, but these figures should help you better understand the gross disparity of land ownership that exists between the ruling class and the rest of us. Most average people do not have the luxury of owning much of anything; instead they are piled into slums and ghettos where they have little privacy or personal property. For the rest of us the idea of *owning* an entire content is not within the realm of our understanding, we are too busy struggling to stay alive and feed our families.

There is no reason why the real wealth of this world should be in so few hands. Literally 99% of the world's population struggles to keep their families fed and in safe housing, while the privileged spend their days figuring out how to hide or whitewash this exploitation. They know that if the majority of people were to figure out that they were being taken advantage of so others could live lives of luxury, things would change very quickly. It is our hard work and creativity that they feed upon. Without having people under them to keep things running, their game would fall apart. The ruling class consists of the people that have given us our corrupt education systems, media, and politicians. All of these institutions have been manipulated in order to imprison the minds of the struggling, hardworking people of this planet.

The elite have stolen nearly every last piece of land on earth and they use their control of this land to keep the world's population under their thumb. Through the strict enforcement of international law and strong-arm collection of property taxes the powers that be are able to use their land to rob their helpless subjects and keep them depended upon the system. This is exactly how the ruling class of feudal lords maintained control over their peasant underlings during the Middle Ages. For all intents and purposes it has been the same royal families that have had control of this land down through the centuries, even before the feudal times of the Middle Ages. So even though the names and financial systems have slightly changed the general structure of our social system and the bloodlines that benefit from it have stayed the same.

QUOTE SOURCES AND SUGGESTED READING
----
[0] The global game for a new world order by Tariq Majid
[SR1] The Leviathan by Thomas Hobbes
[SR2] The tax-exempt foundations by William H McIlhany
[SR3] Undue Influence: Wealthy Foundations, Grant Driven Environmental Groups and Zealous Bureaucrats That Control Your Future by Ron Arnold
[SR4] Who Owns the World: The Surprising Truth About Every Piece of Land on the Planet by Kevin Cahill

"I have no doubt that we will be successful in harnessing the sun's energy.... If sunbeams were weapons of war, we would have had solar energy centuries ago."
- Sir George Porter [0]

Cursed Dinosaur Blood

Anyone with open eyes can look around and see that our world is dying. Looking deeper we see that a small group of very powerful people have taken control of how we live and the mark we leave on our planet. Dangerous and destructive resources such as oil are not needed for energy or product development. There are countless other natural renewable resources that could completely replace oil. The natural alternatives to oil would make energy and household products cheaper for the average consumer in the long run, but would cost big business a considerable amount of money and radically change the balance of power on this planet. As usual it all comes down money and power, just as we have seen countless times throughout history in the horrors of slavery and war.

The ruling elite push for oil dependency because it is a resource that they have a monopoly over. Having total control of our primary source of energy is one of the fundamental scams that they have used to maintain power over humanity. If we were to progress as a species and discover cheaper, cleaner solutions and no longer need their oil, they would not only lose one of their main industries, but they would also lose their ability to restrict travel among the general public. Most ecofriendly energy would be free and can be grown or harvested by anyone, which completely takes away the ability to control the market and the population by manipulating the energy supply. So it makes perfect sense that they would buy the media, bribe government officials, and use their money to stifle any kind of progress in developing cleaner fuels.

Today, one of the biggest businesses in the world is the tightly controlled oil industry. At the very height of this goliath sit is the same people who control the media, the banking industries, and most multinational corporations. The very first oil company in the world was none other than John D. Rockefeller's Standard Oil, established in 1853. He inherited an abundance of petroleum resources from his father William who peddled oil for 25$ a pint as a cure for warts, snakebites, cancer and impotency. To this day control of the entire oil industry has remained in the hands of the Rockefellers and a few other aristocrats spread across the world.

John D. Rockefeller formed Standard Oil in 1853 and shared a monopoly on the world's resources with a handful of elite families for a number of years. Eventually, the public became extremely suspicious and the company was forced to splinter off into a handful of different subsidiaries that are all still a part of the Rockefellers globalist network. It has been almost impossible for any other companies to compete with these giants, so of course after time any contenders end up fading away. The oil cartel that started with standard oil and still controls the oil trade to this day has been called the "seven sister's oil cartel" or more commonly known today as "OPEC'. Many people have the misconception that OPEC is influenced by Arab "leaders" just because the oil is being exported from Arab states, but in reality this cartel was formed by the leading American and European companies, then were later handed off to puppet regimes in the area.

The first trace of this cartel was an agreement signed on September 17, 1920, between Royal Dutch Shell, Anglo-Iranian (aka Amoco aka BP), and Standard Oil. This agreement was set up to fix prices and dominate the market, but came under the guise of an innocent trade deal. Over the years these large companies have splintered off into many smaller subsidiaries to create the illusion of competition and to divert attention away from their monopoly over this prime resource. For example, the company that we know today as BP was once Amoco, before that it was Anglo-Iranian, before that it was Anglo-Persian, and before that it was just plain old standard oil. That is at least 5 name changes in a hundred years and no doubt their going to be forced to change their name again after the BP deep horizon oil spill in the Gulf of Mexico. Rockefellers Standard Oil has today splintered off into many different companies, but remains in the same hands. Who is standard oil today? Almost everyone! Exxon, Mobil, Chevron, BP, Texaco, Gulf, Sunoco are all products of standard oil! Crazy is not it!?

By owning all of the major oil companies and guarding the pipelines, the cartel is able to control the flow of oil to refineries that gives them the power to raise or lower the price of the commodity. With this kind of monopoly on the world's primary source of energy and trade this cartel has an extreme interest in suppressing the development of any other possible energy source. It is a tried and true business model of the elite to eliminate any possible competition in order to maintain dominance of the many industries that they have their hand in. A monopolized industry is the only option for these people; John D. Rockefeller once said "competition is a sin." It is an insult to the intelligence to suggest that this one finite limited resource is the only way that we can power our societies. It does not even make logical sense for our species to build our lives around a resource that will not be around for much longer, to do so is to ensure widespread panic when the resource inevitably runs out. This is not the logic of the people who dominate the industry, their motives rest solely in profit and social manipulation.

Real technological progress is not accepted in our society if it threatens to upset the established order, this point was made abundantly clear almost a hundred years ago when revolutionary genius Nikola Tesla announced to the world that he discovered a way to wirelessly harness free energy from thin air! This project was met with total objection from the establishment and they destroyed his whole campaign because it would put an end to their stranglehold on energy. Throughout his life Tesla made countless contributions to science and the development of human understanding. Unfortunately, due to the fact that most of his ideas would have worked to free humanity from economic slavery, his work was silenced and the powerful implications of his discoveries were covered up for generations.

Tesla could never get any investors to implement his free energy plans because the investor would never get a return on their investment, since the products goal was to not make any money. From an investors perspective it would be a very foolish thing to invest in, so Tesla died a broke man with many of his ideas stolen by people who then implemented those ideas in such a way that they were profitable or violent, thus undermining the original intent of the invention. When Tesla died in 1943 his house was raided by the FBI and all of his plans, notes, experiments, and inventions were stolen to be used for military purposes. He refused to work with the establishment during his lifetime because he knew that they would use his knowledge for war, a concept that he was morally opposed to

We have the intellectual capacity to pretty much decide the fate of the planet, this is no mistake, this is our responsibility, and as a whole we are failing desperately. This responsibility will not be met sitting on the couch waiting for the fools in power to fix the problem. We must educate ourselves about how things work so we ourselves can offer better solutions that will render their oppressive ideas obsolete. Instead of working to lower emissions or improve gas mileage we need to push our technology in a more innovative direction. We should take a direction that would leave fossil fuels and big business completely out of the equation while offering consumers cheap renewable energy. This is not the approach that is currently being taken to solve the energy crisis. The solutions that are being offered by the establishment are only temporary "Band-Aids," which still use their controlled commodities as resources. This approach is an effort to direct attention away from the problem while still maintaining control over the worlds energy supply.

QUOTE SOURCES AND SUGGESTED READING
----
[0]'Sayings of the Week.' The Observer, London (26 Aug 1973). Quoted in Barbara K. Rodes and Rice Odell, A Dictionary of Environmental Quotations (1992)
[SR1] Free Energy Pioneer: John Worrell Keely By Theo Paijmans
[SR2] Nikola Tesla: Free Energy and the White Dove by Commander X
[SR3] The Tesla Papers: Nikola Tesla on Free Energy & Wireless Transmission of Power by Nikola Tesla, David Hatcher Childress
[SR4] The Secret Power Beneath by Frank Acland
[SR5] The Hockey Stick Illusion: Climate-gate and the Corruption of Science by A.W. Montford [SR6] The Great Global Warming Blunder by Roy W Spencer

"There is no crueler tyranny than that which is perpetrated under the shield of law and in the name of justice."
- Charles de Montesquieu [0]

The Climate Industrial Complex and the Hoax of State Sponsored Environmentalism

The human species has a unique responsibility because they are the only creatures on this earth that possess the power to destroy everything living here. We are self-aware creatures and when we are paying attention we can actually comprehend the impact that our actions will have on the world around us. At this time, we are doing a horrible job as a species in fulfilling our responsibility to our home. We have put this sacred responsibility in the hands of governments and corporations who wish only to exploit the earth and everyone on it. We look in the opposite direction as the most ruthless among us transform our beautiful planet into a toxic wasteland.

For the past century there has been a consistent trend of manmade disasters resulting in tremendous environmental damage all over the world. These completely avoidable environmental disasters have all been a result of the greed and carelessness of big business and the military industrial complex. Oil companies are the worst offenders in this regard, as their industry is completely obsolete to begin with. Clean, inexpensive energy is a very necessary possibility, so the fact that we are even still bothering with oil when we see all the problems it causes is completely insane from a humanitarian or environmental perspective. The only reason we are still using oil-based products is because the people who maintain a monopoly over this resource spend billions to ensure that they are the only game in town.

2010 alone saw a tragic amount of oil spills that have completely poisoned some of the most vital ecosystems on the planet. The worst of these spills is the infamous deep horizon BP oilrig explosion in the Gulf of Mexico. This explosion was possibly the worst manmade environmental disaster in human history and could have been easily prevented if BP and Halliburton had spent some money to upgrade their safety mechanism. Unfortunately, during a time of record profit is the companies running this oilrig were unable to spend the meager amount that was required to prevent this catastrophe. These cut corners led to a horrific 3-month ordeal that dumped 185 million gallons of crude oil in to the Gulf of Mexico.

The reaction of the government and media regarding the spill made it obvious that they were on the same team as the oil companies. Homeland Security acted as hired goons for the corporations, kicking activists and environmentalists off the beaches under threat of arrest. Mainstream news sources actually tried telling people that the oil had vanished! After insulting our intelligence with these lies the media completely dropped the story and it disappeared from the news forever. Sadly, the problem is far from solved. The whole Gulf of Mexico is completely contaminated with oil and the toxic chemicals that were used to treat the spill. All of the sea creatures in the gulf are now poisoned, and it will not be safe to fish in these waters for years. There is no telling whether the damage from this disaster will ever be fully repaired. The Exxon-Valdez oil spill in 1989 was a fraction of the size and it is still being cleaned up.

The oil corporations were not the only shady business to leave their ugly mark on the planet in 2010. Many companies that refine toxic metals and very volatile chemicals often set up their refineries in developing countries where the public has even less power to fight back than we do here in the west. When bauxite is refined into aluminum a very toxic, acid like byproduct is left over, resembling a red sludge. This toxic waste is typically stored in large reservoirs until it dries and can be more easily disposed of. In Hungary an aluminum plant unleashed a wave of red toxic sludge onto neighboring villages and ecosystems when their reservoir gave way. This toxic flood poisoned the Danube River and affected the lives of thousands of people. 7 different towns were evacuated and a state of emergency was declared by the government of Hungary. The areas that were affected by this disaster will not be habitable for at least another decade because the environment has been completely poisoned.

Ironically enough, the same people that are responsible for most of this environmental degradation also set up nature based foundations and other phony environmental organizations. These organizations are used to launder money and to advance eugenics depopulation programs. The elite understand that human beings naturally have an interest in preserving the environment and typically will not question or criticize actions taken in the name of environmental protection.

The latest scheme of the ruling class is exploiting environmentalism and fears of "global warming" to establish a carbon credit taxing system. The rationale of this theory is that human beings are creating environmental destruction via their use of carbon, so the suggested solution is to tax the average people and control their energy use. Yet, the average citizens are not responsible for the majority of the world's environmental destruction, nor are they responsible for the majority of the world's carbon output. In fact, the 50 largest transport sea vessels produce more carbon than all the cars in the world. These are military vessels, oil tankers and other transport vehicles for corporations and governments.

Howard Zinn's incredible research in "A Peoples History of the United States Of America" reveals that "In 1992 more than a 100 countries participated in the earth summit environmental conference in Brazil. Statistics showed that the armed forces of the world were responsible for two thirds of the gasses that depleted the ozone layer. But when it was suggested that the earth summit consider the effects of the military on environmental degradation the United States delegation objected and the suggestion was defeated."[1] The general public is not to blame for the environmental crisis that stands before us, we have inherited it from the careless governments and corporations who suppress clean energy and are responsible for the vast majority of the world's pollution.

Despite their obvious guilt, the perpetrators of these crimes place the blame everywhere but themselves and use their political power so they can actually benefit from all the destruction they are causing. Al Gore is currently the main spokesman for the carbon based global warming theory, he is also one of the primary advocates for a worldwide carbon tax, and he is closely involved with businesses that stand to reap large profits as a result of his various legislative moves in Washington.

His primary efforts involve reducing the energy uses of the general public, yet he has a mansion in the Belle Meade area of Tennessee that consumes more electricity every month than the average American household uses in an entire year, according to the Tennessee Center for Policy Research, citing data from the Nashville Electric Service. When this information went public he defended himself by saying that he pays a "carbon offset," but what he did not say is that he paid it through a company that he owned called Generation Investment Management. In other words, he paid the money to himself! Carbon taxing was not a plan that Al Gore came up, that was his good friend and Founder of the embattled ENRON Corporation, Ken Lay. This makes perfect sense considering the fact that ENRON was an energy company that had very close ties in Washington, and they were notorious for concocting brilliant yet deceitful schemes to fleece the public out of their hard-earned money.

If climate change actually was a result of manmade carbon output then surely taxation would not be a realistic solution, yet according to the establishment this is the ONLY possible solution. To make matters worse most of the evidence paints a picture quite different from the "official" stance on global warming. On a very basic level the global warming narrative really does not make any sense when you actually think about what we are being told. Plants depend on carbon dioxide for survival; they breathe in the carbon dioxide and breathe out oxygen.

These politicians are trying to tell us that a compound, which plants need to survive, is bad for the environment. If that does not take a stretch of the imagination, they go on by citing the earths changing temperature and climate as evidence for the damage that is apparently being caused by carbon dioxide. The earth's temperature and climate has been changing and fluctuating since the beginning of time on account of various factors, namely solar activity. Drastic changes in weather have been recorded throughout history, it is a natural process. To claim that a natural process that has been happening forever is evidence of a recent threat defies logic.

Since the "Climate-gate" scandal broke in November of 2009 the carbon based global warming theory has lost support and is now under extreme public scrutiny. Despite the mainstream media and political circles insisting that their theory is fact, more and more people are starting to question the details of the carbon theory and rejecting the idea of carbon taxing. Recently in 2011, NASA confirmed these doubts by releasing a study of satellite data showing that a great deal of heat is being released from our atmosphere out into space, far more than is suggested by most computer models. Around the same time a CERN hadron collider experiment researching cloud formation discovered new evidence that the current global warming dialogue is invalid, and that warming is most likely caused by the sun. Unfortunately, the scientists have been gagged by the government and are not allowed to release the detailed findings of their experiment to the public; their research has been declared confidential.

While all of this discussion and controversy is taking place over this very specific theory there are a host of other environmental issues that are being ignored. Our energy resources are being poorly mismanaged by the organizations that control them. These governments and corporations are destroying the planet and placing the blame on us so they can justify making us foot the bill. Sinister applications of genetic engineering are creating new species that pose an unprecedented threat to our ecosystem. Toxic radiation and pollution has become commonplace in our everyday environment, mostly due to corporate carelessness and military exercises. There are very serious environmental issues that we need to correct, but it is not limited to one chemical compound and we are not going to solve anything by taxing the average consumer.

QUOTE SOURCES AND SUGGESTED READING
----
[0] Charles de Montesquieu – Liberty Quotes (p67) by Christopher Kalabus
[1] A Peoples History of the United States of America - Howard Zinn
[SR1] The First Global Revolution by Alexander King, Bertrand Schneider
[SR2] The Return of the Kings: Rise of the New Feudalism by Thomas Purcell
[SR3] Climate-gate by Brian Sussman
[SR4] www.climategate.tv

"Politics is the entertainment branch of industry."
- Frank Zappa

Section 5

Politics

35. -Newspeak: A Language of Deception
36. -Right? Left? WRONG!
37. -Beyond the Good Guy and the Bad Guy
38. -Classified Corruption
39. - Illegal Information
40. -Who Owns Congress?
41. -Illegitimate Bureaucracy
42. -Fascism...For your safety
43. -The Prison Industrial Complex
44. -Dare to Resist the War on Drugs
45. -Tricks of the Trade

"I just want you to know that, when we talk about war, we are really talking about peace."
- George W. Bush [0]

Newspeak: A Language of Deception

    Anytime a politician speaks to the citizens of their country a con job is taking place, there is always some kind of angle or tactic being used to persuade the people. The most popular tactic used in America's current political landscape is "newspeak," which is basically when someone sugarcoats what they are saying with fancy language so it comes across fewer offensives, and hides the true nature of what they are saying. This term originated from George Orwell's famous dystopian novel "1984, "where politicians manipulated language to deceive the public.
    The best description of this phenomena is revealed in Orwell's essay "politics and the English language." In this piece Orwell says "The words democracy, socialism, freedom, patriotic, realistic, justice, and have each of them several different meanings which cannot be reconciled with one another. The word "fascism," he said, had no meaning "except insofar as it signifies 'something not desirable.' Statements like 'Marshal Petain was a true patriot,' 'The Soviet press is the freest in the world,' 'The Catholic Church is opposed to

persecution,' are almost always made with intent to deceive."[1] If politicians were clever in Orwell's time, they really have perfected their game over the years to be even more conniving.

    Newspeak has infected American politics on such a level that politicians almost never say what they actually mean. The most oppressive pieces of legislation to come through our government always have names with positive connotations, using words like "freedom" "safety" or "peace" when in reality the language within the legislation sets up a completely different policy than is implied in the title. The most popular example of newspeak in recent legislation is the infamous "patriot act" which I have discussed many times throughout this book. If they were really being honest they would have called it the "welcome to fascism act," or something to that effect. Unfortunately, the oppressive patriot act is not alone, every single day our government passes new laws with happy, joyful names that contain the most abusive, and autocratic policies you could possibly think of. This is reminiscent of when the department of war changed their name to the department of defense in 1949 and then proceeded to carry out more wars of aggression than any dictator in recent memory.

    In 2010 alone there have been countless attacks on our civil liberties and freedoms through oppressive legislation riddled with newspeak. The "Food Safety Bill" did not make food any safer it just gave the FDA more control over the food supply and allowed biotech food corporations to become even more powerful in the food market. This bill actually made food more dangerous, controlled, and expensive, yet it was called the food "safety" bill. A similar situation was that of "net neutrality," which the belief is held by most Americans that the internet should be free, open, and unregulated. The government obviously does not adhere to this belief because they are threatened by the ability for normal people to have a voice through the internet. So in order to slip through legislation that allowed them to regulate the internet they had to give the bill a name that would not tip the public off about what they were actually doing.

    They called their bill, the "net neutrality act" which once again was anything but. The government claimed that this bill would regulate the current internet service provider's not American citizens, but this really just opened the door for the government to get their hands on the internet. As usual, had the politicians actually told the American people the truth about what was going on and told them what they actually wanted to do there would be outrage among the public. This is the same way that President Obama promised the American people that he would end the Iraq war by 2011, only to leave 15,000 troops in the country who were then renamed as "diplomats."

    This type of trickery takes place literally every single time a piece of legislation is voted on in Washington. The most dangerous deception that we face from our politicians is when they pretend to be concerned about our wellbeing or about the environment. There are some issues that they know most people will generally not object to and not investigate, so they take advantage of that and push along whatever kind of policies that they wish. The government has no interest whatsoever in the environment or in the wellbeing of the American people. Their actions have proven that their loyalties are with their corporate masters and their own bank accounts so when they tell us they are trying to help the poor or save the environment, watch out!

QUOTE SOURCES AND SUGGESTED READING
----
[0] From a speech at the Dept. of Housing and Urban Development in Wash. DC, 6/18/02.
[1] Politics and the English Language - George Orwell (1946)
[SR1] 1984 by George Orwell
[SR2] Anatomy of Slavespeak by Frederick Mann
[SR3] Big Brother: The Orwellian Nightmare Come True by Mark Dice
[SR4] The New Doublespeak: Why No One Knows What Anyone's Saying by William Lutz
[SR5] Orwell's Warning: The Greatest Amerikan Paradox By Erik Blaire

"Constantly choosing the lesser of two evils is still choosing evil."
- Jerry Garcia [0]

Right? Left? WRONG!

Most Americans in the 21st century are totally convinced that they live in a free society, where they have a say in how their country is run by electing officials to represent them in government. Unfortunately, these assumptions are unfounded because the voting system in America as well as many other countries is rigged to meet the needs of the ruling class. An illusion of choice is presented, but there is no choice. Even those who are still duped by the voting scam will admit that they are forced to choose between "the lesser of two evils." We are told this is our only option, to choose one of the rich elitists that will no doubt bring us war, poverty, corruption, and corporate control. This is not freedom! To choose between evil and evil? What kind of choice is that? What kind of freedom is that?

In the realm of politics, economics and religion there exists many "false dichotomies" in which there seems to be a narrow field of two options to choose from, when there is actually a larger set of possibilities beyond those guidelines. In other words, you are asked to choose between black and white, leaving you to think that the only colors in existence are black, white, and maybe gray, when in reality there is a whole palette of different shades and tints that were left completely out of the discussion. The statement, "If you're not with us, then your against us" is a classic false dichotomy, because it presents two options, both of which amount to violence, while completely neglecting the option of remaining neutral. Likewise, the traditional two-party political system in the West is a striking example of a false dichotomy.

Regardless of party affiliation the vast majority of politicians are completely out of touch with the people whose lives they are in control of. Most politicians come from wealthy families and know nothing of the struggle that most of us experience on a day-to-day basis. Whether the candidate is a democrat or a republican they will still be making decisions from the perspective of a wealthy shareholder with corporate connections. Both parties are bought and sold in every election. Lobbyist and their bribes carry more weight than public outcry or moral obligation.

Our country is run by greedy, power hungry goons that see themselves as a higher class of people than the rest of us. They will never tell us this directly, because they know we would not stand for it. However, quite often politicians slip up and their inhuman lack of compassion shows through. For example, during hurricane Katrina one of the worst disasters in our nation's history, a member of the Bush family showed just how much compassion the ruling class has for the rest of us. While visiting an overcrowded refugee shelter in Houston, Barbara Bush said on live television *"What I'm hearing, which is sort of scary, is that they all want to stay in Texas. Everyone is so overwhelmed by the hospitality. So many of the people in the arena here, you know, were underprivileged anyway, so this is working very well for them."*[1]

This lack of compassion is just as prevalent in the Democratic Party as it is in the Republican Party, although the democrats try to portray themselves as the heroes of the working class. While running for president in 2008 Barack Obama showed his disdain for the working class of this country when speaking about the economic struggles in small towns. He Said *"You go into some of these small towns in Pennsylvania, and like a lot of small towns in the Midwest, the jobs have been gone now for 25 years and nothing's replaced them ... And it is not surprising then they get bitter, they cling to guns or religion or antipathy to people who are not like them or anti-immigrant sentiment or anti-trade sentiment as a way to explain their frustrations."*[2] Instead of addressing the serious concerns that these people had, Obama ridiculed them showed a total lack of respect for their lifestyle as well as some of their natural born rights.

The current two party systems is not just failed, it is inherently corrupt. The very concept of representative government itself is in no way free. Our elections are ceremonial at best. When power changes hands between political parties only the banner changes, the agenda stays the same. Regardless of which party is in control war, oppression and corruption is the dominant policy. Outside of the two "main" political parties there are some decent hardworking politicians out there who are actually trying to do the right thing. These independent parties would win by a landslide in every election if only there was an even playing field. But the playing field is far from even, most people do not even realize that there are more than two parties to vote for! They get confused when they enter the polls and see there is more than just two options!

In 2008 there was a great deal of hype surrounding the possibility of there being the first African American or woman president. All that hype was of course surrounding the pro war, pro globalization corporate candidates Barack Obama and Hilary Clinton. Meanwhile, there was a black woman with much more progressive ideas running for the same office. Cynthia McKinney represented the green party in that year's election and wanted to end the war, end the illegal income tax, legalize marijuana, and clean up Wall Street. These are all issues that would appeal to your average American in such a way that if she were given a shred of media coverage or an equal chance to debate she would easily have been the most popular candidate. Unfortunately, new ideas that would benefit the people and take power away from the elite are smothered by politicians, Wall Street, and the media alike.

Barack Obama won the presidential election in 2008 because the public was fed up with what they saw as "Bush era republican policies" and they wanted a change, which is what Obama was promising. The people were tired of wars, corporate corruption, and police state legislation like the patriot act. Obama promised to put an end to all that, but as soon as he was "elected" he forgot about his promises and continued business as usual in Washington. Nothing changed about foreign or economic policy, more troops were sent to war, more lies were told and more bailouts were given to corporations who were responsible for the economic collapse. The democrats and republicans may have some small insignificant differences that play on people's emotions, but when it comes to all the important things that effect everyday life for average people there is a "bipartisan consensus" to protect elite business interests. This basically means that there is an agreement between both parties that they will not budge on issues that affect the global elite and their corporations.

This bipartisan alliance against the working class citizens results in a one party system that gives the illusion of being a two party system. This leaves no choice for the majority of the country who just want to live honest lives without wars and Wall Street scandals. Sadly, that is not an option here in the "land of the free"; we do not have a choice about those things. The only thing that Obama *apparently* did in the best interest of the American people was his highly publicized healthcare reform. Yet the changes in the healthcare system were primarily to benefit the large pharmaceutical and insurance industries that are extremely powerful in Washington. None of that really ended up mattering though, because the promised legislation never even became a reality anyway.

The democrats and the republicans are like the Crips and the Bloods of the political realm. One is Red, One is blue and it is a bad idea to get them in the room with one another, but when it comes down to it, they're both gangsters in a turf war. The democrats may provide a maternalistic form of authoritarianism while the republicans offer a more paternalistic authoritarian approach, but both options are still authoritarian. This country cannot take four more years of madness, war, and corruption. This volley back and forth between red evil and blue evil has brought our society to the brink of total collapse. Both evils only offer us more of the same corruption that got us into the mess we are in. It is not difficult to see that democrats and republicans represent two sides of the same oppressive coin. It is like being forced to choose between Coke and Pepsi, when what you really want is a glass of water. Both options given are the same well-disguised poisonous garbage while the healthy alternative is left completely out of the discussion.

QUOTE SOURCES AND SUGGESTED READING
----
[0] The Columbia dictionary of quotations - Robert Andrews (1993)
[1] Floodlines: Community and Resistance from Katrina to the Jena Six By Jordan Flaherty, Amy Goodman (2010)
[2] An Election to Remember: Obama, Clinton and the Never Ending Primary of 2008 - Kyle W. Bell (2009)
[SR1] A Peoples History Of The United States Of America by Howard Zinn
[SR2] Matrix of Power by Jordan Maxwell

"If you want government to intervene domestically, you're a liberal. If you want government to intervene overseas, you're a conservative. If you want government to intervene everywhere, you're a moderate. If you do not want government to intervene anywhere, you're an extremist."
- Joseph Sobran [0]

Beyond the Good Guy and the Bad Guy

The history books show a world drama in which the good guys and the bad guys battle it out for military and economic supremacy. Those who fit into the good guy role change depending on which nation's history book you are reading. Each story is very different yet all of them have their own respective "official account" of what has happened in the past. These official versions of events are always handed down to the people by the governments and rulers who play starring roles in these historical dramas. This situation shows an extreme conflict of interest and bias on the part of those who are writing history. The issues are crafted to shift blame, whitewash crimes against humanity, and project a good guy/bad guy mentality. This results in a cartoonish view of history where war, conquest, and blind nationalism are painted as laws of nature.

It is this good guy/bad guy mentality that shields most of us from the truth and brutality of what has taken place at the hands of politicians and monarchies. These labels attach a characteristic image to historical "leaders' and allow us to skip right over the issues that made these people who they are. Regardless of nationality, political party or belief system our world "leaders" are responsible for the most unspeakable crimes against humanity.

The prepackaged history that is fed to us insists that entire countries were to blame for the atrocities that were committed by various political organizations in the past. However, it is the specific policies, attitudes, systems, and leaders of these movements that are to blame for these social injustices, not their flag, nationality, or country. It is the use of institutionalized control systems that are responsible for the darkest, most shameful events in history. In the name of socialism, communism, democracy or just plain old "progress" our governments have created social inequality and genocidal military machines to expand their dominance over the human family.

The most ironic example of this situation exists within the historical American portrayal of the Nazi party. Most people in America have a negative opinion of the Nazi party from the third Reich in Germany and rightfully so. This was a political system responsible for genocide, racism, extreme social dominance, and dehumanizing programs that terrorized the whole planet. What is interesting about this situation however is that American history does not necessarily condemn the Nazis social policies, but only sheds light on the political party and the bad guy?

Following the cold war the western democratic governments presented the idea that the authoritarian rulers of Europe and Asia were so harsh because that is just how people in those countries were. In reality the atrocities that were committed under authoritarian rule are typically carried out against the wishes of the public. If we look beyond the good guy/bad guy mentality that we have been taught to accept we can see that both sides of the fence are responsible for the same horrors. Each government has their own brand of torture, imperialism, and greed, while the average citizens are scared, docile people who just want peace.

It is important for us to take a hard critical look at the policies that all governments are carrying out instead of just identifying with nationalistic labels. There are no "good guys" in war, anyone who is responsible for genocide, poverty or extreme social dominance should not be exempt from criticism because of the flag that they fly. This is the kind of attitude that Hitler expected of his people and this is the same attitude that the US government is expecting from us. If the United States government participates in genocide, torture and terrorism which official records show that they do, then they are in reality no better than the Nazis. This is obvious when seeing what our government did to the Native's during colonization, Africans during the slave trade and Japanese during World War 2.

In 1942 Executive order 9066 was passed by Franklin Roosevelt that called for the "relocation" of Japanese Americans living within the United States. It was this executive order that allowed the US government to keep hundreds of thousands of Japanese Americans in internment camps for the duration of the war. These Internment camps were eerily similar to those used in Germany by the Nazis, yet these details are many times left out of our history books. The Americans were never on any kind of moral high ground in World War 2, they were just as bad as the Nazis, and they still are.

The only thing that sets modern day America apart from Nazi Germany is the different flag, different corporate economic system, and a different set of gimmicks and scapegoats. Both are examples of institutionalized control systems that lied to their citizens so they could expand their empires across the world. Both empires used racism, propaganda, and economic warfare to control their enemies as well as their own citizens. We have seen the detrimental impact that these dominating control systems have had on societies in the past so we must have the good sense to put an end to this cycle of tyranny. Any regime that wages wars creates poverty, and exploits people is inherently evil, regardless of what flag they are waving or what is written in their constitution.

QUOTE SOURCES AND SUGGESTED READING
----
[0] Spam Revisited - Scott Horner (2004)
[SR1] Asian Americans and the Supreme Court: a documentary history by Hyungbychan Kim (1992)
[SR2] And the Truth Shall Set You Free by David Icke (1997)

"In a time of universal deceit, telling the truth is a revolutionary act."
- George Orwell [0]

Classified Corruption

Since the beginning of history our "leaders" have been corrupt and have committed horrible acts. The atrocities that we are actually aware of are most likely a drop in the bucket compared to what has actually taken place. If everything our "leaders" ever did wrong had actually surfaced the political situation in the world would be drastically different then it is today. Just a small amount of information exposing the corruption that exists within our government can have a profound impact on how whole civilizations view political policy. It is for this reason that most governments have large bureaucracies and public relations firms to clean up their tracks. This is why the vast majority of their actions are considered "classified" and hidden from the public.

According to Minnesota Governor Jessie Ventura there are over 16 million documents that are classified annually by the US government. Their argument for keeping information secret is that it is for our own protection or matters of national security. They are basically saying that they do not want their enemies to know what their military plans and capabilities are. This excuse is viciously abused so they can carry out unpopular policies without the knowledge of the American people. If the people were to fully understand the extent to which the government is going against their wishes they would realize that they have absolutely no control in the decisions that their "leaders" make.

Today this government secrecy is just as prevalent as it has ever been, but now with the explosion of the internet ordinary citizens have the power to expose the corruption that exists within the upper echelons of society. In the current struggle against globalism and western imperialism a journalist by the name of Julian Assange has made incredible progress in exposing the sick reality of the war machine. He developed a website called "Wikileaks" where he published politically sensitive material that would otherwise not have been available to the public. The pentagon and other military organizations that have been exposed through this website have been persistently trying to get it shut down since its inception. Institutions threatened by Wikileaks have even fabricated false criminal charges against Assange and have run an extensive media smear campaign. American citizens have been told to stay away from this website as it is "dangerous," but only because once these files are released, the truth is out there for everyone to see, thus putting the establishment in great danger.

War is always a sham, and the end of war usually comes not when one side defeats the other but when the public learns the truth about what is going on. During the Vietnam War, a famous whistleblower named Daniel Ellsberg smuggled a 7,000 page top-secret study revealing the true nature of what was going on in Vietnam. This study would come to be known as "the pentagon papers." The pentagon papers played a major role in ending the pointless Vietnam War and the corrupt Nixon presidency. More recently a brave soul by the name of Bradley Manning has been accused of providing Wikileaks with classified files that showed video evidence of war crimes.

Manning is a United States soldier who saw the corruption in the Middle Eastern conflict first hand and did what he knew was right for humanity. Fearing that more rogue soldiers would divulge their secrets, the US military wanted to intimidate any future whistleblowers from surfacing. They made an example of Bradley Manning by kidnapping him and keeping him detained in a foreign country where he was subject to torture and not protected by US law. At the time I am writing this Bradley Manning has yet to be released.

The documents that surfaced after Manning's arrest showed mass corruption in the highest levels of government in most major world powers. The United States military was exposed for their brutality in Iraq and Afghanistan; there was even video footage of US soldiers firing on civilians. Ironically the soldiers in the film have not been brought to justice, but the person who allegedly released the footage is being held in a military prison. Other documents showed private conversations between diplomats that exposed such incriminating information that the pentagon tried to hack Wikileaks just before the files were released. Although the pentagon was able to temporarily down their server the Wikileaks crew simultaneously sent all the information to various news organizations all over the world. These diplomat files revealed that the United States and their allies were funding and weaponizing their so-called enemies and even carrying out espionage missions against the United Nations.

The government was outraged at the release of these reports, but only because they do not want to be held accountable for their actions and do not want the public to know what they are really up to. This was around the same time that Jay Rockefeller was attempting to impose draconian online restrictions while saying that the internet should have never been invented. Whistleblower organizations like Wikileaks should be applauded and protected because they create the kind of transparency that is necessary for a truly free society. When our "leaders" carry out unpopular wars they are selling out the public for their own personal gain. That is why it is so important for everyday people to get involved and start questioning these policies and authoritarian organizations.

QUOTE SOURCES AND SUGGESTED READING
----
[0] My Few Wise Words of Wisdom (2000) - Charles Walker
[SR1] 63 Documents The Government Does not Want You To Read by Jesse Ventura

"I did not know I was a slave until I found out I could not do the things I wanted."
- Frederick Douglass [0]

Illegal Information

Many people today see the free speech issue in distorted terms; they do not realize that this is the right to dissent against the government. The freedom of speech has very little to do with hate speech, profanity, sexuality or any of the trivial issues that free speech has been recently marginalized to in the media. Free speech and the freedom to express disagreement with government policy is the very basis of a so-called "democracy." If a democracy is defined as the people having a voice in government, then that voice would come in the form of speech. For any kind of progress to be made in a democracy it is pretty safe to assume that the speech from the people would not just be cheers of praise, but would include criticism as well. The publics ability to be involved in government and dissent against the established order was intended to be one of the primary "checks and balances" of our political system.

Today we have a government that hides the truth from the people and only allows them to speak if they have a pro establishment agenda. They are able to constantly establish unpopular policies by keeping the details hidden or just spinning the story. If what they say about the founders of this country is true then they would be rolling over in their graves to learn that information vital to the democratic process is being hidden from Americans under the guise of national security. They came from a place where they were lied to by their "leaders" and apparently they did not want that kind of government for America. The founding fathers were not idealistically perfect and it is true that they were themselves slave owning aristocrats with their own agendas in manipulating the people. However, after fighting a war against the tyrannical British government, the prominent colonists wanted things to be as free as possible without threatening the existing class structure. This is still a rather nefarious attitude in my opinion, but it is sadly much more democratic than what we are seeing from government presently.

An informed public is necessary in a free society and in most of the world that is certainly not the case. This is why in the harshest of economic times the entertainment industry is still booming. The government and multinational corporations that support it want to keep the public distracted, entertained and uninterested in what is going on in the real world. Today there are a lot of shiny distractions to keep people from even seeking information and many forget that in order to have any kind of freedom they have to actually be paying attention to what is going beyond the government mandated media sources. As I discuss in other sections the political and financial interests have total control of the corporate media through the FCC and the few corporations that run the broadcasters.

Even if the public is paying attention and wants to be informed it is impossible for them to get a handle on what is really going on because the government keeps a good portion of their actions completely confidential. What we see take place through the legislature and through the mainstream media is a very small and whitewashed version of what actually takes place on a day-to-day basis between the governments and major corporations of the world. Whenever someone tries to bring the more sensitive information to light they are labeled as a criminal by the establishment just as the church labeled dissenters during the middle ages as heretics.

If activists, whistleblowers and even journalists are criminals then that would mean that any information that the establishment does not like would be illegal. When people who want to make positive political change are considered enemies of the state it seems that our system of government is anything but free. This authoritarian system resembles more of a fascist dictatorship where tiny elite have all the control, than a free society where the people rule themselves.

QUOTE SOURCES AND SUGGESTED READING
----
[0] The Black Americans: a history in their own words, 1619-1983 - Milton Meltzer (1987)
[SR1] Information Feudalism: Who Owns the Knowledge Economy? By Peter Drahos

"Never be deceived that the rich will allow you to vote away their wealth."
- Lucy Parsons [0]

Who Owns Congress?

The rise of corporate lobbyists and special interest groups in the 20th century has encouraged further political corruption in a system that was already being used to oppress the common people to begin with. Although, at least the politicians from Americas heyday were somewhat emotionally invested in the decisions they made. Today, politicians are rarely informed about the issues they are voting on, sometimes they do not even know what they are voting on. They simply vote however their lobbyists and PR consultants tell them to. In most western pseudo-democracies, the lower classes are able to vote between various aristocrats to rule over them, but there is never a chance for the working people to actually have a say in specific legislation. This process gives the public the illusion that they actually have a say in politics so they are more likely to accept the unfair conditions of their society. In most countries where this takes place the ruling elite actually tells the public that they are living in a free society and that their opinion matters to avoid the kind working class backlash that is common in open dictatorships.

The aristocracy in America is always changing their figureheads through elections, but the corporate interests that pay these figureheads always remain the same. Under the circumstances regardless of which party or politician is in office the agenda will be set by the corporate interests who are silently controlling the government through making large financial contributions. In order to make sense of this process it is important to know what a special interest group is and how they operate. These groups have also been referred to as lobbyist and they work for various corporations to "persuade" lawmakers into devising legislation and voting for or against different bills that would affect the business that they are representing. The persuasion usually comes in extremely large contributions that many times far exceed the politician's salary. So for the politician to keep their real source of income flowing they have to vote along the lines of whichever corporate agenda that they are following.

In theory, the legislators that are essentially taking bribes from these large corporations are supposed to be voting in accordance to the wishes of their constituents. Yet it is becoming more and more apparent that what is important to the public is of no concern to the politicians, they are more concerned with pleasing their special interest groups so they can continue to collect their bribes. Typically, what is in the best interests of the public conflicts with the best interest of the corporations, and nine times out of ten the public's concerns are overlooked and the special interest groups get their way.

Every day in the halls of congress, these groups are pressuring politicians to create laws that would benefit their corporate bosses. In many cases whole packages of bills are actually written by the lobbyists, not even read by congress and then voted on according to who is paid off by who. Meanwhile, the

American people have no representation in this process. We are not welcome in the halls of congress to discuss our grievances with our "elected" officials. Even when we protest outside their offices and flood their phone lines with pleas of mercy these crooked weasels still give their vote to the highest bidder with little regard for the welfare of the American people.

Among the most powerful lobby groups in the country are Monsanto, big oil and pharmaceuticals, but the political power of banking trumps them all. The financial sector by far has the most powerful special interest groups in the United States government. Above all else our politicians cater to the financial sector, which has resulted in a government that is completely controlled by Wall Street banks. With that in mind, it makes perfect sense that every financial branch of our government is filled with people from Goldman Sachs, Merrill lynch, Bank of America, Citigroup and other mega banks. The people that are in charge of making all the financial decisions in our government and even those who are in charge of regulating wall street have either came from wall street banking firms themselves or they are deeply in bed with them.

Since the elite insist on having their way they have found (and created) various loopholes in our political system which allows them to buy votes in congress without technically doing so. They do this by referring to their payments as "donations" instead of what they really are, bribes. Beyond this tricky wordplay special interest groups rarely even try to keep their agenda a secret. It is common knowledge that lobbyists are in constant contact with our politicians and make a lot of money pushing corporate policies through congress.

QUOTE SOURCES AND SUGGESTED READING
----
[0]Lucy Parsons: Freedom, Equality & Solidarity - Writings & Speeches, 1878-1937
[SR1] While We Sleep; A Story of Government Without Law by Alan R. Adaschik
[SR2] Washington on $10 Million A Day: How Lobbyists Plunder the Nation by Ken Silverstein
[SR3] Selling Out America's Democracy: How Lobbyists, Special Interests, and Campaign Financing Undermine the Will of the People by Alan L. Moss
[SR4] Obamanomics: How Barack Obama Is Bankrupting You and Enriching His Wall Street Friends, Corporate Lobbyists, and Union Bosses by Timothy P. Carney

"I never would have agreed to the formulation of the Central Intelligence Agency back in forty-seven, if I had known it would become the American Gestapo."
- Harry S Truman [0]

Illegitimate Bureaucracy

In the 100 years since our country was taken over by the banking interests our government has sprawled into a collection of independently ran bureaucracies that operate outside of the checks and balances of the United States constitution. Since these political extensions of the government are not held accountable by the taxpayers they have grown out of control and have become one of the biggest obstacles in between the American people and freedom. The CIA, the FBI, the FCC, and the Department of Homeland Security are just a few of the organizations that are working together to expand the American empire and create a controlling police state at home.

Every single one of these organizations are unconstitutional and they were only created as a means to bypass the checks and balances that our government is supposed to have. Their public relations presents the idea that these organizations are run through the American government on behalf of the people. This is not true, the government usually has no oversight over these organizations, and they often work closely with foreign intelligence agencies and corporations. The CIA works very closely with the UK's MI6 and Israel's Mossad on projects that the president might not even know anything about. Furthermore, even if the government did have some sort of say in what was going on with these bureaucracies that would not mean that the public had a say, because the government does not represent the public.

The CIA is by far the most powerful and the most corrupt division of the white house and many believe that they have more influence than even the president or congress. On a daily basis the CIA is responsible for overthrowing democratically elected governments by stealth all over the world, conducting experiments on its own citizens and carrying out other clandestine missions. Many people on the inside have seen the unacceptable policies carried out by this organization and have spoken out to expose the truth. Former "economic hit men" like John Perkins have come to the public with stories of how they were employed by the CIA to wreak havoc in the affairs of countries that refused to allow our corporations to harvest their natural resources.

Dehumanizing social programs like project MK Ultra and the Tuskegee experiments have been exposed and show the CIA to be criminally responsible of human rights violations. These elaborate programs and military exercises are all paid for by the American taxpayers who are not allowed to know what their money is being used for. This is the same government agency that makes billions of dollars selling weapons and drugs on the black market all over the world.

Since the false flag attacks on the trade centers in New York in 2001 the government has created even more bureaucracies to drain taxpayer money and further destroy the constitution. In the aftermath of the trade center attacks the

Bush administration put the Department Of Homeland Security in place. This organization had been a goal shared by the elite and the CIA for years and 9/11 gave them the opportunity to carry out their plan. By far the worst policy that we have been handed by Homeland Security is the Patriot Act. This piece of legislation was forcefully passed through congress and takes away a good majority of the personal liberties that we are supposedly guaranteed through the Bill of Rights. Because of this piece of legislation the government is now allowed to spy on its own citizens without warrants, and even worse it allows them to detain someone indefinitely and torture them without even charging them of a crime. This is the future that the government is building for us through their many new militant branches.

To keep the details of our reconstructed unconstitutional government secret there is yet another senseless bureaucracy in place, the federal communications commission. This organization exists solely to censor information that appears through the mainstream media. Through the FCC the government is able to select what information is broadcast through television and radio. If a broadcaster should put out information that the FCC did not approve they will be heavily fined and in some cases lose their communications license. This is similar to the techniques that have been used in communist Russia and China to keep the public in the dark about political issues. The FCC is constantly trying to establish new laws to limit free speech and expand their power over other aspects of media.

The founders of America specifically designed the constitution to limit the power and size of the government. By creating bureaucracies that are immune to the checks and balances of the United States constitution, the establishment has undermined the democratic process and taken away our right to have any real impact on political affairs, the very little impact that we had to begin with, that is. These organizations are absolutely unacceptable and we must demand that they are put to an end immediately.

QUOTE SOURCES AND SUGGESTED READING
----
[0] Winter is Coming - James Goulding (2003)
[SR1] Confessions of an Economic Hit Man by John Perkins

"Those who would give up essential liberty to purchase a little temporary safety deserve neither liberty nor safety."
- Benjamin Franklin [0]

Fascism...For your safety

Recently there has been a lot of discussion about capitalism in the news and among activists. Many people are taking stances on either one side of the issue or the other, but very few are stopping to consider the fact that capitalism may have never even existed. This concept may come as a surprise to some, but it should not. If you examine most of the words used to describe our society such as democracy, freedom, representative, or capitalism, you will find that these words are simply abstract euphemisms that are used to disguise the true nature of authoritarian civilization.

We are supposed to believe that we are represented by people who do not represent us, that we are somehow "free" in a situation where we are constantly being exploited and ordered around. Much in the same way that we are told we are "free" in our personal lives, we are also told that we are "free" in our financial lives. The word "democracy" is used to make our oppressive political system seem more benevolent and legitimate, while the term "capitalism" is used to give the impression that we operate under a "free market" economy. Obviously, neither is true.

Capitalism itself has been defined many different ways, but the rights to private property, as well as private production of goods and a free market economy, cross over between all of these definitions. Currently none of the above rights are being fully respected in the United States and most Western countries that claim to be capitalist. Sure, at face value it may seem like these ideas are prevalent in Western culture, but when you take a look at property taxes, government subsidies for big corporations and the mountain of red tape faced by entrepreneurs it should become painfully obvious that capitalism has probably never existed in this country; perhaps it has never even existed in this world.

The system that we have in place today could more accurately be called fascism, mercantilism, or cartelism. These words describe a system where the elite use their power in government to control the rest of society, as well as prop up their businesses by eliminating competition through the political system. The monolithic corporations that now exist would have never been able to grow into what they are today without the help of government intervention and protection. Without government intervention, the infamous lobbyists in Washington would become obsolete because there would no longer be any ability to manipulate the marketplace through bribes or coercion. Government intervention and protection is the primary means by which the world's biggest corporations have devastated their competition and developed massive monopolies.

For any authoritarian government to stay in power they must convince their subjects that they are providing them with safety and security. This is the typical public relations scheme of every oppressive government, the idea that they are providing worthwhile services. This is sadly a myth. The government does not provide services, they monopolize services. In other words, they make sure that they are the only organization that can provide schools, hospitals, roads and other utilities to the public because this creates a situation where the people are completely dependent upon the state for survival. This does not mean that a government is the only type of organization that is capable of providing these services. In fact community groups and entrepreneurs would most likely do a far better job at providing these services because they would actually be judged by the integrity of their work, unlike politicians and corporations who get paid regardless.

In fascist countries there is really no line between government and big corporations; both types of organizations use legislative power to establish and maintain monopolies. When it comes down to it, both of these organizations rely on violence and threats of violence as a means of getting their way in the marketplace. Essentially, the government is an organization that is used to justify violence, from the military to the tax collectors to the police. In most cases this violence is used on behalf of the corporate class, this is how these two interests work in concert to screw over the American people. This constant use of force is said to be keeping us safe, but in reality it just instigates further conflict and makes our lives more chaotic and violent.

Often times when the government is providing a service they are actually doing a very poor job, but no one can really tell the difference because there is no competition to judge it by. If you look at the goals that government organizations apparently set out to achieve, you will see that they always fail miserably. Therefore, if the government is claiming to provide maximum safety and security, it would be safe to assume that this goal will not be achieved. In the most authoritarian countries where the "leaders" claim to have established an extreme level of security, things are actually very unsafe and citizens in these kinds of countries live in constant fear. Just because there is a very high level of control does not mean that there will be adequate safety or order within a society.

The most controlling type of government in today's world is without a doubt a fascist one. Fascism is defined as an authoritarian system of government that has strong nationalist and corporatist values. Fascist governments often have strong military cultures and use force to establish themselves as authority figures, both at home and abroad. A Fascist government never refers to themselves as such; to do so would be to admit that they run unjust and oppressive regimes. Fascism exists in many economic systems that claim to be capitalist or communist and can develop even in countries that call themselves democratic. In fact, most fascist "leaders" tell their people that they live in a free and democratic society so the public takes their grievances to the polls, instead of taking them into the streets where they could actually make an impact. Currently one of the most fascist nations on Earth is called the "Democratic Republic of North Korea." Likewise, the governments in America and the European Union are some of the most fascist regimes in history, yet they still claim to operate under systems of "capitalism" or "democratic socialism." Like anything else in politics and economics, it is a word game that is designed to disguise the truth.

When the conditions for Fascism begin to develop in a country, the public is told that the increased security, taxation, militarization, and corporatism is for their own good. This is of course always an insidious and blatant lie, if history shows us anything it is that increased government power and control is never in the best interests of the people.

The public is needed to run the factories, fire the rifles, build the bombs, and develop the empire, so for them to do all of this they have to be thoroughly convinced that it is in their best interest somehow. This is the only way a fascist regime can stay in power, by convincing their subjects that the institutions that are in place to enslave them are actually there to protect them. The easiest way to do this is to create a culture of fear, where people are so afraid that they allow the government to take extreme measures in the name of safety. This has been admitted by various politicians, even the former Secretary of Homeland Security Tom Ridge admitted that he was pressured to raise terror alerts to help Bush win the 2004 presidential reelection.

In the decade since 9/11 the terror hype has led to the rollout of a massive surveillance grid, draconian security legislation, multiple wars, and a police state that would have been considered martial law two decades ago. This fear that is generated is nothing but baseless hype; technically you are statistically more likely to be killed by your own government than by a foreign terrorist. According to the National Safety Council you are 8 times more likely to be killed by a police officer than by a terrorist, 17,600 times more likely to die from heart disease and 404 times more likely to die in a fall. Crossing the street, having sex with strangers, driving to work, or having a surgical procedure is seriously more dangerous for the average American than any existing terrorist threat in the world.

Unfortunately most Americans do not realize that the biggest threat to their happiness is not a foreign enemy but the tyrants in charge of their government. Early US president James Madison warned *"If Tyranny and Oppression come to this land; it will be in the guise of fighting a foreign enemy."* [1] Then 2 centuries later George W. Bush told the Iraqi people *"Your enemy is not surrounding your country, your enemy is ruling your country."* [2] Most Americans did not understand the sad irony in Bush's statement, because it was something that could be said for Americans as well. Although George Bush was just a puppet, it was his presidency that brought us the TSA, The Department of Homeland Security, The Patriot Act, and other authoritarian measures.

Police brutality and bureaucratic authoritarianism are now commonplace in America, and nearly every public place is now monitored. It is very rare for a terrorist to be stopped or apprehended with the help of the new laws and surveillance equipment, but it is very common for these measures to help law enforcement fine or otherwise penalize citizens for nonviolent infractions. With this in mind it should be very easy to see what the true intention behind the growing police state is, and who it is really intended for. It is not intended for the terrorists, but for me and you.

Today the most cutting edge technology is being used to set up intricate databases to catalog and keep records on every person on the planet. This is typical of fascist societies, the very same kind of measures were seen in Nazi Germany and Soviet Russia. The citizens of both countries were in constant fear of terrorist attacks, and helplessly gave up all their civil liberties to control freak governments, who then in turn carried out mass genocides against their own citizens. Joseph Stalin himself revealed the plan quite clearly saying *"The easiest way to gain control of a population is to carry out acts of terror. The public will clamor for such laws if their personal security is threatened."* [3] Adolph Hitler Echoed *"Terrorism is the best political weapon for nothing drives people harder than a fear of sudden death."* [4].

Surely an authoritarian ruler would never get away with making such a bold public statement in today's world, so nowadays they keep these kinds of thoughts to themselves. Both countries also had extremely brutal police states set up, using the best of the day's technology to keep their herds in line. The security grid in Nazi Germany was truly unprecedented due to the regimes access to advanced technologies such as IBM's famous Hollerith machine. The function of this machine was innocent in nature; it was merely a counting and organizing machine. But the Nazi party used this technology to keep track of their population and easily identify people that they saw as a threat. As I discussed earlier this was the machine that numbered human beings who were to be put in concentration camps.

The Hollerith was just the World War 2 era of big brother technology, but tools have been used for these kinds of oppressive purposes throughout history. Before the Hollerith there was the first official census in Ancient Rome and today we have RFID transmitters. RFID stands for Radio Frequency Identification, and RFID transmitters are tiny microchips that send and receive information via radio waves. These chips are already being used by corporations like Wal-Mart to keep track of merchandise and there are also various political organizations suggesting that they actually be used for tracking citizens.

The Verichip Corporation is the company who has developed the technology that is currently being tested in human beings. Thousands of people throughout the world have already been implanted with these chips for clinical research, incarceration or military and medical purposes. The VeriChip Corporation advertises the implantable microchip as a method of accessing medical records in an emergency, for use as a payment device, and as a way to control entrance to secure facilities. However, aristocrats like Nicholas Rockefeller and other members of the Trilateral Commission, Bilderberg Group and Council on Foreign Relations have said they want to implant the whole population with microchips for more social control.

In 2009 the extensive and controversial health care bill that was championed by the Obama administration actually discussed beginning the process of micro chipping the population. In section 2521 of bill HR3200 you will find the following information: "The Secretary shall establish a national medical device registry (in this subsection referred to as the 'registry') to facilitate analysis of postmarked safety and outcomes data on each device that is or has been used in or on a patient; or a class II device that is implantable, life-supporting, or life-sustaining." In other words a database will be built to store information that will be gathered from a "self-powered implantable device, "which is the very definition of an RFID transmitter.

Implantable RFID chips are not just an attack on our civil liberties and an obvious attempt to dominate the public, but they also cause extreme health hazards. In many cases malignant tumors have developed in people as a result of radio signals constantly flowing through their body to an implanted microchip. Despite the dangers that are associated with this technology major corporations and political organizations are still pushing for the widespread application of the RFID program because it would allow them to hold incredible power over the entire population. Anyone who has a chip implanted will have all of their medical, financial, and personal information reviewed and controlled by the corporations that develop the technology and the political organizations that run the database. These groups have rolled out massive public relations campaigns to promote this program, using the mainstream media that they own and control. Advocates for VeriChip implementation have been on various news programs praising RFID technology and suggesting that the public have these chips implanted in their newborn children for "safety" purposes.

The advertising campaign that has been designed for the public is seemingly innocent, but the personal admissions of CFR and banking cartel members show the sinister nature of the VeriChip program. By their own admissions the goal of the program is to get everyone chipped so the whole society can be controlled by the elite at the flick of a switch. Just before 9/11 Nicolas Rockefeller revealed such a plan to politician and film director Aaron Russo in a telephone conversation. Rockefeller told Russo that the banking elite wanted to reduce the world population by at least half in the next few decades and would do so by waging "endless" wars in the oil rich middle east and taking away civil liberties at home. When Russo refused to join and said he had no interest in "enslaving people, "Rockefeller replied by asking him why he cared about the "serfs." This was to be the end of their political and personal relationship, and in the following years Russo worked to expose his former associate's evil plans. Russo changed his whole career path and became an activist for the truth movement until he died of cancer in 2007.

We may not personally be able to stop these elitist from building atomic weapons, but every single one of us has the individual power to refuse participation in the RFID program. They will phase this program in by first requiring all citizens to carry a national ID card that they will keep on them at all times. Once the national ID card is in use they will then begin installing the ID cards with RFID chips. Then eventually once the public is already familiar with the technology they will begin to push mandatory implementation of RFID chips. This is the biggest danger to human rights in the whole course of history; if we participate in this evil scheme and allow them to commit this extreme invasion of privacy then we are giving away our children's freedom and lives. Boycott stores like Wal-Mart that are using these devices. Refuse to participate in the national

ID program and refuse to have RFID tracking devices be a part of your life at all.

The RFID prospect may sound futuristic but this is something that is already in progress. Even today we can see the growing control that the state has in our everyday lives. Before we wake up in a world of unimaginable oppression we need to reverse this trend by continuing to protest laws like the patriot act and stand up against illegitimate bureaucracies such as the TSA, FBI, CIA, ATF, and DHS. If we conform to this insanity and do not voice our opinions then we are slaves with no hope of salvation, but if we stand up for what we deserve and what is right then we are only prisoners who still have a fighting chance. The difference between a slave and a prisoner is that a slave has no clue that they are in captivity, they think that is simply the way things are, and they can't do anything about it. The prisoner on the other hand understands that he is being held captive against his will and understands that there is a greater world beyond the bars.

QUOTE SOURCES AND SUGGESTED READING
----
[0] Respectfully quoted: a dictionary of quotations By Library of Congress
[1] Liberty Quotes By Christopher Kalabus page 56
[2] George Bush State Of The Union address 2003
[3] Vile Acts of Evil - Volume 1 - Banking in America By Michael A. Kirchubel
[4] Telling It Like It Is By Paul Bowden
[SR1] Snitch Culture: How Citizens are Turned into the Eyes and Ears of the State, Jim Redden [SR2] Orwell's Warning: The Greatest Amerikan Paradox By Erik Blair

"We cage the drunken car thief up like an animal, but if you accidentally invade the country of Iraq because you did too much blow in college and did not listen during the class on weighing the pros and cons of spotty intelligence, then you not only do not go to jail, you get a million-dollar book deal and your portrait in the Smithsonian."
– Lee Camp [0]

The Prison Industrial Complex

The prison industry is one of the fastest growing and top earning businesses in the United States. In the past 3 decades this enterprise has grown into a monstrous system of oppression that now houses over 2 and a half million people in the US. That is by far the largest prison population in the world, no country on earth has as many inmates as the "land of the free." Ironic is not it? Since 1991 the violent crime rate in America has dropped at least 20%, while the amount of people in prison has increased by 50% in that time. These numbers show that the rapid increase in prisoners is largely due to over prosecution of nonviolent crimes. This has nothing to do with "cleaning up the streets" or making our society safer, this is a big business and it is all about money. The prison system as it stands now does not make our society any safer, but instead turns average nonviolent offenders into hardened criminals by exposing them to such a harsh environment.

The sad truth is that the way our prison system has been structured has actually outlawed more than half of the US population. Nonviolent offenders have no place behind bars, if anything the savage conditions of prison will turn most people into violent offenders once they get out. Which is exactly what the prison establishment wants, return customers. The establishment that I'm referring to is the collection of state and private industries that make up the "prison industrial complex. " Billions of dollars are made every year in this industry, one company alone "Wackenhut Corrections" makes over a billion dollars a year and they are not even the biggest prison service in the country.

That is not even considering the many satellite businesses that surround this industry, there are over 1000 vendors that specifically sell correctional paraphernalia. Even local phone companies cash in on the operation and install payphones for free because those phones can generate 15,000 dollars per year just from each inmate making 1 phone call every day. Those companies are just the tip of the iceberg that is not even counting the police, lawyers, wardens, politicians, and food distributors that line their pockets through the incarceration of peaceful Americans.

Most of the people caught up in the prison system are from the working class and are doing time for petty nonviolent crimes. Usually if someone has enough money or influence they can avoid incarceration by cutting deals with the prosecution or paying off officials, this obviously is not an option for most Americans. It has always been rare for someone from the upper class to end up behind bars. In the middle ages peasants who were not able to pay high taxes or debts were thrown in dungeons called "debtors prisons", sometimes for their entire lives. Since these times incarceration has traditionally been a struggle of the working poor and lower classes and a tool for the ruling class to maintain power. It is quite common for political dissenters and protestors to be locked away simply for refusing to comply with the government, and in our culture it even goes several steps further.

The growing police state and the constant influx of oppressive, complicated laws are responsible for the massive increase in the prison population that has taken place over the past decade. Every single day for hundreds of years new laws have been spit out of our legislative system, most of which have been designed to benefit the ruling class who work in finance and politics. The average citizen has very little time to spend contributing to the legislative process and even if they did their opinion would hold very little weight next to the powerful lobby groups that dominate Washington. The ruling class is guilty of the most horrifying crimes against humanity and is responsible for the exploitation, displacement, and murder of millions of people. These are the biggest criminals on the face of the earth, but the prison system was not built for them, it was actually built BY them. So the legal system does not represent absolute moral authority like it claims to, but it is simply a tool that has been created by the elite to maintain dominance over the population.

Our legal system has been specifically designed to oppress and weaken the lower class so the elite can better control them. This is because the majority of the laws have been written by the establishment and most of the bureaucracies that enforce these laws have been created by them also. So they are the owners of this "casino," which means they call the shots. The inequality of the American prison system is illustrated by the high amount of illiterate, mentally ill, and unemployed people that are incarcerated. It seems that the "least employed" in our society are the ones that are more likely to end up in prison, their lack of privilege leaves them more vulnerable to getting caught up in the system.

70% of the prison inmates in America are illiterate, and about 80% have a history of substance abuse. Despite these numbers the amount of drug treatment programs have been cut in half and opportunities for education have been greatly reduced in the past decade. That is because their goal is not to rehabilitate these people and groom them into productive members of society; their goal is to keep as many people in the system as possible. This serves two purposes, the first of course being money and the second is dealing with social control. The underemployed people who have been mistreated by the system are the citizens who would be most likely to speak out against the injustice and inequality in our society. So if the establishment has them in and out of prison for most of their lives, chances are they will not be much of a threat, instead they will spend their time struggling to keep their heads above water in the corrupt legal system.

The worst thing about this whole situation is that this system is doing nothing to keep anyone safe. The propaganda that the police are "the good guys" here to "serve and protect" is the big lie that cloaks the violence and corruption of the state in an air of legitimacy. The first step to removing this false legitimacy and revealing the truth is to simply stop sugarcoating this violence in newspeak and stop pretending that the state actually does anything to prevent violent crime.

There are a lot of ideas and concepts in that last sentence, so let's delve deeper for a better understanding. As I alluded to earlier, a cold hard violent criminal is hard to come by in most holding cells and most county jails. This is because most people are naturally good and typically are not drawn to lives of violence until they are broken down and corrupted by years of moving through the system being treated like an animal. Another reason why there are not a whole lot of violent offenders in prison is because it is a lot of hard work to catch them!

Cops get paid the same for locking up a pothead as they do for locking up a serial rapist, as long as there is a warm body in the cell then Dudley Do-Right makes his quota. So it really makes sense that most cops go into work hoping for a good "easy" day where they do not get shot at. They are not benevolent saints that wake up in the morning and think about nothing else but trying to make the world a better place, although many of them may have convinced themselves of this much. Just like the rest of us, most cops take the easy way out in their day to day, which basically means letting thieves, murderers and rapists roam free while chasing around nonviolent offenders all day because they are easier to deal with and they pay the same.

Now onto the newspeak, which is one of the most fundamental propaganda tactics used to defend this growing police state. Luckily, this is one aspect that we do have a great deal of personal control over because instead of using the same deceptive language that police use to describe their actions, we can simply call it like we see it. Soft sounding words like "detainment," "arrest" and "police officer" subtly change our perception of the actions taken out against us. Police are people who are paid money to go around with weapons and force people to submit to the arbitrary edicts of a central government, so rightfully we should call these people mercenaries, instead of police, because that is what they are. Furthermore, when someone takes you from your home, or any other place that you want to be, they are kidnapping you and holding you hostage. Is this not exactly what happens when one of these mercenaries puts a nonviolent offender in a cage? Again, all these "legal fees" and "fines" are forms of extortion that are dressed up in pretty language to disguise the corrupt nature of what is actually taking place.

There are millions of solutions to these social problems that do not involve violence, unfortunately there just is not enough people out there trying to develop these solutions. Most of the population spends their time rationalizing the current system and learning how to cope with it instead of actually working to devise solutions that would improve our society. Luckily, more and more people are coming to the conclusion that it is time for our species to advance past this kind of brutal approach to dealing with crime.

Stefan Molyneux for example, is a philosopher and writer who has dedicated years of his life towards developing nonviolent solutions to the many social problems that are currently being butchered by the establishment. He has created dozens of future propositions for how life would work in a free society.

This includes the "*Dispute Resolution Organization*," or DRO, which is a system designed to deal with social problems in the most humane and voluntary ways possible. These social problems range from violent crime to trade and property disputes. This is just one person, and he has come up with plans that would replace every brutal aspect of the state with realistic and peaceful solutions. Maybe some of his ideas would work; maybe some of them would not. Personally, I think they are great ideas, but that is not the point. The point is, if one person is capable of coming up with a few simple ideas that have the potential to make human interactions more peaceful, then just imagine what we can come up with if we are openly talking about these issues and working them out together.

QUOTE SOURCES AND SUGGESTED READING
----
[0] Lee Camp – Moments Of Clarity (The Book)
[SR1] Adventures in Legal Land by Marc Stevens
[SR2] Stefan Molyneux at www.freedomainradio.com

"The war on drugs is a war on people... And people's rights are being violated. And your incarcerating and caging human beings often times who are simply victims of the sickness of addiction, Who have become sucked up in this giant war on drugs, Which in fact is a crime against humanity. The war on drugs is a war on people."
– Corporate Avenger [0]

Dare to Resist the War on Drugs

Addiction to mind numbing street drugs like opiates and amphetamines are definitely a serious problem that our generation must overcome in order to have control of our own minds. Although the establishment groups theses poisons in with psychedelics, they are actually nothing like psychedelics. While psychedelics elevate consciousness and have little physical effects on the body, synthetic street drugs diminish the consciousness and do considerable damage to the body. The addictive properties of these toxic substances cause extreme turmoil in the life of anyone who is caught in their grip. Heroin, cocaine and methamphetamines have enslaved a large portion of the lower class, who were just looking to momentarily ease the pain of poverty with substances that were everywhere in their communities.

The government has taken a strong public stance on the issue and has declared a "war on drugs, "whatever that means. Yet lower income communities continue to be flooded with drugs despite the harsh legal penalties that go along with their possession. In the two decades since the war on drugs began, evidence has surfaced that explains why the drug trade has continued to flourish. There have been many cases confirming that the CIA and DEA have been importing and exporting drugs all over the world for decades. Even with the testimony of ex agents and air traffic control operators the mainstream media has continued to ignore the evidence because they fear losing their jobs and ability to broadcast.

The first person to expose this secret operation was an air traffic controller by the name of Rodney Stich. While investigating CIA drug trafficking this former pilot became acquainted with a long list of ex agents that gave him classified information proving the CIA's involvement in importing drugs. Once Stich's research surfaced it exposed the true nature of the drug trade and encouraged other witnesses to come forward. The information that surfaced showed that the international drug trade was a booming business that the US and British covert organizations had a total monopoly over. Although Stich's work was all documented fact his story was covered up by the puppet media and most Americans never even heard about it. Since Stich there have been countless others who have spoken up and have subsequently been slandered by the media and attacked by the government.

In many cases the government and its agencies have gone beyond intimidation and have actually murdered witnesses. The most tragic of these situations to actually surface is the case of Kevin Ives and Don Henry, two innocent teenage boys who were murdered by police in august of 1987. The murder took place in a rural community just south of Little Rock Arkansas. The area is a hotbed for government drug smuggling activity and the boys accidentally stumbled upon a high profile drug deal-taking place. This high profile drug deal was actually involving several CIA assets and was being protected by local police. When police discovered that their operation was uncovered they quickly took out the witnesses. After shooting the two young boys in cold blood the police put their bodies on a set of train tracks and began a massive cover up that lasted several years.

Through her own investigation Kevin's mother Linda began to expose the conspiracy that was behind her son's death but has yet to bring the officers that committed these acts to justice. There were also 6 people who had information about these murders who were hunted down and killed by the CIA one by one so the plot could be kept under wraps. Keith Mckaskie, Jeff Rhodes, Keith Coney, Gregory Collins, Richard Winters and Jordan Ketelson were all closely involved in the case and had sensitive information regarding government involvement in drug trafficking. Every single one of these people died mysteriously in the years following the initial murders. This whole case and everything about it was ignored by the media and all of the politicians including the governor of Arkansas, who was Bill Clinton at the time. Clinton is said to also have very close ties to the drugs and ammunition that was coming in and out of the Mena Airstrip while he was working in the area.

Clintons extracurricular activities were exposed when a man named Larry Nichols was hired as marketing director of the Arkansas Development Finance Authority. Turns out that this organization was just a front for Clinton to launder black market money, and this all surfaced when Nichols was interviewed by the citizens for honest government organization. In the interview he said "For about two months I watched accounts accumulate money. And at the end of the month they zero-balanced. They're laundering drug money. There was a hundred million a month in cocaine coming in and out of Mena, Arkansas. They had a problem. They were doing so much money in cocaine, a hundred million. You, you create a problem in a little state like Arkansas. How do you clean one hundred million dollars a month? ADFA until 1989 never banked in Arkansas. What they would do is they would ship the money down to Florida, a bank in Florida that later would be connected to BCCI. They would ship money to a bank in Atlanta, Georgia, which by the way was later connected to BCCI. They would ship to Citicorp in New York, which would send the money overseas."[1]

Even with the media blackout the facts are on public record and government drug trafficking is so widespread that more cases are surfacing every day. In September of 2007 a CIA jet crashed in Mexico with 3.2 tons of cocaine onboard.

The jet was on its way from Bolivia when it was spotted by Mexican helicopters that followed in pursuit. The chase resulted in the crash of the jet and the seizure of the cocaine. Upon inspecting the wreckage site the Mexican authorities found no body or survivors but did find several thousand pounds of cocaine. The serial numbers on the plane were eventually traced back to a company that transported terrorists for the US government. This story is not uncommon; there have been many cases where government planes have crashed in south and Central America with tons of illegal drugs onboard. On April 10 2006 Mexican police seized a DC-9 aircraft that was carrying 5.5 tons of cocaine, flight records showed this aircraft to be another CIA "terrorist transport" plane that was used to transport drugs. The pilot of the DC-9 aircraft also managed to escape from Mexican authorities.

Many times in recent history the CIA has expanded its drug cartel to include the US military. During the Vietnam War the US government used their occupation as a basis for covert drug operations, which in turn helped fund the war and other secret projects. Drugs were transported on military aircraft and brought back to America, where they were eventually sold to the mafia and distributed on the streets. The same techniques are being applied today during the occupation of Afghanistan. When the US invaded Afghanistan in 2001 there was an immediate hike in the amount of heroin that was flowing out of the country. According to the United Nations Office of Drugs and Crime, after the US invasion in 2001 opium production in Afghanistan rose from 7,606 hectares in 2001 to 193,000 hectares in 2007. That is a 96% increase of opium production since the US has occupied the country. Now that the CIA has control of Afghanistan 93% of the world's heroin comes from inside its borders. It is certainly no coincidence that in recent history we have seen a surge of drug exportation from war torn countries that were being occupied by western nations. During the Vietnam War the area surrounding Vietnam was known as "The Golden Triangle," a hotbed for heroin production. Now the Golden Triangle has taken a back seat to the "Golden Crescent," which refers to the area in and around Afghanistan of course.

Historically it is extremely common for governments to import and export drugs to fund covert operations and control populations. While this corruption takes place it is always hidden from the public because it would create an obvious backlash and show the hypocrisy of government policy. After the years pass things come to the surface and it becomes more difficult for the establishment to keep their drug operations secret. It did not take many years for the details behind the opium wars in China to be exposed to the world. This was probably one of the most historically famous situations where drugs were used by a government to get extremely wealthy at the cost of impoverishing others.

During the opium wars the British government told their people that China was a threat to their way of life, but in reality the whole war was over the government trafficking drugs into Chinese ports. For years the British were making a fortune importing opium into China. The Chinese government was not happy about the opium trade considering its detrimental impact on their society, so they outlawed the drug in 1839 and tried to prevent British ships from importing the cash crop into their harbors. This attempt to clean up the Chinese harbors infuriated the British and they launched a full-scale naval attack on China. From 1839 all the way through to the 1850's there was intense fighting between these two countries until China was eventually defeated. Upon defeat China was forced to sign treaties that gave up their trade rights, opened up their ports to foreigners, and made the prohibition of opium completely impossible. These agreements would go down in Chinese history as "the unfair treaties," and rightfully so. This situation is ironically familiar to the current "opium war" being waged in the deserts of Afghanistan. Just before the US invasion of Afghanistan the Taliban made the cultivation of opium illegal just as the Chinese government did at the start of the opium wars.

As I'm writing this book there is a massive drug war developing around the Mexican border and thousands of innocent civilians are being killed. If it was not for drug prohibition this would not even be taking place, Mexico would not have descended into lawlessness and an untold number of lives could have been saved. By now it should also come as no surprise that the US government is heavily involved in the trafficking of these narcotics. In 2011 Mexican drug kingpin Zambada Niebla testified that his gang the "Sinaloa Cartel" was protected by US law enforcement for years before he was apprehended, the case is still pending today.

The war on drugs is an insult to the intelligence of the American people. There are mountains of evidence proving that the biggest importers of harmful, addictive, mind diminishing street drugs is the government. The drug laws that exist do not apply to the government agencies that bring these substances to our country. They are only designed to keep everyone else from this extremely lucrative business and give the establishment another reason to oppress people. We have seen this all before during alcohol prohibition, where the government, law enforcement, and organized crime were all working together, and making an unbelievable amount of money in the black market.

When black markets are created the crime rate goes up, taxes go up, prices go up and the police become more corrupt, all of this is inevitable. These are in fact the very consequences that any type of prohibition intends to create. To solve these problems all that we have to do is end all prohibitions, this would cripple the black market and drastically reduce violence. This would also drastically reduce the reach of the state, which is why it is looked at as such impossibility. Drug laws do not do anything to prevent drug problems in our society, they only encourage violence, raise prices and criminalize half of the population.

QUOTE SOURCES AND SUGGESTED READING
----
[0] Corporate Avenger – FBI FILE – Freedom is a state of mind
[1] Larry Nichols Interview with the citizens for honest government organization
[SR1] Why Our Drug Laws Have Failed: A Judicial Indictment Of War On Drugs by James Gray
[SR2] Smoke and Mirrors: The War on Drugs and the Politics of Failure by Dan Baum
[SR3] Drug War Crimes: The Consequences of Prohibition by Jeffrey A. Miron
[SR4] American War Machine: Deep Politics, the CIA Global Drug Connection, and the Road to Afghanistan by Peter Dale Scott

"Government: is derived from the Latin word gubernare, a verb, meaning —to control‖ combined with mente, a Latin noun, meaning mind. Government means: To control the mind."
- Anonymous [0]

Tricks of the Trade

There is a war that has been raging for longer than any other political or religious conflict on the planet, and that is the struggle between the aristocracy and the serfs, the "exploiters" and the "exploited". This elite class of politicians, bankers, and aristocrats has always been comprised of about 1% of the world's total population and for centuries each generation has spent their lives bitterly clutching onto their family's fraudulently acquired wealth. In order to continue a legacy of exploitation they concoct a wide variety of deceptive plots that mislead the public and push them to accept their financial servitude. The same kind of trickery is used to silence dissenting viewpoints and extinguish antiestablishment movements when they manage to gather enough public support. These people have lived in luxury at the expense of the masses for centuries so it should come as no surprise that they carry out mischievous deeds in order to uphold their public image and continue their slave driving traditions.

The economic system as we know it is the fundamental scheme used by the elite to keep the masses in servitude. The economy is their game, which they have created and maintained with no concern for the public interest. By nature a centralized economy favors monopolies and mega corporations that are owned by the richest people in the world. In today's economic climate it is nearly impossible for someone to start a small business and succeed because the big corporations have such an unfair advantage, due to government intervention and the use of force.

Most of the largest corporations in the world are exempt from taxes and regulations because of their heavy influence in politics. Many of these corporations even push for higher taxes and regulations through political favors as a clever way of stamping out their competition. This means that small businesses will suffer and everyone will end up working for some different corporation, earning a menial income instead of having the freedom to work for themselves and earn a decent living, or even having the ability to work for a locally owned business.

This is what our government calls "free trade" which basically enables the richest corporations to create monopolies all over the world and use any means to squash out the competition. When the competition disappears the decent paying jobs and low prices disappear with it. This results in economic depression that only affects the lower classes. American History is filled with cycles of long financial depressions due to the monopolization of industry. Many people believe that there was only one depression in the history of this country but there have actually been several each century. During these times of economic turmoil was where the elite greatly extended their fortunes by bleeding the lower classes and using them for slave labor.

These conditions within a society are enough to create rebellion among the underclass even if the elite does have the most elaborate public relations campaign in history, which seems to be the case today. During times of social unrest every facet of the establishment goes into self-defense mode and attacks any group that may threaten to disrupt the current order. This is especially true with law enforcement and the military. We are deceived into believing that they are in place to serve and protect the public but when push comes to shove it becomes obvious they are only here to serve and protect the elite and the status quo. Any time in history that oppressed people have peacefully resisted the establishment they were met with police in riot gear and soldiers with guns drawn. Police have attacked civil rights leaders, union workers and other peaceful protestors in America for over a century.

In 1970 the National Guard murdered four students and badly wounded a dozen others at Kent State College in Ohio. The Students had assembled to protest the United States senseless invasion of Cambodia when they were shot by troops; all of the victims were unarmed. This incident sparked outrage across the country and prompted millions of students to hold national strikes. The Kent State Massacre was not an isolated incident, to this day our government uses tax funded physical force against activist groups that are speaking out for the good of the people and the environment.

In most cases political protestors are nonviolent and do everything they possibly can to avoid clashes with the police. Demonstrators are well aware that they are out matched and are only assembling in groups and taking to the streets as a way of promoting their political ideas, this is the essence of free speech. This is an extremely powerful political freedom that is why it is met with such hostility from the establishment. Almost every single time there is a public demonstration the authorities are unsympathetic and use heavy force to discourage protests from taking place in the future.

However, they do not attack the mob with guns blazing because they know it will further expose their oppressive nature and add credibility to the revolutionary movement. So agent provocateurs are used to instigate physical altercations between activists and authorities. Agent Provocateurs are people that work for the authorities but pretend to be a part of an antiestablishment mob. While under cover these agents commit acts of violence and vandalism to give the police a pretense to use force against the demonstrators. Once the agent smashes one window or throws one rock on behalf of the group they have infiltrated, the authorities are able to send in the Calvary and turn the demonstration into a war zone.

Agent provocateurs have a long history of instigating violence at protests in the United States; this is why almost every time there is a public demonstration there are also police riots. The 19th century in America was filled with labor strikes and protests because of the horrible living conditions that new immigrants and the working poor had to endure while working in overcrowded factories. In

1886 there were 700,000 workers on strike throughout the US due to the inhumane conditions that the lower class faced working for the elite. That year in Chicago a large protest began on May 1st. Two days into the strike on May 3rd, 4 workers outside the McCormick Harvester company were indiscriminately killed by police during protests, and dozens of others were injured. The following day the protests grew as a result of the murders and prominent activists of the time began to call national attention to what was going on in Chicago.

The next day on May 4th a bomb was set off in the midst of the protests and although there was no indication of who was responsible for the bombing, the blame was placed on the demonstrators and a witch-hunt ensued. 8 of the most prominent antiestablishment speakers and writers of the time were rounded up for "inciting a murder" and executed. Their only crime was exercising their right to free speech and speaking out against the establishment. 3 of the 8 activists that were executed were speaking and were nowhere near the explosion; the other 5 were not even in town at the time. The evidence that has surfaced since the Haymarket incident show that the blast was most likely set by an agent provocateur, in order to give the establishment an excuse to silence the growing political movement that surrounded workers' rights.

This strategy is still used to this day, every year at political conventions police double agents have been exposed while posing as protesters. By turning the protests into violence the establishment is able to divert the attention of the protests away from the real issues and towards the chaos that is taking place in the streets. The media, which is merely a tool of the establishment, always paints protestors as violent and unreasonable people to keep their revolutionary messages from gaining political backing. An incident similar to the Haymarket bombing occurred in Greece in 2010 in the midst of antigovernment sentiments sweeping the nation. Agent Provocateurs set off two bombs in different government buildings and later blamed the bombing on youth revolutionaries to discredit their movement.

This practice again reared its ugly head in Wisconsin during massive union protests in the winter of 2011. Senator Scott Walker was extremely corrupt and was strong-arming the public into accepting austerity cuts. Austerity is a process where public services are cut but taxes, bailouts and inflation increases. In the midst of the protests an activist prank called Senator Walker pretending to be his billionaire financier David Koch, and recorded the conversation. The conversation was lengthy and among many revelations Senator Walker discussed the possibility of using agent provocateurs to justify the use of force on protesters.

When the audio of the conversation surfaced Madison Police Chief Noble Wray played damage control and issued a statement demanding answers from the embattled senator. His statement said "I spent a good deal of time overnight thinking about Governor Walker's response, during his news conference (Wednesday), to the suggestion that his administration 'thought about' planting troublemakers among those who are peacefully protesting his bill. I would like to hear more of an explanation from Governor Walker as to what exactly was being considered, and to what degree it was discussed by his cabinet members. I find it very unsettling and troubling that anyone would consider creating safety risks for our citizens and law enforcement officers.

Our department works hard dialoging with those who are exercising their First Amendment right, those from both sides of the issue, to make sure we are doing everything we can to ensure they can demonstrate safely. I am concerned that anyone would try to undermine these relationships. I have a responsibility to the community, and to the men and women of this department -- who are working long hours protecting and serving this community -- to find out more about what was being considered by state leaders." [1] I'm sure that the police chief had a lot of different things to say behind closed doors and only made this statement because the plot was exposed, but at this point only Scott Walker's involvement can be proven. Either way you can expect every government facing underclass uprisings to use this kind of deceptive terrorism as a tactic to maintain political power.

The political system itself is another arm of the elite used to control the masses. Most politicians are just puppets for the lobby groups and financial institutions who put them in office. Although they may have some power to actually make a difference for the people, they usually play the part and pander to the business interests who paid for their campaign. However, every once in a great while one of our "leaders" find a shred of humility in their soul and attempt to use their power for the good of the people. When this happens the elite becomes outraged and uses all their political, media and financial power to destroy the politician's reputation. When a president takes action that creates a serious enough disturbance among the elite they are typically assassinated under very suspicious circumstances. It is absolutely impossible to bring about any positive change by "working within" the parameters of the political system because the system is specifically designed to enslave the population and preventing anyone from actually doing anything about it.

When all else fails and the public finally begins to understand what the establishment is up to there is one final trick that they use to keep their power. When a revolutionary force rises amongst the people that cannot be stopped by the establishment, the establishment then pretends to accept the revolutionary force and assimilate their own organizations into that movement. This tactic dates back to ancient times and is used so frequently it is unbelievable that people haven't caught on yet. When the revolutionary message of early Christianity threatened to overthrow the Roman church, the church simply made the Christian savior a part of their religion so they could then shape the future of "Christian" ideology.

This same kind of takeover happened in the beginning of the 20th century with the first organized worker unions. When trade unions first originated they were very outspoken and were constantly demanding that radical changes be made to their social and political structures. Most of the people involved in these unions were also a political force in the country as well, most of that force being very critical of big business and government corruption. Trade unions really were making serious progress in changing the slave wage system that was an integral part of American life, so they were of course a problem for the establishment.

Back then the unionists were called "communists" or "anarchists," now surely today they would be called "terrorists." After years of reacting aggressively with trade unions the establishment decided to take another approach and they gave the leaders of the unions a limited amount of political pull and convinced them to use the electoral system to air worker disputes instead of striking and protesting. The establishment then got what they wanted, the unions may have kept their organization and their title, but they no longer went on strike or protested but directed all their energy into worthless elections. Sure union protests still take place, but nowadays they are only aimed at slightly tweaking the oppressive policy that is I place, as opposed to radically changing the whole system.

A similar situation took place during the civil rights movement for African Americans, at the very march on Washington where Martin Luther King JR. made his most famous speech, "I have a dream." When the government learned that the oppressed black people of the country were coming to Washington with revolution on their minds, they instantly switched up their approach and pretended to welcome the marching protestors with open arms. After the march Malcolm X describes how the protest was hijacked and watered down by the establishment. When speaking of President Kennedy he said *"that old shrewd fox said 'I will endorse it. I will welcome it. I'll help it, I will join it! This is what they did with the march on Washington....They joined it, they became a part of it, took it over. And as they took it over, it lost its militancy. It ceased to be angry, it ceased to be hot, and it ceased to be uncompromising. Why, it even ceased to be a march. It became a picnic, a circus. Nothing but a circus, with clowns and all... No, it was a sellout, it was a takeover. They controlled it so tight, they told those Negroes what time to hit town, where to stop, what signs to carry, what song to sing, what speech they could make, and what speech they could not make, and they told them to get out of town by sundown."*[2]

Malcolm X's description was spot on; even Martin Luther King JR. was insulted by how the civil rights march was taken over by the establishment. After the march on Washington was a letdown to the civil rights movement King began to call for a new wave of nonviolence that was "massive and militant," and it was not much after that when he was assassinated. Towards the end of his life due to his outspokenness on poverty and the Vietnam War he became a hot target for the FBI in their COINTELPRO operation. King received many threats from the FBI and it is widely speculated that the establishment did have a hand in his assassination.

Again but more recently, after the economic meltdown of 2008 an antiestablishment movement was brewing called the "tea party." The people in this movement started out asking very serious questions about the criminal Federal Reserve Bank, the massive corporate bailouts and the unconstitutional income tax. Obviously this was a huge thorn in the side of the established order so immediately they made steps to hijack the tea party. In just a few short months leading members of the Republican Party started identifying themselves with the tea party image but not the tea party message. Corrupt republican financiers such as the Koch brothers, began funneling millions of dollars into these "tea party" efforts. Just when it finally started to get any kind of media attention, the movement was co-opted and became represented by people who had nothing to do with the original messages or goals of the tea party.

In 2010 a financial blogger and ex-CEO credited with being one of the original "founders" of the tea party posted a very critical blog concerning the direction of the movement, saying it had been hijacked by the very people it was protesting against. His name is Karl Denninger and when denouncing the new tea party he said "Tea Party my ass. This was nothing other than the Republican Party stealing the anger of a population that was fed up with the Republican Party's own theft of their tax money at gunpoint to bail out the robbers of Wall Street and fraudulently redirecting it back toward electing the very people who stole all the fucking money!"[3]. Trade unions, the new tea party, the civil rights movement and one of the most popular religions in the world, these cases show just a few examples of the elites most sacred trick, be assured that they do this every single time they are faced with opposition. This trick can be described as the infection and subversion of counter culture movements.

The most deceptive and cunning villains of all time are not the work of fiction but are the wealthy families who control the world's economic systems and the bureaucrats that do their bidding. Whenever someone stands in the way of their growing financial empire, they immediately move into action and take out the threat in the stealthiest way they can imagine. If these interests were to publicly declare war and their agenda was exposed to the world then they would be looked upon with more disgust then the most brutal dictators in history. They only remain in power and in the good graces of the people because of their intricate web of deception and lies that they manage and perfect with every passing second.

QUOTE SOURCES AND SUGGESTED READING
----
[0] Peace Revolution Podcast Episode 23
[1] http://www.channel3000.com/news/26979885/detail.html
[2] We want freedom: a life in the Black Panther Party - Mumia Abu-Jamal (2004)
[3] http://market-ticker.org/akcs-www?post=16976

*"All my life I been waitin' for, I been prayin' for,
for the people to say, that we do not want to fight no more,
There will be no more wars and our children will play.....one day"*
- Matisyahu

Section 6

War

46. -Who Wins In War?
47. -The War Industry
48. -The Privatization of War
49. -Order Out of Chaos
50. -False Flag Attacks
51. -The Only Way to Truly Support the Troops is to Save Them from War
52. -Controlled Conflict in the Middle East

"Colorful demonstrations and weekend marches are vital but alone are not powerful enough to stop wars. Wars will be stopped only when soldiers refuse to fight, when workers refuse to load weapons onto ships and aircraft, when people boycott the economic outposts of Empire that are strung across the globe."
-Arundhati Roy [0]

Who Wins In War?

As we discuss the basics of warfare in the following chapters, keep one question on your mind. What is accomplished from war? War serves absolutely no productive purpose whatsoever; it only causes destruction and pain. We are told by those who write the history books and the news stories that war is a natural part of human existence. We are expected to believe that human beings killing each other and living in pain is unavoidable and that we should just continue the violence until there is nothing left of this world. Make no mistake about it; war is a primitive, mundane aspect of humanity that we should have evolved past many ages ago. Just like the abhorrent ideas of slavery and racism, we must learn to grow past the inhumane practice of war. In order to overcome the disease of war we must first understand why these conflicts are taking place to begin with, and who is benefiting from them.

Most of the people on this earth are naturally opposed to war; it is only a small percentage that keeps this cycle going. The average citizen of every country wants peace, yet it is the average citizen that is on the front lines torn away from their family and friends, risking their life for someone else's gain.

Every single time there is a war the people are lied to and manipulated into fighting for land, natural resources or strategic advancement that only benefit the government and the wealthy business interests that back it. For them war is a business and the casualties in battle are just a number on a spreadsheet. Our brothers and sisters that die in war are merely pawns to the ruling elite, and just like in a game of chess the pawns are sent by the crown to die with little concern for their wellbeing.

Different governments throughout the world and throughout history have applied the same techniques to manipulate their people into war. This point was made quite clear by Hermann Goering, founder of the Gestapo and one of the main architects of Nazi Germany when he said *"it is the leaders of the country who determine the policy and it is always a simple matter to drag the people along, whether it is a democracy or a fascist dictatorship or a Parliament or a Communist dictatorship… All you have to do is tell them they are being attacked and denounce the pacifists for lack of patriotism and exposing the country to danger. It works the same in every country."* [1] This same approach is used by our government today, just as it was used by one of the most murderous and oppressive regimes in history, the Nazi party. The people in Nazi Germany during World War II are no different from the flag waving Americans who got caught up in nationalistic fervor during the so-called war on terror; both were manipulated into fighting by their "leaders" in the same fashion.

Governments are never honest to the public about war; in fact, it is a crime in most countries to expose the lies and corruption behind the hype, essentially making honesty about war illegal. In the U.S as recently as 2010 a young soldier named Bradley Manning has been held without a warrant and tortured by the military for exposing the horror of the American occupation of the Middle East. This is just the most recent public account of someone standing up for human rights and then becoming a target for oppressive governments. The governments and large corporations that start wars have no interest in human rights; their only interest is to gain more wealth and power. It is completely impossible to have any kind of human rights on this planet as long as we have war.

The honest hardworking people that make up a countries population have absolutely nothing to gain from all this violence. We are the ones who die in wars, our brothers and sisters, mothers, and fathers die in war. Yet the spoils of war are not seen by the people who fight or their families that is saved for the people who are behind the war industry. Companies like Dick Chaney's infamous Halliburton, which gets paid billions of dollars to rebuild the countries destroyed by his own government's war. Halliburton is just one example, there are countless arms dealers, weapons manufactures, and other wartime industries directly tied with banking and the government. This kind of monopoly creates a huge conflict of interest within the highest levels of our government. How can we expect our 'leaders" to make decisions that are in the best interests of the people if they stand to make billions of dollars for sending us to our deaths on a battlefield?

QUOTE SOURCES AND SUGGESTED READING

[0] Public power in the age of empire - Arundhati Roy (2004)

[1] War made easy: how presidents and pundits keep spinning us to death - Norman Solomon (2005)

[SR1] War made easy: how presidents and pundits keep spinning us to death by Norman Solomon (2005)

[SR2] Weapons Systems and Political Stability A History by Carroll Quigley

"Come you masters of war, You that build the big guns, You that build the death planes. You that build all the bombs, You that hide behind walls, You that hide behind desks, I just want you to know, I can see through your masks."
- Bob Dylan [0]

The War Industry

Billions of dollars in tax money from Americans is spent every year so our military can wage wars across the planet. There is a whole industry built around wars, in fact it is one of the most lucrative industries in the world. There is an unspeakable amount of money to be made by the people who sell weapons and ammunition to countries at war. The arms dealers and weapons manufactures never take sides, but are always happy to take billions of dollars from opposing nations of every war so their customers can destroy each other. To people in this industry the idea of peace is bad for business, if there is peace then surely the weapons industry would not be the least bit successful. This gets even more complicated when we discover that the war industry is very deeply tied to our government and the multinational banking institutions; this alliance is what has often been called the "military industrial complex."

The military industrial complex is responsible for most of the wars going on around the world; they instigate conflict and use their wealth and positions of power to keep us in a constant state of war. This racket is nothing new but has been going on for generations and the danger has even been recognized by American presidents. In 1961 the term military industrial complex was first used by Dwight D. Eisenhower in a speech when leaving office. Eisenhower said "In the councils of government, we must guard against the acquisition of unwarranted influence, whether sought or unsought, by the military-industrial complex. The potential for the disastrous rise of misplaced power exists and will persist.

We must never let the weight of this combination endanger our liberties or democratic processes. We should take nothing for granted. Only an alert and knowledgeable citizenry can compel the proper meshing of the huge industrial and military machinery of defense with our peaceful methods and goals so that security and liberty may prosper together."[1] After serving as a high-ranking military official during World War 2 and serving as president for the aftermath of the war, Eisenhower had a morbidly clear picture of the reality of war. However one must ask if he cared so much then why did not he do anything about it during his presidency? I'll leave that one to your own research and imagination.

Since Eisenhower gave us his grim warning in 1961 our country has remained in a constant state of war and the military industrial complex has grown to be one of the most powerful and dangerous organizations in the world. Even in times of peace the establishment is always preparing the public for different conflicts. There is no movement towards peace, no progress made. There are only plans for the next battle, for the future war and the future enemy. Every time the public has managed to have our military pulled out of a war, there is already another one being planned. This perpetual state of war has created a limitless demand for weapons and a cash crop for arms dealers all behind the backs of the American people.

If it is the government who decides when there is peace and when there is war then is not it an obvious conflict of interest for them to be in bed with the people who are selling bombs? It is not rare for a high-ranking member of our government to sit at the head of one of these companies and act as chairmen or CEO. Their paychecks and bonuses are a direct reflection of whether or not the country is at war, and the bonuses are usually enough to drown out the dissent of the American public. Any politician that makes their way to a high-ranking position is bound to get their hands in the war industry and those interests will take priority over the interests of the public. This is why there is never truly an "antiwar" president, because the war industry is now a vital part of American politics and the people in power all agree that peace is not an option.

Although corruption within the military industrial complex is open and documented it is rarely discussed. The wealthy financial interests behind this network control all of the major media outlets, so it is easy for them to keep the nature of their business away from the public eye. If the public was actually aware of how this industry worked there is no way that they would go along with these senseless wars. People all over the world need to realize that our enemies are the people who are building the weapons and instigating the wars, not the people in the front lines from both countries that are dying as a result of their "leader's" ignorance.

QUOTE SOURCES AND SUGGESTED READING
----
[0] Bob Dylan - Masters Of War - The Freewheeling (1963)
[1] Our Documents: 100 Milestone Documents from the National Archives, Michael Beschloss (2006)
[SR1] The Prince by Machiavelli
[SR2] The Art of War by Sun Tzu
[SR3] War is a Racket (The Antiwar Classic by America's Most Decorated Soldier) by Smedley D. Butler
[SR4] Winter Soldier: Iraq and Afghanistan: Eyewitness Accounts of the Occupations

"In the eyes of empire builders men are not men but instruments."
-Napoleon [0]

The Privatization of War

Since the dawn of the technological age the politics and language of war has been changing in order to justify its existence in a more empathetic age. In many ways the human consciousness has evolved greatly in the past few centuries which has made us a more caring, peaceful and unified people. The governments and business interests that have been manipulating innocent people into war for centuries are now facing resistance from the public like they have never seen before. Words like war or genocide are rarely mentioned in the media. To keep the masses calm we now live in a world of "peace keeping missions" and "police actions." The image of war that is given to the west is processed and grossly distorted in order to keep dissent at a minimum. The reality of war however, is still the same as it ever was and it shows no sign of changing its direction anytime soon, regardless of public opinion.

In the summer of 2010 when president barrack Obama declared that U.S troops were finally coming home from Iraq, the war was very far from over. The military may have officially left but the occupation along with all of its horrors was handed over to the "private military companies." These companies employ hundreds of thousands of mercenaries or "contractors" who are beginning to replace traditional soldiers on the battlefield. Mercenaries are paid large salaries by multinational corporations that are in the business of war and natural resources. It is very difficult to tell the difference between a modern mercenary and an army soldier, they perform the same duties and are all working to help the NATO alliance, and the corporations take over the Middle East. In all reality there really is not much different at all between mercenaries and army soldiers, one is paid to kill people by the state while the other is paid to kill people by quasi-state corporations. That is really the only difference. Since police are also paid to commit violence I would also consider them mercenaries, but for the purpose of this discussion I am specifically talking about hired soldiers that are not directly on the states payroll.

It is important to make this distinction because private military contractors are not considered a part of the war effort, therefore the violence that they take place in is completely off the record. When a mercenary dies in war it is not listed with the official body count, and the damage that they inflict on their enemies or civilian populations are also never counted. With little concern for the collapse of the western economy over 100 billion tax dollars per year are spent on mercenaries, which does not even include the on the record military spending. Since private military companies are held accountable to corporations instead of countries it is not necessary for our government to declare war to send in mercenaries either. It is through this loophole that the CIA has managed to occupy over 50 countries while rarely seeking approval from congress or the American people.

Private armies are just one of the many deceptive techniques that the world governments are using to keep the harsh reality of war hidden from the public. If the public were to know the full-unbiased truth about war and world events there is no way we would be living in the constant state of conflict that is seen now. Using private armies allows the government to maintain a military presence in as many countries as they wish without any resistance or public scrutiny. This situation also highlights the merger of the corporate and military establishments. Either way, as a rule of thumb, killing people for money is a bad idea; it does not matter if it is a government, a mobster, or a corporation that is signing the checks.

QUOTE SOURCES AND SUGGESTED READING
----

[0] Napoleon Bonaparte, Maxims [1804-1815], ed. by A. G. De Liancourt, London 1903

[SR1] Blackwater: The Rise of the World's Most Powerful Mercenary Army by Jeremy Scahill

"We are on the verge of a global transformation. All we need is the right major crisis and the nations will accept the New World Order."
- David Rockefeller [0]

Order Out of Chaos

Almost every single human being on this earth just wants peace, and order. Our "leaders" tell us that they can bring us order, some of them even claim to have already done so, but these are obviously all lies. We still have war, poverty, greed, and extreme confusion in nearly every civilization on the planet. The sad irony of this situation is that the people who are responsible for all this confusion are the same people who are apparently here to protect us from it. Our "leaders" are the ones that bring us war, corrupt financial systems, and neurotic social structures. This is much the same way that a lot of computer software companies actually put out viruses of their own, just to provide a need for their product, same idea.

The great swindle of all this is that we are being told that these harmful institutions are the path to salvation and that they are an absolute necessity for society. This mindset creates an unending cycle of chaos that is very destructive to humanity as a whole, but very good for the politician. The politician thrives in chaos just as a malpractice lawyer thrives at the scene of a 5-car pileup. Without car accidents the lawyer might have to look for a different line of work, and without chaos the politician might have to do the same. When I refer to the politician I am also speaking of the corporate ruling class that controls the politician. Their "job security" is measured by the chaos that they create around the world.

Since the beginning of pseudo democracies the elite has created chaos in their societies so they could be given more power, under the pretense that they would clean up the mess that they actually created. The first ruler that we know of to perfect the art of creating chaos was the Roman emperor Diocletian who came to power in 284 AD. This is the "leader" that was responsible for changing Rome from a developing democracy into a covert dictatorship. Since the Roman people had a history of freedom and financial prosperity they were not going to give up their rights unless they were carefully manipulated into doing so.

Diocletian needed to create an enemy that he could use as a scapegoat so he could raise taxes, expand his military, and take away the rights of the Roman citizens. His policies were unpopular and he was having difficulty getting his people to fall in line so he set his own palace on fire twice in two weeks and blamed it on a minority religious group, the Christians. At this time in Rome Christians were a relatively new religious sect and made up only about 10% of the population. After the fires, Christians were labeled as terrorists and either crucified or fed to lions in giant coliseums. With his new powers Diocletian completely reorganized the Roman political system to work like a dictatorship, but he continued to call it a democracy so the people would still think they were free.

Diocletian's approach has been used over and over by authoritarian rulers throughout history who manipulated their people into giving up their freedoms. His technique would eventually be called "The Hegelian Dialectic" or more simply "problem-reaction-solution." The Hegelian Dialectic has existed since the times of Rome, but it did not have a name until aristocratic philosopher Georg Wilhelm Frederick Hegel came along and gave it a full description. This is a strategy where the government creates a problem, waits for the expected reaction from the public, and then offers them a preplanned solution to the problem that they themselves created to begin with. The solution was their plan, the whole reason why they created the problem, but if they were to offer their idea to the people without the problem no one would go for it.

This strategy is still used today, even by major world powers. The parallels between Diocletian's Rome and modern day America are made clear by some creepy remarks George Bush JR. made just after 9/11. Bush made statements like "it'll take time to restore chaos and order - order out of chaos."[1] and *"If this were a dictatorship, it would be a heck of a lot easier, just so long as I'm the dictator."* [2] These comments showed his true feelings regarding what kind of government he was looking to build and how he was going to build it. Bush is just one of the most obvious and comical examples of rulers that use this method, current administrations, and the United Nations still continue to create problems to this day, just so they can fix them.

This process was described in very intricate detail by researcher Jordan Maxwell in an interview conducted by William Cooper. In the now famous interview Maxwell reveals that *"The idea was that if you could create enough chaos that people will be sufficiently frightened and will give to you the political power to bring back law and order....the idea is that if you're going to pull a scam on somebody if you're going to pick someone's pocket or something you always have a diversion, you do something to draw that persons attention while you're picking their pocket. If you're going to break out of a prison you always have a gang fight down at the far end while the guys are crawling out the hole on the other end. The idea is you set up a diversion, you cause chaos, and out of that you will get control. They do not pay these people big money to make mistakes, anytime the president or the government does something they know what they are doing. It may not make any sense to you but according to other plans if you understand what is going on behind the scenes it makes a lot of sense."* [3]

QUOTE SOURCES AND SUGGESTED READING
----

[0] David Rockefeller speaking at the UN, Sept. 14, 1994.
[1] Message to Iraqi people, Washington, April 2003, Bush - the Dark Night of America - G. P. Geoghegan (2008)
[2] Phoenix Rising: The Rise and Fall of the American Republic - Donald G. Lett, Jr. (2008)
[3] Jordan Maxwell – Mystery of Babylon interviews with William Cooper
[SR1] Utopia by Sir Thomas More
[SR2] The Republic by Plato

"When the tyrant has disposed of foreign enemies by conquest or treaty, and there is nothing more to fear from them, then he is always stirring some war or other, in order that the people may require a leader."
~ Plato [0]

False Flag Attacks

Traditional monarchies and dictatorships were always in a state of war because the military policies were determined entirely by the ruling class who would be seeing the spoils of war. Typically wars were fought over land and resources and to expand empire. The lower class that would be fighting in these wars for no benefit of their own did not have any say in military policy because they had no civil rights and were living under authoritarian rule. Under a democracy the "leaders" are naturally still interested in expanding their empire and claiming land and resources for their personal companies. The public in a democracy however is usually reluctant to go to war because they will be the ones fighting and dying in the name of conquest and greed that will not benefit them or their families at all. So here develops a major conflict of interest in where the "leaders" attempt to coerce the people into going into war when they do not want to.

With the ever-growing military industrial complex and the many wars of the past hundred years we can see that the establishment has managed to somehow push the American people into wars that they would never even consider. One of the most effective methods that many different regimes have used is the "false flag attack." This is essentially when the government stages an attack against their own citizens or provokes attack from another nation in order to carry out a preplanned war.

In recent history false flag operations have been carried out many times by many different governments. The sinister Nazi party actually set fire to one of their own government buildings and blamed it on terrorists in order to pass a law that would take away many of the peoples civil liberties. This event came to be known as the Reichstag fires, after the names of the buildings that were burned. Immediately after the fires the Nazis passed a piece of tyrannical legislation called the "decree for the protection of state and people."

This scenario is eerily familiar to the September 11th bombings in New York City and the following PATRIOT ACT, which stands for "United and Strengthening America by Providing Appropriate Tools Required to Intercept and Obstruct Terrorism." Scary how similar they are, huh? Both mentioned regimes carried out these false flag attacks against their own citizens in order to strip away the people's rights so they could enter into wars of conquest. After the fire at the Reichstag building Hitler was incredibly excited that he would now have an excuse to impose his Nazi policies, he was quoted as saying *"You are now witnessing the beginning of a great epoch in German history...This fire is the beginning."*[1]

The Bush administration was somewhat less candid after 911 but they were equally as excited. Chants to "never waste a good crisis" were heard on television sets all over the country as the government immediately put some of the most restricting legislation America has ever seen thru congress and declared unending war on an invisible enemy. It is no coincidence that a poll taken by TNS Emnid showed that over 90% of Germans do not believe the official 9/11 story as told by the US government. The German people have been the victim of tyranny in recent history, and many of them remember the tricks that are used by authoritarian rulers to push their people into wars. In both the first and second world wars the German people were conned into playing a major part in the militarization and violence that took place. The same study also found that 80% of surveyed Germans believe that the CIA conducts covert operations on German soil. In Germany the public has a much more realistic perception of the inner workings of government then we do in the United States, as they are constantly reminded of their government's role in the horrors of World War 2.

There is so much evidence that has come to light since the collapse of the world trade centers that it is now quite clear that there was a massive cover up involved in this situation. There were also many members of the establishment, employees of the CIA, FBI, NSA, and other organizations who caught on to the cover up while it was happening. These whistleblowers successfully exposed the cover up beyond a reasonable doubt, but their stories were largely ignored by the mainstream media. The testimony of people like Sibel Edmonds, Richard Andrew Grove, William Bergman, Coleen Rowley, J. Michael Springmann, Robert Wright, Indira Singh, and Barry Jennings totally blows the official government account out of the water. Among the piles of scientific and anecdotal evidence, there are now over 1300 architects and engineers who have signed a petition demanding of Congress a truly independent investigation. This independent investigation is necessary because the 9/11 commission was a total puppet committee, who just pushed the story that the pentagon ordered them to.

The Bush administration was not the only American regime to use this false flag strategy to convince the people to go to war. Information released in 2005 by the National Security Agency showed that the Gulf of Tonkin incident on August 1964 was deliberately falsified to make it appear North Vietnamese gunboats attacked an American destroyer patrolling in international waters when in reality they did not. This was the event that the US military used as an excuse to go to war in Vietnam and was surrounded in mystery and controversy until 40 years later when the official facts were released. Perhaps many years after 911 when the dust has settled a classified government report will surface showing the true nature of the events that took place on that day. Until then we can only continue to demand a new independent investigation that is not a total sham like the 911 commission report was.

The wars that are happening around the world, the police state that is expanding in the western world and general lack of privacy and peace worldwide is justified by the official story of the world trade center attacks on 9/11. Almost every specific point of the general story contradicts all evidence and eyewitness accounts. The 9/11 commission, which was developed to investigate the issue was a set up. How do we know this? Most of the people who sat on the 9/11 commission have since come forward admitting that they were not allowed to look into most of the evidence and that they were tightly controlled by the pentagon. One commissioner John Farmer has even came out and wrote a book called "The Ground Truth" in which he reveals the details of how the 9/11 commission report was basically written by the government. This means that a kangaroo court was responsible for investigating the crime of the century, is not this good enough reason to support a legitimate investigation?

The very popular false flag approach is a part of the political strategy that I mentioned in "order out of chaos" called The Hegelian Dialectic. This is a strategy where the government creates a problem, waits for the expected reaction from the public, and then offers them a preplanned solution to the problem that they created. This is by far one of the most effective strategies that democratic governments use to scare their populations into war. This approach is becoming increasingly prevalent in US policy as the establishment works to strip away more of our civil rights so they can expand their empire.

In late 2010 the Obama administration carried out some false flag scenarios of their own in order to restrict travel and subject citizens to invasive searches. These policies were apparently in response to foiled airplane bombings that were later proved to be orchestrated or aided by the federal government. This second wave of false flag incidents started in 2009 when a man was escorted through customs onto an airplane by CIA agents and then was later found with a bomb. Several other questionable incidents would pop up in the next year and allow the US government to impose authoritarian policies that would forever change everyday life for American citizens. The most obvious of these false flag attacks came at the very same time that the Obama administration was attempting to install dangerous radioactive scanners in all US airports. Just days before holiday travel began; a US security firm was caught sneaking a bomb past airport security in Germany. Upon questioning all government parties involved stated that the bomb was merely a decoy to "test airport security."

It sounds horrible and it is hard for most people to believe that the government would carry out an attack against "their own people," but one must remember the true opinion that the ruling class has of their citizens, we are seen as slaves to them, not equals. We are the pawns in their game of conquest so our lives do not mean anything to them. In reference to Berkley California students protesting the Vietnam War Ronald Reagan made some chilling comments about how they would be handled. He said *"If there has to be a blood bath, let's get it over with."*[3] That statement illustrates the typical mentality that the government has regarding the lives of their citizens. Later during those protests students were teargased and fired at with shotguns, one was killed and over a hundred injured. Our "leaders" are told what to do by the business interests that support them, and the goals laid out by these business interests are more important to our "leaders" then the lives of their citizens. So do not think for a minute that these people care about us or that our lives mean any more to them then the lives of their enemies.

QUOTE SOURCES AND SUGGESTED READING

[0] Plato - The Republic
[1] Hitler's Piano Player: The Rise and Fall of Ernst Hanfstaengl: Confidant of Hitler, Ally of FDR - Peter Conradi (2006)
[2] Ronald Reagan (Governor of California), cited in the San Francisco Chronicle, early morning edition, May 15, 1969
[SR1] 9/11 Synthetic Terror: Made in USA, First Edition, and Webster Griffin Tarpley
[SR2] The 9/11 Commission Report: Omissions And Distortions, David Ray Griffin
[SR3] The Ground Truth: The Untold Story of America Under Attack on 9/11 by John Farmer
[SR4] What I Saw That Day by Phillip Tourney

"Without him Caesar would have stood alone, He's the one who gives his body As a weapon of the war, And without him all this killing can't go on. He's the Universal Soldier and he really is to blame, His orders come from far away no more, They come from here and there and you and me, And brothers can't you see, This is not the way we put the end to war." – Donovan [0]

The Only Way to Truly Support the Troops is to save them from War

The most unfortunate thing about our over militarized culture is not the financial or political costs but the human cost. The poor souls that are conned into war on either side not only put their own lives at risk, but they put many other innocent lives at risk as well. It is the job of the military to kill or be killed and this profession is glorified in our culture despite the fact that we all recognize murder as being a horrible thing. In almost every single society throughout the world violence and murder are seen as the most deplorable of all acts that can be committed. If this is the case then why are we sending hundreds of thousands of our young citizens out to commit acts of violence and be victims of violence? Even worse why are we applauding this kind of violent behavior by calling these people heroes and holding them to be examples of a model citizen? No one that signs up to kill people should be praised in any way.

I am not saying that we should hate these people, much the opposite in fact. We should pity these poor souls because they have been misled and manipulated by our militant government into giving up their lives for a senseless cause. We should embrace these human beings with open arms but we should condemn their profession. It is not their fault that they grew up in a society that molded them for the battlefield, but we should still encourage these people to leave that dehumanizing lifestyle behind. Our message of love and compassion must be louder than the battle cries and drown out the violent ideals that they have been corrupted with.

We are not the first country to strap our young impressionable citizens with weapons and send them off around the world to expand an empire. This kind of exploitation has been going on for centuries. With the weapons of war becoming more destructive in the 20th century, the carnage that took place on the battlefield became even worse than before. The first and second world wars are among the most horrific and shameful times in human history.

Following the genocide and devastation of the Second World War, everyone agreed that the war crimes that took place were unacceptable and inhumane. To help prevent these kinds of horrors from taking place in the future, the Geneva Convention was ratified through the Nuremburg trials. The Geneva Convention is a set of international rules that dictate what is legal and illegal in times of war. The Nuremburg trials have been the most recent update to the international war crime laws, this update is said to protects citizens' rights in times of war as well as hold specific members of the military accountable for their actions. These laws were a response to the cruel and unusual treatment that many members of the military carried out against their own citizens. This happened in

Germany, The Soviet Union, China, and many other nations as well. These trials ended up being somewhat of a circus because they were not followed through on very well and if they really wanted to make a difference they would just outlaw war. However, a few important things were recognized and established on an international level. It was decided at the Nuremberg trials that even if a member of the military was "just following orders" when they committed a crime, they were still to be held personally accountable for their actions. The sad thing is though, even though they have committed horrible crimes, these are mostly good people who were being forced or conned into doing bad things for bad people.

After the Nuremberg trials a professor by the name of Stanley Milgram set out to discover if good people can really be coerced into doing bad things by authority figures. He conducted an experiment in 1961 that involved average test subjects being ordered to administer electroshock therapy to another "test subject." Only there was no shock and the participant that was apparently receiving the shock was just an actor. The study was designed to discover if the test subject would continue to do what they were told, even if it meant harming another human being. Before the tests were conducted, a poll was taken to predict the percentage of test subjects that would refuse to follow orders once the experiment seemed to become life threatening.

Those who were polled believed that 97% of the test subjects would refuse to administer anything higher than a "strong shock" to the other "participant" or actor. Unbelievably it turned out that only 35% of the subjects actually were able to do the right thing and resist authority. All of the other participants continued to administer what would have been very high levels of electricity to the apparent victim in the study.

Stanley Milgram summed up the findings of his experiments quite well by saying "The legal and philosophic aspects of obedience are of enormous importance, but they say very little about how most people behave in concrete situations. I set up a simple experiment at Yale University to test how much pain an ordinary citizen would inflict on another person simply because he was ordered to by an experimental scientist. Stark authority was pitted against the subjects' strongest moral imperatives against hurting others, and, with the subjects' ears ringing with the screams of the victims, authority won more often than not. The extreme willingness of adults to go to almost any lengths on the command of an authority constitutes the chief finding of the study and the fact most urgently demanding explanation. Ordinary people, simply doing their jobs, and without any particular hostility on their part, can become agents in a terrible destructive process. Moreover, even when the destructive effects of their work become patently clear, and they are asked to carry out actions incompatible with fundamental standards of morality, relatively few people have the resources needed to resist authority"[1]

All over the planet we have been conditioned for thousands of years to obey the orders of authority even if it means committing acts of violence against one another. This cycle of war and violence has brought us to the brink of catastrophe and has removed almost all traces of humanity from our species. This kind of horror cannot continue and it is up to us to stop obeying orders and stop joining the military. If the public was aware of the carnage that they would witness and the impact that it would have on their mind most people would never sign up. Even if someone survives war and comes back home they will join the millions of veterans with extreme depression and post-traumatic stress disorder. They will be forgotten and abandoned by the government who they just risked their lives for. When veterans return from war they are more times than not mistreated and neglected by the establishment and really are seen as nothing more than pawns or cannon fodder for the ruling elite.

Henry Kissinger is a feudal crusader who has been pulling the strings behind the scenes in government for over 50 years. He had a major part in the planning of the senseless war in Vietnam as well as the war of terror that has ravaged the Middle East. This man has made decisions to start wars that have changed and threatened the lives of millions of human beings, but he has never served in the military himself and he has a sick contempt for his loyal soldiers. He played a heavy role in the Watergate scandal during the Nixon administration. As a result of that scandal many tape recordings and classified documents that revealed the inhumane nature of the administration were made public. In the revelations that came from the scandal Henry Kissinger was quoted as saying "Military men are dumb, stupid animals to be used as pawns for foreign policy." [2] This is the general sentiment among the policy makers in government, not just towards the military but towards the bulk of the working class!

The government or media certainly is not going to inform the public about the true horror of war, so it is up to everyday citizens. If someone you know is thinking about joining the military encourage them not to. Talk to them about what they can do to improve their lives here at home, and help them in any way you can. If they are joining for financial reasons, help them find a good job at home so they do not have to sell their soul to the devil and go fight a war. Inform them of the senseless atrocities that they will be faced with and let them know that the government is lying to them. If a life away from war is more attractive and logical then life in a battlefield then people will not join the military. People are only joining now because they do not feel that they have any other options or they have been caught up with the romanticized idea of the military that our country projects. If we can help them find options and we debunk the glorified vision that the people close to us have of the military then we will begin to save our brothers and sisters from the war machine.

It is also extremely important not to be negative towards people that are already in the military, but still encourage them to do the right thing and stand up for their brothers and sisters, instead of fighting for the corrupt regime that keeps them imprisoned. The wars that they are fighting and dying in are making the corporate elite that have hijacked our government richer while further impoverishing the American people and removing our natural born rights. In 1908 Theodore Roosevelt said "*Patriotism means to stand by the country. It does not mean to stand by the president or any other public official save exactly to the degree in which he himself stands by the country. It is patriotic to support him insofar as he efficiently serves the country. It is unpatriotic not to oppose him to the exact extent that by inefficiency or otherwise he fails in his duty to stand by the country.*" [3] This was most likely just campaign talk, but Roosevelt's message is more relevant today than it has ever been, and it is up to us to relay that message to our brothers and sisters in the armed forces. They are apparently here to protect us from authoritarian governments, even if that government happens to be our own.

The once innocent young men and women in the military play a critical role in preventing further genocide and violence on this earth. They are the final line of defense between bloodthirsty tyrants and the struggling masses. If the soldiers refuse to fight an unjust war, for an unjust cause they have the ability to save billions of lives. This is why the military is so strict on their enlistees and discourages freethinking; they do not want the soldiers to actually weigh the morality of what they're doing.

Though the fact has been strongly suppressed there have been many times throughout history when soldiers have stood up against wartime authority in the name of truth, justice, and human rights. There has not been a single war in history where the public and the soldiers were told the complete truth, because if they were familiar with the reality of war they would never support it or allow it. When the soldiers discover that they have been lied to (and they usually do by the time they are forced to kill civilians) they react in some of the most inspiring ways.

Refusing military service is not a new idea at all; people have been doing it for as long as warfare has been around. This is of course yet another very much ignored and glossed over part of history. Wars are always started under false pretenses, and when the truth eventually comes out the people who have been used and taken advantage of are not going to just continue on as usual, they are going to demand answers and accountability. When this happens the establishment uses words like "mutiny" "desertion" or "treason" to condemn the actions of any soldier who was brave enough to stand up against the malicious practices of their so-called superiors. Yet despite the wartime rhetoric of the establishment many courageous soldiers have done just that, rebelled against their inhumane "leaders." This is most apparent in times of revolution and civil unrest where armed forces are ordered to harm the very people that they are sworn to protect. This is when the soldiers realize that they have not been serving the people of their country like they have been led to believe, but were in fact serving the ruling class who was oppressing the people.

It is now when the veil of deception is automatically lifted and soldiers are left with monumental decisions. They are forced to choose between the people of their country and the "leaders" of their country. In most cases the fate of revolutions have depended upon the public's ability to form a bond with the military that will supersede any orders that they may get from so called authority. This scenario makes it easy for a soldier to make the right decisions, but it is a bit less clear-cut when they are sent into a foreign land to fight an unknown "enemy." Even then many soldiers have a difficult time coping with the orders they are being given and have a change of heart when they are exposed to the reality of the situation. In the most recent US wars there has been a very strong culture of resistance in the military, even though you may not have heard about it.

The Vietnam War is today known throughout most of the world as a war of aggression and imperialism on the part of the United States government, and rightfully so. However, if it was not for the courage and defiance of a large number of American soldiers, the world may have never known the true story of what actually happened in Vietnam. Like many wars this was said to be a noble cause, where the Americans were apparently "liberating" the Vietnamese people. Many good-hearted people in America and throughout the world actually bought that excuse for a period of time. Behind the scenes there were very different discussions.

In June of 1952 a secret memo from the National Security council stated *"Communist control of all of Southeast Asia would render the U.S. position in the Pacific offshore island chain precarious and would seriously jeopardize fundamental U.S. security interests in the Far East."*[4] What are those "fundamental security interests"? Well, the memo goes on to explain why the area is so important "Southeast Asia, especially Malaya and Indonesia, is the principal world source of natural rubber and tin, and a producer of petroleum and other strategically important commodities" [5]. Then in 1953, a congressional study mission reported reconfirmed the US governments interest in the region, the study said that "The area of Indochina is immensely wealthy in rice, rubber, coal and iron ore. Its position makes it a strategic key to the rest of Southeast Asia." and *"If the French actually decided to withdraw, the U.S. would have to consider most seriously whether to take over in this area."*[6]

On January 31, 1968 came the "Tet offensive" which was to be a turning point in the war and an awakening for many American soldiers. This was a full-scale attack launched by the North Vietnamese forces that America was fighting against, but they also had many South Vietnamese civilians on their side as well. These are the people that the Americans are supposed to be "liberating"! It then became apparent to the soldiers that they were not welcome in this country, and the story they have been told by their government and their so-called superiors just did not add up. That battle would begin the slow retreat of the US forces in Vietnam and as that retreat progressed the commanding officers became even more brutal. These commanding officers ordered attacks on civilians and were responsible for many untold horrors, as time went on the soldiers began to resist their bloodthirsty masters and make efforts to end the war.

In the years leading up to the end of the war there were countless protests, rallies, sit ins and other peaceful methods of resistance enacted by thousands of American soldiers. Hundreds of independent anti-war magazines were being printed on US military bases throughout the entire world and a culture of peaceful defiance was growing in the American armed forces. Exactly two years after the Tet offensive on January 31, 1971 an activist group called "Vietnam Veterans Against The War" held a 2 day media event called "The Winter Soldier Investigation" to publicize and expose the war crimes that were carried out on the behalf of the American people. Their stories highlighted the brutality of the high-ranking officers and immorality of the whole campaign.

The final blow to the US government's fairy tale about Vietnam came when Daniel Ellsberg, one of Washington's most well respected political analysts revealed classified documents to the world that proved multiple presidential administrations blatantly lied to the public on a daily basis about the war. These files came to be known as the "Pentagon Papers," which I discussed earlier on. Without these brave soldiers taking a stand and refusing to be a part of the violence that their government was ordering, the Vietnam War could have gotten a lot worse and many more lives on both sides would have been lost.

For people who were alive during the Vietnam War the various conflicts today in the Middle East are a haunting reminder of another war that should have never happened. The story seems very much the same, various corrupt administrations that belong to the same club of elitist have lied through their teeth over many years and misled the American people into a brutal war that they have no place fighting. The horror and injustice of these wars are eerily similar, but luckily the resistance is just as strong today as it was years ago. Many American soldiers are coming home from the Middle East and speaking out against the imperialism and brutality that is taking place. Groups like "Veterans For Peace" have created a strong antiwar movement among the military and individual soldiers are taking brave steps to expose the reality of what is going on, just as Daniel Ellsberg and others did during the Vietnam war. Classified information is being anonymously submitted by soldiers to the press via the new independent media on the internet. Droves of videos and official documents have poured in, showing evidence of corruption and war crimes on the part of the US government.

William J. Astor is a retired lieutenant colonel (USAF) and professor of history who writes regular antiwar articles for a website called tomsdispatch.com. Over the many years of the various occupations in the Middle East he received thousands of letters from disgruntled troops who had a different opinion of their government after being exposed to the realities of the war. In a February 2011 article, he shared some of those letters with his readers. One soldier writes "*I am on my second tour of Iraq. My unit has been plagued by suicides and psychiatric problems. Our guards-men even prior to deployment come from compromised social and economic environments, leaving them very susceptible [to military recruiters]. Many of our soldiers are almost forced into volunteering for multiple tours due to the lack of economic opportunity and the cold fact that there is no other way to support their families. I have seen blatant corruption among the [private] contractors [in Iraq] and even cases of outright human trafficking and forced prostitution among female third country nationals… My hope is that the U.S. can withdraw from this senseless war… This war has bankrupted the U.S. and caused untold suffering among U.S. Forces and women.*"[7] This man is not alone either, as the lies of the occupation in the Middle East are exposed a great number of soldiers are having second thoughts about the war that they are in and the orders they are being given.

There has long been a history of rebellion within the highest levels of the United States armed forces. This is because many very great people get involved with good intentions only to discover that the whole thing is a racket. Just as General Smedley Butler revealed in his famous book "War Is a Racket" in 1935. Smedley was the most decorated war hero of his time and during his 34-year career as a Marine, he participated in military actions in the Philippines, China, in Central America and the Caribbean during the Banana Wars, and France in World War I. He would receive dozens of medals throughout his career including the Medal of Honor, twice!

His short but insightful book was no doubt inspired by the 1934 "business plot" in which he was approached by business and finance leaders about a plan to overthrow the constitutional government and instate a feudal dictatorship. Smedley blew the whistle and submitted testimony to a congressional committee to expose the wealthy industrialists and their plot to the American People. The final report of the committee admitted that there was evidence backing up the general's claims, but no charges were ever filed. A year later he released his book that outlined in detail what he witnessed behind the scenes as a decorated general in the United States military throughout the course of various wars. Smedley dedicated the rest of his life to speaking out against war and the growing military industrial complex. The following passage is an excerpt from "War is a Racket," which shows in detail the kind of military operations that our country has been running for at least the past century. Smedley writes:

"It may seem odd for me, a military man to adopt such a comparison. Truthfulness compels me to. I spent thirty- three years and four months in active military service as a member of this country's most agile military force, the Marine Corps. I served in all commissioned ranks from Second Lieutenant to Major General. And during that period, I spent most of my time being a high-class muscle- man for Big Business, for Wall Street and for the Bankers. In short, I was a racketeer, a gangster for capitalism. I suspected I was just part of a racket at the time. Now I am sure of it. Like all the members of the military profession, I never had a thought of my own until I left the service. My mental faculties remained in suspended animation while I obeyed the orders of higher-ups. This is typical with everyone in the military service. I helped make Mexico, especially Tampico, safe for American oil interests in 1914. I helped make Haiti and Cuba a decent place for the National City Bank boys to collect revenues in. I helped in the raping of half a dozen Central American republics for the benefits of Wall Street. The record of racketeering is long. I helped purify Nicaragua for the international banking house of Brown Brothers in 1909-1912. I brought light to the Dominican Republic for American sugar interests in 1916. In China I helped to see to it that Standard Oil went its way unmolested. During those years, I had, as the boys in the back room would say, a swell racket. Looking back on it, I feel that I could have given Al Capone a few hints. The best he could do was to operate his racket in three districts. I operated on three continents."[8]

There is no such thing as a noble or honorable war, all war is genocide and a violation of basic human rights. It takes a lot more courage and dignity for a soldier to stand up against authority for the wellbeing of humanity then it does to follow orders. Albert Einstein said *"The pioneers of a warless world are the youth who refuse military service"* [9] and he was right. The battles that are being fought by our brothers and sisters are not their battles to fight. They are the battles of the aristocracy who plan and benefit from wars. Warfare, like slavery is one of the most brutal forms of intolerance and it is in the best interest of our species to abandon these kinds of abhorrent practices. Unless war becomes just another shameful part of our primitive past then it will surely be the destruction of our future.

QUOTE SOURCES AND SUGGESTED READING
----
[0] Donovan – Universal Soldier
[1] Ethicability - Roger Steare (2006)
[2] America's Disposable Soldiers - Robert S. Miller (2002)
[3] The Great Adventure - Theodore Roosevelt (1918)
[4] Communism in history and theory: Asia, Africa, and the Americas - Donald F. Busky (2002)
[5] Crimes of the American nuclear state: at home and abroad - David Kauzlarich, Ronald C. Kramer (1998)
[6] A grand delusion: America's descent into Vietnam - Robert Mann (2002)
[7] http://www.tomdispatch.com/archive/175357/
[8] Smedley Butler – War is a Racket
[9] Ten excellent reasons not to join the military By Elizabeth Weill-Greenberg
[SR1] War is a Racket (The Antiwar Classic by America's Most Decorated Soldier) by Smedley D. Butler
[SR2] Behold a Pale Horse by William Cooper

"All war must be just the killing of strangers against whom you feel no personal animosity; strangers whom, in other circumstances, you would help if you found them in trouble, and who would help you if you needed it."
- Mark Twain [0]

Controlled Conflict in the Middle East

The war in the Middle East between Israel and Palestine is by far one of the most serious issues of our time; it is also one of the most controversial and misunderstood. Most any place on earth has a history of conflict, and the Middle East is no different. There were many crusades fought in those areas mainly carried out by invading European Christians in the name of religion, but for the sake of empire. Prior to World War 2 Jewish and Muslim people lived in relative peace in the territory which is now Israel, at the time it was just known as Syria. These were all remnants of the once unified Ottoman Empire that was divided and split apart by British imperialism. Most of the people that lived in Syria at this time were of Arab descent, but there was also a much smaller portion of society who was Jewish. Regardless of this discrepancy there was very little hostility among the different religions until British influence and western intervention brought a whole new dynamic to the situation.

The state of Israel developed during a very important time in world history, between the first and second world wars. The end of the First World War brought with it the League of Nations who rewrote borders and territory lines all over the world. The League of Nations was an organization that was proposed by the international banking interests that funded and instigated the war. This institution was designed so the elite could have more control over world events and use the politicians that they employed to do their bidding. Many of the policies established by the League of Nations after the First World War were specifically designed to cause future conflict in Europe. For example, the harsh penalties enacted on the German people caused years of economic turmoil that eventually left them vulnerable enough to be exploited by the tyrant Adolph Hitler. The elite planned to profit off of future wars by selling weapons, making loans and expanding their world dominance using the puppet regimes they had in place in the British and United States governments. The territory lines and policies set up after World War 1 in Europe established the conditions that would eventually lead to World War 2.

When the Second World War became even more profitable than the first, the elite decided to once again set a pretense for future wars. Once again they used the League of Nations that at this point had changed its name to the United Nations, to escalate hostilities in areas they wished to dominate. This is how the great rivalry between communism and capitalism and the resulting cold war developed. The cold war resulted in a massive arms race that sold a lot of weapons for the elite and it allowed them to further divide the most powerful nations, in turn making them easier to influence and take control of. This also gave them an excuse to use military action on self-sustaining rebel nations that were not compliant with western policies.

One of the main areas they wished to instigate trouble in was the Middle East, due to its abundance in oil, a natural resource that became extremely important on the global stage during the First World War. The Middle East was the new frontier for the multinational business interests and exploiting the people and resources of that area has been on their agenda since the crusades of the Middle Ages. Through diplomatic maneuvers following World War 2 the Rothschild's and the rest of the western oligarchy were able to establish an avenue for their future conquest in the region.

There was a massive Jewish refugee population in the years following the holocaust and the elite have very little sympathy for people in these kinds of situations. Refugees of any creed, color, or nationality are treated by all governments as if they were lepers and despite the hardships that the strong Jewish people had just been put through they were seen as nothing more than a "problem" to the United Nations. At the same time another "problem" being discussed behind the scenes at the UN was how to maintain a stronghold in the oil rich Middle East. The western powers were having a difficult time exploiting the predominantly Arab region, and many "leaders" in the area were also being "uncooperative" with western companies who sought to move in and plunder the regions natural resources.

Nothing makes the global elite happier than "solving" two or more of their "problems" at the same time, in a single action. The creation of the state of Israel did just that. Seeing that Jewish people had a biblical connection to the area, the UN claimed that their motivation was to establish a Jewish homeland, not set up an imperial colonial government that the west would control politically and economically. Unfortunately for both the Israelis and Palestinians the latter was what ended up happening. Sure, a great number of Jewish people do live in Israel but they do not have control of their government, economy or their military, but are in fact oppressed and manipulated by all of those institutions. The elite in Great Brittan has more control over Israel's domestic and foreign policy then the people actually living everyday lives inside the country, the same goes for people living in America as well. The British elite have much more say in major American policies than the taxpayers and voters inside the country do.

The creation of the state of Israel is extremely similar to the creation of both Australia and the United States. In each case the aristocracy within Great Britain wanted to set up a colony in a faraway land where there was already an established native civilization. In every single case they did not launch a military invasion but simply sent exiles, refuges and prisoners of war to live in the area and establish a stronghold. Of course the prisoners were always told they were being sent to a promised land or paradise, but in reality they were being used much like pawns are used in a game of chess. They are sent to the frontlines of the area that the elite wish to conquer, and they fend for themselves until a workable civilization is established. At that point the civilization is exploited and overtaken by the colonial powers that sent the refugees there to begin with. Although things are somewhat different in America because of the revolutionary war, Great Britain still has a lot of control over our economy and thus our political system as well. This same situation is taking place but to an even greater degree in both Australia and Israel.

When the state of Israel was created in 1948 anyone that happened to be living within the borders drawn by the United Nations who was of Arab or Palestinian descent was forcibly expelled from their homes. This is not slander or speculation this actually happened, and it created the world's largest refugee population. 6 Million People were forced into exile, in different parts of the world because of their heritage. Since then these refugees have lived in camps or on their own in the ghettos of Palestine because they are not permitted to buy or sell property and are banned from employment. This goes for refugees inside Palestinian territory, the west bank, the Gaza strip, Lebanon, and other parts of the Middle East. They are given no chance of obtaining citizenship and are denied many of their basic human rights. A young Palestinian by the name of Ali Abdul Bari runs a peaceful activist organization called Esha. In an interview with the independent press he said "The media talk about Gaza as a centre of starvation, but that is not true. What we are lacking is our freedom: We have a sea, but we can't use it. We have air, but we are not allowed to build an airport. We want to be able to depend on ourselves." [1] This is the true sentiment of the Palestinian people, not the crazed rhetoric of the areas so called "leaders."

The people of Israel have a nationalistic militant government that does not represent their will, while on the other end the people of Palestine also have a nationalistic militant government that does not represent their will. The so-called "leaders" of the Palestinian territories are Hamas and Fatah; they are two militant Islamic factions that in no way represent the people of Palestine. They are at war with each other, at war with Israel and at war with the people of Palestine as well, their regimes are a massive barrier in the peace process. They refuse to negotiate with each other and refuse to take place in any peace processes, as ceremonial as they may be. They openly spit hateful rhetoric that gets people on both sides fired up, and escalates the tension in the region. Israeli people begin to hate Palestinian people for things that their government did or said and vice versa. Hamas often calls for the complete destruction of the state of Israel and exile of the current Jewish population. This is obviously a bad idea and would simply compound the regions problems by creating yet another human rights crisis and refugee population. This political stance also ensures an ongoing conflict, because if both sides will not quit or negotiate until the other is destroyed then conflict could go on forever.

To understand how Hamas and Fatah really work and who they serve one must ask themselves a few questions. How did they get so powerful if they do not have popular support? Where did they get their weapons and resources from in a poverty-stricken area like Palestine? Most of all, who benefits from them being in power? The answer to all of these questions is short and simple, The UK, the United States and Israel, or more appropriately the MI6, CIA and the Mossad. Remember secret service organizations operate together, many times without the knowledge of the governments that they apparently work for. In June of 2008 the

Prime Minister of Israel Ehud Olmert admitted that Israel's secret service Mossad transferred millions of dollars to the Hamas government every single month for years. The same people that are being condemned in public by the west and Israel as being terrorists are receiving millions of dollars for weapons from these very governments. This allows the conflict to escalate and serves the elite at the expense of the average people in every country.

In spite of Hamas refusal to negotiate there has still been a very one sided and controlled "peace process" of negotiations that have taken place between the Zionist government in Israel and another Political group called the "Palestinian Liberation Organization". The Palestinian Liberation Organization claims to represent the Palestinian people but of course just like Hamas and Fatah, they do not. The details of the peace conferences were hazy in the media for years until 2011 when 1,700 declassified diplomatic cables were released through two different international media outlets, The UK's "Guardian" and the Arabic "Aljazeera". These cables showed detailed exchanges between the Zionist regime and Palestinian Liberation Organization that were hidden from the whole world.

The files showed that a whole decades worth of behind the scenes negotiations took place between representatives on behalf of both nations (With the US as a strong 3rd party of course). The problem with the content of these negotiations is that both the PLO and the Zionist government were both making decisions that were in direct opposition of their nation's public interest. The Zionist "leaders" of Israel refused to accept various peace offers suggested by the PLO that the people of Israel would have had no problems coming to terms with. The reason why these terms were not accepted is because the war on the Palestinians provides the Zionist Government a pretense for constant militarization and homeland police state. This is the same tactic used by the American Government in their ongoing "war on terror"; a constant war state is perpetuated and drawn out by the establishment to ensure the central government more power. On the other end, tyrants of the Arab world take advantage of this crisis to impose the same kind of wartime mentality on their people. The global elite also stand to make a lot of money in both the war on terror and the Zionist war in Palestine through their arms dealers, oil companies, and other multinational corporations.

So the western governments and corporations, the Zionist elite in Israel, and the elites of the Arab world are all benefiting politically and financially from the continuation of this horrible conflict in the Middle East. This is exactly why the aforementioned parties just can't seem to come to terms and bring an end to this bloodbath. Like in any major war it is the common people of each nation who are the biggest victims and the elite of those same nations who reap all the benefits and use the lives of their citizens as bargaining chips behind closed doors. The Palestine papers resulted in the resignation of Saeb Erekat, chief negotiator for the PLO. The leaked documents proved that he was willing to abandon millions of refugees and showed no consideration for the needs of the people he was apparently representing. This is the typical nature of the relationship between politician and citizen throughout most of history.

It is also important to mention that the creation of Israel was not an issue that was brought forth by the Jewish refugees but was championed by the elite of the United Kingdom through the United Nations. Although the state of Israel was created after World War 2, the push for Zionism and a Jewish homeland in Palestine Began on the record in 1917, when the "Balfour Declaration" was printed. This declaration was not something that developed in parliament or among the Jewish people, but it was actually a letter between British aristocrat Lord Arthur Balfour and Lord Lionel Walter Rothschild. Some researchers even believe that it was the work of Rothschild himself, but either way Lord Balfour is quite easily linked as a close associate of the Rothschild dynasty, which strongly implicates their involvement. Rothschild was the representative of the "English Federation of Zionists." This was the same group of people that would fund Hitler's rise to power and ignore the genocide of the Jewish people who they claimed to be so concerned about.

In the western media and Israeli schools people are taught that the state of Israel was created specifically so there could be a Jewish homeland in the Middle East. The United Nations apparently did that out of the kindness of their heart for the Jewish people, the same Jewish people that they turned their backs on just a decade earlier when Hitler and the Nazis began their genocide. I highly doubt that there were not any ulterior motives on the part of the western aristocrats that initiated the creation of Israel. The United Nations was simply carrying out policies that they already wished to establish by exploiting the crisis that the Jewish refugees were facing. In other words the creation of a Jewish homeland was only one side effect of the western powers establishing their base in the Middle East, a side effect that they used to their advantage as a public relations tool.

The people who are truly behind Zionism are not Jewish nationalists they are elitist globalists who use nationalism and religion as a political tool to cultivate support for their non-ethnic imperial agenda. The Rothschild's may claim to be of Jewish descent but they are only "Jewish" in the same way that George Bush is "Christian", it is just a part of their public image that is in place so the common people can relate to them. Along with apparently being Jewish, the Rothschild's are also prominent Catholics and they basically run the treasury department at the Vatican. They play every possible side they can to gain as much control as possible and to more or less buy anyone who might stand in their way.

In reality the global elite and their puppets are the ones calling the shots in the US, Israel, and the UK. These people are not Catholics, Christians, or Jews but they are in fact practicing Satanists. I know it might sound a little bit farfetched at first to think that the most powerful people in the world are Satanists, but if you do some research into what Satanism is all about it makes a whole lot of sense. The modern satanic religion actually has nothing to do with "devil worship," as described by Anton Lavey, author of the satanic bible. Modern Satanism is rooted in hedonism, self-indulgence, and attention to very primal human triggers that perfectly describes the kind of lifestyles that are led by the elite, and the societies they create share these same values as well. Think about it! War, domination, destruction, exploitation, taxation, mind control, manipulation, and deception. Do those sound like the ideals of a Christian, a Catholic, a Jew, or a Satanist? I think the answer should be obvious. Actions speak louder than words, especially when those words are coming from a group of people that have a consistent record of violence and pathological lying.

As I explained earlier The Rothschild's were one of the primary sponsors of the Third Reich in Germany. Without their loans and oil companies Hitler would have never been able to turn the Weimar republic into a threatening military superpower in such a short amount of time. The Rothschild's were not the only prominent family to claim Jewish heritage yet betray the Jewish population of Europe during Hitler's genocide. George Soros the billionaire globalist who has been responsible for crashing markets all over the world admits himself that "his character was made" when he was working for the Nazis as a teenager snitching on other Jewish families so they could be robbed by the thuggish regime and sent off to concentration camps.

On December 20, 1998 during an interview with Steve Kroft on "60 Minutes" Soros admitted that he worked for the Nazis in this fashion. When asked in the interview if he had any sense of guilt he replied "Well, of course I c–I could be on the other side or I could be the one from whom the thing is being taken away. But there was no sense that I should not be there, because that was–well, actually, in a funny way, it is just like in markets–that if I were not there–of course, I was not doing it, but somebody else would–would–would be taking it away anyhow. And it was the–whether I was there or not, I was only a spectator, the property was being taken away. So the–I had no role in taking away that property. So I had no sense of guilt."[2]

So when the elite and so-called "leaders" claim to be a part of some ethnic, religious, or social group remember to pay attention to their actions instead of their words. Many times actions that are taken by the elite result in the death and impoverishment of the very people they are claiming to represent. Their loyalties are centered on wealth and power and are not influenced by any other social, ethnic, or religious factors; those are merely the false divisions that they use to splinter the slave class into feuding sects.

The UK is the base of operations for the elite, and most of their policies are carried out through the politicians in that country as well as their colonies. Coincidentally, just after World War 1 the League of Nations mandated Palestine and Mesopotamia to the UK in 1921 just 4 years after the British oligarchy produced the Balfour Declaration. After World War 2 since the UK was already in control of various Middle Eastern states, the elite began drawing more lines in the sand that would disrupt local diplomacy and open up the region to civil war and western influence. Another quick example is that of Afghanistan and Pakistan, it was once one nation with one people and was split up by British imperialists as a part of their divide and rule strategy. This happened all over the Middle East but is far more pronounced in the areas around Israel because of the refugee populations.

The main issues that are still controversial today are the displacement of the Native Arab's that once occupied the region and the constant expansion of new Israeli settlements. There is a bitter war raging between the Zionist government and the Arab people that inhabit the Middle East due to these issues. This feud is extremely tragic when considering that the people on both sides of the conflict who are caught up in the fighting are both refugees and victims of imperialism. Many of the Jewish people that are now inhabiting the Middle East are descendants of people who were displaced themselves at the hands of Hitler's evil regime. Even living within the state of Israel much of the Jewish population are themselves subject to oppression at the hands of the Zionist government.

When the state of Israel was created instead of integrating the Arab and Jewish cultures together the elite put policies in place that would force the Palestinian people onto unfertile ghettos, separated from water sources and food growing lands by giant walls. The Palestinians were also not given the right to establish a state of their own, without this they remain refugees and live in the most intolerable conditions. These policies would result in a growing hostility between the two groups that eventually flared up in physical violence. This violence has spread all throughout the oil rich Middle East and has allowed the elite to have a permanent involvement in the regions affairs, just as they planned.

Israel is facing a situation much the same as the United States, where their major political parties are heavily influenced by global banking interests. The international bankers use these nations and their militaries as pawns to carry out their globalist agenda. In America we have the Democrat and Republican parties that appear to be different but are really controlled by the same global interests, while in Israel the elite pushes their policies through the dominant "Zionist" political party. It is many times misunderstood in the media but Zionism has no link whatsoever to Judaism or to Jewish heritage, it is simply a political party just like the American Republican party or the British labor party. The Zionist party is the long arm of the elite in the Middle East, who have hijacked the Israeli government since its inception and are forcing its military to take actions that the Israeli people would not agree with if they had all the information. This is exactly the kind of situation that the United States is caught up in.

The United States and Israel are essentially colonies that are controlled financially and militarily by the elite from within the United Kingdom, which is why there is such an unbreakable alliance between the governments of these 3 countries. This is also why all 3 countries have the same economic and military policy, because they are not independent nations who act in the best interests of their people, but are actually a part of an elite alliance of bankers and aristocrats. The American government and military conducts its business overseas against the will of the public and on behalf of the corporations that run the country via the economy.

These corporations are primarily the banking and energy cartels that are owned by the Rockefellers, Rothschild's and other elite families. Israel works in very much the same way, the government has an agenda that is against the wishes and the best interests of the people, but they use propaganda and fear to push public opinion in a direction that suits their agenda. The issues unfolding in the Middle East have absolutely nothing to do with religion or ethnic conflict, but are politically and economically charged issues that have been propagated by western imperialism. Antagonizers and so called "leaders" on both sides of the conflict use nationalism and racism as a tool to manipulate their people into the battlefield, but that is not the reality of the situation.

Though the issues in the Middle East may seem complicated with how drawn out the peace talks are and how much the media confuses the issue, things really are not that difficult. It is important to address the corruption that exists within the Zionist government or else the international business interests will continue to use Israel and its people for their own imperialistic needs. They are the ones who are creating and profiting from these conflicts, not the Israeli or Palestinian people. The Israeli people are forced into military lives and convinced to fight a war that is not theirs, while the Palestinians are sold out and manipulated by their "leaders" as well. Both the Palestinian and Israeli people are honest, decent human beings that just want peace.

The average citizens of both groups are tired of the fighting and really wish to live in harmony with their fellow human beings. A Palestinian writer named Talal has written for Palestine's "Al Yam" newspaper for 15 years and has a pretty good grip on the situation. In a 2011 article he said "Even before the events that split our government and pit Hamas and Fatah against each other, youths were not well organized. They did not get much support from outside, or inside. The political factions were only interested in using them as employees or fighters." [3] This is the same way that the Zionist government looks at their people, and this attitude is common among the elite in the US and the UK as well.

The Palestinians have been tossed out into the wilderness, displaced from their homes and are striving to establish their own state. This would prevent them from being displaced again and would establish a proper economy so the Palestinian people can have a fighting chance to become a thriving society. The American government, which is also an arm of the elite, used these same policies to wipe out the native people that inhabited North America. The Native Americans were also not allowed to form a state of their own on their land and were pushed further and further away from their homes until the only places left for them were small reservations that were mostly in the desert. This is the kind of policy that the elite wish to carry out in Palestine using the Zionist party as a political front.

The development of a Palestinian state would prevent the kind of land takeover and genocide that occurred in the United States. This is a fair deal for the Israeli people, but for this to take place a more populous controlled political system is needed to replace the elite controlled Zionist party in Israel. It is only the economic and political situations surrounding the leadership of these nations that is bringing so much violence and disorder to the region. This is not an ethnic issue that is what the "leaders" of these countries want people to think because it distracts people from the real, political issues that are at the root of these problems.

The refugee crisis is not something that the Palestinians should hold against the Israeli people as they were just refugees themselves at the time when the state of Israel was created, besides the citizens within the country have no say in their governments actions anyway. The root of the crisis lies with the United Nations who actually made the decision to expel the native population and the interests that forced the UN to take these actions. The militant rulers like Hamas and Fatah are also responsible for escalating the conflict as is their counterparts in the Mossad and the current Zionist regime. Even the PLO who was apparently making an attempt at peace was ready to sell their people down the river for some political advancement.

It is extremely important to emphasize that the people of Israel should not be vilified and punished for the actions of their "leaders." They are very much in the same predicament that the citizens of the US and most of Europe are faced with. In all of these areas including Israel there is a strong counter culture movement among the youth. The young people in Israel are not happy with the actions of their government and their military. Military service is required for all male citizens which gives the young people a constant reminder of the realities of war. This is actually having the same kind of effect on the youth that the draft did for the youth in America during the 60's and 70's, its waking them up.

A large number of potential Israeli military enlistees are growing disenfranchised with their government and they are rebelling, partying, and seeking a less aggressive lifestyle than the one that has been chosen by their "leaders." Not every Palestinian is not a terrorist, nor is every Israeli a trigger-happy jarhead. This may be the image that Hamas, Fatah and the Zionist regime want for their people but this is not the kind of future that the young people of both territories wish to create. In 2011 there was social unrest and mass protests all over Israel, because Israeli citizens were unhappy with the actions of their government. There is also a very strong antiwar movement growing among orthodox Jewish Rabbis who are coming out and saying that the actions of the Zionist government are a complete contradiction to the teachings of Judaism and that the current regime is actually doing more harm than good for the Jewish community.

There has been a very strong but unreported resistance to Zionism within the Jewish community long before the creation of the state of Israel. On April 20, 1922, Rabbi David Philipson, testified before the House Foreign Affairs Committee, disagreeing with the proposition to make Palestine "the national home of the Jewish people." He insisted that, "No land can be spoken of as the national home of the Jewish people, as Jews are nationals of many lands." Rabbi Phillipson was a part of a powerful but largely ignored movement that is still a force today. Yakov M. Rabkin is a professor of history at the University of Montreal and he has recently written a book about this resistance called "A Threat from Within: A Century of Jewish Opposition to Zionism". In his book Rabkin says "Zionism constitutes the most radical revolution in Jewish history.

Opposition to this nationalist conceptualization of the Jew and of Jewish history was as intense as it was immediate. Even those rabbis who at first encouraged settlement in Palestine in the closing decades of the 19th century felt obliged to turn against Zionism. What made the Jews unique, they declared, was neither the territory of Eretz Israel nor the Hebrew language, but the Torah and the practice of mitzvahs."[4] These Rabbis and many other people of Jewish faith feel that the emphasis on Zionism takes away from the true teachings of their culture and that the Zionist regime does not embody Jewish values or properly represent Jewish people of the world or those in Israel.

These problems that face this region can actually be resolved quite easily but it would only happen under conditions that the elite would absolutely detest and refuse to accept. The people who have been displaced and are refugees as a result of this crisis must have any kind of employment blocks removed and should be offered citizenship to whichever nation they happened to be displaced in. This will at least improve their quality of living while they decide where they are going to start anew. When it is time for them to start anew they should be given amnesty and citizenship of any country in the area that can economically sustain them. Any funds that would be needed to make this better life possible should be provided by the United Nations and their subsidiary groups, the World Bank and the International Monetary Fund as these are the powers responsible for creating the refugee crisis and pillaging the entire planet. I definitely do not agree with how these groups acquired their resources to begin with, but now that they have managed to steal a great majority of the world's wealth, we should make sure that money is actually returned in a way that will benefit society.

An equal Palestinian state needs to be established by a government that actually represents them (if such a thing exists). By the same token the Israeli people need to take control of their government from the grips of the western elite. The Zionist regime and their financial backers in the west have done the Israeli people a great injustice, using them as cannon fodder and political pawns to establish a stronghold in the Middle East. Both groups have been misled, abused, and exploited by their self-appointed masters. As with almost every large-scale conflict in the world, the key to a peaceful resolution lies with the ability of the people to realize that there is no reason for them to be fighting. The feuds and conflicts of history have been orchestrated by and for the ruling class not civilians or army recruits. Bring the power to the people and bring the people together and there will be peace, but this is not what the "leaders" in the area want so they continue to prevent the advancement of human rights in the Middle East.

QUOTE SOURCES AND SUGGESTED READING
----
[0] The portable Mark Twain - Mark Twain, Tom Quirk (2004)
[1] http://www.globalissues.org/news/2011/02/27/8681
[2] Dec 20, 1998, 60 Minutes, Steve Kroft interview with George Soros
[3] http://www.globalissues.org/news/2011/02/27/8681
[4] A threat from within: a century of Jewish opposition to Zionism - Yakov M. Rabkin (2006)
[SR1] A threat from within: a century of Jewish opposition to Zionism by Yakov

M. Rabkin (2006)
[SR2] The Controversy of Zion by Douglas Reed
[SR3] The Invention of the Jewish People By Shlomo Sand

"Remember this revolution is born out of love for my people not hatred for others."
–Immortal Technique

Section 7

Peace

53. -An Error in Communication
54. -Peer Pressure in a Divided Culture
55. -The Global Consciousness Crisis
56. - The Illusion of Race
57. - Who are you callin crazy?
58. – Future Physics
59. - Positive Vibrations

"Political language is designed to make lies sound truthful and murder respectable, and to give an appearance of solidity to pure wind."
- George Orwell [0]

An Error in Communication

Language is without a doubt the most important and profound development in human history. It has allowed us to describe the world we live in and express ourselves to one another. Language lays the foundation for our belief systems, possibilities, and idiosyncrasies. Our view of the universe is shaped by the words that we use to describe what we see and experience. Written language is especially important because it immortalizes information and makes it possible for humans to record an extremely detailed history. This literary advancement in language was highly suppressed among the early monarchies that had control of their population's education. These oppressive rulers understood the incredible power that was represented by written language and made sure that they were the only ones who possessed that power.

Literacy was extremely uncommon until well after the industrial revolution. Before the renaissance of the middle ages, reading and writing was a secret art mainly reserved for the ruling class. Thus it was the story of the elite that got passed down through the generations and presented as history. The slaves and peasants were not able to contribute their perspective to history because their messages would not last many generations as an oral tradition. With no true past and no frame of reference our oppressed ancestors were unable to recognize the inhumane conditions that they suffered at the hands of their rulers. In many feudal societies throughout medieval Europe it was actually a punishable offence if someone from the underclass was caught with personal reading material or even calendars. The authoritarian rulers feared that if the peasants were to become educated then they would no longer be content with their slavery. The current view of history would be drastically different if the people who lived through slavery, poverty and political tyranny had an equal chance to pass their message to future generations.

In addition to literacy suppression, our entire vocabulary has been manipulated to carry subliminal implications. This hijacking of the vocabulary affected not only written language but the spoken word as well. Language manipulation was highly effective for the early establishment and is still used by governments all over the world today. In the United States our vocabulary has been crafted to support a male dominant, white, upper class perspective. By setting the parameters of our linguistic possibilities they can to an extent control the direction of the dialogue. They have been in wars all over the world but have called these wars everything from "police actions" to "peacekeeping missions." America is apparently an equal and free society yet everyone who is not a rich white male is considered a "minority." The "patriot act, "which is anything but patriotic, has set up a carefully named "homeland security" agency to act as a modern day Gestapo. This "newspeak" that I touched on earlier is found everywhere in American culture, especially in the political arena because if they actually straight up said what was going on in plain English there would be a huge civilian uproar.

Many people do not think of it this way, but human language is a technology, and like any form of technology it can be used for good or for evil. Language can be used to enlighten and inspire or imprison and control, just as nuclear energy can be used to heat homes or destroy the planet. However, language that helps people describe the true nature of their reality has been long suppressed and discouraged. It is absolutely absurd that there is a book of terms to describe the different parts inside a computer, but only a handful of words to describe human emotion or other natural phenomena. This is why it is so difficult to describe unexplained phenomena or articulate the difference between something like religion and spirituality, because the words are simply not there.

What we must do to counteract this problem is to expand the limits of our vocabulary and create new terms and new words to describe the indescribable. If you come up with a new word or new way of explaining something in your day-to-day conversations then by all means continue to use it! If it sounds good to you than your probably right and your addition to the language will most likely catch on, as long as it works. Terms like vibe, synchronicity, ego trip, or civil liberties have revolutionized philosophical dialogue just as terms like inertia, gravity, or relativity have revolutionized scientific dialogue. Imagine how hard it would be to have a conversation about the state of our society without words like "freedom," "oppression" or "autonomy." These philosophical terms are all fairly new to our vocabulary and allow us to better describe things that were at one time just beyond our descriptive possibilities. Some of these terms were created by philosophers, scientist, and psychologists, others by college students and hippies.

Anyone can contribute to the positive expansion of their cultures vocabulary and tear down the linguistic barriers set by those who keep us mentally enslaved under their cultural paradigm.

Advancing our communication skills is an essential step towards achieving world peace, one man who proved that fact in our lifetime is a traveler and psychologist by the name of Marshall Rosenberg. Rosenberg is responsible for developing a new way of speaking which he calls Non Violent Communication (NVC) or Compassionate Communication. This method of communication is simple and has had profound success all over the world, from the feuding tribes of the southern hemisphere to the broken homes of modern America. Marshall recognized that all human language is filled with traps that inevitably lead to conflict; these traps are trigger words that he referred to as "jackal language."

Jackal language consists of words that imply guilt, humiliation, shame, blame, coercion, or threats. Marshall believes that this kind of language and interaction is not a natural process but is the result of the "culture of domination" that he believes has consumed our species for at least eight thousand years. I would tend to agree with his assertion. To resolve conflicts it is necessary for us to avoid using jackal language and learn to be empathetic when working out our problems. According to NVC conflict arises between two or more people when someone in the equation has needs that are not being met. This is the root cause for humans acting out and the reason why some people are oftentimes unhappy with the actions of others. In most conflicts these issues are never addressed, instead of identifying everyone's feelings and needs to work towards a solution, the two parties begin a battle of blaming which neither side can ever truly win.

Nonviolent communication is a very easy method to explain but can be difficult to master. One of the most difficult parts of the process to actually grasp is the very first step, observation. In times of conflict many of us are very quick to confuse judgments with observations. An observation would be "our project is due next week." In this case you are only stating the facts of the situation; you are not making any judgments. A judgment relating to this observation would be *"our project is due next week and you haven't done a damn thing, I have done all of the work, your lazy."* This is an example of the kind of judgments that cause a lot of arguments and miscommunication. It is very common for conflicts to be filled with judgments and labels that only push the conversation into a more negative direction. Do not get discouraged with yourself if you find it difficult to speak without passing judgments or using jackal language, these are both things that are fundamentally woven into our language and seem natural to most people. A wise eastern Philosopher once said *"Observation without judgment is the highest form of intelligence."*[1].

The philosopher was right, this is an amazing achievement, but with some practice it can become second nature. Once an observation is made its time for the parties involved to express their feelings on the subject to establish a mutual understanding. Relating to our example scenario, to include the feeling aspect we could say the following: "our project is due next week, and I'm very worried about our grade, what we can do to make sure we pass?" In situations of conflict it is an unmet need that is causing discontent so the objective of the conversation is to identify the needs that are causing the feelings. Once everyone's needs are on the table it becomes very easy to see a possible solution in which everyone's needs are met and the conflict can be resolved.

This was a very quick and basic introduction to nonviolent communication but there are many books written by Marshall Rosenberg that discuss this in greater detail so it is better understood. This is by far one of the most important topics that I have covered in this book and I truly believe it has the potential to save the world. It is also extremely useful if applied to everyday life situations and can drastically change ones interactions with others for the positive. However, Marshall Rosenberg is just one great mind in a sea of millions and it is very possible for his method to be someday improved upon, or for an entirely different communication method to develop. In fact it is probably necessary for each generation to constantly be working to improve our language so it can be a tool of expression rather than a tool of oppression.

QUOTE SOURCES AND SUGGESTED READING
----
[0] Understanding management research: an introduction to epistemology - Phil Johnson, Joanne Duberley (2000)
[1] J. Krishnamurti - Nonviolent Communication: a Language of Life: Create Your Life, Your Relationships, and Your World in Harmony With Your Values - Marshall B Rosenberg, PH.D. (2003)
[SR1] Nonviolent Communication: a Language of Life by Marshall B Rosenberg
[SR2] Politics and the English Language by George Orwell
[SR3] Practical Spirituality: The Spiritual Basis of Nonviolent Communication by Marshall B Rosenberg
[SR4] Speaking Peace: Connecting with Others Through Nonviolent Communication by Marshall B Rosenberg

"The Matrix is a system, Neo. That system is our enemy. But when you are inside, you look around, what do you see? Businessmen, teachers, lawyers, carpenters. The very minds of the people we are trying to save. But until we do, these people are still a part of that system, and that makes them our enemy. You have to understand, most of these people are not ready to be unplugged. And many of them are so inured, so hopelessly dependent on the system that they will fight to protect it." – Morpheus {'The Matrix'} [0]

Peer Pressure in a Divided Culture

In modern pseudo democracies such as the United States, the establishments top priorities are to mold public opinion in a way that suit is the goals of the elite and preserve the institutionalized control systems that keep the people in check. This is often referred to as "social engineering" which basically just means large-scale social manipulation. There are a variety of ways that this is done but the most basic fundamental step is creating false divisions amongst the public, this is known as the "divide and rule" political strategy. They know that if all of the impoverished, downtrodden people of the world or even in a single country were to band together to fight for equality then their stranglehold on the human race would literally topple within days. So it is essential for them to keep the masses divided and in disagreement so they do not join together and overrun the empire. This has been the policy political systems all over the world for many centuries.

In American culture, women are played off against men, blacks against whites, Jews against Catholics and so on. Sadly, even the many civil rights struggles that sought to bring equality to this nation were all eventually co-opted and used to further divide the public. Oppressed African Americans were led to mistrust the white man down the street instead of the white men on congress and in Wall Street. Likewise women were led to mistrust the men in their families and communities, instead of the men in government who had long labeled them as second-class citizens. Many white males have been led to mistrust everyone that does not look like them, while at the same time blindly respecting authority. Every so-called "social group" has been played off against each other, which keeps everyone distracted from the true source of their oppression. Everyone is convinced that the problems in their society are caused by their neighbors, instead of the few crooked members of society that claim positions of "authority."

The Middle East has been tormented with authoritarian governments and oppressive "caste" systems for generations. Different castes relate to different classes within the social structure, creating a hierarchy that ranges from the poorest of the poor to the ruling elite. Every caste within these societies is oppressed by the ruling class, but they never rise up because of the mistrust and stereotypes that have been created between the lower and middle castes. For centuries the elite in the west and middle east alike have lived in luxury while the other 99.9% of the population lives in different levels of poverty constantly fighting and bickering over the small rations that are handed down to them by their rulers. This is just a culture where the class system is divided in a painfully obvious way, but it is certainly not the only area of the world where this policy is in place.

Early on in American history even before the revolutionary war, colonial governments used this tactic to keep their slave and working poor populations at bay. In colonial America the disparity of wealth was just as great as it is today and there was a very large population of working poor whites, many of which were considered "servants." There was a great fear among the so-called "masters" that the white servants would join up with the massive African slave population and revolt against the ruling class. Most of the servants at this time had no racial hatred whatsoever towards African slaves but had an extreme animosity towards the white aristocrats, who were responsible for the difficulty of everyday life. So to prevent the coming insurrection the ruling class gave the white servants a limited amount of freedom and respect. They were given the "privileges" of owning property, weapons and the right to vote for which aristocrat would rule over them. This created a divide between the lower class and the slaves and made the whole population easier to manage for the establishment. While the poor whites were able to have their limited rights they became more loyal to the ruling class and developed a false sense of superiority towards the slaves. These conditions would insure that there would be no insurrection.

This divisive strategy was also used to prevent organization within the plantations as well. The so-called "masters" imposed a class system on the slave populations which they held in captivity. Some slaves were given a limited amount of freedom and treated with a bit more respect, they were allowed to stay inside the mansion and were well fed and clothed in comparison to their brothers and sisters that were subject to the most cruel of conditions just outside the walls of the mansion. This is where the term "house slave" comes from. Whenever one of the slaves in the field would start talking about escape, they were usually told by one of the house slaves that "they have it good and they should stay where they are at."

These strategies were used to keep enough of the population comfortable so the comfortable portion of society would be convinced to protect the riches of their so-called masters from the less fortunate, while thinking that they were protecting their own. This also worked to divide any groups that threatened or questioned those riches. It is the Native American and African races, who have suffered more than anyone at the hands of the Anglo aristocracy, but the oppression of these elite transcends color lines, it even transcends class lines. Rich, poor, black, white, woman and man all experience oppression and manipulation from this very tiny portion of society. These people that call themselves the "masters," the elite, they have wronged us all and they have been frantically hiding the truth for generations. The atrocities that they have committed haunt them only in the sense that they are incredibly paranoid that someday we will come between them and their precious riches. So in their mind, it is necessary for them to devise schemes and plots to separate and weaken those that they see as a threat, which is pretty much the entire planet.

The divide and rule strategy is still a vital part of American politics to this day and has corrupted the foundation of our social structure. All of the issues that are sensationalized in politics create divisions by design and turn the working class against one another. The division that exists in our culture creates a deep need within most people to be accepted and to belong to some kind of social group. While this is obviously a positive thing and something that we should all strive to achieve, this desire often pushes us further away from the truth. Many people who understand the injustice that is taking place and realize that the status quo is insane are too afraid to speak out because they are afraid of what their parents, friends or even what total strangers will think of them.

Deep down most people do not accept the status quo, but since its socially unacceptable to question it everyone goes on thinking that they are alone, weak and powerless. Most self-respecting people can't go on feeling like that, so they rationalize what is going on around them, tell themselves it is the only world that is possible and then proceed to ridicule anyone who challenges their unconsciously created facade. This is why many people go on putting up with circumstances that they find to be intolerable, they are afraid of being alienated from their peers. Unfortunately, if your peers are ostracizing you for talking about peace and freedom then you might want to think about the company your keeping.

Remember that most of these people are just afraid. Just like a battered child who cries when being taken away from the safety of their abusive parents, we also feel comfort in unacceptable situations simply because we are familiar with them. Much like the child we need to break free from the familiar confines of our abuse and oppression. This situation is actually so common that the condition is actually classified medically as "Stockholm syndrome." Stockholm syndrome is typically used to describe hostages who develop positive feelings for their kidnapper because they are dependent upon them for sustenance. When we apply this concept to the macrocosm of our civilization we find that people living under a system of authoritarianism exhibit these exact same characteristics.

Our political and economic systems have been structured to protect the wealth of the elite and to add to it. It seems to be only simple logic that over enough time they will control just about all of the land and resources in the world and everyone will be dependent upon them for their basic needs. Under those circumstances we would be indebted to these people just for attaining our basic needs as human beings, and they have spent their whole lives creating a political environment where the only option to survival is through them. This is obviously some sort of slavery or serfdom, but it is tolerated by the masses because they place the blame amongst each other instead of where it really lies which is in the hands of elite, as it is their policies and maneuvers that impoverish the world.

QUOTE SOURCES AND SUGGESTED READING
----
[0] The Matrix Film

"There are no political solutions only technological ones, the rest is propaganda."
- Jacques Ellul [0]

The Global Consciousness Crisis

Our world is facing violence, political violence, economic violence, cultural violence, and spiritual violence, in its simplest form that is our root problem, violence. So then, it would make little sense for the solution to be violence. Then you're bringing more violence, into being. Offering more of the problem is not a proper way of solving it, what is needed is a completely new idea entirely. That in reality is what a solution is. Our oppressors have used violence as a means of control and dominance for thousands of years, and time after time we respond with more violence to bring them down. This chain of madness is what has gotten us to where we are at today, and this planet cannot afford another cycle.

We first must understand that although the threat we are facing is on a physical level it was formed at a conscious level. This basically means that the negativity we see in the world around us is a direct result of the turmoil within us. Our misguided thoughts and actions over many generations have built our current existence and before we can even think about tackling the physical problems we must come to peace within ourselves. Once we come to peace within ourselves we will think and act in a way that creates a more positive future. Revolutionary scientist Carl Jung articulated this problem quite well by stating *"The gigantic catastrophes that threaten us today are not elemental happenings of a physical or biological order but psychic events. To a quite terrifying degree we are threatened by wars and revolutions that are nothing other than psychic epidemics. At any moment several millions of human beings may be smitten with a new madness, and then we shall have another world war or devastating revolution. Instead of being at the mercy of wild beasts, earthquakes, landslides, and inundations, modern man is battered by the elemental forces of his own psyche."* [1]

There is a very close relationship between human thought and the balance of the world around us. Ancient philosophy recognizes this relationship, and modern science now recognizes this relationship as well due to countless breakthroughs in quantum physics. Scientists and researchers all over the world are working to show the unseen connection between our species and the world around us. In Japan for example, a doctor by the name of Masaru Emoto made an astonishing breakthrough with his study of how unseen vibrations in human speech and thought can cause distilled water to form beautiful crystals, much like snowflakes. In 8 years of experimenting with different water structures, and using what he calls "hado water" DR. Emoto was able to cure tens of thousands of patients. These patients all came from different medical, economic and spiritual backgrounds and saw the same positive results.

The term "hado" means "wave" or "move" which refers to the vibrations that cause these crystals to appear in water. Emoto proved that vibrations within music, written word, spoken word, and even silent human thought can change the physical world around us. Positive vibrations and thought patterns caused lifeless distilled water to flower into miraculous water crystals, while negative vibrations and thought patterns actually made the frozen water seem even more dull and lifeless then before. This experiment confirms that our thoughts have a profound impact on the physical world. If positive thoughts can have this kind of effect on water then just imagine what it could do when applied to humanity.

On a deeper level you can see how the discovery of hado water sheds some light on the crisis we are facing. The vast majority of the people on the planet are constantly putting out negative energy, damaging the natural world around us on a molecular level. This destruction that we cause ultimately comes back to us, because we rely on nature for our health and survival. If people were to start walking a different path, and began to transfer positive energy around the planet instead of negative energy, then much like DR Emoto's hado water our planet would transform into something infinitely more beautiful than what we see today.

QUOTE SOURCES AND SUGGESTED READING
----
[0] The Technological Society by Jacques Ellul
[1] The Collected Works: Civilization in transition - Carl Gustav Jung (1964)
[SR1] Messages from Water by Masaru Emoto

"I do not care if you're gay, black, Chinese, straight. That means nothing to me. It is all an illusion."
– Joe Rogan [0]

The Illusion of Race

Every human being is a unique individual. We each have different thoughts, different inspirations, different hair, and eye and skin color. These differences should all be embraced as it shows that everyone is bringing a unique and enlightening perspective to the table for humanity. Sadly, those who seek to control us use these differences to put us against each other, and take the heat off themselves. Throughout the history of imperialism our "leaders" have conditioned us to be frightened and hostile towards those who are not under their rule. That is because our rulers either wish to enslave this other people, or take their land and resources, or both.

In order to carry out war and conquest it was necessary for rulers to infect their subjects with blind nationalistic ideologies. People were trained from birth to think of their nationality as being superior to all others. Citizens were taught that people who lie outside the domain of their ruler were sub human, their lives were said to be less valuable than those that were inside of the kingdom. Imposing this kind of twisted worldview made it possible for kings and emperors to use their citizens as mercenaries and gatekeepers. This is how racism was invented, as a mental justification for conquest and the brutality of the ruling class. By using fear tactics and generalizations the powers that be have managed to turn everyone in the world against one another so they can play war games amongst themselves, using us as the pieces.

Some of the darkest moments in human history were the result of mob frenzies fueled by racist ideologies. The crusades, the German holocaust, the Native American holocaust, the African holocaust, and various forms of slavery have all been carried out under the racist visions of various elite psychopaths. Each time it has been a different control freak from a different corner of the earth with the same list of excuses and a similar set of dehumanizing epitaphs. This is happening in any country with an imperialistic, dominating system of government, just as it has for centuries. Although the mass majority of people are more conscious now and are opposed to racism, the elite still project a very racist message through the media and through their social policies. This influence has a very serious impact on the acceptance of the current occupation in the Middle East and the corporate rape and pillaging of the 3rd world.

Humanity as a whole wants to move past this barbaric self-destruction but the elites and their dominant political systems create a social environment where certain groups are at a disadvantage due to their ethnicity. The establishment is constantly promoting racism and creating social injustice under the radar, regardless of what they say in the public arena. This has been the policy of the ruling class for centuries and is still very much alive today just in a more subtle subliminal form.

Unfortunately, racism is alive and well today in the form of ethnocentrism and nationalism. Both of these words mean the same thing but ethnocentrism would be a more realistic description that carries a more negative stigma. The Merriam Webster Dictionary defines ethnocentrism as "the belief in the inherent superiority of one's own ethnic group or culture" and defines Nationalism as "loyalty and devotion to a nation; especially: a sense of national consciousness exalting one nation above all others and placing primary emphasis on promotion of its culture and interests as opposed to those of other nations or supranational groups". Both of these definitions sound like a dressed up form of racism to me. These ideologies are an attempt to justify or rationalize aggression against another group of people. These are cultural assumptions that are rooted in falsities and continue due to a lack of understanding.

Regardless of the color of our skin, the language we speak or the cultural ideologies we subscribe to, we are all a part of the same human family. In every country throughout the ages we have been deceived by our oppressors. People of all nationalities struggle and suffer at the hands of conniving elitists who tell us that other oppressed people in some far away land are the reason for our unhappiness. In reality the oppressed people of all nations have more in common with each other than they do with the people in charge of their governments. Unfortunately, we have all been lied to and conditioned to be suspicious of our brothers and sisters. Our real enemies are the snakes that promote subversive racist political systems and put the human organism on a path of self-destruction.

QUOTE SOURCES AND SUGGESTED READING
----
[0] The Joe Rogan Podcast

"Our society is run by insane people for insane objectives. I think we are being run by maniacs for maniacal ends and I think I'm liable to be put away as insane for expressing that. That is what is insane about it."
- John Lennon [0]

Who Are You Callin Crazy?

We live in a crazy world, a world where war is peace, lies are truth, and ignorance is wisdom. Our species as a collective is speaking the language of hate, with its wars and its divisions and all the other injustice we have come to accept. So I guess it only makes sense for those who speak the language of love to be written off as "crazy", "irrational," or "idealistic." Most of the greatest thinkers to walk the earth have been called "lunatics," simply for questioning the status quo. It is important for us to pay close attention to these people, they are the greatest teachers that we have and without their contributions we would understand even less about the world around us then we do now.

Now in modern times when we hear of Socrates we think of him as being the father of philosophy, one of the first great thinkers recorded in this age. Though in death his achievements have been respected and remembered, in life this was unfortunately not the case. Socrates spent his whole life asking questions, as most philosophers find themselves doing and towards the end of his life those questions led him to some politically forbidden answers. Athens had a sort of pseudo democracy much like the governments we see today in the west, where a ruling class were actually the ones running the country, not "the people" as was advertised. This ruling class was not very fond of Socrates because he saw through their game and was always questioning their authority, and even worse encouraging the public to question it as well.

Eventually the aristocracy grew very afraid of this great teacher and like many other great teachers Socrates was put to death by the ruling class. This all happened in ancient Greece, the apparent birthplace of democracy, yet in reality this was a place where slavery was still common and a great thinker was killed because he wanted people to have freedom over their own minds. 2000 years later an Italian astronomer and mathematician by the name of Galileo Galilei was condemned to medieval house arrest for his radical ideas. What was this heresy that Galileo committed? He insisted that earth revolved around the sun and that the earth was not the center of the universe.

Even in contemporary American culture it is easy to find free thinkers that have made their mark on history, and changed the way we look at the world around us. For example let's take a look at Mark Twain, the legend of American literature. In his own time Mark Twain was a rebel, who was constantly speaking out against authority. He seemed to have a pretty good idea about where our government might have been heading and was always dropping underhanded knowledge in his writings. Closer to our generation we saw John Lennon, a pop music icon that would sacrifice everything, even his own life in the fight for peace. In the years before his death Lennon was extremely outspoken when it came to the war in Vietnam and was very critical of the government and corporations that were impoverishing the world. He became such a threat to the establishment that they actually deported him from the U.S and then finally assassinated him when he was able to reenter the states. Another great musician that fought the struggle was Bob Marley, one of the most popular recording artists of all time. All that one needs to do is listen to any album by "The Wailers" with an open mind, and it will become obvious that this is very revolutionary music. It is almost eerie to see how much of Bob Marley's music is relevant in today's world.

If you were watching the news in the 1960's you would have seen that Martin Luther King was out to destroy America and that the good policemen were doing their jobs beating and arresting civil rights protesters. At that time the civil rights movement was a serious threat to the establishment, so much so that the C.I.A. developed a program to target and silence civil rights leaders, this program was called "cointelpro." It is this program that many researchers believe is responsible for the deaths of Martin Luther King, Malcolm X and other civil rights activists. The fact that Martin Luther King was an enemy of the state did not silence his message, and even in his death that message was not silenced.

Kings message is so strong because he was undeniable; he was so positive and non-violent that it demanded respect not only from his followers but his oppressors as well. It is possible that King was inspired by our greatest teacher of the past few hundred years, Mahatma Gandhi. Gandhi brought a whole imperial nation to their knees without a single gun being fired; he did this through promoting peaceful resistance. It is interesting that Gandhi was one of the most radical people of the 20th century, an "idealistic extremist" and at the same time one of the most peaceful people to walk the earth. What would the world be like if we were all a bit "crazy" like Gandhi was? I would say it would be a world worth living in, and a world worth working towards.

The alchemists, artists, and revolutionaries such as Gandhi, Socrates, Martin Luther King, and others who have risked their lives to speak a message of peace were far from mentally unsound, if anything they were true examples of human sanity. They were only labeled as insane because they represented ideals that were radically different from those of the existing power structure. If we actually look at the definitions for various forms of insanity we can see that being different, radical or out of the ordinary has absolutely no relation to mental illness. In modern clinical terms aggressive insanity is described as psychopathic behavior.

Characteristics of a psychopathic mind would be selfishness, ruthlessness and a lack of empathy for other people. Psychopathic behavior is often confused with psychotic behavior but these are actually two very different things. A psychotic person is more prone to violence and overt aggression because they have little self-control and no regard for consequence. Meanwhile a psychopath is well aware of his or her actions and their possible consequences, so they display more subtle but equally destructive violent behavior. The actions of a cunning psychopath can actually be far more destructive than that of a person who is psychotically deranged because they are better able to conceal mental instability, thus allowing them to impact more victims over greater periods of time without getting caught.

Psychopaths are known to be dishonest, manipulative, and impulsive and have a completely different thought process then the rest of society. Most of us make our decisions with the wellbeing of other people in mind while psychopaths are not only incapable of doing this but they actually realize this fact and see their cold mentality as an advantage that they have over their peers. They actually view empathy as a weakness and with this perspective they manipulate people by playing on their natural concern for others. Psychopaths never accept responsibility for their cruel actions and always blame others, especially their victims to further justify the negative situations that they have created.

Psychopaths make up a very small percentage of the human population but they come from various walks of life and many times their ruthless and manipulative disposition lands them in positions of great power. In reality the only thing that separates a serial killer from a wartime tyrant or Wall Street robber baron is social status, opportunity, and intellectual capabilities. Unfortunately it is actually quite common for psychopaths to come into positions of power simply due to the fact that they are obsessed with dominating their peers and will stop at nothing to get what they want.

It is so typical for our "leaders" to be manipulative, deceitful, callous, and ruthless that most people actually expect this kind of behavior from a politician or businessperson. Yet these are the very personality traits that characterize the most violent and dangerous element in our society, so this means that psychopathic behavior is actually accepted simply because it is being exhibited by those with authority. To make matters worse the general public actually begins to mimic the psychopathic behavior displayed by their "leaders" since it has been established as acceptable. This is why our values are demoralized and twisted, because they have been established by control freak rulers based on their psychopathic worldviews. They make sure that their perception of reality is the dominant view within the culture, so they can use that culture to impose their will on the general population.

Only an extremely selfish and deranged person with no empathy for other human beings would take place in starting wars, carrying out genocide or neglecting suffering people, but these are the kind of things that our so called "leaders" do on a regular basis. Yet, unfortunately many of these acts are carried out through a proxy such as a government or corporation. In other words, these psychopaths hide behind a group or organization and basically say "I am committing all of these horrors on behalf of this group of people and if you want to come after me then you have to get through them first." Many people on both sides are convinced by this argument, even those who are being taken advantage of. In the case of America, the American people are convinced that their "leaders" are carrying out wars of conquest in their best interest when in reality they are being used as workhorses, scapegoats, and political pawns. Sadly, the insanity does not end with political and social violence; many of these elites lead extremely depraved private lives that are hidden from the mainstream culture. Some of the things they do are so downright careless and sick that in today's connected world the deranged behavior of our illegitimate rulers is starting to see the light of day.

The most common traits that psychopathic elites share is sexual deviancy, abuse and overall predatory behavior. There have been countless stories that have surfaced in recent memory where some of the most powerful people in the world are caught up in a rape case, human trafficking ring, or child prostitution racket. The most recent and high profile rape case involving a member of the aristocracy occurred in the spring of 2011 when the chief of the International Monetary Fund, Dominique Strauss-Kahn was charged with sexually assaulting a hotel maid while he was staying in New York. When the story broke women from all over the world came forward with similar stories about Kahn, saying that it was dangerous to be alone in a room with him. These people are so arrogant because most of the time they suffer little consequences for their depraved actions, even when they are caught.

A perfect example of this came less than a year before Kahn's now infamous hotel maid encounter when British banker and close friend of the royal family, Jeffrey Epstein got off with a 13-month sentence after being convicted of sex crimes including pedophilia. Conchita Sarnoff writing for the online newspaper "The Daily Beast" explained the horrific background of Epstein's sex crimes. According to her article "Some of the most shocking allegations against Epstein surfaced only after the conclusion of an FBI probe, in civil suits brought by his victims: for example, the claim those three 12-year-old French girls were delivered to him as a birthday present.

The feds did identify roughly 40 young women, most of them underage at the time, who described being lured to Epstein's Palm Beach home on the pretense of giving a "massage" for money, then pressured into various sex acts, as well as the "Balkan sex slave" Epstein allegedly boasted of purchasing from her family when she was just 14. More recently, a big cash payment from Mail on Sunday coaxed one of Epstein's main accusers out of anonymity to describe what she claims were her years as a teenage sex toy. This victim, Virginia Roberts, produced a photo of her with Prince Andrew in 2001 and reported that Epstein paid her $15,000 to meet the prince. Then 17 years old, she claims that she was abused by Epstein and "loaned" to his friends from the age of 15." [1]

After hiring some of the best lawyers in the world and using ruthless witness intimidation tactics Jeffrey Epstein was able to escape any serious charges like so many others in his position. Epstein was closely connected with the British royal family who also has a scandalous history in human trafficking, recently one of their victims William Arnold Combes was able to get away from the situation and tell the world about the horrors he was subject to, by some of the world's most powerful people.

The human trafficking industry is so elusive and difficult to prosecute because trials are shut down, cases are dropped, or the investigation is completely diverted whenever evidence surfaces that implicates the aristocracy, which happens more often than not. The elite has been organizing and profiting from the human slave trade for many centuries so it really does not take a stretch of the imagination to consider that they are still behind the business today, especially when the evidence is constantly implicating them. There are almost too many cases to list in which high profile public figures or organizations were accused in pedophilia or human trafficking cases, but quickly dodged any prosecution or public scrutiny due to their control of the legal system and media. The rampant child molestation accusations that have been brought upon catholic priests are by far the most obvious examples of how people in positions of power claim the moral high ground while at the same time leading a predatory lifestyle.

There have been many cases in recent memory where aristocrats have been caught up in child prostitution rings and quickly had the story swept under the rug. One such case was on June 29 1989, when the Washington Times' Paul M. Rodriguez and George Archibald reported on a Washington D.C. prostitution ring that had intimate connections with the White House and President George H.W. Bush. It was suspected that this was connected with the Franklin prostitution ring that was being exposed at the same time, in a different part of the country. That story involved the manager of the Franklin Community Federal Credit Union in Nebraska. His name was Lawrence "Larry" King and he was also a prominent republican politician.

Various unconnected victims accused him of transporting them around the country to be used as sex slaves for politicians. When the accusations finally came to light, the victims were railroaded out of court and threatened into recanting their statements, thus making themselves guilty of perjury in the process. This was unfortunately enough to drop the case and actually send the victims to jail. The truth of the matter did not come out until former Nebraska State Senator John DeCamp went back to reexamined the case and discovered that the accusations were indeed true.

Human trafficking is an industry of the elite, it always has been. Your average blue collar, white-collar people are not buying slaves, and they certainly are not selling them either! The slave trade has been going on for a very long time and it has always been an industry ran by the elite. This is still very much a part of western culture, even companies with major government contacts have been accused of organizing full-scale slave rings. These companies have not only been protected by their governments, but they were also able to keep the contracts and subsidies that they had prior to the accusations.

Some of the world's largest multinational corporations such as DynCorp and Halliburton were exposed as major players in the global human trafficking market. These companies did not work alone, but cooperated with each other through various subsidiaries and had the luxury of government protection. When suspicion was brought upon these companies it was swept under the rug by government officials, even high-ranking members of the establishment such as Donald Rumsfeld were implicit in covering up this scandal. On March 11th 2005 he was questioned by Congresswoman Cynthia McKinney and he admitted on the record that the allegations did have credibility, but he pushed the blame off onto a few "rogue" employees. He used the "few bad apples" line that the government always dishes out when they are caught up in scandal. Although Rumsfeld and other high-ranking officials claimed that they would look into the case, they actually prevented any serious investigations from taking place. This happens every day, even organizations like the UN and NATO have come under fire for running slave rings out of third world countries when they are on "peacekeeping missions"

The things I have just discussed are absolutely crazy and depraved, but they are sadly true and what I'm about to talk about is actually even more disturbing. What is more cruel and disgusting than human trafficking? I'm talking of course about, human sacrifice, mass murder, and cannibalism. I know it sounds too outrageous to be true, but these horrific practices have been commonplace among elites in various different cultures throughout history. In most modern cultures, mass murder and human sacrifice still takes place out in the open under the cover of warfare, while cannibalism also still takes place but behind closed doors.

It is only in the past few hundred years that the practice of cannibalism among royals was forced underground. In Europe around the time of the American Revolution "corpse medicine" was very popular among elites; Charles II even brewed his own. Today this aspect of royal life has been kept secret, but many other bizarre practices of the elite have been exposed to the public. Strange rituals have been infiltrated and videotaped at prestigious country clubs such as "The Bohemian Grove." Almost every single elite organization is associated with some sort of depravity, and there is plenty of evidence to verify the truth of these claims.

For most people this information is a lot to take in and may be very hard to believe because it is just so sick and extreme. This level of insanity and cruelty is very hard for most people to understand, because most people are kindhearted individuals that would not like to see anyone get hurt. The majority of the general public also believes the great myth that people in authority are to be trusted and can do no wrong. If history has shown us anything, it shows us that power makes people do very crazy and illogical things, pretty much across the board. When people are in positions of power and have authority over others it literally changes their whole psychological process and seems to make them far less empathetic than they were before they attained their power. Authority seems to make it easier for people to justify or rationalize immoral actions and it tends to create a mentality in which the lives of others are less valuable.

Deborah Gruenfeld, a psychologist at the Stanford Business School did a study that analyzed over 1,000 decisions made by the United States Supreme Court between 1953 and 1993. She found that as the judges ascended the power structure of the court, or became part of a majority coalition, their written opinions became vague and they also became less considerate of outside perspectives. Many psychologists refer to this phenomena as "the paradox of power" and its characteristics are visible anywhere you find authority. That is not to say that every person who ever had authority over someone else was a pedophile and a cannibal, that is only in very extreme cases where people have had somewhat global authority for many generations. There are many good people involved in the establishment who do genuinely believe that their doing the right thing, but unfortunately most days they are taking orders from complete lunatics.

      Every president, chairmen of the Federal Reserve, corporate CEO, decorated general and many other agents of the aristocracy lead lifestyles of violence and deceit with a total lack of empathy for the people whose lives are negatively impacted by their actions. Yet when someone speaks out against the cruelty of these traditions they are the ones who are written off as mentally unstable? Sanity is not something that should be judged by observing ones thoughts or opinions, rather it should be judged by observing their actions. If ones actions are detrimental to the wellbeing of others and there are no signs of remorse then there is a pretty good chance that you are dealing with a person who is mentally unsound. On the other hand just because someone is unusual, or different does not mean that they are insane, as long as they are still peaceful in their interactions.

QUOTE SOURCES AND SUGGESTED READING
----
[0] John Lennon, Interview BBC-TV (June 22, 1968)
[1] http://www.thedailybeast.com/articles/2010/07/20/jeffrey-epstein-billionaire-pedophile-goes-free.html
[SR1] Political Ponerology (A Science on the Nature of Evil Adjusted for Political Purposes) by Andrzej M. Lobaczewski
[SR2] The Authoritarian Personality (Studies in Prejudice) by Theodor W. Adorno, Else Frenkel-Brunswik, Daniel J. Levinson
[SR3] Emotional Wellness by Osho
[SR4] EMOTIONS: Freedom from Anger, Jealousy & Fear by Osho

"Evolution has exponential timing. It'll be half as long 'til the next breakthrough that blows our mind. It is up to people to brave on with experimentation. Move forth the species by using our imagination."
– 311 (Rock/Reggae Group) [0]

This chapter contains personal theoretical assumptions of my own; please do your own research after reading this to form your own opinion.

Future physics

Many of us who have been brought up in the technological age of satellites and wireless communication take for granite the impossible feats that are taking place right before our eyes every day. In just a few generations our knowledge of the universe has grown at a pace never seen before in the history of humankind. This new knowledge has allowed us to do things that were unthinkable just a short time ago. If someone 50 years ago were to be shown today's cutting edge technology, it would appear to them as magic.

As intelligent of a species that humans are, it is surprising to see how arrogant they can be when it comes to the limits of their own knowledge. Yet, time after time our theories about the nature of existence are proven wrong by those who come after us. Even brilliant scientists in the past that were bold enough to call something "impossible," were eventually proven wrong. In 1825 the philosopher Auguste Comte declared in his *"course de philosophie"* that it was impossible for science to determine what the stars were made of. Lord Kelvin, the prominent Victorian scientist who is buried next to Sir Isaac Newton insisted that airplanes, X rays, and radio were absolutely impossible.

Many life changing technological advances have been made possible by complex mathematics and a new revolutionary field of science called "quantum physics." Quantum physics represents a new and more imaginative era in scientific research. Science as we know it at the beginning of the 21st century is a very mundane and close-minded institution. As a result of hundreds of years of religious oppression the scientific community would immediately dismiss any kind of paranormal or spiritual answers to their questions. This kind of arrogant approach is certainly not scientific or unbiased. In the long battle of wits against the Catholic Church, the scientific community had become exactly what they were trying to destroy. Science has become a dogmatic, mind imprisoning institution itself. Luckily quantum physics has forced the mainstream scientific dialogue to be somewhat less rigid, but that is not to say that the scientific establishment is not still a completely dogmatic and mind imprisoning institution to today, even with the recent addition of quantum physics.

It is true science has brought us many great things, and the scientific method specifically has helped us decode our reality better than any of our ancestors. However, as I explained earlier, the direction of scientific progress and research has been misdirected and tightly controlled by the ruling class. This is the point that I am making, I am in no way attacking science itself or the scientific method. The Soviet government in Russia used falsified "science" on a regular basis as a means of distorting reality and controlling the public discourse. This is still happening in Russia today but to a lesser degree, and it is definitely happening in the west at an ever-increasing rate. This does not mean that that there is something wrong with science; it just means that science can be used as a weapon of oppression and control when it is controlled by such a small portion of society.

There are a lot of positives though; the discoveries within Quantum Physics put serious doubt on the "if I can't physically touch it, it does not exist" philosophy taken on by conventional science. String Theory, The Uncertainty Principal, and studies involving extremely small atoms and very complicated mathematics have torn down a lot of the barriers that were separating conventional science from a clear picture of reality. Through these studies we have learned that there is an endless world of life and energy that is not detectable by our 5 senses. Quantum physics show us that the world is far more complex and unpredictable then conventional science believed it to be.

QUOTE SOURCES AND SUGGESTED READING
----
[0] 311 - Evolution - Sound system (1999)
[SR1] Quantum Enigma: Physics Encounters Consciousness by Bruce Rosenblum, Fred Kuttner
[SR2] Taking the Quantum Leap: The New Physics for Nonscientists by Fred A. Wolf

"Our senses enable us to perceive only a minute portion of the outside world. Our hearing extends to a small distance. Our sight is impeded by intervening bodies and shadows. To know each other we must reach beyond the sphere of our sense perceptions. We must transmit our intelligence, travel, transport the materials, and transfer the energies necessary for our existence."
- Nikola Tesla [0]

This chapter contains personal theoretical assumptions of my own; please do your own research after reading this to form your own opinion.

Positive Vibrations

Modern science has finally began to catch up with the sacred knowledge that was possessed by the ancients thousands of years ago. Ancient people may not have had the advanced technology that we do today but they had a far greater understanding of consciousness, energy fields, astrology, and other mysteries of the natural world. Indigenous Cultures were aware that there are many invisible layers of our existence that are not detectable by our 5 senses, as we have recently been shown through the discovery of atoms, germs and energy. Just a few hundred years ago most of these ideas would have come across as either completely insane or would have been labeled as black magic.

Through quantum Physics we have learned that energy waves of all kinds play a huge role in how the world around us works. We have also learned that our consciousness has a profound impact on how our reality unfolds. The idea of "waves" transmitting information is actually very common in modern science. Our technological society is made possible by invisible vibrations such as radio waves, or satellite transmissions, for example. The room that you are sitting in right now is filled with many different vibrations or "waves. " Some of these vibrations are synthetic and come from machines that our species have created, and then others come from the human consciousness. The natural "Vibes" that occur as a result of consciousness travel from person to person in waves, just as Wi-Fi waves travel from transmitter to transmitter.

Brain waves are organic vibrations that originate in our psyche and are constantly being projected out to the universe. It is these brainwaves that are responsible for mysterious phenomena like telepathy. Telepathy is not reserved for psychics and gurus, every human being is capable of telepathy. It is simply the transmission of signals from one consciousness to another. Have you ever thought about someone then right away got a phone call or email from that person? Has someone ever taken the words right out of your mouth when the words were not even relevant to the conversation? These situations come up often in most of our day-to-day lives and are made possible by the sending and receiving of brain waves. Right now our world is in danger because too many people are operating on a low vibrational frequency, it is these negative vibrations that are responsible for the destructive forces we see around us. The power to manifest a better reality is hidden within every soul, but in order to uncover that potential one must be operating on a higher vibrational frequency.

QUOTE SOURCES AND SUGGESTED READING
----
[0] The Nikola Tesla Treasury - Nikola Tesla (2007)

"There is a spiritual obligation; there is a task to be done. It is not, however, something as simple as following a set of somebody else's rules."
-Terence McKenna

Section 8

Shamanism

60. - The Psychedelic Inquisition
61. - Why Shamanism?
62. - Meditation
63. - Responsible Shamanism in the 21st Century
64. -Marketing Illness and Addiction
65. -Fundamentals of Firewater
66. -Marijuana: Miracle not Menace

"Prohibition will work great injury to the cause of temperance. It is a species of intemperance within itself, for it goes beyond the bounds of reason in that it attempts to control a man's appetite by legislation, and makes a crime out of things that are not crimes. A Prohibition law strikes a blow at the very principles upon which our government was founded."
-Abraham Lincoln [0]

The Psychedelic Inquisition

It is a matter of provable fact that psychedelics are the safest compounds within the modern drug culture. The strongest hallucinogen known to man dimethyltryptamine is actually less damaging to the human body than America's favorite fix, caffeine. Many substances that are deeply imbedded in American culture such as alcohol, caffeine, nicotine, or pharmaceutical narcotics are in fact toxins, while psychedelic compounds are actually physically benign and many times already occur naturally in human metabolism. What this means is that the chemicals that make psychedelics do what they do are actually naturally occurring compounds that are already inside your body.

Study after study confirms the safety and natural composition of these substances, yet psychedelics are vilified in our media, politics, and other cultural institutions. This massive public smear campaign exists because the establishment fears the impact that psychedelics would have on the materialistic society that keeps them rich and powerful. You see, these drugs are not dangerous to the individual or the community but they make us seek our own answers about the world around us, instead of swallowing the line of garbage we have been fed by the establishment. Psychedelics will break down the personal ego and cultural barriers that our materialistic society has corrupted us with and will make negative cultural norms such as war; poverty and oppression seem completely insane. This kind of social clarity could be very dangerous for the establishment and their control system, which is why they insist that these substances are bad and cannot be introduced into society.

The government is not against all drugs, they shove drugs down your throat every day through your food, drinking water, prescriptions and the street drugs that they smuggle into the country via the CIA. What the government is against is the practice of shamanism, the oldest religion in the world that connects the practitioner to his environment and his fellow human beings. Shamanism is a possible antidote for the cultural poison that plagues this age. Whether it is through meditation, psychedelic journeying or spiritual healing the practice of shamanism can very quickly free a person from the mental restrictions of a dominating culture.

Terrence McKenna, one of the frontrunners of the modern psychedelic age understood the nature of this situation very well and toured around the world to speak with audiences about the wonders of psychedelic shamanism. In one of his lectures Terrence articulated the psychedelic inquisition quite well by saying *"all cultures are involved in the culture game and psychedelics transcend the culture game, and whether you're a citizen of Jerusalem, a Tokyo stock broker or a tribal islander when you take psychedelic substances your cultural values will suddenly be much more relativistically revealed to you. And that is political dynamite. Psychedelics challenge the assumptions of any cultural or political system and that makes them dangerous to every culture or political system. So if there is anything a Marxist dictatorship, a high tech industrial democracy or a theocracy, they can all get together on one thing that is that psychedelic drugs are a knife poised at the heart of community values, well this is just simply nonsense, and all the reasons brought forth are a red herring. Psychedelics are among the safest substances known for human ingestion. Considering the depth of their impact on human mental functioning the fact that you pick yourself up 6-8 hours later and go on about your business with an expanded point of view is quite remarkable."*[1]

McKenna's point is highlighted in recent American history by the counter culture explosion of the 1960s. Psychedelic research began in the late 1950s and became a regular part of the youth culture by the mid-1960s. The explosion of psychedelic use interestingly coincides with the explosion of cultural freedom and antiestablishment sentiments of that decade. It is for this reason that the American government took quick action to make these substances illegal and to vilify them in the public arena. Laws were passed which imposed strict penalties on anyone involved in psychedelic use, manufacture, or even scientific study. Yea that is right, psychedelic drugs are actually the only subject that science is almost completely forbidden to explore, only recently have any serious studies into psychedelics been able to take place. The establishment knew that the psychedelic movement was a threat to their control system and that if enough of the population were exposed to this experience then their whole system would be in jeopardy. If psychedelics were tolerated and further explored they knew that they would see more counter culture movements, protests and overall more questions on their ill-gotten authority.

Luckily there have been some brave researchers over the years. Psychiatrist Dr. John Halpern, of Harvard medical school did a study of people with cluster headaches and discovered that the majority of patients who took LSD or psilocybin noticed a drastic reduction in their pain. In the past few years more and more of these studies have developed all over the world, researching the possible therapeutic uses for psychedelic compounds. From Rick Strassman's experiments into consciousness and DMT to the many experiments that have conclusively shown LSD and Psilocybin to be beneficial for people with anxiety, substance abuse problems and troubles with creativity. Yet despite the mounting evidence that they can be used for positive means, research into psychedelics has remained extremely taboo in most mainstream circles. And remember, the mainstream is not just completely disregarding all this scientific and anecdotal evidence, but they are also completely ignoring the recent history of psychedelics influencing important technological breakthroughs.

Without the creative application of psychedelic drugs it is very possible that the personal computer never would have been invented and DNA may have never been discovered. This is not rumor or speculation, Steve Jobs, the mind behind the first Apple computers, iPods, iPhones and other revolutionary inventions, has frequently said that his experience with psychedelics were among the most important events in his life. Steve Jobs was not the only technological pioneer who was using psychedelics to boost creativity, Douglas Englebart the inventor of the computer mouse was also a psychonaut. Likewise, Francis Crick, the scientist credited with discovering DNA was taking psychedelic drugs when he made his groundbreaking revelation. Years later, another scientist and LSD user by the name of Kary Mullis advanced our knowledge of DNA even further with the development of the polymerase chain reaction (PCR) technique, a process that made it possible for scientists to better study how DNA works.

These psychedelic compounds are so important that we cannot let them be suppressed in the extreme manner that we see in western culture. Psychedelics offer us a glimpse into the final frontier of humanity, the consciousness. With these substances we can explore the human imagination for profound insight that will help us in our own personal lives and the bigger picture as well. We must push for new legitimate scientific research into the therapeutic uses for these drugs. These studies will prove, as they have in the past that psychedelic compounds have many medical and spiritual uses that are necessary for our species to continue the evolution of our consciousness.

QUOTE SOURCES AND SUGGESTED READING
----
[0] Abraham Lincoln (1809–1865), U.S. president. Speech, December 18, 1840, to the Illinois House of Representatives.
[1] Terrence McKenna - Personal Collection of Recorded Lectures

[SR1] The Invisible Landscape: Mind, Hallucinogens, and the I Ching by Terence McKenna
[SR1] The Politics of Consciousness: A Practical Guide to Personal Freedom by Steve Kubby and Terence Mckenna
[SR3] The Encyclopedia of Psychoactive Plants: Ethnopharmacology and Its Applications by Christian Ratsch
[SR4] The Pharmacratic Inquisition DVD Directed by Jan Irvin
[SR5] The Entheogenic Evolution: Psychedelics, Consciousness and Awakening the Human Spirit by Martin W. Ball
[SR6] Pharmakon: Plato, Drug Culture, and Identity in Ancient Athens By Michael A. Rinella
[SR7] What the Dormouse Said by John Markoff
[SR8] High Society: The Central Role of Mind-Altering Drugs in History, Science, and Cult by Mike Jay

"This is my simple religion. There is no need for temples; no need for complicated philosophy. Our own brain, our own heart is our temple; the philosophy is kindness."
- Dalai Lama [0]

Why Shamanism?

Shamanism may be a taboo subject in today's society but it was actually the world's first religion. Before royal oligarchies gave spirituality a strict set of rules and guidelines indigenous cultures had a much more personal and open religious tradition. Through shamanism these cultures were able to advance their spiritual knowledge with every age that passed, because each generation would play an active role in building their cultures understanding of the universe. This happens much like our scientific research is conducted today, generation after generation puts in work to slowly chip away at the mysteries that they are trying to uncover. Shamanism does very much this same thing but it deals with exploring the realm of the spirit, instead of the material realm which science deals in. Generations of scientific research has allowed our species to create incredible technology, but our spiritual growth seems absolutely crippled due to lack of exploration.

What has happened in the modern world in the past few thousand years is that the exploration into the spirit realm has ended. The religious institutions that have had control of the spiritual dialogue for the past few millennia have made any kind of research into these realms completely forbidden. They tell us that no new questions need to be asked because they already have all the answers and to bring any kind of question is heresy. It is this kind of strict stubbornness and arrogance that has caused so much of our generation to be completely uninterested in spirituality at all. The fact that these institutions are trying to keep us from asking questions and preventing us from thinking philosophically should tell us that they are not to be trusted. They do not want us to study these matters because it could threaten their political power and influence. This should come as no surprise, because let's face it, religious institutions are and always have been power and capital seeking political organizations that have very little honest interest in spirituality.

Shamanism is different from our modern religious institutions because there is no agenda or hierarchy. There are no cloaked figures to tell you that you are not worthy and then take your money. There is no inquisition to condemn you to death if you happen to disagree with the metaphysical conclusion that other people have come to. There are no politics or heretics either, no one is going to benefit from you financially or tell you how to think. No one is going to call you evil and demand that you be killed because you do not comply with their edicts.

Shamanism is less of a belief system and more of an advanced form of philosophy. Belief systems many times claim to have every single correct answer in the universe, and this approach can have a negative impact on people and society. If people really believe that there are no intellectual frontiers then they will stop looking and stop questioning, and when this happens they are cutting themselves short. Any major human advancement has come from individuals trying to expand the collective pool of knowledge. Not by recycling information that has been in constant circulation for centuries and handed down by authoritarians.

Life is a forever-unraveling mystery, every time a question about our universe is answered ten more pop up in its place. Even if someone were to live for a hundred years in daily research and meditation they will still have questions, there will still be more left to uncover. Every great teacher that has walked this earth has recognized the infinite mystery of life. This is the kind of attitude that is necessary to investigate the spirit world through shamanism. This path will not give you a prepackaged set of ideals and convictions wrapped with a bow and carried by a savior. You will be forced to create your own belief structure that will change every day with every new situation you encounter. Really it should not even have a name; the fact that I even call it shamanism is merely because I have to attach a term to the philosophy to be able to articulate the idea. Spirituality is a personal, individual thing that should be a mutual respect and interest between everyone instead of a division or a barrier.

The fact that various groups of aristocrats from different cultural backgrounds have managed to stamp a copyright on spirituality is itself a complete sacrilege. Everyone should have their own religion that they ponder on and share with one another. The good ideas would be shared more often and become more popular while the bad ideas would dwindle off pretty easily. The best ideas would be passed along to the next generation to be changed and molded based on whatever new information came in during their lifetime. This would essentially be a constantly changing collective religion that was actively being built by everyone in the society.

This is the kind of social structure that a shamanic culture would have. This would eliminate a lot of the spiritual segregation that is caused by modern religion because participants are encouraged to learn from one another instead of look down on one another. If people were actually talking to each other philosophically on a regular basis and reaching into the spirit realm using meditation and psychedelics we would be able to achieve the same kind of break troughs in the spirit realm that we have in the material realm, and we would be much closer to peace.

QUOTE SOURCES AND SUGGESTED READING
---

[0] The Dalai Lama, a policy of kindness: an anthology of writings by and about the Dalai Lama - Sidney Piburn, Claiborne Pell (1990)
[SR1] Food of the Gods: The Search for the Original Tree of Knowledge A Radical History of Plants, Drugs, and Human Evolution by Terence McKenna
[SR2] The Archaic Revival: Speculations on Psychedelic Mushrooms, the Amazon, Virtual Reality, UFOs, Evolution, Shamanism, the Rebirth of the Goddess, and the End of History by Terence McKenna

[SR3] True Hallucinations: Being an Account of the Author's Extraordinary Adventures in the Devil's Paradise by Terence McKenna
[SR4] True Hallucinations: Being an Account of the Author's Extraordinary Adventures in the Devil's Paradise by Terence McKenna
[SR5] The Psychedelic Experience: A Manual Based on the Tibetan Book of the Dead (Citadel Underground) by Timothy Leary
[SR6] Entheogens and the Future of Religion By Robert Forte, Albert Hofmann, R. Gordon Wasson, Eric Sterling, Rick Strassman, Thomas Roberts, Thomas Riedlinger, Dale Pendell, Robert Jesse, Ann and Alexander Shulgin, Terence McKenna, Jack Kornfield, Brother David Steindl-Rast

"The mind is constantly talking. If the inner talk can drop even for a single moment, you will be able to have a glimpse of no-mind. That is what meditation is all about. The state of no-mind is the right state. It is your state."
- Osho [0]

Meditation

The art of meditation dates back many thousands of years, and is just as natural as dreaming. Throughout history, the practice of meditation has had a profound impact on the intellectual and spiritual growth of billions. Even in today's materialistic societies many people still meditate, a 2005 Newsweek study showed that one in three adults meditate on a daily basis. Yet in our modern institutions of control like the education system or the media, we see a very sarcastic and even negative attitude towards meditation. Meditation is presented by the establishment as a sort of tribal ritual that has no place in the so-called "civilized" world. Many people buy into this mentality not knowing what meditation is and go through their whole life with an unclear perspective of their own consciousness.

Meditation is a much simpler and more natural act then most people realize and can be extremely therapeutic in the fast paced, high stress world we are living in. It is simply the act of taking personal time to relax, focusing your attention and clearing your mind, no "witchcraft" or "voodoo" involved. Anyone that has counted sheep to fall asleep before has meditated. All that you have to do is set aside some time to yourself, in a quiet comfortable area somewhere away from distraction. Once you have found this place, sit, or lay down in a comfortable position. The traditional lotus posture seen in most kung'fu movies works for a lot of people, but many find that uncomfortable and prefer laying down or sitting in a different posture. As long as you are comfortable, that is all that matters. Now instead of thinking about the daily dramas or your aspirations just put your mind at ease. This may be difficult for you at first, some find it helpful to count their breaths or repeat meaningful phrases, and this can help you center your focus.

That is all that you have to do to get started. There are many techniques that go beyond this to bring the practitioner into deeper states of meditation and there is a lot of free material out there that help teach these techniques. OSHO is perhaps one of the most enlightening philosophers of our time and has his own "meditation resort" in India where people visit from all over the world to learn the inner workings of meditation. He has written many books and has a very informative website that I would highly recommend (osho.com). If meditation is an idea that is foreign to you then it is really important to look into it and do some research for yourself. There are countless different techniques that work for different people and which technique works for you is a very personal thing. Therefore, it is best for you to discover your own style of meditation using the techniques that you are most comfortable.

There are many advantages to meditation, which are now being confirmed by scientific studies. We have learned through scientific research that meditation can relieve pain, enhance creativity, relieve stress, and boost immune systems. In 1998, a breakthrough study published in the Journal of the American Medical Association, by a DR. Dean Ornish showed that meditation could actually reverse heart disease. This study lasted for over 5 years and involved various control groups that all had coronary artery disease and only one of these groups practiced meditation. Amazingly, the group that practiced meditation had actually managed to reverse the effects of the illness.

Meditation can also help to heal mental disturbances and correct psychological issues. In 2006, a doctor by the name of Ron Cavanaugh started a meditation program at Donaldson high security prison in Alabama. His course was called "Dhamma Brothers" and included a 10-day session in which inmates refrained from speaking and took on 100 full hours of meditation during the session. The results of this program were profound and greatly improved the lives and attitudes of the inmates. You can feel the sincerity in their words. One man named Omar Rahman says, *"For the first time, I could observe my pain and grief. I felt a tear fall. Then something broke, and I could not stop sobbing. I found myself in a terrain where I had always wanted to be, but never had a map. I found myself in the inner landscape, and now I had some direction."* [1]

Another man named Edward Johnson says "On the third day of meditation, I began to feel calm. Moreover, immediately, for the first time in my life, I was really ready to deal with me. Many people were afraid to deal with Big Ed. And now I was ready to take him on, right there on that meditation mat." [2] Yet another Dhamma brother Benjamin "OB" Oryang says, "Well, it is over. However, the vibrations are still here. The memories of those last 10 days on the mat, the experiential wisdom which was gained, and all the prospects of peace which were found here, that is always going to linger." [3] Many of the inmates said that they wished they only would have known about meditation before they made the decisions that landed them in prison.

Even in light of all the positive findings that would encourage meditation, the subject is still approached with sarcasm and ignorance in most mainstream circles. This taboo exists because meditation is a path toward the spirit realm and the far reaches of the human imagination. This whole process is a great threat to the established cultural institutions because it opens a connection to deeper levels of the psyche. The establishment wants the public to be cut off from their higher realms of consciousness. These higher realms of consciousness actually have the capability of showing people the insanity of the status quo. These realms also give people the insight and the tools to devise real solutions to the problems created by the establishment. This is the same reason why they made psychedelic drugs illegal, but they cannot outlaw meditation as they did psychedelics, so instead they create social taboos to discourage people from practicing it. Just as they have dumbed down our education and passed legislation to keep us away from psychedelics, they have created social stigmas to discourage us from reaching meditative states of consciousness.

QUOTE SOURCES AND SUGGESTED READING

[0] www.oshoquotes.com
[1] www.dhammabrothers.com
[2] www.dhammabrothers.com
[3] www.dhammabrothers.com
[SR1] The Book of Secrets: 112 Meditations to Discover the Mystery Within by Osho
[SR2] The Psychedelic Sacrament: Manna, Meditation, and Mystical Experience by Dan Merkur Ph.D., Dan Merkur
[SR3] Shamanism: A Biopsychosocial Paradigm of Consciousness and Healing Shamanism: A Biopsychosocial Paradigm of Consciousness and Healing By Michael Winkelman

"I think psychedelics play a major part in what we do, but having said that, I feel that if somebody's going to experiment with those things they really need to educate themselves about them. People just taking the chemicals and diving in without having any kind of preparation about what they are about to experience tend to have no frame of reference, so they are missing everything flying by and all these new perspectives. It is just a waste. They reach a little bit of spiritual enlightenment, but they end up going, 'well, now I need that drug to get back there again.' The trick is to use the drugs once to get there, and maybe spend the next ten years trying to get back there without the drug."
- Maynard James Kennan [0]

Responsible Shamanism in the 21st Century

Long before the days of western medicine and pharmacists sponsored by multibillion-dollar drug companies, indigenous cultures had a sacred understanding of the plants that shaped our evolution. The knowledge that ancient cultures had about the complexity of our reality make our current spiritual conceptions looks primitive at best. It was this deep knowledge and understanding of the universe that led these ancient tribes towards the path of shamanism. Meditation, yoga, psychoactive plants, herbs, and various philosophical traditions allowed indigenous people to look far beyond the limits of our conventional wisdom. Shamanic cultures oftentimes held rituals where dancing, storytelling, and psychedelic intoxication took place, but there was a sacred respect for the psychoactive plants and the earth from which they came. Many of these tribes still exist today and practice these methods in various places throughout the world, although their numbers are far less due to the Indigenous genocide that has been going on since the Middle Ages.

The Traditional indigenous perspective of psychedelics is drastically different from the current western view. Due to the overindulgent lifestyle that is prevalent in the west, psychedelics are grossly misunderstood throughout most of the so-called "civilized" world. In modern western cultures intoxication is not about connecting with the depths of consciousness, instead it is seen as a method of sedation, a way to escape the troubles of life. Our culture teaches us from a very young age that there is time for work and time for play, and most of us work so hard throughout the week that come Friday we just want to forget everything before it all starts over again on Monday. When work time is over, westerners play hard and they usually put their bodies through a great deal of torment in the process. The substances available to most westerners are far more damaging to the mind, body, and spirit than most shamanic psychedelics and they are also far more addictive.

Alcohol and Tobacco companies spend billions of dollars every year to target their future customers, these future customers being impressionable kids. If there was ever such a thing as a gateway drug, alcohol and tobacco would be the only drugs in that category, they are widely accepted, easily available and some of the leading causes of death and social problems in this country today. These drugs in their modern forms do not just diminish ones consciousness but are also extremely addictive and will build up a habit of abuse that will go unchecked because of the ignorant acceptance of these substances by the general population. These substances are largely responsible for misconceptions about shamanism because they teach entire civilizations that altered states of consciousness are "playgrounds" and as a result, people have absolutely no respect for the psychedelic experience.

Today many see the psychedelic experience as just another high, another variation of uppers, downers, whatever's and this could not be farther from the truth. Indigenous cultures understood that their ancestor's souls were somehow imprinted into the psychedelic experience, so they treated these altered states with great care and dignity. I am not trying to attack anyone who might enjoy alcohol or tobacco products, but it is a fact that their excessive use is encouraged in our society and they are far more damaging to body and mind than any psychedelic.

The overindulgent nature of a consumerist culture typically results in a lack of respect for many sacred things, including the psychedelic experience. Beginning with the discovery of LSD and reemergence of psilocybin in the later part of the 20th century, the sheltered youth of America began to handle psychedelic drugs much as they handled a bottle of whisky. Children that grew up with shopping malls, liquor stores, infomercials, and Marlboro now have access to the shaman's tools, but they do not have access to the shaman's teachings, so it is near impossible for them to use these tools correctly and have the proper respect for their power.

During the cultural revolutions of the 1960s, this is exactly what happened, suburban teenagers were using psychedelics to "get high" and oftentimes were taught a very harsh lesson in the process. The youth of this generation entered the psychedelic realm expecting a front row seat at a Hollywood movie, but what they got was a rude awakening. That rude awakening was a conscious flow of ideas that told them things that their culture did not prepare them for, many times they were told things about themselves and their society that their ego did not want to hear. Without the Shaman present to explain the lessons and to put what is going on into context, this kind of experience results in what is now days called a "bad trip."

Although his wares were free for all who sought after them, the shaman kept a very watchful eye over his stash. He was well aware that if someone without the proper knowledge and assistance were to go into the psychedelic experience blindly, it would be taken out of context and the whole village would have an interesting problem on their hands for the next few hours. Today things are unfortunately much different, young people have easy access to intoxicants and are given all the wrong information about them. Sure, there may be laws and social taboos to keep young people away from intoxicants, but these only result in stimulating more curiosity. It is not even very difficult for young people to get illegal drugs; all that they have to do is go looking for long enough. Since psychedelics are outlawed, their care and distribution responsibilities fall on the black market. Unlike the shaman, the black market has no interest in the people who are consuming their products. Whether it is legal or illegal intoxicants, they are easy to come by in the western world and overindulgence is encouraged for the sake of profit either way.

There are pockets of various counter cultures in the west that have a better-rounded understanding of shamanism than mainstream society does. Those who are in the rave and festival scenes are more familiar with psychedelics, but some of them still do not have a proper respect for the experience. This is because they have come from a materialistic consumer culture that teaches them that everything is a competition and reinforces that it is not important to take care of your body, mind, and spirit. The same opportunity for discovery and expansion of consciousness that existed in the 60s & 70s is reemerging again today, but many of the same obstacles are still standing in the way.

There are still many who escape the mainstream to seek refuge in the counterculture, but in doing so they bring along a lot of the baggage that is associated with mainstream thinking. Most of us are introduced to intoxicants through drinking games, frat parties or other situations that encourage excessive drinking and drug use. The rave and festival scenes are intended to create a different kind of atmosphere, one of peace, freedom, and creativity. Some who are brought up in a culture of gluttony are given personal freedom and feel that they are no longer required to be responsible for themselves, when in reality it is then actually much more important for them to be responsible for themselves.

In times of struggle, the counter culture experiences explosions in popularity, because there are so many people who become fed up with the mainstream and seek out new ways of living so they can be more fulfilled personally. When these times of growth occur, there is an excess of people who do not properly understand the meaning behind the events that they are attending and sometimes their irresponsibility can cause trouble for the entire culture. Such is the case when a misinformed teenager goes overboard and hurts him or herself at a show, as we saw in Los Angeles in 2010 at Electric Daisy Carnival. That was the biggest event in the US and it can no longer take place in the city of Los Angeles because overindulgence was causing a problem for the city and a concern for local parents. The victims in these situations are not necessarily to blame, many of them do not even know what they are doing and were raised in a society that has taken away their ability to be responsible for themselves. Still, this is a serious issue that needs to be addressed or more people can be needlessly hurt.

Since the brain, goes into overdrive when under the influence of psychedelics it is important to enter the experience with a process of critical thinking so we can accurately decipher the messages contained within the psychedelic experience. When critical thinking is applied there is no need for a shaman to be present, you become the shaman and are able to make proper sense of your experience. Within the psychedelic experience, you will be subject to an onslaught of emotions, intuitions, and opinions that you will never have any hope of understanding without some method of organizing and analyzing the incoming data. Establishing a clear goal for the experience and finding the appropriate setting are some extremely important steps for getting the most out of psychedelics. Setting is vital to having a good experience, if you are in a place that is going to make you feel uncomfortable or with people who are not going to respect your state of mind, then you are setting yourself up for bad times. Keeping journals and records of experiences are also helpful when using psychedelics to figure out long and complex problems.

It is not my business or the business of anyone to tell you what to do with your body and what decisions to make in your life, but it is still important that people know how to take care of them. People should be free to do what they want but there are some general things that everyone should know in order to keep him or herself safe. It is generally a bad idea to mix drugs with alcohol. It is important for people to understand that overindulgence and habitual use is not only dangerous but it also makes it impossible to get any kind of shamanic value out of the experience. Psychedelic drugs are tools, and just like any tool, they can help us if we use them correctly but they can also harm us if we misuse them.

QUOTE SOURCES AND SUGGESTED READING
----
[0] Unleashed the Story of Tool - Joel McIver (2009)
[SR1] Plant Spirit Shamanism: Traditional Techniques for Healing the Soul by Ross Heaven
[SR2] The Doors of Perception and Heaven and Hell by Aldous Huxley
[SR3] The Psychedelic Explorer's Guide: Safe, Therapeutic, and Sacred Journeys by James Fadiman Ph.D.
[SR4] LSD Psychotherapy by Stanislav Grof M.D.
[SR5] Mushroom Wisdom: How Shamans Cultivate Spiritual Consciousness by Martin W. Ball
[SR6] Psychedelic Healing: The Promise of Entheogens for Psychotherapy and Spiritual Development by Neal M Goldsmith

"They do not want you to see the remedies; you can stop influenza with vitamin D for free. Herbal medicine is all that you need but they can't charge a fifty dollar fee, Unless They injects you, they infect you, they stick that needle in your arm and chemically wreck you."
– Michael Adams {Organic Food Activist} [0]

Marketing Illness and Addiction

In western society our school systems fail to educate, our businesses have corrupted our economy and our "elected" "representatives" do not represent the people that elect them. Everywhere that you find powerful cartels providing a public service you will also find policies that are extremely oppressive to the consumer. Energy companies have had the ability to break away from fossil fuels for decades, but continue using them because it is easier to manage and exploit a controlled commodity. Therefore, it should come as no surprise that the pharmaceutical industry has destroyed the nation's health and wellbeing, in order to provide them with steady flow of income.

Like many of the business issues we are facing today, the problem with the drug industry is that it is controlled by a government protected corporate cartel. This allows a select few mega corporations to dominate the market, preventing entrepreneurs from developing new products that could threaten this monopoly. Without having to worry about any kind of competition this cartel can make their products as harmful and ineffective as they like. Thanks to government protections, they are able to make their products more addicting and less effective so they can create return customers and extend their profits. If a medication is effective in curing a patient then they will not continually use and purchase that drug because they will have no need to do so. However, if the drug is mediocre and has addictive properties then it will become a regular part of the patient's monthly budget.

This deceptive strategy proved to be quite lucrative so the drug companies launched a massive advertising campaign to peddle a wide variety of ineffective and unnecessary drugs to a trusting and ignorant public. This industry actually spends more money on advertising then they do on research and development every single year. That fact alone shows that they are more interested in making sales than producing a well-researched and effective drug. Today's television and radio commercial spots are dominated by advertisements for mediocre pharmaceuticals. Companies pay billions of dollars per year on advertising alone and their investment comes back many times over. This advertising budget includes "incentives" for personal care providers to overwrite prescriptions, or in other words bribes for doctors to sell more drugs.

The arrogance and carelessness of the pharmaceutical industry has had a detrimental effect on society since its inception. This industry is responsible for creating and marketing the most toxic substances that our species has ever seen. In the 19th century morphine and cocaine were being peddled by pharmacists as wonder drug cure all's. Patients were told that these drugs were not addictive if they were injected directly into the bloodstream. I know it sounds unbelievable but this kind of stupidity actually passed for medical science less than 200 years ago. This act of ignorance resulted in widespread addiction all throughout America and Europe.

      A Scottish physician by the name of Alexander Wood was the first to inject morphine directly underneath the skin with the hypodermic syringe almost immediately after it was invented. Ironically, his wife became the first needle addict and the first person in the western world to overdose and die from injected opiates. When morphine addiction finally became recognized as an issue, doctors rushed to find a cure for this problem, so they invented heroin. Wrong again doc! This creation was many times worse than morphine and spawned a drug problem more ferocious then any seen in the world. Sadly, even a century later doctors are still peddling toxic drugs containing amphetamines, opiates and other addictive chemicals.

      The most over prescribed, unnecessary, and problematic drugs on the market today are antidepressants, ADHD medication and opiate based painkillers. Clinical depression and attention deficit disorder are both fabricated conditions that were made up by the pharmaceutical industry to create a new market where they could push more of their dangerous and ineffective drugs. The medications that are currently on the market for these conditions have extremely harsh side effects and very low rates of success, yet they are still over prescribed by thousands of doctors.

      People are depressed because they live in a society where injustice and exploitation run rampant not because they are "sick and need medication. " This medication is even known to make people feel more depressed and in extreme cases even lead to suicide or violent outbursts. Clinical ADHD is also a myth, children are supposed to be hyperactive, playful and disorderly; this is no "sickness." The drug companies wish to create a culture where everyone can be labeled with some kind of sickness that will require him or her to be on maintenance medication.

      Prescription painkillers are among the most abused narcotics in the United States. These drugs are just as addictive and harmful as the hardest street drugs, but because they are legal and prescribed by doctors, they are greatly underestimated by our society. This is what makes these drugs so dangerous, since they are somehow socially acceptable many people ignore or overlook their addiction until it is become a serious problem. In most cases when someone finally faces their problem they go right back to the doctor that got them hooked on the drugs in the first place to ask for help. At that point, they are actually given more drugs that are supposed to wean the patient from their original addiction. This is seen in the popular but ineffective methadone and suboxone programs, which are responsible for keeping millions of addicts dependent on synthetic drugs. Many of the drug programs in the United States are actually designed to keep people disempowered and dependent. People fighting addiction are told that they are helpless and have a "disease" which they will suffer with for their entire lives, regardless of their ability to overcome their current habitual drug use. This kind of rhetoric makes it more difficult for people to channel their will power and lays the foundation for future relapse.

The pharmaceutical industry has created a dependent pill popping generation that is riddled with addiction issues. People are taught from a very young age to over consume mass produced drugs at the slightest sign of physical or mental discomfort. While the medication that is available on the market is typically far less effective than a healthy diet, exercise, and natural remedies. These options are never mentioned in mainstream circles because they would put the pharmaceutical monopoly in danger. However, due to a growing public distrust of the industry, many people are taking a more holistic approach to their healthcare.

In 2010 a consumer reports study showed that a staggering 80% of patients felt that their doctors were so influenced by the drug industry that they would deliberately write a drug prescription even if a better, safer, non-drug option were available. This blatant corruption has resulted in a renewed interest in herbal medicine; there are many cures and remedies waiting to be discovered deep in the rainforests. This is one of the many reasons why it is so important to preserve the world's rainforest, because they contain plants that can cure every ailment known to us. The solutions to the pathological threats that humanity faces lay within nature, not a corrupt multibillion dollar industry.

QUOTE SOURCES AND SUGGESTED READING
----
[0] Michael Adams (Healthranger)
http://www.naturalnews.com/Dont_Inject_Me_The_Swine_Flu_Vaccine_Song.html
[SR1] Selling Sickness: How the World's Biggest Pharmaceutical Companies Are Turning Us All into Patients by Ray Moynihan and Alan Cassels
[SR2] A Dose of Sanity: Mind, Medicine, and Misdiagnosis by Sydney Walker III, M.D.
[SR3] 1000 Cures for 200 Ailments: Integrated Alternative and Conventional Treatments for the Most Common Illnesses by Marshall Editions
[SR4] Alternative Science: Challenging the Myths of the Scientific Establishment by Richard Milton
[SR5] America Fooled: The Truth about Antidepressants, Antipsychotics, and How We've Been Deceived by Dr. Timothy Scott
[SR6] Antioxidants Against Cancer: How to activate your bod natural healing powers with today's most protective and immune-boosting supplements and foods By Ralph Moss, PhD
[SR7] Attaining Medical Self Sufficiency by Duncan Long
[SR8] Bartram's Encyclopedia of Herbal Medicine: The Definitive Guide by Thomas Bartram
[SR9] Beat Diabetes Naturally: The Best Foods, Herbs, Supplements, and Lifestyle Strategies to Optimize Your Diabetes Care By Michael T. Murray
[SR10] Beating Cancer with Nutrition by Patrick Quillin, Ph.D., RD, CNS

[SR11] Beating the Flu: The Natural Prescription for Surviving Pandemic Influenza and Bird Flu by J. E. Williams

[SR12] Before You Take that Pill: Why the Drug Industry May Be Bad for Your Health by J. Douglas Bremner

[SR13] Inventing the AIDS Virus by Peter H. Duesberg

[SR14] World Without Cancer By G. Edward Griffin

[SR15] Toxic Overload: A Doctor's Plan for Combating the Illnesses Caused by Chemicals in Our Foods, Our Homes, and Our Medicine Cabinets By Dr. Paula Baillie-Hamilton

[SR16] Too Profitable to Cure By Brent Hoadley, Ph.D.

[SR17] Psyched Out: How Psychiatry Sells Mental Illness and Pushes Pills That Kill By Kelly Patricia O'Meara

[SR18] The MD Emperor Has No Clothes By Peter Glidden

"The fight could have been won But we sit stunned As we get drunk and forget once we were tricked And now they can complete their goal 'Cause we are convinced that dung heaps are gold People sold to keep our souls dug in Deeper holes than we could know we are stuck in."
– Sweatshop Union [0]

Fundamentals of Firewater

Throughout the course of history, the human mind has been constantly sedated by alcohol. In our modern society, this poison elixir is the only option that most people have in legally reaching an altered state of consciousness. Unfortunately, this altered state is a far lower realm of consciousness where confusion and aggression run rampant. It is this state of consciousness that the ruling class wants us to experience, because we are much weaker and do not think very deeply under the influence of alcohol. A weak and uncreative population is much easier to control and they are far less likely to complain about the unfair conditions that they are forced to experience on a day-to-day basis.

The alcohol issue is far more complicated than most people realize. In 2010 the "Centre for Crime and Justice Studies," based out of London, did some research to discover which drugs were the most harmful on an individual and the people around them. This study concluded that alcohol was the most damaging controlled substance in our society. Illegal poisons such as cocaine and heroin actually ranked just below alcohol, but showed to be close to equal in destructive potency. At the end of the list were psychedelics, they were found to be the least dangerous drugs in the study, ranked far below alcohol, tobacco and poisonous street drugs such as heroin or cocaine.

The findings in this British study only confirm what many of us already knew. The legal drugs are far more dangerous than the illegal ones! Why is this? Why do drugs like DMT, LSD, or MDMA carry strict legal penalties while more harmful substances like alcohol and tobacco are available in every storefront? It has nothing to do with health and has everything to do with social control and keeping the average people docile. They know that a person on alcohol may wrap their car around a tree, abuse their family, and squander their paycheck. Of course, this is not the kind of behavior that is exhibited by all drinkers, but alcohol does increase the risk of violence, accidents, or foolishness, that much we must admit. Oddly enough, this is exactly the kind of behavior that the establishment finds acceptable! These are the traits of a subservient consumer who needs to be told what to do in order to survive, or perhaps a citizen who causes enough trouble to keep the government in business. This is the kind of population that the aristocracy and the governments that they support are looking to create. It may sound somewhat crazy, but this is how they stay in business.

On the other hand, how will a person react after a shamanic experience with DMT? Maybe that person will feel a deeper connection to their true self and turn their back on the sick consumer culture they have fed. Maybe after someone has a profound experience on psychedelics they will be less likely to march off to war! Imagine someone who does not want to take another human life! What a problem he has made for the establishment! It would be far easier to convince a regular alcohol user that war is somehow a good idea, as opposed to someone who uses psychedelics.

The "Fire Water" as the natives called it, took away their sense of spirit, and allowed them to be easily manipulated by the conquering Europeans. To this day alcohol remains a serious problem for the few Native American communities that have not been eradicated by early Europeans or the US Government. In fact, this issue is commonplace in most native cultures that were colonized by the Europeans and Americans. In South Africa, the situation is far more blatant under a policy known as the "DOP" system. This is a system of employment that developed during apartheid where native farm workers were actually paid in alcohol for their labor. This practice led to widespread alcoholism and a complete lack of spirit among the native people. These are just some of the extreme instances where alcohol is obviously used for social control.

Overindulgence in alcohol can cause people to become tired, unimaginative, and extremely easy to manipulate by the authorities. The substance is also very addictive which serves to keep people in the same imprisoned state, until they are able to break the chains of addiction on their own. Due to the seemingly endless supply of revenue that this substance creates for the people that manufacture it, and the sedative properties that is has on the population, alcohol has been chosen as one of the favorite weapons of the ruling class.

From a young age, we have seen our elders and our media set the stage for future alcohol use. While we have been taught to stay away from mind-expanding psychedelics, the poison firewater remains a part of our culture leaving a nation completely helpless and sedated. There is nothing wrong with relaxing with some friends and enjoying some drinks, but when that happens, do not lie to yourself and think that you are not partaking in drug use. Alcohol is a drug just like any other and is actually one of the most dangerous and addictive drugs out there, so it should be treated as such despite its legality. If you are going to drink there is nothing wrong with that, but do not judge someone that decides to relax or party in a different way. It is possible to use alcohol responsibly, but the misconceptions about its effects on the body and mind in relation to other chemicals needs to be understood and came to terms with in our society.

QUOTE SOURCES AND SUGGESTED READING
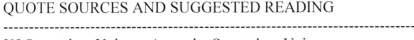
[0] Sweatshop Union – Ascend – Sweatshop Union

"If the words "life, liberty and the pursuit of happiness" do not include the right to experiment with your own consciousness, then the Declaration of Independence is not worth the hemp it was written on."
- Terence McKenna [0]

Marijuana: Miracle not Menace

Marijuana has been proven to be one of the safest drugs known to man, less harmful than alcohol or anything you will find in a pharmacy. This plant has been called a miracle drug by many and is quickly growing in popularity for its medicinal properties. Yet despite the growing evidence of the incredible advantages and benign nature of cannabis, there are powerful business interests that are very intent on keeping this drug illegal.

The system that incarcerates people for using marijuana is a multi-billion dollar industry. Politicians, law enforcement and prison developers all see great financial benefits from the prohibition of marijuana. These agencies as well as other government and corporate interests all share in the profits made from the seizure of drugs and cash as well as the fines imposed on the victim for breaking said law. Police officers get bonus's for these arrests, politicians get campaign donations to keep this harmless substance illegal, prison developers get paid a cash amount for every human being that they put in a cage. This is a huge business, where the cash crop happens to be human lives.

The law enforcement system is its own unique fraud as I covered in detail earlier, but there is also a long list of financial reasons behind the prohibition of this plant. The primary lobby groups you will find supporting laws that criminalize marijuana are alcohol companies, oil companies, tobacco companies, prison developers and pharmaceutical manufacturers. These companies are threatened by the many industrial and medicinal uses that the marijuana/hemp plant has. If marijuana were to be made legal, many of these industries would lose their monopolies because their products would no longer be necessary or practical for widespread use. A plant that can grow almost anywhere and is in completely limitless supply cannot be used by a corporation to exploit people and make money; therefore it is not in their best interests for this plant to be legal.

We all know politicians do not really do what they believe in; they do what they are told and what they are paid to do. Every single piece of legislation that goes through our government has "special interest groups" on both sides of the argument. Whichever side is most "persuasive" or donates the most money to the politician is the side that ultimately decides whether the legislation passes or not. Since large multinational corporations have much deeper pockets than activist and community, groups they are able to develop lobby groups that can control the direction of our legal system.

The pharmaceutical drug industry spends an incredible amount of money to ensure that marijuana remains illegal. This is because marijuana is much safer and more effective than synthetic prescription drugs in treating a wide variety of illnesses. There are many conditions that marijuana can improve greatly without risk, even cancer. A study by Manuel Guzmán of Madrid Spain showed that THC, the active chemical in marijuana could actually inhibit tumor growth. Dr. Ethan Russo, a neurologist and world authority on medical cannabis explains the process in which THC fights cancer in this statement. *"Cancer occurs because cells become immortalized; they fail to heed normal signals to turn off growth. A normal function of remodeling in the body requires that cells die on cue. This is called apoptosis, or programmed cell death. That process fails to work in tumors. THC promotes its reappearance so that gliomas, leukemia's, melanomas, and other cell types will in fact heed the signals, stop dividing, and die. However, that is not all. The other way that tumors grow is by ensuring that they are nourished: they send out signals to promote angiogenesis, the growth of new blood vessels. Cannabinoids turn off these signals as well. It is truly incredible, and elegant."* [1]

This extreme breakthrough has been known about by the establishment since at least 1974 when studies at the Medical College of Virginia showed the ability that THC had in fighting cancer. The results of these tests were reported in the Washington post on august 18th 1974 and then completely disappeared from the news due to a media blackout backed by the anti-marijuana lobby groups. Despite the media blackout, many independent scientific investigations have been carried out over the past 20 years that reconfirm the healing power of cannabis. If these details were presented to the public, the pharmaceutical industry would lose billions of dollars.

The alcohol and tobacco industries have an obvious conflict of interest when it comes to marijuana prohibition. Alcohol and tobacco are Americas top vices and both of them are extremely addictive, unhealthy and honestly pretty repulsive when considering the natural cannabis plant as an alternative. These companies are well aware of the threat that marijuana legalization poses on their yearly earnings so they lobby for politicians to vote for prohibition just like many other industries have. There are many corporations in addition to the ones I mentioned putting a lot of money through our government to keep the drug laws as they are. That includes the oil, cotton, and paper industries all of which would lose their cash crops at the hands of industrialized hemp.

Marijuana can cure cancer, heal countless other physical ailments, reduce our dependence on oil based products and prescription pharmaceuticals. All research shows that this plant is not only harmless but can be extremely beneficial to our environment and our society. Hemp was even used to clean up radiation after the Chernobyl disaster in 1986. The current social stigma against marijuana is only the result of the propaganda put forth by those industries that benefit financially from marijuana prohibition as well as the overarching control system that wishes to keep our minds enslaved. By exposing the corrupt nature of the drug laws and the system that is enforcing them, we can shatter that unjust social stigma and have a fair and sensible dialogue regarding legalization.

QUOTE SOURCES AND SUGGESTED READING
----
[0] Personal Collection of Lectures – Terrence McKenna
[1] New Study Explains How Pot Kills Cancer Cells by Steve Kubby, Sierra Times, 11/10/ 03
[SR1] The Emperor Wears No Clothes by Jack Herer
[SR2] Hemp: Lifeline to the Future By Chris Conrad
[SR3] The Great Book of Hemp By Rowan Robinson
[SR4] Why Marijuana Should Be Legal By Ed Rosenthal, Steve Kubby

"Seek truth, Observe Nature, Educate Yourself"
- Kottonmouth Kings

Section 9

Imagination

67. -Living The Dream Awake
68. -Synchronicity

"A dream you dream alone is only a dream. A dream you dream together is reality."
– John Lennon [0]

This chapter contains a mixture of facts and personal theoretical assumptions of my own please do your own research after reading this to form your own opinion.

Living the Dream Awake

The human psyche is one of the most mysterious frontiers of modern science. The study of consciousness has been developing in the west for the past few hundred years and at best, we have been able to catch up with the knowledge of our indigenous ancestors. Our knowledge of the brain consists of mostly observational or recordable information, for example, we know which parts of the brain are responsible for our mechanical functions and we know which parts of are brain are responsible for creativity. However, there are still many brain functions such as dreaming, telepathy, intuition, and meditation that still remain a mystery to modern science. The material world of the west does their best to ignore the more mystic and unexplainable realms of the human psyche which is why their knowledge in these areas is so mundane.

The dream realm was always held sacred by indigenous cultures, it was believed that dreams held the key to not only our inner struggles but also gave us a glimpse into the future and a connection to the spirit world. Throughout the centuries, most mystic traditions have been lost in the overwhelming materialistic cultures that dominate our world, and the spiritual connection to dreams is no different. Many of us pay very little attention to our dreams, and when we do pay attention we do not know enough about the dream realm to understand what is going on and put things into context. Recent studies have found that dreams and even near death experiences may be traced to a specific region of the brain. This region of the brain is known as the pineal gland and to this day, it remains an anomaly to modern medicine. The pineal gland is located in the very center of the brain and is extremely delicate, but it is well protected by the rest of the brain and skull.

Although there has been little mainstream interest in the pineal gland advanced civilizations of the past, all recognized this gland as the "3rd eye." The third eye represented the seat of consciousness to these cultures and linked the human body with the spirit world. Egyptian tombs were decorated with animals coming out of the center of the pharaoh's head, to depict the power of the third eye or pineal gland. Art all over Asia and ancient America also show countless depictions of the third eye and its connection to other realms. What makes matters more interesting is that in the past few decades some western scientists are actually conducting studies on the pineal gland and its effects on the human condition.

Over the past 20 years, a doctor from the University of New Mexico named Rick Strassman has been conducting experiments on a chemical called DMT or dimethyltryptamine that is produced naturally in the human brain. Strassman's 5-year study included test subjects from all backgrounds and gave new insight into the pineal gland and its role in the human body, as well as possible links between DMT and consciousness. Strassman's studies do not conclusively prove a relation between the pineal gland and DMT, but does show a strong correlation. Based on the research so far, many believe that the pineal gland releases stored DMT in times of REM sleep and extremely high doses are released at the time of death, this could explain the popular phenomenon known as "near death experiences." If this chemical really is released, every night when we sleep and at the time our soul passes onto the next life, than this reconfirms what our ancestors believed about the pineal gland being the seat of consciousness. This relationship also tells us that dreaming is very much an important spiritual experience just as passing to the next life is.

The DMT research study was extremely difficult to fund and there were many bumps along the way, but they ironically received a large grant from some high up places to start their work. The Scottish Rite Freemasons actually made a considerable donation towards Rick Strausman's work. There is no doubt that secret societies and elite groups are interested in occult knowledge, so it makes perfect sense that they would be interested in knowing more about this pathway to the dream realm. Now that we understand the importance of the dream realm to our human psyche, we must cherish the times spent away from our material consciousness. For all we know every night our souls could be transported to a universal dream world where all the great mysteries of life are revealed. Meditation is also very important to uncovering this territory; we need to start thinking more about the health of our consciousness, not just our surface mental and physical health.

The same cultures that knew about the importance of the pineal gland also shared spiritual systems that were deep rooted in meditation and other realms of consciousness. In these meditative states, people would learn about their inner selves as well as their relation to the rest of the world and their impact on it. Our ancestors paid close attention to the lessons they were taught in the dream realm and while in meditative states. On a mass scale, adopting this kind of mentality could help people make better decisions that are more centered on the progression of our planet instead of the progression of our current self-destructive ideologies.

QUOTE SOURCES AND SUGGESTED READING
----
[0] All we are saying: the last major interview with John Lennon and Yoko Ono
[SR1] DMT: The Spirit Molecule by Rick Strassman
[SR2] Ayahuasca in My Blood: 25 Years of Medicine Dreaming by Peter Gorman
[SR3] The Entheological Paradigm by Martin W. Ball
[SR4] Tryptamine Palace: 5-MeO-DMT and the Sonoran Desert Toad By James Oroc

"Synchronicity hints at the unified world behind the illusory veil of the material universe."
- Roger S. Jones, Associate Professor of Physics at the University of Minnesota [0]

This chapter contains a mixture of facts and personal theoretical assumptions of my own please do your own research after reading this to form your own opinion.

Synchronicity

Since Human beings were able to contemplate the nature of their existence in the universe, they have asked for signs from beyond to aid them in their spiritual journey. These signs have always come in the form of "synchronicities" which are also known as "cosmic coincidences. " This takes place when something that you are thinking about actually presents itself in the real world as a result of your thought. Over the generations our limiting cultural institutions have led us to believe that these signs from beyond are merely randomly occurring events and that our mind has no impact on or relation to the physical world around us. These events are passed off as insignificant and are largely ignored by the general population. However, if one pays close attention to what is going on around them they will find that nothing is random and that everything happens for a reason.

Carl Jung was one of the most well respected figures of modern science, and was the first person to use the term synchronicity. He used it to describe the significant coincidences that occur when something in a person's psyche manifests in the physical world. Jung was inspired to this concept when treating a patient in his psychology firm. The night before a therapy session, the patient had a dream about a golden scarab. The next day during the session when he was discussing this dream with his patient, a real golden scarab randomly hit against the cabinet window. This strange occurrence was the basis for Jung's "acausal connecting principle" which linked mind and matter through the process of synchronicity. The synchronicities that take place every day demonstrate that there is a connection between our consciousness and the physical world around us. Every one of us experiences this phenomena on a daily basis, whether we realize it or not.

When someone is actively looking for synchronicities in their daily lives, every day becomes a new meaningful adventure where magical things happen all the time. The magic is always there, in every event that everyone encounters, but it is only visible to those who are actually looking for it. The modern idea of this is more commonly recognized through a principal called "the butterfly effect. " This is the observation that every action that someone takes, no matter how small has a direct and profound impact on how the future will unfold. Synchronicity just takes it a step further and recognizes that thoughts as well as actions are somehow related to future events.

The most visible occurrences of synchronicity in our everyday lives are surrounding the important relationships that we develop and important places that we encounter. When you meet a best friend or significant other through an odd circumstance, or a new job drops into your lap just when you need it the most you are witnessing synchronicity take place. I am sure you can think back through your past and remember a few unbelievable circumstances that were in no way just coincidences. Now in the future when these events occur you will understand that they are significant and you will pay close attention to what you are feeling, thinking and what is taking place around you. Taking in as much information at this pivotal moment is important because it will give you the intuition that will lead you down the right path. That path may not present itself immediately, but whatever was learned through your synchronistic experience will prove to be vital at some point in the future.

Synchronistic experiences teach us that the world is more complex then we can imagine and that our psyche has an unseen relation to the events that unfold in our everyday lives. The alchemists of the European Renaissance paid close attention when these events would manifest because they believed that synchronicities occurred during important moments that would significantly change the future. This acted as a sort of a guide for many philosophers who were seeking to solve the world's mysteries. If a synchronicity were to occur which had a relation to something that the philosopher was thinking then that was taken as a sign that they were on the right track and to follow their intuition.

This kind of mystical approach to life was not limited to just the alchemists, many indigenous tribes throughout the world also observed synchronicities as signs from their gods. Tribal elders would use these signs to choose where to set up their village, where to hunt or for guidance in times of struggle. Nothing has changed since our ancestors took this path; the universe still behaves in the same way even if many cultures have forgotten this fact. We may never fully understand these phenomena or their origins but they are so apparent in our everyday life that it would be careless to ignore them. Synchronicity shows us that the universe is not just a collection of random events thrown together in a meaningless space, as today's pop culture would lead you to believe. The universe is a place of cosmic intelligence where every thought and every movement has a deeper meaning then we can perceive.

QUOTE SOURCES AND SUGGESTED READING
----
[0] 'Time and Time Again' American Theosophist, The (Dora Kunz, Executive Editor)
[SR1] Intuition: Knowing Beyond Logic by Osho
[SR2] The Collected Works: Civilization in transition by Carl Gustav Jung (1964)
[SR3] The Sync Book: Myths, Magic, Media, and Mindscapes: 26 Authors on Synchronicity

"Religion is a common motion and is like a river that may flow through one country, but may have its headwaters in another."
– Manly P. Hall

Section 10

Legend

**Note: This whole section is just my interpretation on the historical research that surrounds these particular religions and the statements of the holy books themselves, I encourage you to do your own research and come to your own conclusion

69. -Mythological Origins of Modern Religion
70. -Your Prophets Were Shaman Revolutionaries?
71. -Jesus the Peaceful Revolutionary
72. -The Birth of Islam and the Arabian Empire
73. -Holy Wars

"There is only one religion, though there are a hundred versions of it."
-George Bernard Shaw [0]

Mythological Origins of Modern Religion

    In the ancient world, human spirituality was guided by mythology, mysticism, and alchemy. In ancient Egyptian, Hindu, and Sumerian mythology, there were countless legends and tales of the gods and ancient people that paved the way for their civilization. The legends laid the foundation for all of these ancient societies and eventually over many generations would splinter into various different spiritual traditions. The stories were spread throughout the known world by merchants who traveled from empire to empire-trading fabric and spices. Eventually the stories that originated in ancient Sumer and Egypt became a vital part of the philosophy within the other major thriving empires.
    Many of these legends were identical aside from the names, dates, and places that lead many researchers to believe that they are all copies of a much older tradition that lies outside of our historical view. These are very sensitive subjects that happened very long ago, and have very distorted histories so it is difficult to nail down the true origin of these stories. However, many researchers are starting to agree that all of these ancient myths are simply allegories with astrological references. In other words, they are stories that have been designed to represent and symbolize the passing of the days, seasons, equinoxes as well as other natural earth and space functions. This is most likely how all of these legends started out, until civilization became more complex and the astrological myths began to take an earthly form with human characters.

As Centuries passed the Roman, Greek and Babylonian philosophies all developed the same themes as the traditional myths, but many of the details and language within the stories were changed to fit the geography and culture of these civilizations. So as time went on the ancient myths still played a role in shaping religions around the world, but they were constantly changing and adapting based on the political and cultural influences that ruled each empire. These cultural differences are responsible for creating an array of seemingly different religious philosophies that all have the same historical origin. As time progressed even further, each culture became more and more familiar with the unique language of their own cultural myths, until they were unable to recognize the similarities between their belief structures and that of their neighbors.

The leaders of these empires also frequently changed the spiritual teachings within their civilizations that resulted in more perversion of the ancient myths. As different kings and emperors added laws to the religious philosophies and converted, their people to monotheism the divide between each empires spiritual structure began to grow. As the cultural differences between these empires deepened, it became more and more difficult to distinguish the origin of their religious traditions. Eventually, due to different styles of governance and different cultural prejudices a once small collection of ancient myths morphed into several full-blown dogmatic religions. It is important to remember that all aspects of spirituality in our early development were totally controlled by the literate ruling class and then dictated to the rest of the civilization. Therefore, it was the different "leaders" of these ancient cultures who molded the traditional myths to fit their own political and cultural agendas.

The Babylonian empire and their rendition of the ancient myths would change the face of civilization for centuries to come. An ancient ruler named Hammurabi developed a complex set of laws and rules based on the "Sumerian Family Laws" and "the Egyptian book of the dead," which governed the ancient societies that came before the Babylonians. This set of laws came to be known as the "Code of Hammurabi." Although the Babylonian codes were not religious in nature, they originated from the Sumerian and Egyptian spiritual traditions that were practiced before the time of Hammurabi. He simply collected ideas from past civilizations that he felt would be best for ruling a society and adopted those ideas to form the basis of his empire.

All of this historical information is extremely important when considering the biblical character of Moses who is the basis for the Old Testament. According to biblical historians, Moses was a prophet that appeared a few hundred years after Hammurabi and was the first to dictate "the ten commandments" to humanity. Because of this apparent historical incident, Moses came to be known as "the law giver." There have been many other "law gives" in ancient spiritual mythology that have strikingly similar stories to that of Moses. Different renditions of this character appeared in many other cultures, "*Menu*" in India, "*Mises*" in Syria, "*Menes*" in Egypt and countless others with similar names are found throughout ancient history.

All of these characters were considered by their cultures to be "law givers" who brought the law of god to their people on stone tablets. Each one of these characters was also pulled out of a basket floating in a river, had a rod in which they performed miracles including parting waters and leading armies across the sea, the parallels are unending. While the laws may differ slightly between cultures, the basic ideals remain the same throughout every civilization. The code of Hammurabi, the Sumerian family laws, and the Egyptian book of the dead all predate these religious traditions and all have the same basic intentions. Therefore, it is safe to say that the Egyptian and Sumerian philosophies are in fact the origin of the bible and everything that came after it.

These basic ancient origins of the world's mainstream religions are one of the best-kept secrets on the planet. If everyone realized that their beliefs were not different from one another at all, it would be more difficult for dominating cultural institutions like churches or governments to maintain control over their subjects. This mentality is typical of the classic "divide and rule" strategy of governance, where societies are divided into smaller sections or cliques so they are easier to control and manipulate. While different cultures fight and bicker over their petty philosophical differences, their "leaders" exploit that cultural bias so they can start wars and expand empires.

However, this deception can be easily put to rest with a comparative look at religious history. Once we compare the language and situations depicted in the different spiritual traditions we can see that they can all be traced back to Egyptian or Sumerian roots. This fact is right under our noses in many cases, especially in Christianity, Judaism, and Islam. For example, at the end of every prayer Christians pay homage to the Egyptian god Amen-Ra when they say "Amen." The vast majority of our modern astronomy, architecture, and politics originated from these ancient cultures, so it would make perfect sense that a lot of our religious philosophy came from these civilizations as well.

QUOTE SOURCES AND SUGGESTED READING
----
[0] Perspectives on Mankind's Search for Meaning - Walter Taminang (2008)

"All major religious traditions carry basically the same message; that is love, compassion, and forgiveness is the important things that should be part of our daily lives." - Dalai Lama [0]

Your Prophets Were Shaman Revolutionaries

There are many established religious orders spread throughout the world, all of them claiming to have a different perspective from the rest. In addition to all these faiths having the same mythological origins, the modern historical figures that represent these different sects have all preached the same message and would not be very happy to see that there is spiritual segregation going on in their name. The "prophets" of the mainstream religions all opposed organized religion and authoritarian government in their time.

Historical records of these figures show that they spoke out against the great injustices that were occurring in their lifetimes and condemned the social institutions that propagated those injustices. The injustices that they spoke out about were mainly war, poverty, and social injustice. The social institutions that these teachers spoke out against included organized religion, even though they were very religious people they understood that to create a social system out of a belief structure was spiritual tyranny. They also understood that corrupt political and religious orders would use spirituality as a tool to control and manipulate people, so they were all advocates of a more personal, less authoritarian religious tradition.

The message that all these prophets brought to us was that we should live in peaceful societies and respect and love one another. They told us not to live aggressive lives and live in harmony with nature. They also warned us not to trust dominating control systems like government, banking, or the church because they were responsible for the separation of human beings and unhappiness within civilization. It was no surprise that every single one of these religious figures was persecuted by establishment authority figures of the time. These were leaders that spoke out for human rights as well as political and economic equality. This is always the part that is left out of the holy books, because the holy books were all written by the establishment. Many times accounts of these prophets were written hundreds of years after their deaths by people who had absolutely no connection to them or their cause. At the time that most of the major religious texts were produced, the only people that could read and write were the nobility, so they were the people that ended up writing the holy books.

The prophets of every religion were true revolutionaries and for their eras, they became a great threat to the establishment. Although they all sprang up in different times and places, their shared message of equality and peace made their local authority figures very nervous. Their teachings were groundbreaking for civil rights and they were in complete defiance of the established orders of the time. The fact that the ruling class was responsible for recording and handing down the history and philosophies of these religious figures is absolutely insane because they were the forces against these revolutionaries were working. There is an obvious conflict of interest on the part of the elite to manipulate the message in order to suit their political needs. The establishment knew that these figures had made such a profound impact during their lives that their legends were never going to go away. Therefore, instead of trying to erase the revolutionaries from history, the elite merely corrupted their message. When translating these stories into the traditional religious texts the established orders of the time presented the information in a way that would reflect ideals that were favorable to their agenda of social dominance.

Both mainstream prophets Jesus and Muhammad believed in the same general philosophy and were promoting the same ideas. The only reason why their messages appear to be somewhat different is that they were recorded at different times, by different rulers in different cultures all over the world. Due to the difference in language, culture, and politics between the rulers who passed along the messages there have arose divisions between the various religious sects. If one looks at the works that these different revolutionaries carried out throughout their lives one can see that they were all very much on the same page. These were people who brought a message of peace and equality to a system gone mad with greed and corruption. These figures fought against the established orders of the time in hopes to put an end to poverty and social control. They were so strong in their lifetimes that the establishment saw them as a threat and in most cases; they suffered extreme persecution at the hands of their local political and religious institutions.

QUOTE SOURCES AND SUGGESTED READING
----

[0] The Greatest Quotations of All-Time - Anthony St Peter (2010)
[SR1] Astrotheology & Shamanism: Christianity's Pagan Roots. A Revolutionary Reinterpretation of the Evidence
[SR2] The Sacred Mushroom and The Cross: A study of the nature and origins of Christianity within the fertility cults of the ancient Near East by John M. Allegro
[SR3] The Holy Mushroom: Evidence of Mushrooms in Judeo-Christianity: A critical re-evaluation of the schism between John M. Allegro and R. Gordon Wasson ... in The Sacred Mushroom and the Cross by J. R. Irvin
[SR4] That Old-Time Religion: The Story of Religious Foundations by Jordan Maxwell
[SR5] Stellar Theology and Masonic Astronomy by Robert Hewitt Brown
[SR6] Occult America: The Secret History of How Mysticism Shaped Our Nation by Mitch Horowitz

"Archbishop - A Christian ecclesiastic of a rank superior to that attained by Christ."
- H. L. Mencken [0]

Jesus the Peaceful Revolutionary

The biblical accounts of Jesus were not consolidated and printed until nearly 300 years after his death. In that time, his followers had caused a massive social upheaval that threatened the established religious institutions of the time. Even in his own time, Jesus was an enemy of the state and an enemy of the church for his radical views of peace, freedom, and equality. The established religious order of the time was the Roman church and they were so threatened by his philosophy that they had him silenced. However, his death did not silence his message and his ideas were starting to spread all over the empire. Fearful that this antiestablishment movement would break down their spiritual monopoly, the church developed a plan to corrupt the message of Christ and use his cult status as a banner for their religious institution. The religious institution that was in fact responsible for the death of Christ and persecution of his followers was now planning to merge the popular image of Christianity with the dogmatic tradition of the church.

In 325^{AD}, the Roman Church held "The Council of Nicaea," a meeting of all the nobles and high-ranking church figures where they discussed how they would deal with the explosion of the Christian philosophy in their society. The church knew that if they let things continue as they were that all of their subjects would convert to Christianity in a very short time. They had to find a way to change this trend and convert the Christians back to the traditional structure and control of the church. To achieve this goal the establishment decided to merge Christianity with their religious teachings in such a way that the radical messages of peace and freedom were replaced with the dogma of the church.

The outcome of the council stated that Jesus Christ was the son of god and that he was to be treated as a divine figure, even though during his life he insisted that he was only a messenger and that people should not worship him, only follow his message. Christian followers who mostly belonged to the working illiterate class were deceived by the church and felt that this was a cause to be celebrated, because their savior was finally formally recognized by the church. Most Christians did not know the true implications of the terms that their rulers laid out at the council of Nicaea. The church then used "the divinity of Christ" as supporting evidence for all of their philosophies, even though the issue of divinity was decided by them at the conference. With the image and following of Jesus now a part of their church, the establishment was able to neutralize the social movement of Christianity from within and assimilate it into their own culture.

Once the church molded the Christian ideologies to fit its own political agenda, they were also able to dictate an "official" but corrupted recording of history. The church focused only on their fabricated depictions of Christ's birth and death and gave very little mention of what he actually stood for and what he did throughout his life. Many historical accounts of Jesus have been suppressed by the religious institutions because the reality of his political struggle would expose many of the primary falsehoods of our authoritarian society. This is the way that they have "watered down" and misdirected Jesus' revolutionary message. This is the most successful strategy employed by the elite to silence and corrupt revolutionary movements. You see them do that to this day with any kind of political or social movement that threatens the established order. They know that attempts to fully eradicate a social movement will only make that movement stronger and give it more credibility so they simply corrupt the message and turn it into a tool of social control.

Even in the accounts of Jesus that have not been destroyed by the church, his opposition towards the oppressive system of government, banking and organized religion is extremely obvious. In all of the biblical depictions of Christ, he has a peaceful state of mind except when he is dealing with "the money changers." He actually used physical force to throw these people out of a temple, which was the only account of him ever getting physical with anyone. The moneychangers were an ancient banking cartel that ruled the ancient world by lending money to governments and applying interest. Through the act of inflation and deflation, these cartels were able to strip the people of all their wealth, the same tactic that has been used by international bankers all the way to present times. Just like today, the moneychangers of biblical times were deeply imbedded in the government. Jesus was also said to constantly condemn authority and those who sought to subjugate others by monopolizing spirituality.

There is a great deal of controversy surrounding the divinity of Christ and many say that he did not want organized churches in his name. Behind the fabricated image of Jesus that the church has been perpetuating for centuries, there was most likely a revolutionary who vehemently opposed the ruling class and fought for the rights of the oppressed throughout his entire life. His whole life was a struggle for peace, equality, and human rights yet the religions that have sprung up in his name have marginalized his work, because it stood up against the kind of blind obedience to authority that they all require.

QUOTE SOURCES AND SUGGESTED READING
----

[0] The Columbia dictionary of quotations - Robert Andrews (1993)
[SR1] The Politics of Jesus by Obery M. Hendricks Jr. (2006)
[SR2] The Christ Conspiracy: The Greatest Story Ever Sold by Acharya S
[SR3] The Book Your Church* Does not Want You to Read: *(Or Synagogue, Temple, Mosque...) by Tim C Leedom (Editor), Maria Murdy (Editor), Bill Jenkins (Introduction)
[SR4] Virgin Mother Goddesses of Antiquity By Marguerite Rigoglioso
[SR5] Who Was Jesus? Fingerprints of The Christ By D.M. Murdock, Acharya S
[SR6] Christ in Egypt: The Horus-Jesus Connection By D. M. Murdock, Acharya S

"There has not been a religious organization in the world that was not a little bit political, and there has not been a political organization that was not a little bit religious." - Jordan Maxwell [0]

The Birth of Islam and the Arabian Empire

Islam is one of the most misunderstood religions in the world today, like most of the other mainstream religions it is even misunderstood by its own followers. The origins of this religion are shrouded in mystery and the state has had total control of the direction of the faith in most of the Arab world for centuries. The faith of Islam sprang up in the 7th century during the reign of the Arabic empire. The introduction of this belief structure into the Arabic society was largely due to the revelations of a man named Muhammad, the prophet of Islam. This was a man who committed many great acts and prompted positive social reform just as many different prophets of different faiths did before him.

Prior to the time of Muhammad, the Arabic world was mostly nomadic tribes that traveled the desert. A prominent group of Arabs called Bedouins were among the most cultured of these nomadic people. The Bedouins invented the camel saddle that allowed them to travel throughout the known empires working as merchants. In their trade journeys the Bedouins learned all the poetry, philosophy and science that the modern world had to offer. It was Bedouin culture that gave rise to the first Muslim cities, including Mecca. From the age of six Muhammad had grown up and traveled with caravans of Bedouin traders so he had the advantage of a philosophical and historical background, but like most of the world's population, he was still illiterate. Muhammad remained a merchant until the age of 40 when he had a vision that inspired him to preach about the need for social and religious reform in mecca. After a few years of preaching, he got involved in politics and became a voice and prophet for the people.

Muhammad did bring many of the reforms to mecca that he intended to but he never assembled a structured set of religious beliefs. He had nothing to do with the writing of the Quran, that actually took place hundreds of years after his death. It is agreed that he was a strict monotheist and also had some very egalitarian social philosophies as well. His insistence on monotheism was a sign of the times; the authoritarian government in the Arabian world at that time was strictly pagan so he associated that religion with the establishment's policies. It is also very possible that Muhammad was actually referring to the Christian or Jewish deity when he was talking of the "one god." Remember, Muhammad spent most of his life along the Bedouin trade routes, where he had a lot of contact with western monotheism, which would have been Christianity or Judaism.

Some of the social reforms that he was able to put into place show his revolutionary antiestablishment philosophy. Just as Jesus Christ "expelled the moneychangers from the temple" several hundred years before the birth of Islam, Muhammad actually managed to make "money exchanging" illegal in the Arab world. The act of "usury" or charging interests on loans was deemed to be a sadistic trick by Muhammad and remains illegal in most of the Middle East to this day. Perhaps that has something to do with why international bankers have made them an enemy, and created constant war in their homelands.

Muhammad was an advocate of social equality and human rights. During his time, he was able to make incredible political changes that shifted power from wealthy nobility to common people. He did this by demanding that people have the right to vote instead of being ruled by bloodlines. Muhammad made many successful attempts to develop thriving classless societies and his ideas began to assimilate into political systems all over the ancient world. This was achieved through demanding that the public have a proper education that was unheard of at the time. Unfortunately, just as many teachers to come before and since, Muhammad's message fell on deaf ears and his social vision was overpowered by the status quo.

Muhammad died in 632^{AD} with a whole civilization under his control and left no successor. This situation resulted in years of battles between different elite classes that wished to take his kingdom. Over the years, different tyrants have continued to fight over the lands that Muhammad once ruled and continually use his name to push their own political agenda, although their philosophies are nothing alike. Just as in the case of Christianity, oppressive cultural institutions have been responsible for handing down the holy book. The Quran has very little to do with Muhammad's philosophy and was produced by authoritarian regimes many years after his death.

The Quran is just a different retelling of the same ancient myths depicted in the bible, just with different cultural and political twists that suited the Arab establishment. Christians, Jews, and Muslims are all praying to the same god, just with different names, being described by different cultures. If Muhammad or any of the other prophets for that matter experienced divine intervention we may never know, but we can be sure that they did not want religions in their name and they had nothing to do with the production of the holy books of their faiths. The Quran in fact was never really an important part of Islamic tradition until "the renewal movement" of the 19th century. The renewal movement was a push by the authoritarian rulers of the Middle East to integrate the Quran into everyday Islamic teachings. It was only after this movement that the words of the Quran were expected to guide the lives of everyday citizens. Muhammad himself strictly opposed authoritarian political and spiritual institutions so the current dictatorial trend in the Middle East is completely against the teachings of Muhammad and the true intent of Islam.

QUOTE SOURCES AND SUGGESTED READING
----
[0] Jordan Maxwell – Religion And Politics Presentation
[SR1] The Book Your Church* Does not Want You to Read: *(Or Synagogue, Temple, Mosque...) by Tim C Leedom (Editor), Maria Murdy (Editor), Bill Jenkins (Introduction)
[SR2] That Old-Time Religion: The Story of Religious Foundations by Jordan Maxwell

"My religion consists of a humble admiration of the illimitable superior spirit who reveals himself in the slight details we are able to perceive with our frail and feeble mind. That deeply emotional conviction of the presence of a superior reasoning power, which is revealed in the incomprehensible universe, forms my idea of god."
- Albert Einstein [0]

Holy wars

Spirituality is one of the many great paradoxes of the human story. Nothing in the world is responsible for so much joy yet at the same time responsible for so much pain and destruction. Even now in the apparently "civilized" world that we are living in today, millions are killed in the name of religion. After centuries of fighting there has been no progress, it has not gotten us anywhere. Different Cultures have different belief structures because we come from different areas of the earth. We use different words to communicate our ideas, so of course the names dates and places in each cultures sacred story are not going to be the same. Every religion tells basically the same story, just with different words to accommodate whichever culture the book is coming from.

A positive spiritual movement usually turns into a violent control mechanism when it is corrupted by a figure of authority. It is at this point when everything changes, the goals are no longer to discover the future, but to fear the future and cling to the past in order to serve another. At our current stage of evolution, we have about the same chances of understanding the spirit realm as a gold fish has of understanding quantum physics, so it is absolutely insane for us to be killing each other in the name of god. At the heart of this ignorance is fear, fear that has been stirred up and manipulated by our oppressors for many generations. They have preyed upon our natural fears of the unknown, of change and the progression of time while only giving us fractions of information about our existence.

We can now look back throughout history and see that most wars and "crusades" in the name of religion were really over land, resources, and empire expansion. The Rulers of the time used their subject's deep fear of god to manipulate them into going on crusades just as our rulers today use fear tactics to con us into fighting and dying in wars. Just like pawns on a chessboard time after time, we are sent out to war by the king, and seen as completely expendable. This kind of senseless carnage is still taking place without anyone really stopping to question it. Insignificant differences among common people of all nations are still used by those in power for the sake of conquest. Whether those differences are religion, race, economic status, or culture, they are used as justifications to commit atrocities.

Our fear of being wrong has pushed us away from our brothers and sisters plunging us all into a world of confusion and pain. We spend all of our time worrying about, and planning for our destruction, while we lose sight of the beautiful complexity and infinite mystery of life. Accepting life as a mystery, only to be solved upon the turning of the final page will allow us to progress spiritually.

What is needed is a more open-ended spiritual culture that can grow with our evolutionary path, instead of keeping us chained to ridged ideologies. None of us even have a fraction of a clue what lies beyond, and accepting that fact is the first step towards discovering truth. If different religions would have been seriously open to the fact that they had more to learn and shared information with each other instead of going to war, imagine the positive impact it would have on our spiritual development and safety here on this planet.

QUOTE SOURCES AND SUGGESTED READING
----
[0] Albert Einstein - Quoted in his obituary in "The New York Times" April 19, 1959

"Putting new world funds in the new world banks
With the new world guns on the new world tanks
New world devils and new world gods
New world jails see the new worlds hard
New world names sing new world songs
New world planes are the new world bombs
New world's flyin, the new world's dying
The new world's crying and the new world's trying
New world sons and new world daughters
They're already selling us new world water"
–Michael Franti and Spearhead

Section 11

New World Weapons

74. -Water as a Weapon
75. -Monsanto's Monopoly
76. -Frankenfood Politics
77. -Fluoride: The Poison in the Well
78. -Quit Smoking
79. -Air Pollution and Chemtrails
80. -MK Ultra

"When you give food to the poor, they call you a saint. When you ask why the poor have no food, they call you a communist."
 - Helder Camara [0]

Water as a Weapon

     Our environment provides us with the resources that sustain our life, the air, the water, and the fruits that grow from the soil. These are our basic needs and basic rights as human beings. There is no price that you can put on these basic needs, just as you can put no price on a human life. Yet all over the world, incredibly rich banking interests seek to make our natural resources a commodity, so they can basically decide who has a right to live and who does not. This is a sad reality everywhere but is much more prevalent in underdeveloped countries where multinational corporations are monopolizing control of the population's water, with the help of the corrupt local governments.
     Every day in Bolivia, South Africa, India, China and other areas throughout Africa and the Middle East people struggle just to get access to

uncontaminated water. Men in suits and ties from distant lands are building their fortunes while at the same time impoverishing the good people of the third world by controlling their most basic need, water. Although they claim to work in the best interests of the native people these business tycoons, have no sympathy for human life and are only concerned with increasing their profits and depopulating the third world.

In Delhi, India, the Suez water company built a dam that massively restricted water flow to the city. Once the dam was in place and the people had less access to water that was rightfully theirs, Suez began to charge the townspeople for the water which they now claimed to own. This kind of story is not unique, it happens on a regular basis all over the developing world as the tyrannical financial institutions ravish the less fortunate. When a site for a dam is decided on, families that live in the area are forced to move from the only homes they have ever known.

The water companies promise to compensate these people for taking their land but those promises is always broken. People are displaced to areas where they no longer have access to water or fertile land, which was plentiful before it was stolen from them. To illustrate the magnitude of this issue here are some statistics. Katse Dam in Lesotho displaced 17,000 people, Xiaolangdi Dam in China displaced 200,000 people, Alosombo Dam in Ghana displaced 80,000 people, and three gorges dam in China displaced 1.3 million people. 80 million people have been displaced because of dam construction in the 20th century.

How did this happen? How did the native people of these lands lose control of their water to these corporate goons? Through the intimidation and manipulation of the International Monetary Fund, the World Bank, the United Nations, and the cooperation of local dictators, that is how. These organizations are very deceptive, well-dressed fronts that the elite use to influence what goes on around the world on an economic level. Recently, these groups have taken an apparent interest in bringing food, clean water, and infrastructure to the struggling third world. However, this is not how things are playing out at all. The programs being set up by the UN, the IMF and the World Bank are actually further impoverishing the poor people in these countries, stripping these people of their water and putting it in the hands of rich companies in which they are financially involved.

If their motives are altruistic then they would allow the people to collect rainwater, but they do not. Under the Irrigation Drainage Act that was set up by World Water Council the IMF and the World Bank, it is illegal for native peoples to collect rainwater. All of these international laws are then enforced by local military, corporate mercenaries and NATO troops. When these interests open up their water plants in the third world they shut down all of the plants that the local people are currently running and operating. The people are left with only one option and that option is so expensive that they cannot afford it. Thousands of innocent lives are taken every single day because they are forced into a position where they do not have access to clean water.

These corporations pump millions of dollars into the western media so the true horror and inhumanity of their actions never reach the public. These third world water grabs are a 400 billion dollar a year industry, one that is far more corrupt then even the oil industry. The international groups responsible for overseeing these companies are in fact the same people that own them! Loic Fauchon is the president of Marseilles Water Company a wealthy business that makes billions taking advantage of peoples basic need for water is also the president of the World Water Council. Michael Comdessus is the former president of the IMF and his top two advisors are the presidents of Suez and Vivendi water companies, both of which are owned by Marseilles!

This is a very calculated, very well covered up genocide on the struggling people of this planet. Whether these atrocities are intentional or not, the blatant disregard of human life for the sake of financial and tactical gain is nothing short of homicidal. When the people speak up for their basic needs they are forced into submission by violent riot police, which are hired by the establishment that is responsible for this oppression. We cannot allow this kind of injustice to go on. The people of these communities know how to run water plants and are more than willing to do so; they should be the ones in control of their own livelihood. No one owns the water of this planet, not the IMF, the World Bank or the companies behind the World Water Council. Just like air, water is a basic resource needed for life and to cut a population off from water is to cut them off from breathing.

QUOTE SOURCES AND SUGGESTED READING
----
[0] Walking Our Talk: Taking radical responsibility for our lives and our world - Bruce Mulkey (2006)
[SR1] Social Power and the Urbanization of Water: Flows of Power by Erik Swyngedouw

"What you are seeing is not just a consolidation of seed companies; it is really a consolidation of the entire food chain."
- Robert Fraley {Monsanto Executive} [0]

Monsanto's Monopoly

The human race is plagued with a long list of cancers, allergies, mutations and other ailments that may seem like the result of a careless industry, but are in fact a part of an intricate assault against the health of humanity. Just a few generations ago, many of these illnesses did not even exist. Now with the use of harsh metals, radiation, and genetically modified food we are being exposed to toxins that our species has never had any contact with in the whole course of our evolution. Most of these toxins come from multinational corporations who are owned by psychopathic elites that are seeking to weaken, control, and thin out the human population.

A company called Monsanto is one of the wealthiest multinational corporations in the world and is also one of the most ruthless. Behind the false image of innocence created by their lawyers and public relations, this company is as evil as they come. Thousands of lawsuits have been filed against this corporate giant worldwide, but because of their incredible wealth, they are usually able to settle out of court for large sums and pay off the media so their crimes are not exposed to the public.

Monsanto has a very nasty history, before they were in the food industry they primarily dealt with chemicals. Since the beginning of the 20th century, they were responsible for the manufacture of various toxic chemicals, which includes anything from caffeine to Agent Orange, along with other dangerous pesticides and herbicides. Monsanto even helped develop uranium for the atomic bomb in the Manhattan Project. Their chemical roundup has been known to cause dozens of different plant diseases and does unknown damage to the ecosystem, just as their other pesticides do. Monsanto does their fair share of destruction to our environment and our food supply, but their genetically modified food programs have taken this corporation a sinister step forward. Through tampering with the genetics of various plants and animals, they are looking to have a complete monopoly over the world's food and agriculture industries. This may seem difficult to believe, but policies that Monsanto had established in the past and the plans they have for the future show very clearly what is going on.

The milk industry was once one of the largest businesses in America, and due to its success, the market has been flooded with companies trying to cash in. Monsanto was of course one of these companies. In the 1980s, Monsanto developed a biological agent called (RBGH) or posilac. This was a hormone that was specifically designed to alter the genetics of cows in order to increase milk production. This horrible abuse of genetic technology resulted in carcinogenic milk, which a large amount of the population was exposed. Many of the lawsuits against Monsanto are involving this tainted milk and the unfortunate people who now have cancer because of it. The livestock that were exposed to this hormone suffered from mutations and diseases that put them in an incredible amount of pain before they ultimately died.

In addition, as a result of the over, production of milk the dairy industry was crippled and average farmers are having a time that is more difficult surviving in today has genetically modified market. The most interesting thing about this situation is the fact that the FDA only approved the patent of this hormone for the Monsanto Company, but denied the other three companies that applied to distribute it. Think back to our discussion about how government regulation is used to stamp out competition for the bigger corporations, like Monsanto for example. Monsanto receives this kind of "above the law" special treatment because of their immense political power. Many members of the FDA are actually Monsanto employees, and those who are not, are probably still on the payroll somehow anyway.

Eventually due to public outcry, their milk growth hormone was silently taken off the market, but this was just a small bump in the road for Monsanto. Their current goal is to completely dominate the whole agriculture industry using their genetically modified food and seeds. Monsanto has genetically modified seeds only produce one plant cycle, what this means is that once a seed has sprouted there will be no more seeds produced by this plant. If their plan works, which it is, farmers will have no choice but to buy every seed for every crop directly from the Monsanto Corporation. Currently, 80-90% of all major crops are genetically modified by Monsanto in some way or another. To make matters even worse Monsanto has used their political pull and financial backing to take independent farmers to court for using their own seeds!

What does all this mean for the average consumer? Well if Monsanto is able to have a complete monopoly on food then they can control the prices and production of all the food on the planet. This can put many farmers out of business and make it impossible for people who are not wealthy to have access to safe and healthy food. In addition, if Monsanto's milk already caused cancer and severe mutations then how can we be sure that their genetically modified food is not going to do the same? Monsanto will not even have genetically modified foods catered at their events and meetings, so that should tell you right there how unsafe they are. If their goal is accomplished and every seed on this earth is genetically modified and sterile, our natural world will be in danger of completely disappearing.

Monsanto's public relations campaign positions the company to be the savior of the earth, but anyone who has done some research into their work knows better. In 2010, an independent website called "naturalnews.com" conducted a survey to determine who the most evil corporation of the year was. Over 16,000 people voted in the poll and a staggering 51% of the votes went to Monsanto, while the Federal Reserve came in second with 20% of the vote. Ironically, just a year earlier Monsanto was at the top of a different list in the mainstream circuits, they were named "company of the year" by Forbes magazine in 2009 because of their incredible corporate power and influence. Despite their clean image in the mainstream press, there are a growing number of citizens who are raising awareness about Monsanto's monopoly.

This growing social movement against genetically modified food and big corporations has threatened Monsanto in such a way that they have actually hired an army to harass and intimidate activist groups. This is no exaggeration, remember those private mercenary companies that I discussed in "the privatization of war"? Well, in 2010 Monsanto actually hired "Blackwater" which is the largest private military company in the world. A corporation that has nothing but good intentions has no need for a mercenary army. This company must be stopped and exposed for the devil that it is, no one gave them the right to disrupt the chain of life of earth. This is our planet, our nature, our food and its time that we take it back! If we let Monsanto continue their destructive policies, it will be the biggest mistake that our species has made since the bombing of Hiroshima. Buy local produce, try to support organic farming or even better set up a garden of your own, and please do your best to raise awareness about this horrible cartel.

QUOTE SOURCES AND SUGGESTED READING
----
[0] The revolution will not be microwaved: inside America's underground food movements - Sandor Ellix Katz (2006)
[SR1] Food, Inc. Mendel to Monsanto - The Promises and Perils of the Biotech Harvest By Peter Pringle
[SR2] The World According to Monsanto: Pollution, Corruption, and the Control of the World's Food Supply by Marie-Monique Robin
[SR3] Seeds of Destruction: The Hidden Agenda of Genetic Manipulation by William F. Engdahl
[SR4] Lords Of The Harvest: Biotech, Big Money, And The Future Of Food by Dan Charles
[SR5] Stolen Harvest: The Hijacking of the Global Food Supply by Vandana Shiva
[SR6] What is In Your Milk? An Exposé of Industry and Government Cover-Up on the Dangers of the Genetically Engineered (RBGH) Milk You're Drinking By Samuel S. Epstein, M.D.

"If people let government decide what foods they eat and what medicines they take, their bodies will soon be in as sorry a state as are the souls of those who live under tyranny."
- Thomas Jefferson [0]

Frankenfood politics

Today we have more and more options of different foods that we can choose from, but it is also becoming harder to find food that is affordable and actually good for you. The sad truth of the matter is most of the things we eat on a day-to-day basis should not even be considered food! Most of the food on the market is created in factories using some natural ingredients with a whole lot of additives and chemicals. This approach has allowed companies to create an array of different products at a low cost. This financial advantage for the manufacturer unfortunately has a negative effect on the consumer because of the low quality of product that is flooding the market.

We all know that this processed food is unhealthy but why do we continue to eat it instead of looking for healthier alternatives? A lot of this unnatural preference for unhealthy food is actually due to advertisement. As we have talked about many other times throughout this book, advertisements have an extremely profound impact on your subconscious whether you realize it or not. Most of the food advertisements that we are subject to are for brand specific, manufactured food distributed by large corporations.

Therefore, because we are subject to subliminal stimuli that represents a certain type of food, that is the kind of food that we will be more likely to crave. Another thing that makes it hard to kick the junk food is the fact that the chemicals that are in them are actually addictive. Recent studies have shown that lab rats actually show signs of addiction and withdrawal from junk food. Scientists observed that after a rat became addicted to the junk food that they would no longer be interested in vegetables or other real, healthy foods. Since a good portion of what goes into our food is protected as "trade secrets" most of us will never know what kind of chemicals we are consuming, even if we are vigilant about checking labels.

A good number of people are finally starting to improve their eating habits and consider a more natural diet. It is important to be careful though even when purchasing fruit, vegetables or meat to make sure that it was not genetically modified. This is another sick little trick that these food corporations are using to save themselves money. They are actually tampering with the genetics of plants and animals so they offer crops that are more plentiful. As always, the financial advantages to these practices are greatly outweighed by their devastating impact on the consumer and the ecosystem.

The companies that genetically modify their products are the dominant force in the industry, but there are an increasing number of farmers that are growing only organic food. Some consumers have taken the matter into their own hands and even started their own gardens so they can have their own safe supply of fresh produce. This practice is extremely important and should be encouraged, however the companies that are intent on genetically modified food being dominant in the market are spending large sums of money on political contributions, in order to pass legislation that would make organic farming impossible. A lot of this legislation has already passed, and the government is actually raiding farms and grocers with guns drawn for selling or producing organic food.

This persecution of organic farming is being carried out by our government, as a favor to the large corporations that specialize in genetically modified food. These corporations have managed to develop a monopoly over the industry through their influence in government. Their ultimate goal is to have their products dominate the market completely and they want to stamp out any chance of people being able to grow their own food. In addition to highly subsidizing the GMO industry, the government also passes legislation to make things difficult for smaller businesses and farmers.

The corruption that exists between these companies and the government was made apparent in late 2010 when a bill called the "food modernization acts s510" passed through the senate. This bill would actually make it illegal for people to grow their own food or "horde seeds," as well as make it even more difficult for organic farmers to contend in the market. Despite massive public outcry and protest, this bill passed in the senate because of bribes that the politicians received from corporations. Luckily, there were new taxes hidden within the language of the bill, when those taxes were discovered days after the bill was signed it was automatically killed, because there are laws against new taxes being included in this kind of legislation without approval. Even though the bill was killed, they are still working hard on other pieces of legislation that would give the FDA an unreasonable amount of control over who is allowed to grow food.

The only way to solve this problem is for people to really get behind this issue and demand that we have access to organic food and maintain the right to grow our own food. We need to support our local farmers and try to do as much organic farming as is possible for our lifestyle and location. Developing a natural organic diet will not only make you feel better and healthier, but it will mean there is one less person putting their support and money into the Frankenfood establishment. If you make these choices yourself and encourage those around you to do the same these corrupt corporations will be powerless, because it is our support that is keeping their industry booming.

QUOTE SOURCES AND SUGGESTED READING
----
[0] European food law - Raymond O'Rourke (2005)
[SR1] Seeds of Destruction: The Hidden Agenda of Genetic Manipulation by William F. Engdahl

"Life is a kind of thievery, right from the days of infancy, too many things taking away the raw sense of freedom. Why did it have to be like this, my condition is clouded in mist? Wear a coat of anxiousness I lay down to sleep on."
– MC Xander [0]

Fluoride: The Poison in the Well

A poison world has sprung up before us in just a few short generations. The water we drink, the food we eat and even the air that we breathe is filled with dangerous toxins that have been consciously unleashed on the population by governments and corporations. Many times this contamination is due to neglect and greed, but there is also proof that it is an intentional practice for social control. Regardless of the motive, be it corporations cutting corners or governments drugging their populations, we are being exposed to more toxic chemicals than any other generation in history.

Fluoride is one of the most harmful chemicals in existence and is a daily part of life for most people in the western world. Fluoride is a carcinogenic waste product of aluminum. It is also the main ingredient in rat poison, nerve gas, and Prozac. This chemical agent has been present in the water supply in America for several generations, but this sick and twisted idea actually began during the Third Reich in Nazi Germany. Nazi scientists discovered that small doses of fluoride would work as a tranquilizer in humans and put them in a subdued and passive condition.

Fluoridating the water supply was not the only attempt by the Nazis to diminish the consciousness of the German people; it was just one of the most successful and subtle. It has been confirmed that the Nazis fluoridated all of the water in their concentration camps and it has been rumored this was also practiced on their civilian population as well. It was necessary for the Nazis to break the spirit of their political prisoners so they were easier to manage. They also needed to debilitate their population because a fully conscious and aware public would never allow them to commit such atrocities as genocide.

Ironically, just after the second world war in 1945 the American government introduced fluoride into the water supply. The US government told their citizens that this chemical was being added to their drinking water to promote dental health. As ridiculous as this explanation was it actually worked. The American Dental Association acted as puppets for the establishment to reinforce the fluoridation program. They even added fluoride to almost every major brand of toothpaste! In the decades following independent research would show the true dangers of fluoride poisoning and prove that there were no positive effects from fluoride on human beings. It was discovered that fluoride caused cancer, sterilization, Alzheimer's disease and even a dental deterioration called fluorosis. That is right, the very reason that fluoridation was said to be in place was not just an exaggeration, but also a complete lie.

In October of 2010, the fraudulency of the fluoridation program was exposed when the American Dental Association posted a report in their monthly journal warning about the dangers of fluoride intake in young children. This development came just months after the Center for Disease Control issued a similar warning. The admissions from these institutions were released quietly and they still maintained that fluoride was necessary to have in the water supply even though it has been known to damage cells and cause serious health issues. On an even deeper level, it is said that fluoride causes calcifications to build up on the pineal gland, the most sacred part of the human brain. This completely shuts off ones center of consciousness as well as weakens the mind and body.

There are temporary solutions that you can take to safeguard yourself against this attack. There are water filtration systems available that work using reverse osmosis. The reverse osmosis system will probably be cheaper and more environmentally friendly than buying bottled water on a daily basis. There is also different toothpaste companies that offer fluoride free toothpaste, these products can usually be found online or at natural food stores. All of these steps are good for individual protection; however, awareness about the dangers of fluoride is extremely important. The facts and evidence are all out in public, even the very institutions that once stood behind these malicious practices are now starting to backtrack and warn against them. Fluoride must be removed from the public water supply and from dental practices. Do not put your faith in the corporate funded media propaganda about fluoride, do the research for yourself and with your family and friends. If you have any kind of public outlet even if it is your own website or social networking page, bring this issue to the public so we can protect ourselves from these harmful chemical agents.

QUOTE SOURCES AND SUGGESTED READING
----
[0] M.C. Xander – Frailty - Eyeopeness
[SR1] Fluoride the Aging Factor: How to Recognize and Avoid the Devastating Effects of Fluoride By Dr. John Yiamouyiannis
[SR2] Water: For Health, for Healing, for Life: You are Not Sick, You are Thirsty! By F. Batmanghelidj
[SR3] SC-Guide/Safe Drinking Water By Scott Alan Lewis
[SR4] The Case Against Fluoride: How Hazardous Waste Ended Up in Our Drinking Water and the Bad Science and Powerful Politics That Keep It There by Paul Connett, James Beck, and H. Spedding Micklem
[SR5] The Fluoride Deception by Christopher Bryson
[SR6] The Devil's Poison: How fluoride is killing you by Dean Murphy

"You know, it is cigarettes that killed Jerry Garcia. Everyone thinks it is heroin, but it was not. It was cigarettes."
- John Melencamp [0]

Quit Smoking

Smoking is one of the leading causes of illness and death in the world. The use of tobacco has become more widespread than ever and the substance itself is far more dangerous than it has ever been before. Tobacco was originally a product of the Native Americans, but it was used by them in a much different way. The Native Americans only used tobacco on special occasions for rituals, gatherings, and feasts. The smoke was also never inhaled by the natives; this was a mistake that the westerners made in their ignorance. Another mistake that they made was mass producing it and encouraging daily use. Today cigarettes are mass-produced and treated with thousands of additives and chemicals. Carcinogenic, poisonous chemicals and toxic metals can all be found in modern tobacco products. These chemicals are present for many reasons ranging from taste and preservation to being purposely addictive. There are over 4000 of these chemicals in cigarettes and all of them are actually not even revealed to the public, they are protected under law as "trade secrets." This means they can be putting anything they want in there without our knowledge.

The tobacco industry is nearly as profitable and deadly as the arms industry. The global cigarette business is valued at over $559.9 billion and the World Health Organization estimates that cigarettes could kill 1 billion people in the 21st century if the current trend continues. Today smoking causes a whole list of adverse health reactions, illnesses, and disease but because it is such a big business, the corporations that profit from the sale of tobacco spend a lot of time and money keeping its use alive. Like all-important industries, the global tobacco market is controlled by just a few multinational corporations who spend billions in advertising and public relations every year to keep their product in demand.

Before the effects of smoking were seen on aging generations, the tobacco companies paid off doctors, dentists, educators, and celebrities to endorse their product. Through these public relations, projects the tobacco companies projected a healthy, socially desirable, and sophisticated image for their product. When cigarettes started, being mass-produced most doctors and dentists were actually telling people that smoking was good for them! It was not until massive amounts of people began to die as a result of smoking that the scientists and doctors actually began to warn the public that it might not be that healthy after all. Now we know the sad truth, smoking cigarettes is one of the worst possible things you can do to your body and mind. As with fluoride, the chemicals contained in cigarettes have even been known to cause unhealthy build-ups on the pineal gland in your brain and make your consciousness "hazy."

Many local governments have been forced by their constituents to ban smoking in most public places, but that does not necessarily mean that the establishment wants you to quit smoking. Most politicians have financial interests in tobacco and are in close ties with the people behind the industry, but it goes much deeper than that. The people that control trade and politics are also heavily involved in the production and distribution of cigarettes, as I am sure you could have guessed. The ruling class sees this product as the perfect tool for population control and a welcome boost to their pharmaceutical business. Due to the toxic chemicals in cigarettes, smokers are always coming down with different respiratory and sinus problems. The companies that are behind the cause of these illnesses are again the same ones that offer you the drugs to treat them. Therefore, it is very much in the best interests of the elite to keep you sick and keep you addicted. This is especially relevant when considering the eugenics agenda that I discussed earlier on in the book.

One of the best ways to keep you in their grip is by making it seem impossible to quit, when in reality it is actually pretty easy. There is a whole market of gums, patches and other quitting devices available that actually make quitting more difficult and have extremely low success rates. Most of these quitting mechanisms actually come from a very unlikely source. That is right you guessed it, the tobacco industry. Through developing faulty quitting programs the tobacco companies are not only able to create another market to fleece you of your hard earned money, but they also make it more difficult for you to quit by giving you the idea that you can't do it on your own.

The financial advantage alone should be enough of an argument to quit smoking. In most states, cigarettes are now over 6 dollars a pack, half of which is taxes. Therefore, people are literally paying the government and rich multinational corporations an average of 10 dollars every day, for a product that destroys their bodies. It is true that there are addictive chemicals in cigarettes but their strength and power has been blown way out of proportion. The psychological addiction is always much stronger than the physical addiction even with harsh narcotics like heroin and especially with nicotine. All you have to do is stop and get through a few days without it. Soon enough the smell and taste will no longer be desirable to you and you will be happy to have that extra 6 dollars a pack in your pocket. It will be easier to breathe, you will not get sick as often, and you will overall be in better spirits. Quitting cigarettes is one decision that you can make that will drastically improve your life in a number of ways and it will give the elite less control of your money and your health.

QUOTE SOURCES AND SUGGESTED READING

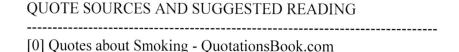

[0] Quotes about Smoking - QuotationsBook.com

"Treat the earth well: it was not given to you by your parents, it was loaned to you by your children. We do not inherit the Earth from our Ancestors; we borrow it from our Children."
- Navajo Proverb [0]

Air Pollution and Chemtrails

Air is definitely the most basic necessity for human life, in just a few minutes of its absence any of us would be risking death. Yet with every day that passes the world's air supply becomes more and more contaminated with harmful pollutants. Even if you do not live in a smog-filled city, you are still subject to air pollution in the form of pesticides and Chemtrails. Many people do not think twice about any of these toxins because they have no immediate visible effect. The effect of these chemicals may not be immediate but they do exist, our species now suffers an abundance of toxin related diseases that were never a problem for our ancestors. The worst of these conditions is cancer, which is now one of the leading causes of death in the world. Cancer is still a relatively new disease and is caused by the toxic chemicals that are everywhere in the modern world. In addition to cancer, air pollution has been known to cause various respiratory, reproductive, and skin diseases.

Pesticides are among the biggest threats to clean air on earth. Pesticides have been used to keep insects and animals away from crops for a very long time. Over 4000 years ago, the ancient Sumerians dusted their crops with sulfur, in the Middle Ages more poisonous chemicals like mercury, arsenic, and lead were developed for pesticide use. Corporations continued to use toxic chemicals all the way up to the 20th century and then in the 1940s pesticide use became even more widespread. This widespread use was brought on by the ability of large companies to mass produce synthetic chemicals. Since this boom in the pesticide industry some breakthroughs have been made towards producing less toxic chemicals, but even the safest products on the market are still hazardous to human health.

All throughout the European Union the pesticide atrazine has been banned outright while it remains one of the dominant chemicals on the American market. Birth defects increase drastically in agricultural areas that use atrazine. Tasmanian cancer rates shot up 200% after heavy use of pesticides became widespread. There are very simple alternatives to alleviate pest problems on farms, but pesticide use is pushed because of the amount of money that it brings large corporations, like Monsanto for example.

Sadly, there is a far more sinister threat to our air than pesticides, that being Chemtrails. Chemtrails are toxic jet streams containing aluminum and barium stearate. These jet streams are not to be confused with contrails, which are the small water vapor streams that evaporate just after leaving the plane. Chemtrails are still a controversial topic because the government has completely denied that they exist until recently. The establishment has insisted that what people are seeing is regular Jetstream contrails, but the jet streams in question hang in the hair for hours until they turn into long clouds and eventually fall onto the ground. Once the clouds fall onto the ground they have been tested many times by people who are paying attention. Every time these clouds are, tested traces of aluminum and barium stearate are always found. These chemicals are extremely dangerous when they come in contact with the skin and have adverse health conditions when present in the air supply.

No one knows exactly why these Chemtrails are being sprayed but we do know who is responsible. You guessed it, the government. After years of denying the existence of Chemtrails in October of 2010, the establishment was forced to admit they existed when the situation was brought up through the United Nations. When confronted about Chemtrails the government claimed that it was a part of a project called "geo-engineering" which was designed to prevent global warming! This laughable excuse was pushed through the mainstream media but the UN still plans to launch a full investigation in their next major report in 2013. Unfortunately, we can be sure that this investigation will be far from unbiased considering the UN is probably implicit in these activities.

There are many theories that are more plausible as to the reason behind this geo-engineering program. Our current government has no interest in environmentalism, and if they are claiming to then watch out. The government is only interested in expanding their military and social dominance. Some say that this is a military program that is experimenting with weather control; others say this is a toxin for social control, much like fluoride. Regardless of the motive behind these programs, they should not be practiced because playing with nature could result in total disaster, especially when using toxic chemicals.

QUOTE SOURCES AND SUGGESTED READING
----
[0] The Daily Book of Positive Quotations - Linda Picone (2008)
[SR1] Toxic Childhood: How the Modern World is Damaging Our Children and What We Can Do About it By Sue Palmer
[SR2] Chemtrails Confirmed by William Thomas
[SR3] Weather Warfare: The Military's Plan to Draft Mother Nature by Jerry E. Smith
[SR4] Contrails, Chemtrails & Artificial Clouds - Dave Dahl

"It is like MK-ULTRA, controlling your brain. Suggestive thinking, causing your perspective to change They want to rearrange the whole point of view of the ghetto The fourth branch of the government, want us to settle A bandana full of glittering, generality Fighting for freedom and fighting terror, but what is reality? Read about the history of the place that we live in and stop letting corporate news tell lies to your children."
– Immortal Technique {Hip Hop Artist} [0]

Project MK Ultra and CIA mind control

In American culture, the topic of mind control is shrouded in fiction and mystery. Most people automatically think of science fiction films or comic books when mind control is brought up without realizing the vital role that it actually plays in government policy. This is not a new idea, for ages the elite has been using various forms of mind control to dominate their civilizations. Monarchs of the past would suppress education among their subjects and make threats of fire and brimstone towards the citizens that were reluctant to submit to their authority. Cultures, laws, religions and other language based mind control have been the dominant method throughout history. For centuries, they have been perfecting various methods of shaping the minds of their citizens, molding them into the perfect worker and soldier drones. Now with the past centuries technological explosion, the elite now has a wide range of new tools to assist them in controlling the masses.

Most of the government mind control programs that exist are kept secret but there is one that managed to draw the attention of the public. That program was a government project called "MK Ultra", a CIA operation that involved very extreme methods of mind control that were tested on the US population. Although the CIA was forbidden to carry out tests on their own citizens, they did so anyway and kept the whole operation classified. The project began in April of 1953, just 6 years after the formation of the CIA and was among the top secret of government operations. There were 150 "sub projects" within the MKU program, many involved advanced brainwashing techniques using psychological drugs, sensory deprivation and electroshock therapy.

After 20 years of testing harsh brain washing methods on unsuspecting US citizens, some of the victims of these tests began asking questions about what had happened to them while they were under the care of doctors that were on the CIA's payroll. Fearing exposure the pentagon ordered the MK Ultra program to be terminated and all documents destroyed. In 1973 CIA, director and chief architect of MKU Richard Helms followed through with destroying the evidence, but some papers were misfiled and overlooked. Just a few years later those misfiled papers would come back and haunt the pentagon as they would expose some of the harsh realities behind the MKU program. After this evidence, surfaced dozens of victims came forth claiming to be test subjects in MKU experiments and filed lawsuits against the CIA.

The most recent lawsuit against the CIA for their brainwashing experiments is by far the largest. Three veterans groups in the state of California have brought a case against the CIA claiming that over 78,000 soldiers were used as human guinea pigs to research biological, chemical, and psychological weapons. In 2010, a federal judge in San Francisco finally ordered the CIA to produce specific records of the experiments that they conducted on thousands of soldiers from 1950 through 1975. The agency has been backpedaling for the past 20 years claiming that the details behind the MKU program are states secrets and a matter of national security. They have tried every trick in the book to avoid exposure in this case, even saying that the experiments in question happened so long ago that they cannot legally be held accountable for what happened.

Project MK Ultra is just one government mind control project that happened to be exposed, there is bound to be countless others that are still classified, possibly even more horrific than MK Ultra is. In fact, there are many parts of MKU that have remained secret for over 50 years and are probably much more sadistic than the parts that have surfaced. The inspector General of the CIA had this to say in the freedom of information act document about the project.

"The concepts involved in manipulating behavior are found by many people both within and outside the Agency to be distasteful and unethical. Nevertheless, there have been major accomplishments in both research and operational employment. Many additional avenues to the control of human behavior have been designated under the MKULTRA charter, including radiation, electro-shock, and harassment substances. Some activities raise questions of legality implicit in the original charter. A final phase of the testing places the rights and interests of US citizens in jeopardy. The MKULTRA program has pursued a philosophy of minimum documentation in keeping with the high sensitivity of the projects. Some files contained little or no data at all. There are just two individuals who have full knowledge of the MKULTRA program, and most of that knowledge is unrecorded." [1]

The CIA has managed to run away from any legal consequences but they have not been able to keep the details of MKU a secret. Congressional testimony showed that not only were many people's lives drastically torn apart by these tests, but also one test subject actually jumped from a 10-story window and killed himself after he was unexpectedly drugged by government agents. The agency themselves admit to still be carrying out the kind of covert mind control operations despite public resistance to the original MK Ultra program. The horrors of this project are a reminder to us that the government does not look at us as equals; they want to control how we think feel and act so they can use us to build their empires.

QUOTE SOURCES AND SUGGESTED READING
----
[0] Immortal Technique – The 4th Branch – Revolutionary Vol 2.
[1] J.S. Earman, Inspector General 26 July 1963, MEMORANDUM FOR: Director of Central Intelligence SUBJECT: Report of Inspection, MKULTRA DECLASSIFIED through freedom of information act request

[SR1] A Nation Betrayed by Carol Rutz
[SR2] Bluebird by Colin Ross, MD
[SR3] Mind Controllers By Dr. Armen Victorian

*"We hold what is to come in the next generation; We hold the key to peace and prosperity.
We have the tools to create a better existence, To end all things bad and to start a new beginning.
This is the time we become something else, We are the future."*
– Toneshifterz

Section 12

The Future

81. -2012: Do not Fear the Renaissance
82. -The Culture Battle Between Art and Propaganda
83. -Peaceful Economics
84. -Peaceful Politics
85. -Kindness and Cooperation
86. -We Are Winning

"2012 It could be heaven, it could be hell. Make a choice, Make a decision, Make a difference, I choose love, Light and Ascension Into 2013 and the fifth dimension." - P.E. {Rap/Rock Group} [0]

This chapter contains a mixture of facts and personal theoretical assumptions of my own please do your own research after reading this to form your own opinion.

2012: Do not Fear the Renaissance

Although few of us realize it, our species is at the dawn of a quantum leap in our development. Things most of us take for granite in our everyday life would baffle those who came before us. Our technology and capabilities would seem magical and perhaps even extraterrestrial to our ancestors. However, this trend is not new, since the beginnings of civilization there have been many quick spikes in human advancement. In history we usually refer to these times of rapid development as "Renaissances," we have seen several of these quite recently with the industrial revolution and the information age. Signs are all around us showing that we are on the brink of a revolution in consciousness. This leap has been foretold for centuries and it is said we will obtain knowledge that will far surpass what we have learned in the industrial and information ages.

Many indigenous cultures including the ancient Sumerian's and Mayan's were master astrologers that pointed to the age we are currently living in as one of great change. They predicted this through careful observation and study of the night sky, and at times they probably knew more about the universe than modern science. The end of the age of pieces the age we are currently living in will occur on 2012 and will be marked by an event called the galactic alignment. The galactic alignment will take place for the first time in recorded history on 2012 when the planets line up with the sun and the center of the galaxy.

Although there are many different things that this alignment could mean, this is where the media sensationalized "2012 doomsday phenomenon" originated. It has been known for many generations that movements and changes in the heavens will affect the psyche of human beings here on earth; this is where the concept of astrology comes from. Therefore, it would make sense that the time of the galactic alignment will coincide with a time of great change here on earth. This change will most likely be inside the hearts and minds of the people on the planet, instead of a cosmic catastrophe that has been suggested by our media.

The doomsday theory is unlikely and overused by power hungry governments that wish to keep their populations in fear. As we have seen quite recently in the past decade in the United States, the establishment constantly uses fear to manipulate the minds of US citizens. This technique is not new either, it has been used for centuries whether it be the fear of economic collapse, natural disaster, the enemy, or the fear of god, fear has been used by the few to dominate the many for ages.

When the Spaniards were conquering the Mayan empire, they learned through missionaries that 1698 was the end of the Mayan time cycle. Therefore, the Spanish waited until 1698 to invade and the Mayans took it as a sign and fled without resistance. One of the most celebrated of all doomsday predictions was made by astrologers who predicted a great flood that would end the world on February 20 1524 based on the conjunction of all the planets in the heavens mercury, Venus, Mars, Jupiter, and Saturn. We have also seen quite recently with the media hoax Y2K, which threatened us with a "cyber Armageddon" at the turn of the millennium. In both cases obviously, the world continued to turn.

To even further discount the doomsday propaganda surrounding 2012 many Mayan elders are coming forward and saying that their prophecy has been greatly misunderstood by the western world. Carlos Barrios is one of those elders and he has interviewed over 600 other senior Mayan elders to get the clearest possible understanding of the situation. In an online interview representing the Organization for Mayan and Indigenous Spiritual Studies, Carlos made the following statement:

"Anthropologists visit the temple sites and read the inscriptions and make up stories about the Maya, but they do not read the signs correctly. It is just their imagination. Other people write about prophecy in the name of the Maya. They say that the world will end in December 2012. The Mayan elders are angry at this. The world will not end. It will be transformed. We are no longer in the World of the Fourth Sun, but we are not yet in the World of the Fifth Sun. This is the time in-between, the time of transition. As we pass through transition, there is a colossal, global convergence of environmental destruction, social chaos, war, and ongoing Earth Changes. Humanity will continue, but

in a different way. Material structures will change. From this, we will have the opportunity to be more human. We are living in the most important era of the Mayan calendars and prophecies. All the prophecies of the world, all the traditions are converging now. There is no time for games. The spiritual ideal of this era is action. The indigenous have the calendars and know how to accurately interpret it -- not others. The Mayan Calendars comprehension of time, seasons, and cycles has proven itself to be vast and sophisticated. The Maya understand 17 different calendars such as the Tzolk'in or Cholq'ij, some of them charting time accurately over a span of more than ten million years."

"All was predicted by the mathematical cycles of the Mayan calendars. -- It will change --everything will change. Mayan Daykeepers view the Dec. 21, 2012 date as a rebirth, the start of the World of the Fifth Sun. It will be the start of a new era resulting from and signified by the solar meridian crossing the galactic equator and the Earth aligning itself with the center of the galaxy. This process has already begun. Change is accelerating now and it will continue to accelerate. If the people of the Earth can get to this 2012 date in good shape without having destroyed too much of the Earth, we will rise to a new, higher level. However, to get there we must transform enormously powerful forces that seek to block the way. The economy now is a fiction. The first five-year stretch of transition from August 1987 to August 1992 was the beginning of the destruction of the material world. We have progressed ten years deeper into the transition phase by now, and many of the so-called sources of financial stability are in fact hollow. The banks are weak. This is a delicate moment for them. They could crash globally if we do not pay attention. If the banks crash -- then we will be forced to rely on the land and our skills. The monetary systems will be in chaos, and we must then rely on our direct relationship with the Earth for our food and shelter. Right now, each person and group is going his or her own way. The elder of the mountains said there is hope if the people of the light can come together and unite in some way." [1]

Ancient calendars were astrology based and far more complicated than the calendars we have today. For example, the Mayan and Sumerian calendars included not only months and years but also very long ages defined through the procession of the equinoxes and solstices, ideas that are foreign to most people in modern times. The ancients saw that everything in the world was connected and that the human psyche was deeply affected by stars and planetary bodies. They believed that events here on earth were reflected in space, and through mapping space, they designed the first calendars.

Early rulers would plan all of their royal duties astrologically, whether it was agriculture, ritual, or war, the placement of the stars and planets played a major role in what decisions were made by those in charge. Many super advanced ancient cultures such as the Sumerians, the Mayans, and tribes in Asia and North America all pointed to the time were living in as one of great change. From the perspective of these cultures, we are living in a dark age, much like the medieval period in Europe before the renaissance we are functioning far below our potential and we are on the brink of discovering just how much we are capable. Many indigenous tribes agree that humankind is in a state of sleep, a lower state of consciousness that is the root cause of all the pain and struggle we see in the world.

The Hopi tribe of North America also has a series of revelations that vividly described many events leading up to the dawn of a new age. These revelations are strikingly similar to events that have unraveled in modern American history, and are still unfolding today. The Hopi foretold the expansion of Anglo European civilization into native lands, the railroad systems that cut through the western terrain, and the development of industries that would lay waste to nature. When the BP oil spill blackened the Gulf of Mexico in 2010 and birds, fish and other animals began, dying in 2011 it seemed that the last signs of the Hopi prophecy were upon us.

The final verses of the prophecies went something like this *"there will come a time, when the fish will die in the streams, the birds will fall from the air, the waters will run black, and the trees will no longer be, a new tribe of people shall come unto the earth from many colors, classes, creeds, who by their actions and deeds shall make the earth green again. They will be known as the warriors of the Rainbow."*

The very animal deaths and environmental destruction may seem ominous but according the Hopi prophecy these are only the wakeup calls that will spring the warriors of the rainbow into action. You are a warrior of the rainbow, so is the soldier who refuses to go to war, the farmer who refuses to work with Monsanto, the scientist who refuses to develop oppressive technology, the police officer that puts down his billy club to join the protesters in the streets, and the average citizen who cancels their cable television subscription and becomes a part of the counter culture. This group of concerned citizens is growing and will continue to grow as the crisis on the planet earth deepens.

Looking at the direction our species is taking this planet it is obvious that a massive change and awakening is needed for us to avoid a complete disaster. We are very much living in a dark age, an age where we must decide to grow and change the way we are living, or continue down the path that has already led to the decline of civilization. This decision will come in our lifetime, it is just around the corner, and it is going to get more difficult to ignore with every day that passes.

To create a better world were going to have to make some changes in the way we do business and how we affect the world around us. We all know change can seem like a scary thing, especially when it is a change this big. It does not help that we have been told our whole lives that there would be chaos and disorder without the institutions that are destroying the earth and exploiting its people. I understand that this may seem like an intimidating leap for many people but we must not allow the elite to continue to control us with fear. It is fear that is responsible for every war that has ever taken place on this earth and almost every single act of aggression.

If we have the courage to work together toward a more humane and peaceful, civilization then we can have it. The reason why the existing cultural institutions so vehemently deny that a better way of living is possible is because they know it is possible. They want us to fear the renaissance and cling to the old ways, but if we stay in line and do not change the course of our civilization then we will miss one of the greatest opportunities our species has ever had, to save our planet and ourselves.

Our world is in ruins and its people are sick, confused, and starving, we need to turn around the ship before it is too late. It is not difficult to live in a world of peace and equality, the only thing that needs to happen is for the people to demand it. If everyone had all the information and were able to conquer their fear then they would immediately demand an end to elitism and aggression. The change is coming, but it will not be something that we witness it the form of an apocalypse, it is something that we will create, in the form of a renaissance.

QUOTE SOURCES AND SUGGESTED READING
----
[0] (HED) P.E - No More Secrets - Truth Rising (2010)
[1] http://preventdisease.com/news/11/030411_mayan_elder_explains_2012.shtml
[SR1] The Myth Of The Great Ending by Joseph M Felser
[SR2] Maya Cosmogenesis 2012: The True Meaning of the Maya Calendar End-Date By John Major Jenkins, Terence McKenna

"We have to stop CONSUMING our culture. We have to CREATE culture. DO NOT watch TV, DO NOT read magazines, and do not even listen to NPR. Create your OWN roadshow. The nexus of space and time where you are -- NOW -- is the immediate sector of your universe. And if you're worrying about Michael Jackson or Bill Clinton or somebody else, then you are disempowered."
– Terrence Mckenna [0]

The Culture Battle between Art and Propaganda

Every individual military conflict and case of economic slavery is made possible by some kind of cultural or philosophical mindset. All of the decisions we make throughout our lives are guided by our philosophical outlook and our cultural programming. Our ideas about the meaning of life, right and wrong and human nature will ultimately dictate our behavior. Tyrants would not be able to walk good hearted, self-respecting people into war and tax slavery if those people were not first instilled with a personal philosophy that was receptive to those orders. This is why they so desperately control the education system and the media, to set the culture and ultimately control the overall mindset of the population. This is also, why the counter culture is often viewed as a threat, because their role is to offset the established culture and push it in a direction that is not controlled by those running society.

At the beginning of this book, I discussed propaganda as a method of controlling culture and public opinion to achieve destructive ends. Now I am going to talk about how the common people of this earth can use the same methods but with benevolent intent in order to push the culture in a more positive direction. If propaganda is what the establishment uses to create a culture of war, then art is what the average person can use to create a culture of peace. In times of oppression it is very difficult for people to speak out against the constant tyranny, even when they do it is even more difficult to get others to listen. Art is a subtle way of getting the message out to the masses. This is useful because many times people are so entrenched in the mainstream culture that they will become defensive when they come face to face with facts that call their worldview into question. However, if these same ideas are presented in the form of art, people are much less defensive and are more willing to approach the information with an open mind. Art is also used by activists who want to send a message but still remain under the radar.

This culture battle is all around us; almost every human creation is in one way or another either art or propaganda. Award winning movies, chart toping songs, children's cartoons, books and pretty much any form of media are filled with various philosophic and political overtones that are intended to speak to the audience. One of the top grossing films of all time "Avatar" may have seemed like a science fiction film at first glance, but with a closer look one will find that the whole plot was making a bold political statement. The creator and director of the film James Cameron discussed the role that his political views played in the creation of Avatar.

In the December 2000 interview, he said "I think it is important for people to see the patterns in history… I think science fiction is a way of making history exciting by putting it in the future and taking you to a new planet and showing you exactly the same shit that is been happening for the last 2,000 years…Science fiction is excellent for that because if you want to make a comment about the Iraq war and American imperialism in the middle east, you're going to get a lot of people pissed off at you in this country, but you do it in a science fiction context where you do it at a metaphorical level, people get swept in by the story and they get to the end of the movie before they realize they have been rooting for the Iraqis"[1] Cameron's other record breaking blockbuster "Titanic" was also very political, a film with class conscious social commentary hidden in a love story.

If you really examine some of the greatest works of art in history, you will find that the vast majority of the time the artist was motivated by some kind of social cause. The art that really moves people and leaves a lasting impression is rarely made with the thought of making a buck or climbing the social ladder. In today's culture massive advertising schemes and flashy graphics are enough to catch most people's attention long enough to make a purchase, but you'll find that the works of art with real staying power are typically sending some kind of social message.

The original Wizard of Oz play was a subtle critique of the banking industry, most popular rock songs during the 60's were speaking out against the Vietnam war, early hip hop spoke out about civil rights and social justice, while at the same time almost everything that is approved by the FCC for television and radio is pure propaganda, designed to glorify materialism, authority and violence. Unfortunately, it is the information that is put out through the mainstream channels that is usually adopted as "truth" by the general public. This is why it is so important for us to not support the mainstream culture and actively work to create our own culture.

Now for the first time in history the internet gives average people access to unlimited, uncensored information and a place to share their opinions, free from fear of persecution. It is very easy nowadays for people to make a YouTube video, or put their music out to thousands of people, or start a podcast, the possibilities are limitless with today's technology. Our ancestors did not really have the option to become the media, but we do. There is no need for us to feel helpless, or to resort to violence because we have the ability to reverse the direction of our culture peacefully.

QUOTE SOURCES AND SUGGESTED READING
----
[0] Terrence McKenna - from the lecture "Eros and the Eschaton"
[1] James Cameron discussing avatar in Vanity Fair" December 11, 2000

"Folks, it is time to evolve. That is why we are troubled. You know why our institutions are failing us, the church, the state, everything is failing? It is because, um – they are no longer relevant. We are supposed to keep evolving. Evolution did not end with us growing opposable thumbs. You do know that, right? There are another 90 percent of our brains that we have to illuminate."
- Bill Hicks [0]

This is just an abstract idea to illustrate that alternatives to the status quo are a possibility, I am by no way saying that this is perfect and I am sure that with some research and brainstorming you can come up with an even better idea.

Peaceful Economics

Since the economic collapse of 2008, the markets in every nation all across the globe are beginning to deteriorate. Cities and even entire countries are going bankrupt. It seems that global corporatism has done nothing but consolidate all of the world's wealth into a few small hands. This is exactly what it was designed to do, despite the claims of the banks public relations staff. The financial systems that we know today have been devised by the ruling elite as methods of resource rationing and social control. They are intended to fail collapse and increase the gap between the rich and the poor, as I discussed at length in "controlled economic collapse."

Anyone who is not on the feds payroll or a victim of the propaganda machine knows that the collapse is coming, but what are we going to do when it gets here? The "powers that be" who are responsible for this mess are suggesting a global currency, which would centralize their control and further strip away the wealth and freedom of the working class. The current economic process is also responsible for a significant amount of the violence in the world, because the system has long been structured around easily controlled finite resources. Rather than going deeper into the control of the deranged aristocracy, we want to completely change how we do business, for once in history we need to be on the offensive with our own ideas instead of accepting ideological Trojan horses that are handed down by our so-called masters. If we are going to take matters into our own hands then there are a few questions we are going to need to ask ourselves first. What would tomorrow's economy be like? How would it be structured and how will it be different from today's economy?

At this point in history, it is not too bold for us to say all of the popular economic methods are all complete failures or they are sadistically rigged. These economic models are unstable because they are feudal systems of control; they are not "free markets" or "community economies" as they masquerade to be. Ideologies like "capitalism" "socialism" or "communism" are simply different systems that are used by the elite of various countries to exploit their working class peons. Essentially all of these systems in their current forms amount to nothing more than feudalism.

As I discussed earlier, capitalism seems like it would be a viable option in a free society, but it honestly cannot exist with legalized monopolies like a centralized government. With that being the case, we can surely say that there is no nation that we can point to as a decent example of a capitalist country. Most places that call themselves capitalist still have government monopolies and protected corporations making them nothing more than centrally planned economies, not all of which would exist in a "free market." The ability for people and to run their own business without any interference is apparently the core values of capitalism.

These are definitely essential values to freedom but unfortunately, these values have not been upheld by any existing "capitalist" country. For us to use words like "capitalism" or "communism" in a discussion about a theoretical economic system would be confusing and counterproductive due to all of the confusion surrounding these definitions. These words mean many different things to many different people. To prevent any confusion I am going to avoid using these words, however it is still important to remember that private property rights and a decentralized economy are absolutely necessary for the development of a free society.

Humanity has been living in scarcity despite the cultural and technological advancements of the past century because our economic systems are all centered on tightly controlled, finite resources and managed from the top down. It has been this way since the pharos, when gold and jewels were horded and hidden away by the civilizations oligarchy. Even in ancient times, people were led to believe that unusable items hold value on account of their supposed rarity. This is a dangerous illusion because true value is rooted in human need, not rarity. If you really think about it, defining value as rarity guarantees that there will be scarcity. On the other hand, if we were to assess value according to human need, instead of fighting over things that were rare we would be able to create a society of abundance. Gold Jewels and paper money cannot feed, clothe, or shelter a human being, so when push comes to shove these objects hold no value in relation to true human need. As the Native Americans have long pointed out "you cannot eat gold." Yet for centuries, we have coveted these worthless objects because we were convinced that they were rare, and thus valuable.

This misconception of reality has led us down a path that is unsustainable and must be corrected, so where do we start? We start by determining value according to human needs instead of determining value according to rarity. What are the very basic things that everyone needs? Healthy food, clean water, a nontoxic environment and protection from violence. What we have to do is put aside politics and prejudices in order to work out a solution that will make these resources plentiful and easily available to everyone, without sacrificing anyone's rights in the process. I am going to imagine for a minute that we are able to put aside all of those superficial obstacles aside (because I know it is possible), and come together to bring about this solution. Now I am going to continue to use my imagination to describe what I believe a possible solution could look like.

As I have said before, our current economic, structure is merely a method of rationing resources, a method which is controlled and exploited by the rulers and aristocracy. Those people have a stake in the widespread use of scarce resources because it is through the control of these resources from which they derive their power. Be it gold, oil, food or information, resources of real or imagined value have been horded by the elite and withheld from the rest of society. It is understandable to want to accumulate and set aside some extra resources for reassurance on a rainy day or some kind of project, or even to hand down to your children. What is not reasonable is for one corporation or banking dynasty to have a net worth greater than that of an entire country. With that being said, I feel that private property is a basic human right and should be the basis of any free economic system. However, while everyone is entitled to his or her own land and property, there must be some discussion on how to go about managing natural resources like food and water.

For us to establish an economic system in which everyone has their basic needs met it is first necessary for us to create an abundance of food, clean water and other resources that we need to survive and live enjoyable lives. The intellectual and technological requirements to put this plan into motion have already been achieved but unfortunately, our current social structure does not allow for these advancements to be properly applied. Unbelievably food abundance has been created in various communities around the world.

In Brazil's fourth largest city Belo Horizonte, local community workers have developed a program that has managed to completely cure hunger by making access to food a top priority. Before this project was developed a great portion of the city's population was in poverty and risked starvation and malnourishment on a daily basis. By setting up urban farming areas and giving local farmers incentives to keep their prices low, the city of Belo Horizonte has managed to completely eradicate hunger among its citizens. The cost of this revolutionary program is only 10 million dollars annually that is less than 2% of the city's budget.

To put these numbers into perspective our country spends billions of dollars every year on the military and has given out trillions of dollars in taxpayer money to Wall Street firms in the form of bailouts. Therefore, this kind of program is an extremely viable option for the United States and is well within their budget. This amazing effort in Brazil shows us that resource abundance is a real possibility if people are willing to come together in creating solutions. Unfortunately, the money for this project is coercively extracted from Brazilians by the barrel of a gun, so this program is far from perfect. Coercive taxation is a violation of non-aggression principles and natural law, so that would not be allowed in a peaceful and free society and it would not be necessary either. In a free society, all taxation would be voluntary, so this would not be a problem in the theoretical economy that I am discussing now. Since more charity money gets to where it belongs than tax money, even in today's world, you can be assured that people would be even more generous when they do not have to fund their own oppression.

To solve the problem of scarcity in a new economic system we are going to need to think outside of the box. One possibility would be backing our currency with resources that everyone needs to survive and that everyone has easy access to. For example, if we were to back our currency with food it would encourage food production and drive down the cost thus making a vital resource more abundant and affordable to more people. Community gardens and small-scale agriculture are essential to a bio-economy, as they allow everyone the freedom and motivation to grow their own organic food. Since the currency would be redeemable in food this means that, anyone has the ability to plant his or her own goldmine whether it is in his or her back yard, windowsill, or community garden. New urban gardening techniques give people the ability to grow food without vast plots of farmland. Every community would have a locally owned food bank that would trade food for currency and vice versa. Food, building materials, Bio fuel and more could all be grown organically within this system, creating abundance in energy as well as food and shelter.

The issue of service and labor has nearly become obsolete due to technological advancement and the capability of machines to take on most of our labor burden. Obviously, there is still going to be a need for active human participation in the society and this will come about naturally through citizens either working for a living or volunteering. In today's materialistic culture, we are led to believe that money is the only motivation that people have to do anything. This is a very narrow minded and unfounded claim because many of the greatest discoveries, inventions, or works of art in history were made with no financial motivation whatsoever. There are many people who make considerable financial sacrifices and dedicate a lot of time towards their community or other larger issues that they are concerned about without being forced to do so. People will naturally want to contribute especially when they are not dedicating all of their time and energy towards turning out widgets and running a rat race.

Most of what happens on the stock market is worthless to society, it is just a place where money constantly changes hands, nothing substantial is created or discovered. Trading stocks is no different than betting your paycheck on a blackjack table, your betting against the card dealer in his house where he has all of the inside information. This madness fills no human need whatsoever it only satisfies the corrupt, so it would not be necessary in a sustainable economy.

For people who are familiar with the popular documentary film series zeitgeist, then you might recognize that a few of these ideas are similar to "The Venus Project" which is featured in the movie. The idea of a "resource based economy" is brought forth in this project and I think it is brilliant. However, there are a few details about their social and political plan that I personally felt could be improved on. For example, I do not feel that it is necessary to do away with private property and I think that it is possible and necessary to have a decentralized debt free currency, while the Venus Project imagines a world without currency. No offence whatsoever to Peter Joseph and Jacque Fresco's work, I have a great deal of respect for their contributions, but I think there is definite room for improvement in their plan, and I feel that some aspects of their plan could actually threaten individual rights if they were to be adopted.

I am hopeful that other concerned people will do the same thing in dissecting the ideas that I am laying out here. At this point in time, all of these proposals for the future are theoretical anyway so we are all welcome to join in work out the details through conversation. The options that we have inherited are not leading us in a positive direction so I commend anyone who puts time and energy towards solutions. Everyone's ideas are vital and important to the success of this planet. Every single one of us has a unique piece to the puzzle and when we get together to expand on our agreements and work out our disagreements is when that puzzle starts to come together.

In short, what is needed is an economic and political system where there is no elite, where a small ruling class does not control all of the resources. Many people may think that this sounds like communism or socialism but every system that has gone by those names has had a very wealthy oligarchy. In reality, both socialism and communism cannot exist without a strong central control system. A truly cooperative egalitarian economic and political system has never been allowed to take form. Sadly, it seems that the governments who claimed to be the most peaceful and equal were actually the most brutal and oppressive.

My proposals for the future may not be perfect, but after years of research, I feel that this is a good place to start the conversation. I am more than willing to adapt my plans if a point is brought to my attention that I was not aware of before. No one has all of the answers but if we work together, we can answer enough of the big questions to save our species and our planet.

Today, almost every economy in the world is totally dictated by the ideas of two long-dead aristocrats. Karl Marx on one end representing communism and Adam Smith on the other end representing capitalism. Our whole way of doing business on this planet has changed very little since the time that these two characters were alive, and that right there is the root of our problem. Imagine if a few people in every city across the world wrote their own economic manifestos and got together to respectfully discuss their ideas. We refuse to accept yesterday's television shows, IPods and PlayStations, but without thinking, we have accepted ways of living that are centuries old. It is time for us to work together in creating strategies where everyone can meet their needs without violating the rights of others.

QUOTE SOURCES AND SUGGESTED READING
----
[0] Bill Hicks –Standup
[SR1] Permaculture A Designers Manual by Bill Mollison

This is just an abstract idea to illustrate that alternatives to the status quo are a possibility; I am by no way saying that this is perfect and I am sure that with some research and brainstorming you can come up with an even better idea.

Peaceful Politics

The growing influence that the elite have over our everyday lives through the government may seem to be overwhelming and unstoppable but we do have the power and the right to fight back against the slave drivers. The politicians and multinational corporations that are responsible for the dismal state of the planet are all convictable under current laws regarding crimes against humanity. These people are not just criminals but they are mass murderers and they should be tried in court just as anyone else would. That is not to say that the existing courts are valid, however these people should still be held to the same standards that we are.

The royal families that have established the World Bank, the IMF and other multinational corporations that deal with international trade have signed business deals that have been systematically impoverishing and starving a vast majority of the world's populations. This land grabs and other pillages can be traced back to the Rothschild's, the Rockefellers and other high profile elite families. Many of the elite have publicly admitted their genocidal goals to the press in addition to the mounting documented evidence against them.

For example, Henry Kissinger is a major player in American politics and lead spokesperson for the bankster's agenda. In 1973, he blatantly told the New York Times *"Depopulation should be the highest priority of foreign policy towards the Third World, because the US economy will require large and increasing amounts of minerals from abroad, especially from less developed countries."* [1] He basically went on the record saying that their goal was to kill people in the third world so they could more easily exploit the land and natural resources. In the many years, since that statement was made we can see that they followed through with their plan. The genocide and displacement that has taken place in the third world at the hands of the global elite should be enough to bring the royal banking cartel to "justice" for crimes against humanity.

Former president George W. Bush openly admitted to ordering the torture of suspects at Guantanamo bay in his memoirs saying "damn right I signed the orders. " This admission has actually caused a great deal of trouble for Bush because every time he attempts to leave the country human rights groups are waiting to arrest him, seriously! On February 12, he was forced to cancel a trip to Switzerland where he was to appear as the main speaker at a fundraiser because various human rights groups were issuing a warrant for his arrest. It is good to see people bringing attention to the issue, but Bush and other aristocratic nation builders still believe that they are above the law. As their scheme for world domination begins to become a reality, the authorities have gotten arrogant and put their agenda out for the public to see. Just as the Templar Knights were not above the law in the middle ages, our oppressors today are not above the law either. While I am not suggesting we burn anyone at the stake here, it is necessary that we bring these criminals to justice and put them on trial. Remember, I am in no way saying that our legal system is at all credible or "just," but they should at least be held to the same standard that anyone else would when faced with such accusations.

A society that fulfills our need for peace and equality would rest upon a foundation of individualism and non-aggression principals. Individualism is a completely new concept that may have been discussed in the past but has rarely been applied in society because it requires decentralization of power, a move that would not be put into effect by anyone who had the power to do so, go figure. Most civilizations thus far, especially authoritarian ones have been collectivist societies. Collectivism allows for the individual's rights and needs to be sacrificed for the state. "The common good" is a vague euphemism that is typically used to describe the goals of the state and the ruling class.

This collectivistic term is always thrown around when people in power are trying to take advantage of us. They usually do this by convincing us that we are helping our neighbors, when in reality we are only helping those in power. On the other hand, Individualism is a philosophy that holds each person's rights as top priority and says that there is no excuse for a person or group of people to violate the rights of others, not even if it is one person, and not even if it is for the "common good." This way the door is no longer open for a tyrant to come in and start manipulating our natural concerns for others just to suit their own selfish needs. This all ties in with the non-aggression principle, which asserts that using force on others through physical violence, psychological manipulation, financial extortion and other means of coercion is unacceptable in every circumstance.

The ability of people to manipulate the opinions of others without their knowledge or permission is ultimately the downfall of the democratic process, but the democratic process can still take place as long as non-aggression principals are adhered to and power is decentralized. In other words, voting is still a valid concept but in a free society, a majority opinion could not justify force or coercion, and the individual cannot be sacrificed for the whims of the majority under any conditions. Much of the manipulation that takes place today is done so by convincing people that they must make personal sacrifices for the "common good" or "national interest." There is no room for this in a free society because it is simply a cop out for justifying the use of force in violating the rights of others. Apparently, this violation of rights is for the betterment of civilization but in reality, it is only for the benefit of the aggressors, who in most cases come from positions of so-called "authority."

The problem with government has always been the same, power leads to corruption and corruption leads to violence and exploitation. The idea that "absolute power corrupts absolutely" has been a notion in the public consciousness for many centuries, but unfortunately, no one has really done anything about it. The revolutions of the 18th and 19th centuries may have officially denounced the divine rule of kings but that honestly had little impact on the lives of the working class. This is because the only thing that changed is that the monarchs were forced to share more of their power with the aristocracy, all the while leaving the majority of the population out in the cold. In other words, we went from a small monarchy to a slightly larger oligarchy.

This is the true structure of a republic, an oligarchy disguised as a representative government. The senators of Rome were not a proper representation of their people, the British parliament is not a proper representation of their people and the US congress is not a proper representation of their people, all of the above are oligarchies that protect the interests of the ruling class. To go from a monarchy to a representative system of government is like being a prisoner who is released from jail only to be put on house arrest.

All over, the world no matter where you go people will agree that they want to live in a free society where problems are solved without institutionalized violence. Sadly, this kind of government does not exist, well at least not yet anyway. The people who are in power now are horrified of this prospect, because they know that it will take away their control of the world, because that is what it is designed to do! To prevent this from happening they tell us we are already free so we remain silent. They tell us we have a voice but when it comes to things that matter like staying out of wars or preventing corporate corruption those voices go unheard, so what is the point?

Sadly, the point is not to guide the society according to the will of the public but it is to guide the public according to the will of the ruling class. Some people, in hopes that their voices will be heard, spend their whole lives voting in and voting out people that do not care about them and only wish to deceive them. They spend their whole lives just waiting for the day that one of these sell out puppets will finally pay attention to their cause, only to see that the establishment has other priorities that do not apply to the general population. Having a representative government and calling it a democracy is a very clever way of subverting a true freedom movement and keeping the power out of the hands of the people.

A truly free society would be decentralized, and place equal power into the hands of every single citizen. A decentralized power structure would also act as one of the primary checks and balances in this system. Developing a forum where every single citizen can voice his or her opinion would be extremely easy by utilizing the internet technology that we already have. There is absolutely no reason for centralized power, we should know by now that this does not end well. The outdated concept of central planning is responsible for the constant violence, misplacement, and monopolization of power throughout history.

Central planning is basically the idea that all-important decisions in a society are to be made by a small group of people on the behalf of the general population. On its face, this idea is a complete joke because a handful of politicians or "planners" could not possibly represent millions of people. Giving a small group of people the power to tell everyone else how to live and allowing them to decide how the collective wealth of the entire nation ought to be spent is nothing short of slavery. With today's closely connected "small world," it seems that it is a realistic possibility for central planning to fade away into obsolescence. It is very possible to have an organized society without central planning, especially with modern technology and communication.

People oftentimes confuse government with culture and have the misconception that without a central planning structure everything that makes a society great would vanish. This fact was recognized by some of the more "radical" founding fathers of America, including Thomas Paine. In his most famous literary effort "Common Sense" there is a section called "Of the origin and design of government in general, with concise remarks on the English Constitution." In this piece, Paine discusses the difference between government and society.

Thomas Paine writes "some writers have so confounded society with government, as to leave little or no distinction between them; whereas they are not only different, but have different origins. Society is produced by our wants, and government by our wickedness; the former promotes our happiness positively by uniting our affections, the latter negatively by restraining our vices. The one encourages intercourse, the other creates distinctions. The first is a patron, the last a punisher. Society in every state is a blessing, but Government, even in its best state, is but a necessary evil; in its worst state an intolerable one: for when we suffer, or are exposed to the same miseries by a government, which we might expect in a country without a government, our calamity is heightened by reflecting that we furnish the means by which we suffer." [3] His statement is as true today as it was during the first American Revolution, culture, society and security is absolutely capable of continuing in the absence of a central control system.

In today's global society, there is an overwhelming list of laws and pointless restrictions that are specifically created for either social control or class warfare. They have absolutely nothing to do with safety. There definitely needs to be codes of conduct for human beings even in a free society. However, any codes of conduct should be set up according to the non-aggression principle, it is that easy. There is no need to control people's actions with laws and taboos, as long as those actions are not violating anyone's rights.

There would have to be a distinction made between individual privacy and public transparency. We all agree that individual privacy is a right to every human being on the planet, but groups of people that have a stake in the civilization do not share that right. It is necessary for any group that has an effect on society to be completely transparent, to safeguard against corruption. Information about individual issues that were up for debate and vote would be widely available through many different sources by using the internet.

This would give people the proper tools to make educated decisions about issues. The issues that would be voted on would be extremely different from the things that are considered by our government today. How to improve cities and towns, what to do about environmental issues, or how to address other real problems that have a chance of making an impact on our lives. These would be the issues that every single citizen will have a part in shaping. This sounds like a free society to me. It seems what we have today is the complete opposite where a handful of people vote on who to bomb or how to divide, criminalize and tax their fellow human beings, that does not sound at all free or democratic.

With the many different views expressed in the mainstream today it can seem like finding solutions is going to be very complicated, but it is not. It is really quite simple, just give us what we have been asking for all along, a free society where the people have a voice and are not constantly threatened by violence and extortion. This may be difficult for some people to understand at first because our education system, media, and other social institutions have been conditioning us for years to believe that we already have freedom and that to be without central control would be violent and chaotic, when In fact the opposite is true. The buzzword that the establishment and their apologists use for the lack of central control is "anarchy," a term that has been vilified by those in authority for centuries.

The term anarchy has been associated with the complete breakdown of society, riots, violence, and the absence of any kind of social structure. We have been led to believe that civilization will fall into total bedlam if there is not a central government to keep people in line through the use of force. This idea is laughable considering the fact that a great majority of the world's pain and chaos has been created or exacerbated by centralized governments. Delving deeper, most of the immoral actions that are carried out by individuals are simply eventual consequences of state conditioning, propaganda, and abuse. Another problem with the public's concept of "anarchy" is the assumption that human beings would not cooperate, advance technology, trade, or uphold justice in the absence of a centralized control structure. Not only would all of this still happen in a free, decentralized society, but also the quality of these human interactions would actually greatly improve! Governments rig economies, suppress technology that threatens the status quo, create unnecessary strife between different groups of people and makes the idea of justice a complete joke by establishing a monopoly on force and not respecting their own rules. If the people were left to govern themselves and were not constantly, being held back by a control structure, then a more coherent, peaceful and advanced society would be able to take form.

If power were decentralized then average citizens would have more of a role in the community, thus bringing more real, genuine order to the social structure. We have been conditioned to believe that there will be chaos in the streets if we are left to govern ourselves, but this is only the point of view of those who already govern us and stand to lose their power if the citizens actually had the ability to influence politics.

We already have chaos in the streets, war, confusion, and division among the world's people because of the corrupt and divisive tradition that we have inherited. Everything that the government claims to be providing us is in short supply, and most of the enemies that they claim to be protecting us from have either been instigated or created by the very same government. In other words, all of the jobs that the government is responsible for are not being done properly, so leaving them in charge is obviously only going to bring us more of the same.

One of the most common misconceptions about life in a free society is that law and order would somehow cease to exist without a centralized control system. This is simply not true; in fact, the law would actually be more just because everyone would be held to the same standards. Currently not everyone is held to the same standards because those sanctioned by the state are enabled to use force without consequence, while everyone else is expected to fall in line with millions of laws and codes, most of which have no relation to morality. The only code that is necessary is non-aggression, do not hurt people and do not damage or steal their property. This would be the common law that would be enforced locally by community groups who work cooperatively in the marketplace and the individuals within the society as well. Almost everyone would have weapons of their own in a free society also, which would actually make things extremely safe. Currently, it is common for the most armed countries to have the smallest and most bored police departments.

Possibly the biggest public relations con that any government has going for them is that they apparently promote the general welfare and offer protection and security for the downtrodden people of the nation. However, these are just words that completely contradict the actions that are actually being taken by government. While it is true that there are some social programs and services established by government, it does not mean that these programs are actually helping in the end. Typically, government programs are aimed at keeping people weak and dependent so the establishment has an excuse for its existence and reason to create more bureaucracies. The government is notorious for figuratively breaking your legs so they can give you crutches and say "see look without us you would not be able to walk." So while there is all this talk about the "general welfare," the true intention of these programs is to keep people dependent and in servitude. In a free society based on non-aggression, self-ownership, property rights and autonomy, citizens would be responsible to defend and provide for themselves but they would also be more inclined to help others. Important social problems will still exist thanks to voluntary charities that would be far more accountable and efficient than any tax funded government program in existence. Without the parasitic monstrosity of a central government people will be much more generous and even those who are disabled would be taken care of better by their neighbors than by a cold and careless bureaucracy. Even in today's world, most governments are doing a very bad job at providing public services and protecting their subjects from harm, but then again that was never their true intentions so we should not be surprised.

There is also a widely popular misconception that communism and representative republics were designed with the best intentions and set out to create a "Utopian society" in which everyone was equal and where everyone had a say. Ironically, these systems are both SCAMS that had intentions that were drastically different from the goals that were projected on a surface level to the majority of the world's population. Both systems were created by elites in order to put down the revolutions that were sweeping the world in the 18th century. After becoming more educated and literate, the peasant classes began to rise up and demand "freedom" and "equality," so the elites created these social systems that were truly designed to control their populations, while convincing them that they are living their lives without bondage and exploitation. Both philosophies are collectivistic in nature and allow governments to justify the removal of the individual's rights for the sake of the "greater good," this is not by mistake. We have been taught to see these as opposing ideologies when in reality they defend the same kind of social structure that has troubled our species for thousands of years.

Some of the worst situations in history were the result of governments using force in order to construct the "perfect society." Hitler, Mao, Bush, Obama, Caligula, and Caesar all had good intentions or at least they claimed to, all the rhetoric was generally the same. It is impossible to create a peaceful society by allowing one portion of society to have a monopoly on the use of force. Force can never achieve anything positive, even in times of revolution. Beware of any violent revolution or rebel movement that seeks to use force in order to replace the existing order with a power structure of their own. This is a false revolution where not much is ever accomplished, and if there is any positive social change it does not take many generations before the power structure descends into despotism yet again. Even if the initial founding fathers of the government were morally virtuous and had the best of intentions eventually they will die and leave their power to someone who cannot handle the responsibility, it is bound to happen eventually. In fact, it is inevitable; because history has shown us, power is not a good thing.

All functions of government can be fulfilled by citizens working together, because after all governments are just groups of people. In the current social system it is true that privatization of natural resources and essential services results in an oligarchical monopoly. This is due to corporate welfare, special treatment, lobby groups, and the use of force, all of which would not exist or be tolerated in a decentralized society built on non-aggression principals. It is true that force and violence will still be a possibility, and will still exist here on earth on rare occurrences.

However, if the power balance on the planet is equalized then people will be less inclined to act violently, and it would be impossible for dictatorships and organized crime to develop because no one would tolerate it and everyone would have the power to prevent it from happening. The kind of carnage and brutality that we have seen throughout history only occurred because those in power were able to morally justify their actions to the rest of the world. If we take away their moral justifications for committing this evil, then it will cease to be.

For the vast majority of human history there was no state, this is a very recent development in our evolution. It is a mistake, a bad idea just like slavery, racism, sexism and other harmful ideas that humans have used to justify their mistreatment of others. Some of the main arguments against the abolishment of slavery were "what will happen to the economy" or "who's going to build the roads"? Now hundreds of years later the same arguments are heard against the abolishment of centralized control.

Although we have been trained to believe otherwise, it is possible to live in an organized society without giving one group of people the right to aggress upon others. As I discussed early on in the book, autonomy and self-ownership are natural born rights that supersede any constitution or royal decree. Every human being on this earth has the right to do whatever he or she wish in any circumstance so long as their actions do not infringe upon the rights or property of others. Likewise, no one should be given a license to kill, and there is no act of violence that can be excused or allowed.

QUOTE SOURCES AND SUGGESTED READING
----
[0] 'Scuse Me While I Kiss the Sky: Jimi Hendrix: Voodoo Child By David Henderson
[1] Henry Kissinger, New York Times, Oct. 28, 1973.
[3] Common Sense. - Thomas Paine
[SR1] The Most Dangerous Superstition by Larken Rose
[SR2] Complete Liberty – Wes Bertrand

"There is no path to peace, peace is the path."
- Gandhi [0]

Kindness and Cooperation

    As our reality descends deeper into chaos it is becoming impossible for the reigning cultural institutions to claim that there is nothing wrong with the way we are living. Our civilizations are built upon values of self-destruction which allow the most ruthless among us to set the general pace and attitude of our species. This means that our basic model of reality is shaped by the self-interest of those who have conned and murdered their way into power. The only ideas that are accepted into society are those that allow the ruling class to conduct business as usual and continue their corrupt existence. This is why insane ideas like "survival of the fittest" and "nice guys finish last" are held with such high esteem in authoritarian societies.

    Our rulers are aggressive and emotionless people so they tell the rest of us that we are supposed to be that very as well. We are given cultural norms based on the beliefs of the elite and are told that this is the way that humans are supposed to think, act, feel, and live. It is very arrogant for people to suggest that simply because we live a certain way now, and have lived this way for some time, that this is the pinnacle of human achievement and understanding. Every generation of our ancestors has had this same kind of arrogance regardless of how mundane their existence was. Things like slavery and human sacrifice were common in ancient life and seen as normal human activity just like our generation looks at war and poverty as some of life's "necessary evils. " These practices were not devised by the average person and they do not benefit the average person. These were all created by one group of people that wished to dominate everyone else.

    The idea of superiority and inferiority was put forth by people who thought themselves superior to their brothers and sisters simply because they could manipulate and overpower them. To carry on these barbaric policies in a sane world where people lived in love and cooperation would be impossible. For the manipulators to get away with their aggressions it is necessary for them to convince the rest of us that what they are doing is acceptable human behavior or "human nature" (whatever that is). This is when all hell breaks loose, because when the "leaders" of a society act nefariously then everyone else has the green light to behave the same way. This pattern is responsible for the depraved form that modern civilization has taken. People are not born violent and manipulative, but are made that way by sick cultures that encourage that type of behavior.

    The cycle of domination and exploitation continues through the ages because we never make an attempt to do things in a different way. Religions, politicians, and cultures may change but the basic way of doing things remains the same. To break this cycle we need a new approach entirely, as Einstein said *"The significant problems we face cannot be solved at the same level of thinking we were at when we created them."* [1]

What he was saying was that if you are constantly trying to solve a problem using the same methods time after time then you are not going to get very far. This is kind of an extension on the idea of "trial and error," which says that when mistakes are made you should try a different approach. This idea has revolutionized science and technology but unfortunately has not been applied to politics because we have governments throughout the world that are carbon copies of the ancient Roman Empire. That traditional model of Roman representative oligarchy fails completely somewhere in the world every decade and is then rebuilt with the same oppressive class structure, and same general policies but a different label. Our planet cannot stand another rehash of this senseless power struggle; we need to find another way.

The solution is very easy but for us to make this transition into a better way of living everyone is going to have to get involved and start being more kind and respectful in their everyday lives. Just because we are ruled by liars, thieves and hotheads does not mean that we have to display them characteristics within ourselves. For our ideas and our way of life to be taken seriously, we will have to be more honest and ethical then those we are standing against. If the issues we are facing are due to a culture of violence and greed then the only way to counteract that is to perpetuate a culture of love and understanding.

While there are many problems that do, need our direct attention like dethroning the warmongers and banking cartels and delegitimizing their authority? For the way and us to truly sustain any kind of real civilization we have to drastically change the way we think we treat each other. All of the peaceful revolutionaries who have helped bring understanding to the world were aware of this solution and made it their life's work to share that message. Dr. Martin Luther King Jr. was one of these people, in one of his famous speeches he said *"Darkness cannot drive out darkness; only light can do that. Hate cannot drive out hate; only love can do that. Hate multiplies hate, violence multiplies violence, and toughness multiplies toughness in a descending spiral of destruction....The chain reaction of evil--hate begetting hate, wars producing more wars--must be broken, or we shall be plunged into the dark abyss of annihilation."* [2] If we want to put an end to the violence and hate that we see in society then we are going to have to drop those ideals from our everyday lives. There is no way that we will ever be able to make a change in the world if we are not able to make some changes within ourselves. We must represent a better way of life and lead by example with our own positive actions.

To get humanity and the planet earth back on the right track we need to take a more cooperative approach at how we run our societies and live our lives.

One person could not possibly create an "ism" that will have the makings of a utopian society, which is not the kind of solution that will bring us peace and prosperity anyway. I've laid out some ideas that I feel are pretty good starting points However, if the world's population was cooperatively working together, sharing knowledge and using their technology for the betterment of all humanity then we be living in a society more advanced then we could imagine. The common people need to get together and cooperatively construct a new paradigm for the future, instead of allowing our wicked "leaders" to decide the fate of humanity. We must work together and form a new society that works in the best interests of all people instead of a select few, while maintaining the principals of non-aggression, of course. This is the only path towards a truly civilized world and for us to be walking that path we cannot participate in the same malicious activities as our corrupt "leaders."

QUOTE SOURCES AND SUGGESTED READING
----

[0] Pavement: reflections on mercy, activism, and doing "nothing" for peace By Lin Jensen
[1] Sustainability by design by John Ehrenfeld (2008)
[2] Strength to love - Martin Luther King (1977)

"They will not force us, and they will stop degrading us, and they will not control us! We will be victorious! so come on! Interchanging mind control, come let the Revolution take its toll……If you could flick a switch and open your third eye, you'd see that we should never be afraid to die, so come on!"
– Muse {Psychedelic Rock Band} [0]

We Are #Winning

At the time I am writing this it has already began. The things that I have discussed in this book are now becoming widely understood around the world and the common people who represent the overwhelming majority of this earth are beginning to see how we have been exploited and manipulated for many generations. With the explosion of the internet, independent media websites have developed and are working to inform people about the reality of what is taking place in the world. Average people are taking advantage of social networking websites and using them as a political platform and a means to connect with likeminded people. In past generations the elite was able to advance their agenda without the knowledge of the public because they had a stranglehold on which information was publicly available. Now with the internet average citizens who are not controlled by the elite are able to become the media themselves and bring uncorrupted information to the rest of the population.

As the truth begins to reach the masses a new subculture of revolutionaries is being born and a whole generation is coming together in a way that has never been seen before. People who once saw one another as enemies are now realizing that they are facing the same struggles, that they are being exploited by their so-called "leaders," just as a slave is exploited by their so-called master. Christians, Mystics, Muslims, and Jews are finally united in a universal fight against tyranny, poverty, and oppression. The rich, the comfortable and the poor are all realizing that they are on the same side in a great "class war" that has been raging for centuries. This class war is really between the people who print the currency and the people who use the currency, not the "rich and the poor. "

People of all financial and ethical backgrounds are realizing that they are all the same in the eyes of the elite. Soldiers are putting down their guns to join the protest lines, police are speaking out against the immoral war on drugs, and scientists who have towed the party line for ages are finally starting to question the government approved, established version of reality. For generations the elite have played off our petty differences in order to divide and control us, but that time is over. People of different political affiliations are also beginning to learn that the people that they elect do not represent them, but represent the business interests that get the politicians into power and keep them there. All of the wonderfully different people on this earth are realizing that they are on the same side, and that living together in peace is not only possible, but it is absolutely necessary for our species advancement on this planet.

Once the people become united and realize the immense power that they have over their freeloading "rulers" they become unstoppable. The practice of massive militant nonviolence is by far the safest and most effective method of removing corrupt regimes from power. When used correctly it works every time, without fail. This is among the biggest kept secrets in the world. No dictator is too strong; no military police state is too powerful to stand against the peaceful masses when they are united, organized, and defiant. What is most important though, is how the aftermath of the revolution is handled. It is incredibly easy for an informed, organized, and morally conscious public to overthrow a corrupt regime, but the complicated part is preventing a power vacuum from developing for a new tyrant to fill.

We are watching a new era of revolution take place, where powerful tools like the internet are bringing people together, making their causes stronger, and allowing them a place to record and express their struggle. The freedom of expression that exists on the internet makes it much more difficult for the elite circles and governments to control the flow of information the public has access to. This is an advantage that our predecessors did not have. If a rebellion happened in one part of the world before modern methods of communication were developed it was very easy for that movement to be disrupted without any other communities finding out about it. Now with the internet activist movements spread out all over the world can join together and be just as informed and tight knit as the elite circles that they are fighting against. The fact that the internet is shut off by the government in times of rebellion proves to us that this is indeed a very strong tool in the fight for freedom.

The internet is simply a tool, but the primary strength that ensures victory for the peoples revolution is the incredible majority advantage that we have within the population, as I have laid out in this book, there are two classes on this earth, the elite and the rest of us. The elite are the privileged few involved in politics and multinational business. "The rest of us" make up more than 99% of the population in almost every nation, we have them tremendously outnumbered. The poor, the middle class, the independently wealthy, the police, the military, the activist, the revolutionary are all on the same side; all these people belong to the 99% that I am referring to. This is an unstoppable force because once the people understand that they are being exploited it is only a matter of time before they refuse to partake in their own enslavement.

When revolution day arrives we must be clear in our intentions and not let our grievances be marginalized by vague terms like "equality" or "democracy." We need to have strong faith in our message and our cause but not put too much trust into one specific "opposition leader." We must be very specific about the changes that are to be made and the future that we wish to build or else we run the risk of being led astray by a new tyrant and thrown back into another oppressive situation.

A revolution would threaten all of the wealth and power that the tyrants and aristocrats have been pillaging and hording over the generations, so they will without a doubt use every trick in the book to maintain their control over the population. These tricks include using controlled oppositions to make it look like someone new is taking over when in reality the new boss is taking orders from the same people and is often times just as bad as the old boss. As I discussed at length in "tricks of the trade" the elite has used many of the same techniques throughout history to maintain their power. To disable and counteract these kinds of sneaky tricks we must make fundamental changes to our political and economic systems. These changes will work to correct the injustice and violence that is threatening the existence of our species.

We can have a social system without having hierarchies, taxes, armies, politicians, and prisons. We can also have an economy without poverty, exploitation, greed, and insecurity. These things are possible; we just need to start making changes with how our societies are structured and how we do business. The steps that need to be taken are easy, simple, and obvious but will result in a transfer of power and wealth from the elite to the masses so my ideas are far from orthodox and will not be well received by those in power. The tyrants that have caused this mess will insist that the sky will fall without them there to hold it up, but these are obviously lies.

This is the same way they have conned us into wars and huge corporate bailouts, using threats and fear. The politicians, the elite, and the military industrial complex have brought us nothing but more problems that were dressed up as solutions. This is because real, honest solutions would leave them powerless and on even ground with the rest of us. The time has come for new solutions to stand in opposition of the status quo, the human suffering and environmental destruction that has taken place as a result of politics and savage military force is inexcusable and will not be sustainable for much longer.

The aristocracy that has kept us and our ancestors imprisoned under debt and propaganda is starting to lose their grip on the human consciousness. Their whole game is supported by us, the very people that they are viciously oppressing and we are finally starting to see through it. We need to stop working for them and start working for each other, and that message is spreading all over the world as average people are taking the revolution into their own hands. People are using their creative time and energy to develop solutions for the problems being faced by the working class. The only way to solve these problems is by creating our own solutions that will actually empower us, instead of just accepting the solutions that the ruling class offers. Any policy that the ruling class wishes to put in place is only to suit them and further exploit the Average people, so we cannot depend on them for any kind of assistance whatsoever.

When the declaration of independence was first signed in 1776 it only protected the white property owners who made up the colonial elite. There was no mention of the freedoms guaranteed to American citizens in the original constitution. It was not until oppressed colonial citizens took to the streets in protest and formed armed militias that our founding fathers actually drafted the bill of rights in 1787. The bill of rights is the document that has officially recognized our natural born freedom of religion, the right to bear arms and the rights of the press, among others. Although many of our founding fathers where the elite of their time and did not have much sympathy for the working class, some of them did understand the importance of rebellion in a free society.

Thomas Jefferson was one of those people, in responding to one of the antiestablishment riots in early America he said *"I hold it that a little rebellion now and then is a good thing, it is a medicine necessary for the sound health of government. God forbid that we should ever be twenty years without such a rebellion."* [1].

I am not condoning violent action in response to our current oppression, I am just saying that it is within our rights as members of a free society to DISOBEY the established order to maintain and advance our level of freedom. It is in fact the only way that any progress has been made for civil rights in America or anywhere else. Without protest and rebellion white males would be the only people that had any rights at all. Luckily for us this is not the case; America has a long history of brave intelligent people who led peaceful antiestablishment rebellions. This is why America has flourished so much in its short history, because of the average citizen's insistence on civil rights and equality. The ruling class would have never handed those rights over if the public had not demanded them in protest. Currently their greatest power over the rest of the human population is the idea that we no longer have to fight for our rights and our freedoms.

When I began writing this book three short years ago, the topics discussed herein were underground and you had to look pretty hard for research and it was rare to come across other people who understood what was going on. Now you can find these topics in the mainstream news every day, in the lyrics of chart topping songs, in the themes of blockbuster films and documented on websites all over the internet. The revolution of the mind that I discussed in the beginning of this book has already begun to take form and a more peaceful and empowering attitude is seeping into the mainstream culture. Sure, things may seem bleak if you are approaching this information for the first time, but if anything this knowledge should give you hope that a better world is possible and that human nature is not rooted in violence. We must not get discouraged by minor setbacks, and we cannot expect the world to be saved overnight. We are facing an enemy with multi-generational goals, so in order to keep up we must think just as long term. We can win this, and the fact that your reading this right now, shows that we are already #winning.

QUOTE SOURCES AND SUGGESTED READING
----
[0] Muse – Uprising – The Resistance
[1] Letter to James Madison Jan 30 1787, The Yale book of quotations - Fred R. Shapiro

"The people who are trying to make this world worse are not taking the day off. How Can I?"
- Bob Marley [0]

About The Author - J.G Vibes

Since as far back as I can remember I largely rejected the cultural traditions that I was born into because they seemed unnatural, irrational, and oppressive. School was difficult because even from a young age I refused to conform and somehow understood that I was not going to learn anything of value in school. Most of my teachers in elementary school resented me because I would bring in books on topics that I was interested in and I would read them to myself while the class was going over their indoctrinating lesson. By the time high school came around I was so sick of the whole thing that I spent my class time sleeping, drinking, and doing drugs, and from time to time I would still read. The oppressive nature of the school system only pushed me to hold greater resentment against authority and mainstream society. Unfortunately, that resentment pushed me toward some naive conclusions.

Although I had my suspicions about society and the status quo I was still heavily conditioned by media and operating on a fairly low level of consciousness. I was still seeing the world in black and white terms and was pushed towards ideas like Satanism and Communism because I was so turned off with the typical mainstream culture that I was subject to. Like many of the pitfalls I encountered this was a necessary adventure along my path and vital to my learning experience. Those interests led me to a wide variety of philosophical studies, but nothing would really make sense to me until many years later when I had enough information to get a clear picture of how things really worked.

Most of my adolescence was filled with misplaced angst and overindulgence, which I hear is fairly typical. Regular drug tests pushed me towards heavy alcohol and pharmaceutical use, so although I was using psychedelics and researching philosophy I was still operating on a fairly low level of consciousness because of the mind numbing chemicals I was putting into my body and the media I surrounded myself with. Through those years I was faced with many synchronistic situations that slowly led me toward a more conscious lifestyle and informed perspective, but it would be many years before I broke free from the state of sleep that I was in.

There is no doubt that every single one of us has our whole perception of reality crafted by our environment and the things we experience, I am obviously no different. Like most of the people on the planet I was born into a life of serfdom and grew up being constantly reminded about the struggles and obstacles that came along with financial slavery. Many times I was shown firsthand the senseless violence of war and the threatening oppression of the legal system, as you can tell my story is not unique, almost anyone can relate. The issues that have affected my life and the ones I discuss in this book affect everyone; they are not limited to my experience.

Things did begin to get a little bit out of the ordinary when I started working at a funeral home at the age of 17. Looking back it is hard to imagine that I was drawn to that kind of profession but at the time I was a very confused person. I ended up spending about 6 years as an apprentice mortician and those were quite possibly the most turbulent times of my life. I am sure that the late teen to young adult phase is no cakewalk for anyone, but my job and my drinking problem seemed to at least keep things interesting.

They say you should never regret anything, and for the most part I agree but if I could take back anything I would not have let my drinking get so out of hand. At the time I was very ignorant and underestimated the toxicity of alcohol due to its cultural acceptance and for that I was left with health problems that I am still trying to sort out today. I was never an aggressive drunk, but that does not mean that I was not an extremely stupid drunk that caused a lot of trouble for myself and other people. Unbelievably it would take an enlightening shamanic experience to make me realize that I was destroying my body and that I should probably phase out my alcohol use. After 7 years of drinking hard liquor on a daily basis it was a lot easier to quit then I ever thought it would be and with every day that passed I became more conscious of what was going on around me.

Due to my own personal experience and my earlier research into philosophy I was always untrusting of power, government, war, finance, religion, and authority in general but I did not have enough of the specific background information to fully understand the true nature of our reality. I had a very limited knowledge of occult history for most of my life and was heavily sedated by chemicals and cultural assumptions that I greatly underestimated due to my ignorance. That all began to change when my physical and mental health began to deteriorate from alcohol abuse, heavy smoking, and extremely poor eating habits. I was partying constantly because I was so disgusted with society and the life that seemed to lie before me, because it just seemed so confusing and backwards. I saw a world consumed with greed, violence, pain and misunderstanding for no apparent reason. This was not the kind of world I wanted to live in. I did not want anyone to be subject to violence and I did not approve of the status quo, but I was so convinced that this was the only world that was possible that I made no attempt to do anything about it and led a hedonistic lifestyle in order to fill a void in my soul.

During that period I was immersed in the heavy metal circuit in Baltimore and although mostly everyone was distracted by sex, drugs n rock n roll, I synchronistically met some activists and artists who were using the scene as a social platform. My new friends and acquaintances taught me all sorts of new information about the monetary system, social engineering and specifically the new world order. After putting a few tidbits together with the research I had done in the past light bulbs went off all over the place in my head and I began to scour the internet for more information. There I found piles of documented evidence that supported what I knew all along but had no clue how to put into words. Eventually after enough research it became easier to find the words and I could accurately explain to myself and others why I disapproved of the status quo and exactly who was responsible for perpetuating it.

Unfortunately, even with my newfound knowledge I was still making poor decisions and still had a very negative outlook. My whole worldview was still heavily conditioned by years of media, schooling, and cultural norms. I was still looking at things in a very nihilistic way, where I had no understanding of the higher spiritual levels that existed or the unbelievable things that could be achieved through love and human cooperation. I really hate to be cliché here but I was to learn all of this at my first hippy festival. I am going to spare the names, dates and places out of respect for the promoters but ill share the basics of what happened. This event was something that I had never experienced before and I had no clue what to expect. It ended up being a whole weekend almost completely removed from the mainstream American culture that had held me prisoner for most of my life.

My many adventures and realizations over that weekend would have a huge impact on my future path and encouraged me to delve deeper into the counter culture. After the enlightening weekend I had at that event I spent the rest of the summer touring similar festivals on the east coast seeking to clock more time outside of the mainstream culture and return once again down the rabbit hole. That summer my travels brought me to an outdoor rave that was on the water. That was probably one of the best parties I had ever been to, until around 3am when fire trucks, cop cars and other emergency vehicles began to surround the event. Things became very frantic at that point and I decided that I should leave the area where everyone had assembled and find another way out. Just before the area was raided I saw a fishing boat and began to shout to them for help and they came ashore to see what was going on. I offered them 20 dollars to take me and my friends out of harm's way toward where we had parked our car and luckily the agreed to help us.

That certainly was not my first narrow escape with the Gestapo that summer. After a few of these encounters I came to realize that the counter culture truly was outlawed in an Orwellian society I had come to find myself in. I always had a deep suspicion of authority, but now that I had the proper information and witnessed this peaceful culture being demonized by those authoritarian forces, I understood the reality of how our "civilization" operates.

In addition to the personal realizations that came to me at that show I had also made connections that would eventually help me establish myself as a rave promoter. At one of these events I met a promoter from Philly who said he hosted parties at a place called "Gods Basement" and that I should check it out sometime. If it was not for that synchronistic random encounter it is highly possible that I never would have written this book, thrown a single rave, or even met my wife. Without Gods Basement and the time I spent there I cannot even begin to imagine what my life would be like today. While I had been to some club and underground events in the past Gods Basement was my official introduction into the underground rave scene.

When I started partying at Gods Basement I was still in that part of my life where I was drinking on a daily basis and working at a funeral home in Baltimore.

Nearly every day after work I would stop at local bars to kill time before traffic died down and most times I ended up at a place that I probably also should not name, for this discussion let's just it "The Zoo", because the place was pretty crazy. Eventually I took on a second job there working the door during rock and hip-hop shows to make some extra money. Eventually, the "The Zoo" began getting involved in raves after a friend of mine made a suggestion to the owner. I helped book and promote a few shows there when things were starting up but was always helping other crews, doing my own shows never really crossed my mind at that point. After a while I began to spend most of my time in Philly and New York networking and promoting for shows at Gods Basement and the "The Zoo" with my wife Kali. At the time we had just recently met, but now we are happily married and I do not know what I would do without her.

    Gods Basement was one of the main party spots on the east coast when I began promoting, and the "The Zoo" was still getting itself established and building its base crowd. Gods Basement is still to this day one of the most awesome venues I have ever been to, and I feel extremely lucky for the time I was able to spend there. As they say though, all good things must come to an end. When Gods Basement came under fire I learned just how corrupt and one sided the media is first hand. At the time I was familiar with media bias but I was still under the impression that the talking heads on the news were just mistaken with good intentions. However, as I would learn the media consistently and deliberately constructs lies, falsifies reports, and intentionally spins stories in order to uphold the status quo.

    I will be the first one to admit that wild things happen at raves but they still offer a much safer and more peaceful environment than the average rock concert that is advertised on mainstream television and radio. It was an ignorant and close-minded mother who did not understand the path her child was taking who decided to run to the corrupt establishment to do her parenting for her. Instead of playing an active role in her child's life and attempting to understand what was going on in her child's mind, this parent decided to force her will onto an entire culture. With her face and voice disguised she appeared on the news calling for the shutdown of Gods Basement. This bigoted testimony was presented with fake video footage of kids doing various drugs, but long time patrons of Gods Basement could see that the clips that showed this were not even filmed at that venue. After the initial story ran the NBC news channel received so much feedback defending the rave that they were forced to run a second story to apparently show the other side of the argument.

    As expected that second segment was a total whitewash, where all legitimate complaints about the hit piece from the day before were mocked and marginalized leaving the viewer with a skewed version of events. The fact that the promotion crews involved with the venue ran regular charity events and gave back to the community was completely left out of the reports and when it was time for the crew to make a statement their words were distorted and put in a context that made us look careless and unintelligent. The lies and attacks from the media eventually did result in the downfall of Gods Basement. When things got too crazy in Philly, I returned to Baltimore with a new direction and new connections that I developed working as a street promoter for Tru Skool Productions, the crew that ran Gods Basement.

By spring of 2008 I began to start thinking about doing my own shows because there were some elements that I had witnessed in the parties up north, which were lacking from the events in Baltimore and DC. The shows up north had an underground feel with themes, hard dance music and decorations, whereas the parties in my area were club events not raves. Therefore, I approached the "The Zoo" with my plan and by June of that year I began hosting my own underground themed events under Good Vibes Promotions. The name was just something that came naturally to me, almost at the same time that I had decided to start a crew.

From the first show on things were great, the parties were awesome, crowds came out of nowhere, and packed the place every month, things were looking very promising. The only problem we really had was that the venue was in a residential area and we were harassed by the cops on a pretty regular basis. The place never backed down though and launched their own lawsuits on the police department armed with video evidence and countless eyewitnesses on their side, including myself. Unfortunately, years later the police launched a full scale raid and shut down the business, bringing an era to an end and putting many nonviolent human beings in cages. This situation was of course one of the many times in which I experienced the corruption of the legal system first hand.

In the beginning I knew I enjoyed themed events but I was having a lot of trouble coming up with themes on my own. The names for the first few events that I hosted actually came from friends, for some reason my creativity seemed to be blocked. This was around the same time where I had really been getting deep in my activist research, spending up to 6 hours a day, or more studying the things I have discussed in this book. It must have been very obvious to everyone around me that occult history and activism had pretty much consumed my interest because many of my friends suggested that I themed my events around the things I was researching. The idea was brilliant and suddenly I no longer had any problem coming up with creative ideas for my shows. I did parties about sacred geometry, the Wall Street bailouts, and free "end the fed" shows on tax day, and many other events aimed at subtly educating the people who came out.

Eventually I was able to get a website set up thanks to the generosity of the raver who set up the domain and taught me the basics of the software. The website allowed me to host hundreds of educational activist documentaries and post independent news in an organized format on a daily basis. The website really took my research to a new level and eventually resulted in the book that you have just read.

I am not the best writer in the world, I am certainly not the best rave promoter, and I am not any smarter than your average person either. I have just spent my life confused about the social structure and why people behave the way they do, so I have continued to seek answers with every passing day. As time passed and I began to piece together more information I realized that most of what

I was taught throughout my whole life was untrue. I had always suspected this but since I did not have all the information I was not able to fully understand or specifically describe what I knew in my soul. I have always had a mentality that was in line with the principals of non-aggression and I was always aware that the major establishments in society did not live up to those standards. For most of my life that vague idea was more or less the extent to my understanding of geo political and financial events. That all changed when I started researching things more thoroughly and came across the ideas and information that are contained in these pages.

Many synchronicities that I experienced during my adventures in the counter culture are eventually what led me to begin writing this book. I never had many resources or major connections so when I began to think of new ways that I could contribute to the freedom movement, writing seemed like the only real option financially. Faster computers for video editing, music production software or podcasting equipment were not a financial possibility for me, but luckily writing does not cost anything. I knew that my path would be some form of art, because as I expressed many times I feel that human creativity is the only way to put an end to the violence and lack of compassion that is so prevalent in today's culture.

There is no way that more violence or aggression is going to bring us out of this mess but at the same time a life of submitting to this unjust culture is not a life worth living. This is the reason why I decided to call my company "Good Vibes," because as I discussed a few chapters ago I believe a world of peace can only become a reality if people are sending out good vibes to the universe and to one another.

QUOTE SOURCES AND SUGGESTED READING
----
[0] Bob Marley as said during interview from I am Legend - Film (2007)

J.G Vibes and his wife Kali at Starscape 2011

ALCHEMY OF THE MODERN RENAISSANCE
By J.G. Vibes

Alchemy of the Modern Renaissance
Leilah Publications
Copyright © 2012 J.G. Vibes Leilah Publications
All rights reserved.

To order wholesale, please contact:
American Wholesale Book Company (205) 956-4151
Ingram Book Company (800) 937-8000
Baker & Taylor (800) 775-1100

Leilah Publications P.O. Box 1863 Tempe, AZ 85280 U.S.A.

Leilah Publications brings a global vision of art & writing for the 21st century, publishing & investing in avante-garde artists, writers, and visionaries. The company was founded on 13 October 2006 to publish the visions of prodigies, leading us into the 21st century under a new generation of visionary artists, lyricists, writers, actors & actors, and poets.

CPSIA information can be obtained at www.ICGtesting.com
Printed in the USA
BVOW041149130113

310484BV00002B/2/P